Green Economy and Renewable Energy Transitions for Sustainable Development

Rui Alexandre Castanho
WSB University, Poland

IGI Global
PUBLISHER of TIMELY KNOWLEDGE

A volume in the Advances in Business Strategy
and Competitive Advantage (ABSCA) Book Series

Published in the United States of America by
IGI Global
Engineering Science Reference (an imprint of IGI Global)
701 E. Chocolate Avenue
Hershey PA, USA 17033
Tel: 717-533-8845
Fax: 717-533-8661
E-mail: cust@igi-global.com
Web site: http://www.igi-global.com

Library of Congress Cataloging-in-Publication Data

CIP Data in Progress

Title: Green Economy and Renewable Energy Transitions for Sustainable Development
ISBN: 9798369312971

This book is published in the IGI Global book series Advances in Business Strategy and Competitive Advantage (ABSCA) (ISSN: 2327-3429; eISSN: 2327-3437)

British Cataloguing in Publication Data
A Cataloguing in Publication record for this book is available from the British Library.

For electronic access to this publication, please contact: eresources@igi-global.com.

Advances in Business Strategy and Competitive Advantage (ABSCA) Book Series

Patricia Ordóñez de Pablos
Universidad de Oviedo, Spain

ISSN:2327-3429
EISSN:2327-3437

Mission

Business entities are constantly seeking new ways through which to gain advantage over their competitors and strengthen their position within the business environment. With competition at an all-time high due to technological advancements allowing for competition on a global scale, firms continue to seek new ways through which to improve and strengthen their business processes, procedures, and profitability.

The **Advances in Business Strategy and Competitive Advantage (ABSCA) Book Series** is a timely series responding to the high demand for state-of-the-art research on how business strategies are created, implemented and re-designed to meet the demands of globalized competitive markets. With a focus on local and global challenges, business opportunities and the needs of society, the **ABSCA** encourages scientific discourse on doing business and managing information technologies for the creation of sustainable competitive advantage.

Coverage

- Economies of Scale
- Customer-Orientation Strategy
- Competitive Strategy
- International Business Strategy
- Differentiation Strategy
- Entrepreneurship & Innovation
- Joint Ventures
- Business models
- Strategic Management
- Value Creation

IGI Global is currently accepting manuscripts for publication within this series. To submit a proposal for a volume in this series, please contact our Acquisition Editors at Acquisitions@igi-global.com or visit: http://www.igi-global.com/publish/.

The Advances in Business Strategy and Competitive Advantage (ABSCA) Book Series (ISSN 2327-3429) is published by IGI Global, 701 E. Chocolate Avenue, Hershey, PA 17033-1240, USA, www.igi-global.com. This series is composed of titles available for purchase individually; each title is edited to be contextually exclusive from any other title within the series. For pricing and ordering information please visit http://www.igi-global.com/book-series/advances-business-strategy-competitive-advantage/73672. Postmaster: Send all address changes to above address.

Titles in this Series

For a list of additional titles in this series, please visit:
http://www.igi-global.com/book-series/advances-business-strategy-competitive-advantage/73672

Smart Strategies and Societal Solutions for Sustainable International Business
Abdelkader Mohamed Sghaier Derbali (Taibah University, Saudi Arabia)
Business Science Reference • © 2024 • 228pp • H/C (ISBN: 9798369305324) • US $275.00

Sustainable Consumption Experience and Business Models in the Modern World
Maria Amélia Machado Carvalho (Business School of the Polytechnic Institute of Porto, Portugal) and Maria Antónia Rodrigues (Business School of the Polytechnic Institute of Porto, Portugal)
Business Science Reference • © 2024 • 300pp • H/C (ISBN: 9781668492772) • US $240.00

Applying Interdisciplinarity to Globalization, Management, Marketing, and Accountancy Science
Vladislav Pavlát (The University of Finance and Administration, Czech Republic) Ladislava Knihová (The University of Finance and Administration, Czech Republic) Lubomír Civín (AMBIS, Czech Republic) Jaroslav Halík (Metropolitan University, Prague, Czech Republic) and Radka MacGregor Pelikánová (Metropolitan University, Prague, Czech Republic & Anglo-American University, Czech Republic & Czech University of Life Sciences, Prague, Czech Republic)
Business Science Reference • © 2023 • 310pp • H/C (ISBN: 9781799886693) • US $240.00

Transformational Interventions for Business, Technology, and Healthcare
Darrell Norman Burrell (Marymount University, USA)
Business Science Reference • © 2023 • 584pp • H/C (ISBN: 9798369316344) • US $295.00

Innovation, Strategy, and Transformation Frameworks for the Modern Enterprise
Anacleto Correia (Portuguese Naval Academy, Portugal) and Pedro B. Agua (Portuguese Naval Academy, Portugal)
Business Science Reference • © 2023 • 431pp • H/C (ISBN: 9798369304587) • US $275.00

Handbook of Research on Designing Sustainable Strategies to Develop Entrepreneurial Intention
Ramakrishna Yanamandra (Skyline University College, UAE) and Logaiswari Indiran (Universiti Teknologi Malaysia, Malaysia)
Business Science Reference • © 2023 • 642pp • H/C (ISBN: 9781668487815) • US $295.00

Strategic Management and International Business Policies for Maintaining Competitive Advantage
Ailson J. De Moraes (Royal Holloway University of London, UK)
Business Science Reference • © 2023 • 411pp • H/C (ISBN: 9781668468456) • US $295.00

IGI Global
PUBLISHER of TIMELY KNOWLEDGE

701 East Chocolate Avenue, Hershey, PA 17033, USA
Tel: 717-533-8845 x100 • Fax: 717-533-8661
E-Mail: cust@igi-global.com • www.igi-global.com

Table of Contents

Detailed Table of Contents

Resource efficiency, environmentally friendly consumption and production, and the green economy's contribution to sustainable development resource efficiency refer to the ways in which resources are used to deliver value to society and aims to reduce the amount of resources needed, as well as emissions and waste generated, per unit of product or service. Sustainable consumption and production aim to improve production processes and consumption practices to reduce resource consumption, waste generation, and emissions across the full life cycle of processes and products. A macroeconomic strategy for achieving sustainable economic growth is offered by the green economy, with a primary emphasis on investments, jobs, and skills.

This chapter reflects on the significant developments in environmental awareness and action over five decades. It discusses the evolution of global perspectives on environmental challenges, tracing the journey from the inaugural Earth Summit in Stockholm in 1972 to the present day. This brief chapter highlights the progress, the challenges, and the urgent need for continued international cooperation to address pressing environmental issues. It also explores the role of subsequent summits and initiatives in shaping policies and promoting sustainable practices, ultimately emphasizing the ongoing relevance of the ecological agenda as we mark fifty years since the first Earth Summit.

The European Union's carbon border adjustment mechanism (CBAM) ratified by the European Parliament as a part of the European Green Deal in 2023 will be in effect in the beginning of the year of 2026. But

EU's CBAM regulation shows that compensatory carbon tax on imports cannot be applied in a non-discriminatory manner in terms of the destination principle. Therefore, it is seen that the paragraph G of Article 20 of the GATT allowing for the measures to protect the exhaustible natural resources, may constitute a more appropriate justification for the EU's carbon adjustment at the border. The EU's border carbon adjustment mechanism will also have a negative impact on international competition, primarily in terms of carbon-intensive industries in the countries such as Turkey. It is considered reasonable for Turkey to introduce appropriate policy tools to price carbon in a way not being subject to the European Union's carbon tax at the border.

A residential energy consumption model was estimated by using socio-economic characteristics, economic activities, mobility, land cover, natural hazards, governance, energy, air quality, and green economy variables for the EU-27 and UK. Regional variations of the energy consumption were also investigated through focusing on European regional typologies including urban, intermediate, and rural regions. The residential energy consumption model was estimated by using spatial econometric approaches as well as specific regression models were estimated for the urban, intermediate, and rural regions. The key variables used in regression analysis were selected according to their importance using the Random Forest (RF) classification method. The results from the regressions confirm that socio-economic, environmental, governance, technology, and natural hazards related variables explain residential energy consumption in Europe. The variations of sign and coefficients of the variables according to different regional typologies were also uncovered.

The pursuit of sustainability, initiated by the United Nations' adoption of the 2030 Sustainable Development Goals, has prompted developed and developing countries to adopt alternative policies. To address energy security concerns, countries have begun implementing strategies and practices to reduce carbon emissions and limit the use of environmentally harmful energy sources. However, unexpected crises like the COVID-19 pandemic and the Russia-Ukraine conflict have brought energy availability to the forefront as a major challenge. This study aims to examine the issue of energy security in the context of these two crises. By utilizing OECD indicators and current reports, the study will provide an overview of the energy security dilemma.

Economics, traditionally centered on the production of goods and utility maximization, has often undervalued the pivotal role of the environment in shaping societal welfare. The environment, as a

Foreword

In *Green Economy and Renewable Energy Transitions for Sustainable Development*, the reader is invited to explore the pragmatic and pressing issue of sustainable development. This book arrives at a critical juncture in our history, where the need for a concerted effort towards environmental sustainability is not just a noble goal, but a necessary one for the continued prosperity of our planet.

The authors, experts in their respective fields, present an insightful examination of the green economy and its role in fostering a sustainable future. They do not shy away from the complexities involved in transitioning to renewable energy sources, nor do they oversimplify the challenges. Instead, they offer a balanced view of the multifaceted strategies required to reduce environmental impact, conserve biodiversity, and mitigate climate change.

This volume is grounded in the reality of our current situation, yet optimistic about the potential for change. It provides a clear-eyed analysis of how sustainable production and consumption, coupled with strategic investments in renewable energy, can lead to meaningful change. The book also highlights the critical role of policy, technology, and behavior in the energy transition, emphasizing the importance of shifting from fossil fuels to renewables like solar, wind, and hydropower.

Education and innovation are central themes, as the book discusses the importance of aligning curriculum and technological advancements with the Sustainable Development Goals. It also touches on the collaborative efforts in shaping a sustainable future.

For policymakers, researchers, educators, and anyone interested in the stewardship of our environment, this book serves as a knowledgeable guide. It is a straightforward, well-researched resource that encourages informed action and thoughtful participation in the global movement towards sustainability.

As we turn the pages, let us approach the content with a sense of purpose and a willingness to engage in the necessary work to protect and preserve our world for future generations.

Sincerely,

Recep Ulucak
Erciyes University, Turkey

Preface

The urgent need to transition to a green economy and renewable energy sources has become increasingly apparent in recent years (Kirikkaleli *et al.*, 2023). Our planet faces environmental, economic, and social challenges that demand immediate attention and innovative approaches (Castanho, 2017; 2021). Climate change, resource depletion, biodiversity loss, and social inequalities are some of the critical issues we face (Duran Sosa *et al.*, 2021; Batista *et al.*, 2022). The way forward is to shift our paradigms and embrace a future rooted in sustainability (Crespo *et al.*, 2023).

This book results from collaboration among experts and practitioners from various fields who are passionate about addressing these challenges and shaping a better future for our planet and its inhabitants. The book aims to provide readers with a comprehensive and accessible resource that delves into the complexities of green economics and renewable energy and offers pragmatic insights and actionable strategies for sustainable development.

The chapters contained within these pages cover a wide array of topics, from the fundamentals of green economics and renewable energy technologies to case studies highlighting real-world applications. Thus, we will discuss policy frameworks, market dynamics, and the role of governments, businesses, and individuals in driving the transition towards a sustainable future. Each chapter contributes a piece of the puzzle, ultimately forming a cohesive narrative that illustrates the power and potential of green economy principles and renewable energy sources.

This book will inspire and empower the reader to become a catalyst for positive change. Whether the public is an academic, a policy maker, an entrepreneur, or an engaged citizen, it is feasible that they will find valuable insights and inspiration within these pages. Together, we can work towards a more sustainable and prosperous future, where the harmony between economic growth, environmental stewardship, and social well-being is not just an aspiration but a reality.

As we embark on this journey, let us remember that sustainable development is not a destination but a path we must walk with determination, ingenuity, and a shared commitment to living a better world for future generations.

Contextually, in the following pages, we embark on an enlightening journey through the transformative landscape of sustainable development and renewable energy. Thus, this monography comprehensively explores our world's pressing challenges and the promising solutions within our grasp.

Many thanks for joining us in exploring *Green Economy and Renewable Energy Transitions for Sustainable Development.*

ORGANIZATION OF THE BOOK

This monograph is organized into 16 chapters. A short description of each of the chapters follows:

Chapter 1 provides a general theoretical overview regarding the Green Economy and how we can understand and perceived it.

Chapter 2 embrace us in a retrospective journey from Stockholm 1972 to Stockholm 2022 - enabling to understand where we are today in environmental protection fifty years later.

Chapter 3 focuses on the EU tax regulation and its possible effects on Turkey's exports in the short term.

Chapter 4 addresses the problems related to the residential energy consumption in Europe from a spatial econometric analysis of the regional variations.

Chapter 5 analysis the hot topic of the Covid-19 pandemic, Russia-Ukraine War and Energy Issues Energy Security Dilemma in OECD Countries.

Chapter 6 emphasizes the theoretical framework about the Conceptual Evaluation on Economy, Environment and Sustainable Development.

Chapter 7 explores a case study organizations from the Global South regarding the contribution of waste management social enterprises to the SDGs.

Chapter 8 highlights the systems engineering. For that the work leads us through Green Economy and Renewable Energy Transitions.

Chapter 9 centers on the momentum to accelerate Indonesia's sustainable economic growth towards green economy through the tax carbon policies.

Chapter 10 studies the energy infrastructure in the scope of rational choices via the analysis of energy infrastructure for sustainable development, using game theory.

Chapter 11, through the literature review examination, allows us to expand our knowledge on the materials for phase change heat storage. Through the example of Scheffler reflectors.

Chapter 12 reminds us about the relevance of engaging stakeholders for a sustainable future - in order to be the catalysts of green economy and renewable energy transitions.

Chapter 13 debates the effects on health the environment, and the importance of environmental education.

Chapter 14 brings the issue related to green entrepreneurship pioneering solutions for climate change. For that, the investigation focuses on an Indian case study.

Chapter 15 deals with a case Study on a beacon of hope, Transition India's Renewable Energy Integration, and the Ujwal DISCOM Assurance Yojana (UDAY).

Chapter 16, finally, focus on the growing issue of the green jobs – from an historical perspective.

Rui Alexandre Castanho
WSB University, Dabrowa Górnicza Poland

REFERENCES

Batista, T., Torre, S., Fermoso, J., Morais, N., Avila, R., Pinto Gomes, C., Castanho, R.A. and Cabezas, J. (2022). Nature-Based Solutions for Climate Change Adaptation in Scholar and Social Buildings: Concepts and Pilot Solutions for Portugal and Spain. *INTECH Book: Urban Green Spaces*. Intech Open. doi:10.5772/intechopen.105701

Castanho, R. A. (2017).*Sustainable Urban Planning in Transboundary Areas: Analysis of Critical Factors for Territorial Success* [Doctoral Thesis, Universityof Extremadura (UEx)].

Castanho, R. A. (2021). *Handbook of Research on Sustainable Development Goals, Climate Change, and Digitalization*. IGI Global. doi:10.4018/978-1-7998-8482-8

Crespo, A., Velázquez, J., Herráez, F., Gülçin, D., Ugur O'zcan, A., Hernando, A., & Castanho, R. A. (2023). Territorial planning of rustic land constructions and their adaptation to climate change in the province of Málaga, Spain. *Land Use Policy*, *129*, 106644. doi:10.1016/j.landusepol.2023.106644

Durán Sosa, R., Araya Ramírez, I., & Castanho, R. A. (2021). *Environmental Sanitation in Heredia: A Relevant Challenge in Costa Rica. Chapter #8 in the IGI GLOBAL Handbook of Research: Handbook of Research on Sustainable Development Goals*. Climate Change, and Digitalization., doi:10.4018/978-1-7998-8482-8.ch008

Kirikkaleli, D., Castanho, R. A., Deniz Özbay, R., Yılmaz Genç, S., & Ahmed, Z. (2023). *Does Resource Efficiency Matter for Environmental Quality in Canada?* (Vol. 11). Front. Environ. Sci. Sec. Environmental Economics and Management. doi:10.3389/fenvs.2023.1276632

Chapter 1
Understanding Green Economy

Anshu Agarwal
Christ University, India

ABSTRACT

Resource efficiency, environmentally friendly consumption and production, and the green economy's contribution to sustainable development resource efficiency refer to the ways in which resources are used to deliver value to society and aims to reduce the amount of resources needed, as well as emissions and waste generated, per unit of product or service. Sustainable consumption and production aim to improve production processes and consumption practices to reduce resource consumption, waste generation, and emissions across the full life cycle of processes and products. A macroeconomic strategy for achieving sustainable economic growth is offered by the green economy, with a primary emphasis on investments, jobs, and skills.

LITERATURE REVIEW

Paul Krugman (2010)

Is it possible to reduce greenhouse-gas emissions drastically without wrecking our economy? Economists generally believe that a market-based program to address the problem of climate change can produce big gains at a small, if not trivial, cost. According to economic theory, free markets are efficient which implies that no one can get better without making somebody else worse off. If there are "negative externalities," or costs that market players inflict on others while not paying a price for their conduct, the assumption that the market economy would do the right thing disappears. He contended that economic actions that impose unjustified expenses on others shouldn't always be prohibited, but rather discouraged. A Pigovian tax, as it is now known, is the proper approach to price negative externalities.

Peter A Victor, Tim Jackson (2012)

In their report, the authors describe the UN Environment Program's (UNEP) report towards a Green Economy, a green economy expands faster than a brown economy in the long term while preserving

DOI: 10.4018/979-8-3693-1297-1.ch001

and recovering natural capital (ibid. p.i). If this is true, people can continue enjoying increased output & consumption of products and services while enhancing social equity and minimizing environmental consequences. The UNEP report (2011a) proposes an attractive but faulty model for transitioning to a green economy that views the globe as a whole. It makes no distinctions between geographical regions or between wealthy and impoverished nations. As a result, generalizations about greener versus brown development based on such a large number of input modeling frameworks are at best premature, and at worst profoundly deceptive.

Maria Kurnia Ayunisari (Ayunisari)

The United Nations Environment Program (UNEP) has issued three studies on the concept of the green economy. It is a reaction to the world's crises in terms of climate, food, and financial turmoil with an alternative model that promises growth while safeguarding the earth's ecosystems. Certain types of spending and investment must be limited to avoid depletion of resources and waste. According to Khors (2011) Ocampo, the renewable energy industry has significant adaptation and mitigation potential for a number of the repercussions of global warming. According to Cosbeys, a sound industrial policy must prioritize new private and public investment. Developed countries should reserve some protective space in order to build their own environmental products and services. Governments should contribute to the development of recognized national or regional capability to test and certify products as compliant. Harmonizing energy performance targets, testing methodologies, and labeling regulations for products would be a big help to small and medium-sized exporters.

Martin Khor (2011)

A green economy creates the appearance of an environmentally friendly economy that is conscious of the need to preserve natural resources. It reduces pollution levels that harm the environment throughout the manufacturing process. The phrase has become contentious as the topic of a multinational negotiating process. Developing countries have expressed concern that the green economy idea may be overused or misapplied. It would be illegal under GATT regulations to impose a trade measure, such as an additional import charge, on a product because the manufacturing method is less ecologically friendly.

Incorporating PPMs and eco-dumping into the WTO would indicate that if a country has weaker environmental laws in a business, the cost of that industry will rise.

Olivia Bina (2013)

Greening documents place a strong emphasis on market forces, investment in innovation and green tech, and green production and consumption. Greening promotes a greater emphasis on economic and social goals, which the ecosystem is called upon to serve through effective systems. All of the materials examined refer to the apparent problem of scarcity, either expressly (UNEP, 2011b) or implicitly (when discussing food or fuel crises and security difficulties). Scarcity is indeed a source of innovation, technological development, investment, and thus GDP growth in mainstream economics. Scarcity levels are directly related to growth success. When scarcity is an issue, growth becomes an issue. Understanding the scarcity issues brought by crises is likely to ensure respect.

Minjian Guo, Joanna Nowakowska Grunt, Vladimir Gorbanyov, and Maria Egorova (2020)

The Europe 2020 plan for smart, ecological, and inclusive growth highlights the following important economic factors: smart growth, which promotes an economy built on information and innovation. Sustainable growth promotes a more resource-efficient, environmentally friendly, and competitive economy. promoting a high-employment economy that provides social and geographical cohesion The promotion of the green economy necessitates extensive research into its formation conditions, system-forming elements, and impact on national environmental sustainability. Market orientation and technology have been shown to drive sustainability impact, hence improving it. Increased corporate investment in social and environmental information sharing helps operational progress. Any country committed to green growth must first address a number of finance challenges. Green financing can be viewed as a component of the economic framework for long-term development. Multiple decision-making frameworks, including such qualitative and quantitative economic research, can allow for different perspectives and approaches to promoting green growth.

Mikhno Inesa, Koval Viktor, Shvets Galyna, Garmatiuk Oksana, Tamošiūnienė Rima (2021)

The goal of the research is to look for effective indicators that take into consideration negative externalities as well as the influence of energy efficient technologies on the growth of the green economy. This article employs economic and scientific modeling, comparisons, induction and reasoning, forecasting, and other techniques. At a preliminary phase of the startup process, predominance of green reasoning over any other reasoning is possible. It is critical to assist the public sector in getting grants, equity, and new kinds of finance in both rich and low-income countries. These funds could provide financing to environmentally conscious enterprises while also encouraging investment in new sectors. The following are the primary tools for stimulating the green economy and leveling the playing field: Subsidies and gifts to businesses having minimum detrimental impact on the economy.

Lucretia Dogaru (2021)

In order to discover future development potential, the shift to a green economy is associated with a rethinking of unsustainable consumption habits. Goal Twelve of the 2030 Agenda outlines the need for integrated environmental, social, and economic promotion. The key drivers of the sustainable future are global pledges and activities to minimize and dispose of waste, use resources wisely, and reduce pollution. The green economy is a set of economic activities connected with sustainability in production, distribution, and consumption. It is the kind of low-carbon economic development that promotes sustainable development and inclusive social progress. UNEP has been promoting the Green Economy Initiative since October 2008, with the goal of encouraging investment in the green economy. The notion of green growth is frequently used to define national, regional, or multinational policies in the current global setting created by Sars2 Covid-19 coronavirus epidemic. On a European level, numerous initiatives have evolved to help the adoption of the green economy.

Hannah Stoddart (2012)

They want to guarantee that the world's largest established and emerging economies receive a good proportion of the world's resources while also leaving enough room for animals and wilderness. Governments (national and international) have to be democratic and responsible, and they must employ mechanisms to hold civil society accountable. Gender equality and equity must be prioritized as conditions for the transition to a green economy and achieving socioeconomic and environmental sustainability.

Tim Jenkins and Andrew Simms (Jenkins and Simms)

Attempts to govern the global environment responsibly and manage the global economy without disruptive crises are hopelessly unconnected two decades after the Earth Summit in 1992. We have survived with an economic model built on debt-fueled overconsumption that coexists with massive levels of impoverishment and inequality since the first Earth Summit. Most economic sectors exhibit comparable patterns. Many people working in the sectors of development and the environment are discovering that systemic problems necessitate systemic solutions. This study proposes six challenges to establish the groundwork for systemic change: Create a national plan of action that places countries on trails to operate within limits of the planet and on time frames sufficient to retain key, environmental life support roles; do not start from the a growth perspective; agree to implement new perspective of financial success; commit to reducing income and wealth disparities between and within nations; place fiscal coverage and policy expenditure at the center of economic transition management and recapture the Other worlds are feasible, but the goal is to mold and manufacture them over the next decade before "business as usual" locks in catastrophic climate change.

HISTORY OF GREEN ECONOMY (SUSTAINABLE DEVELOPMENT)

The term "green economy" was coined by a group of top environmental economists in a groundbreaking 1989 study for the Government of the United Kingdom titled Blueprint for a Green Economy (Pearce, Markandya and Barbier, 1989). The study was conducted to advise the UK Government on whether there was a common definition of "sustainable development," as well as the consequences of environmental sustainability for measuring economic success and evaluating projects and policies. Apart from the title of the paper, there will be no further mention of the green economy, and it seems that the writers used the word as an afterthought. Blueprint 2: Implementing Green the World Economy, published in 1991 and 1994, was a follow up to the previous study.

Blueprint 3 is about measuring sustainable development. While the first Blueprint report's thesis was that economics can and should help environmental policy, the subsequent reports extended this message to global economic challenges such as climate change, ozone depletion, tropical deforestation, and resource loss in the developing world. All studies are based on decades of environmental economics study and experience.

The phrase was reintroduced in 2008 in the light of talks on governmental responses to various global crises. In the midst of the financial crisis and fears of a worldwide recession, UNEP advocated for "green stimulus packages," identifying specific sectors where large-scale public investment might kick-start a "green economy" (Atkisson, 2012).

As part of the economic recovery efforts, numerous countries implemented major "green stimulus" programs.

UNEP started the Green Economy Initiative in October 2008 to provide research and policy assistance for green sector investment and greening environmentally unfavorable sectors. As part of this Initiative, UNEP appointed one of the original writers of Blueprint for a Green Economy to produce a report labeled a Global Green New Deal (GGND), which was published in April 2009 and suggested a mix of policy actions that'd stimulate economic recovery while also improving global economic sustainability.

Main Focus of Green Economy (UNEP)

1) Using regional, sub-regional, and national sites to promote the macroeconomic approach to sustainable economic growth
2) Green Economy ideas will be demonstrated, with a particular emphasis on investments, technology, and financial access.
3) Assistance in developing and implementing macroeconomic policies in order to help nations transition to a green economy.

Green Economy Components (Kaushik, 2021)

Have you ever pondered what the world might look like through a green lens? A world having zero carbon dioxide emissions is a dream that is slowly becoming a reality. The following are the key elements of the sustainable future that are gradually transforming the future.

Green Buildings: These structures are often constructed in an environmentally beneficial manner. Green buildings are equipped with suitable ventilation and recycling technologies. Solar panels are installed on rooftops to generate power.

Green buildings are built using non-toxic materials such as clay plaster, cement, and straw bales. Sustainable buildings feature flexible designs that can survive any climate situation. It imposes parameters to ensure the tenants' quality of life.

Finance for the Environment: is a discursive word that encompasses several concepts such as investments, debts, loans, and securities under a single umbrella. Eco investing is investing in firms that encourage environmentally friendly activities. Green finance integrates the financial and environmental worlds.

Green finance investments are made by both the public and commercial sectors for the solar panel installation and hydropower projects. Loans are also made available to encourage the widespread deployment of solar panels and the construction of wind energy facilities.

Social Inclusivity: To put it another way, a socially open community cherishes all of its inhabitants. In perspective of such an economy, being socially inclusive entails offering resources to individuals of various socioeconomic backgrounds.

Examples in Practice (Kaushik, 2021)

Samples of the green economy may be found in people's daily lives. People contribute towards the green economy in a variety of ways, including significant development in the organic agricultural industry, the establishment of plant-based housing, and the use of bicycles as a mode of transportation.

1. Plant-based dwellings: Plant dwellings are both healthful and long-lasting. They have adequate rooftop harvesting systems, and the mix of healthy housing with a touch of history is allowing individuals to experiment with traditional ways of life. These dwellings are superior to regular residences because they include a specific small recycling arena and suitable ventilation systems. Traditional homes typically take a year to build, while plant-based dwellings may be completed in six months. Plants used in home construction include teak, bamboo, and sundari. Plant-based houses are environmentally friendly and will shape the future of living. Plants used in home construction include teak, bamboo, and sundari. Plant-based houses are environmentally friendly and will shape the future.
2. Lithium Battery Recycling: Laptops and mobile phones use lithium-ion batteries. Because cobalt and lithium are extracted through mining, these batteries cause global warming. While they are the lifeblood of processing systems, their environmental effect cannot be underestimated. Lithium ion batteries burn and are not environmentally friendly. Recycling lithium ion batteries is the most effective solution to address the current issues. To recycle lithium batteries, a sophisticated Li-cycle technology is used. Stationery items are made using lithium batteries. Materials from post-conversion batteries are treated and recycled. Recycled battery packs are a green approach to save energy for the future.
3. Organic Agriculture: Natural agricultural manure is the most effective technique to boost crop yield without using pesticides or fertilizers. Organic farming employs a unique combination of farmyard manure, bone meal, and compost meal, as well as exclusively organic fertilizers. Organic farming has been a popular notion in the modern day, and there are various benefits to eating organic foods. They boost the body's resistance to antibiotics, improve flavor, support general health, and lower the likelihood of pulmonary problems. This kind of gardening improves the soil's nutrient supply. Organic farming is beneficial for the ecology as a whole. It protects nature since it is chemical-free, minimizes the danger of soil erosion, and aids in the conservation of biodiversity.

Partnerships To Promote Green Economy: (UNEP)

To accelerate and solidify sustainable changes in consumption and production patterns, multi-stakeholder collaborations for the development of a green economy are encouraged. UN Environment has extended its involvement with the corporate sector, which is a key player in promoting efficiency and the green economy, in addition to governments and non-profit organizations.

Figure 1. Sustainable consumption (UNEP)

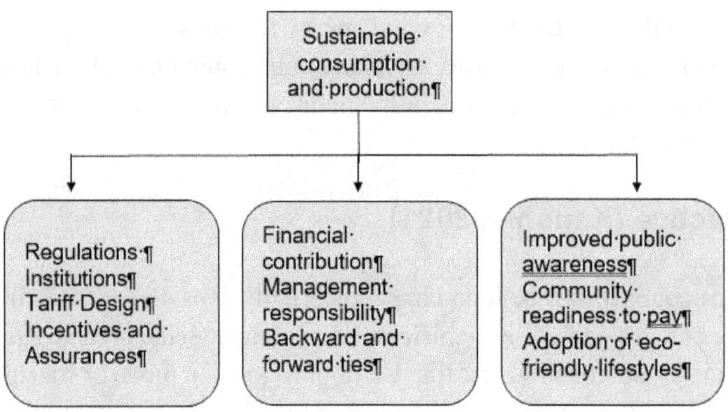

Green Innovation Statistics in Top Ten Countries: (Compare Your Country)

See Figure 2.

Figure 2. Share of environmental patents in per cent vs. countries

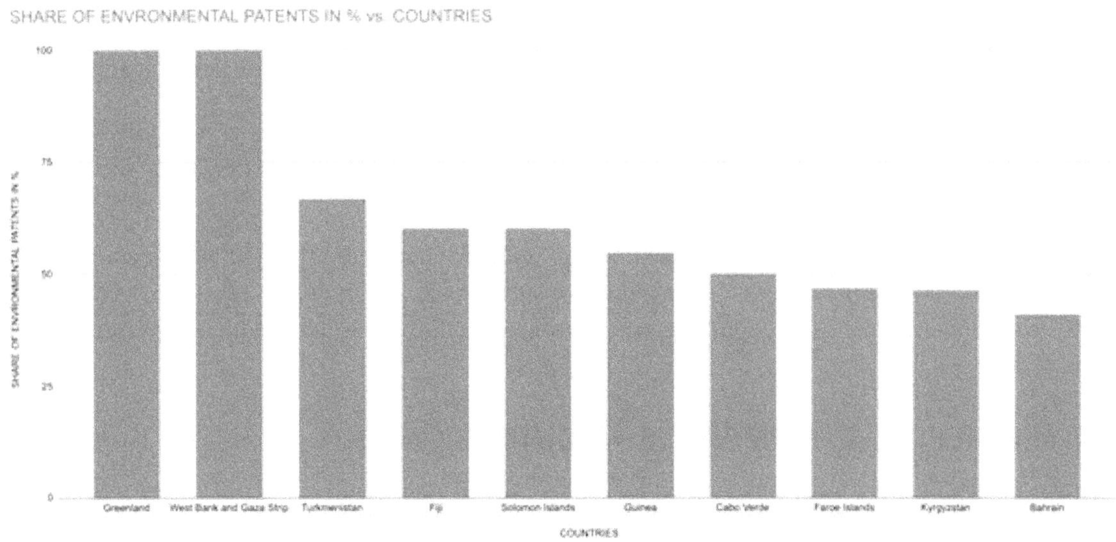

Four Dimensions of Green Economies: (UNRIC)

The planet's and people's health are given top priority in a green economy, and both are seen as interdependent. Prioritization and the green initiative's execution aid nations in achieving a variety of sustainable development objectives.

1) SDG 3 - Wellness and good health

Numerous major investments in the energy and environmental sectors would lead to the development of thousands of new employments. The emphasis on clean energy and rising wealth all assist the growth of natural, human, and social capital, creating job possibilities for businesses, organizations, and livelihoods that promote sustainability. Additionally, the sector - based activities will open up opportunities for education, sustainable infrastructure, and training that will benefit everyone.

2) SDG 16 - Justice, stability, and good institutions

There is data to support the green economy and its benefits to the economy and society. Institutions must be multidisciplinary in order to achieve a sustainable green economy, utilizing science, economics, information from other industries, and local expertise. A green economy will develop a financial system that serves the interests of society by fostering local economies while upholding common norms and practices by taking into account the various facets of communities.

3) SDG 13 - Climate change

A green recovery invests in, protects, and restores the environment; a key component of green economies is biodiversity restoration and climate mitigation. Recovery and expansion of water, soil, and natural systems are given top priority because of the constrained sustainability of natural capital. A circular economy, a production and consumption model that emphasizes recycling and reusing resources and goods for as long as feasible, is also closely related to a green economy.

4) SDG 12 - Controlled production and consumption

The circular economy and the green economy are related. There should be a change in consumption to limit the use of natural resources to levels that are sustainable. An inclusive economy welcomes and includes contemporary forms of economic growth whose goal is to spread wealth across the earth.

SUSTAINABLE DEVELOPMENT: (SD-COMMISSION UK)

Although there are many ways to interpret the idea of sustainable development, at its core it refers to a method of growth that seeks to strike a balance between various, frequently incongruent needs and an awareness of the social, economic, and environmental constraints that our society is subject to.

All too frequently, development is fueled by a single demand without adequately accounting for its wider or longer-term effects. The harm that may emerge from this sort of strategy is already becoming apparent, from the large-scale financial crises brought on by reckless banking to the changes in the planet's climate brought on by our reliance on fossil fuel-based energy sources. We must act now because the longer we pursue unsustainable growth, the more probable it is that its effects will become frequent and severe.

Three Pillars of Sustainable Development: (Collins, 2021)

- Economic sustainability: which attempts to decrease severe poverty and ensure that everyone has access to well compensated jobs.
- Environmental sustainability: attempts to preserve the planet's natural equilibrium while minimizing the effects of human activity.
- Social sustainability: attempts to ensure that everyone has access to fundamental goods and services.

Objectives For Sustainable Development: (Kth, 2020)

1) Eradicate all types of poverty worldwide.
2) Eliminate hunger, provide healthier diets and food safety, and advance sustainable agriculture.
3) Ensure everyone's wellbeing and encourage health at all ages.

4) Make sure all students get high-quality, inclusive, and equitable education, and encourage lifelong learning for everyone.
5) Obtain gender balance and improve the status of all women and girls.
6) Ensure that everyone has access to water and sanitation and that these resources are managed sustainably.
7) Ensure that everyone has access to modern, sustainable, cheap energy.
8) Encourage enduring, inclusive, and sustainable economic growth, complete and productive employment, and respectable employment for all.
9) Increase innovation, encourage inclusive and sustainable industrialization, and build resilient infrastructure.
10) Lessen inequality both inside and across nations.
11) Make settlements and cities inclusive, secure, adaptable, and sustainable.
12) Make careful you follow sustainable production and consumption habits.
13) Combating climate change and its repercussions requires swift action.
14) Seas, lakes, and marine resources should be preserved and used sustainably for sustainable development.
15) Reducing desertification, slowing and reversing soil deterioration, and halting the loss of biodiversity are all examples of sustainable forestry.
16) Encourage inclusive and peaceful communities for sustainable development, ensure that everyone has access to justice, and create inclusive institutions at all levels.
17) Renew the Global Partnership for Sustainable Development and strengthen the implementation mechanisms.

PRINCIPLES FOR A GREEN ECONOMY (STODDART, 2012)

1. Equitable wealth distribution

Promote equitable income distribution within and across nations in order to eliminate inequities between wealthy and poor and achieve economic and social equality while using a sustainable and good amount of the world's resources and leaving enough space for animals and wilderness.

2. Economic justice and equity

Create economic alliances that would convey major financial and technological aid to less developed nations, in order to help narrow the gap between the developing and industrialized worlds and promote the sustainable development of both.

3. Intergenerational Equity

Natural sources and habitats must be carefully monitored and conserved so as to maximize the value of environmental\assets for future generations, so as to meet their requirements and allow them to thrive.

4. Conservative Approach

Science should be used to improve social and environmental consequences by identifying environmental risk. Scientific uncertainty about environmental hazards should not be used to justify avoiding environmental protection measures. Those asserting that there would be no substantial environmental repercussions should bear the "burden of evidence."

5. Developmental Rights

Human evolution in balance with the environment is critical to achieving sustainable development, as it empowers individuals and societies to achieve beneficial social and environmental results.

6. Externality Internalization

Policy should prioritize the creation of actual social and environmental benefit. To that purpose, market prices should reflect true social and environmental costs and advantages, so that the polluter pays for pollution. Tax and regulatory systems should be used to 'tilt the playing field,' making 'good' products cheap and 'bad' items highly expensive.

7. International Collaboration

Environmental norms must be implemented within nation-states in collaboration with the international community, with an appreciation of the potential impact on the growth potential of many other states. Environmental trade policies should minimize unjust protectionism, but should also ensure that trade promotes sustainable resource use, environmental protection, and progressive labor standards, supporting a "race to the top" rather than a "race to the bottom."

8. International responsibility

Recognizing that acts within national borders can have environmental consequences that extend beyond national jurisdictions, necessitating collaboration in the establishment of international law that provides for independent legal remedies in such circumstances.

9. Transparency, participation, and accountability

All citizens must have access to environmental information and the ability to engage in decision-making processes. To guarantee that environmental challenges are addressed with the involvement of all concerned individuals, organizations at all levels (national and international) have to be fair and accountable, and they must use mechanisms that allow civil society to hold them accountable. In this regard, citizens' access to justice for grievance and redress in environmental problems is a critical component of increasing accountability.

10. Consumption and production that is sustainable

Introduce sustainable production, as well as resource use that is both sustainable and equitable. Reduce and remove unsustainable production and consumption habits, i.e. minimize, reuse, and recycle the materials utilized, and recognize the limitation of resources on Earth.

11. *Planning* that is strategic, coordinated, and integrated in order to achieve environmentally friendly development, the green economy, and poverty reduction.

Through strategy development with civil society and stakeholders, as well as with all key government ministries, an integrated approach must be taken at all levels to accelerate the accomplishment of socioeconomic and environmental sustainability.

12. Just Transition

Making the shift to a low-carbon, green economy in pursuit of sustainable development will incur expenses. Some governments and individuals can tolerate these costs better than others and they are more resistant to transitional shifts. Most vulnerable must be assisted and safeguarded during the change process; developing nations must have access to sufficient financial and technical aid, and individuals and communities must have access to the new skills and jobs.

13. Redefine Well-being

GDP is insufficient for evaluating social well-being and environmental integrity. Many socially and environmentally destructive activities, such as fossil fuel extraction and financial speculation, boost GDP. Human well-being and quality of life, as well as environmental health, should be the overarching goals of economic development.

14. Gender Equality
    Women's rights and equity are necessary for achieving sustainable development and transitioning to a green economy. Women play an important role as change agents in environmental management and development; their efforts must be recognized and their talents developed.
15. Maintain wildlife and prevent pollution in any aspect of the environment

Preserve and restore wildlife and natural habitats as essential to human development and well-being and build a governance framework that protects ecosystem resilience to avoid permanent damage.

16. The Happiness Principle (GEC)
    a) A green economy allows everyone to generate and enjoy wealth.
    b) People are at the heart of the green economy. Its goal is to foster true, shared prosperity.
    c) It focuses on building riches to promote happiness. This richness is not just financial, but also comprises personal, social, physical, and ecological capital.
    d) It prioritizes investment and accessibility to the sustainable biological ecosystems, infrastructure, knowledge, and education that all people require to thrive.
    e) It provides chances for sustainable and dignified living, businesses, and jobs.
    f) It is based on people's choices while relying on community action for public benefits.

17. The Principle of Justice
    a) The green economy fosters equity both within and across generations.
    b) The green economy is non-discriminatory and inclusive. It distributes decision-making, benefits, and expenses evenly, resists elite capture, and promotes women's empowerment in particular.
    c) It encourages the equitable split of opportunity and result, minimizing gaps among people, while also providing adequate space for animals and wilderness.
    d) It adopts a long-term view of the economy, producing wealth with resilience that benefits future generations while also moving quickly to address today's multifaceted poverty and inequality.
    e) It is founded on solidarity & social justice, and it promotes civil dignity, the rights of employees indigenous peoples, and minorities, as well as the right to environmental sustainability.
    f) It encourages MSMEs, social entrepreneurs, and sustainable livelihoods.
    g) It aims for a quick and equitable transition while covering its expenses, leaving no one behind, empowering vulnerable populations to be transition agents, and improving in social welfare and reskilling.
18. The Principle of Planetary Boundaries
    a) The green economy protects, restores, and invests in the environment.
    b) An inclusive and sustainable economy acknowledges and promotes nature's varied values, including functional values of supplying commodities and services which underpin the economy, cultural values that sustain society, and ecological values that guide all of life.
    c) It recognizes natural capital's limited substitutability with other capitals, applying the safeguards to avoid the loss of important natural capital and exceeding ecological limitations.
    d) It invests in biodiversity conservation, growth, and restoration of land, water, air, and biological ecosystems.
    e) It is creative in regulating natural systems, guided by features such as circular logic, and aligned with biodiversity and natural system-based livelihoods in local communities.
19. The Principle of Efficiency and Sufficiency
    a) The green economy promotes sustainable production and consumption.
    b) A green economy that is inclusive is low-carbon, resource-conserving, varied, and circular.
    c) It accepts innovative economic development strategies that solve the difficulty of achieving wealth within global boundaries.
    d) It recognizes that there must be a huge worldwide change to reduce natural resource use to physiologically sustainable limits if we are to stay within planetary bounds.
    e) It acknowledges a social floor of fundamental products & services that is necessary to satisfy people's wellbeing & dignity, along with undesirable consumption 'peaks.'
    f) It matches pricing, subsidies, and incentives with genuine societal costs through methods in which the 'polluter pays' and/or benefits flow to those who provide inclusive green services.
20. The Principle of Good Governance
    a) A green economy is led by institutions that are interconnected, responsible, and resilient.
    b) An inclusive and sustainable economy is evidence-based, with transdisciplinary norms and institutions that employ both solid science and economics, as well as local knowledge, for adaptive strategy.

c) It is backed up by organizations that are integrated, collaborative, and cohesive - horizontally across sectors as vertically across governance levels - and have the capacity to carry out their various duties in an effective, efficient, and responsible manner.
d) It necessitates public engagement, prior informed permission, transparency, social discourse, democratic accountability, and the absence of entrenched interests in all institutions - public, private, and civil society - in order for intelligent leadership to be supplemented by societal demand.
e) It encourages decentralized decision-making for regional industries and natural system management while retaining strong shared, centralized standards, processes, and compliance mechanisms.
f) It creates a financial structure with the goal of producing happiness and sustainability, structured up in methods that safely serve society's interests.

The European Green Economy Framework

Since the start of 2015, the EU has approved an ambitious green economy action plan with the goal of supporting the transformation to a competitive Community sector and accelerating sustainable economic growth. The European Commission's September 2017 Communication, "Investing in a Smart, Innovative, and Sustainable Industry." A "revised EU Industrial Policy Strategy" aims to boost industry's capacity to respond to the demands of creating new technologies that will enable the shift to a green economy. According to the aforementioned publication, encouraging use of smart technology across industrial value chains related to low dioxide emissions is critical for enhancing competitiveness. The eco-design laws, as well as the Environmental Working Plan for 2016-2019, are also components of its European framework again for transition to a green economy.

As per Eurostat data (Eurostat 2018 a, Improving resource statistics; Eurostat 2018 b, Improving resource increases in the European Union), the household consumption of raw materials in the European Union in 2010 was approximately 14 tons per capita, while it decreased to 13 tons per capita in 2017. At the same time, resource productivity improved by almost 40% in Europe between 2002 and 2018, despite a fall in household material consumption (DMC) owing to the 2008 economic crisis, which had a severe impact on the metallurgical industry.

According to official Eurostat data, Romania's household demand of materials used immediately in the economy was over 485 thousand tons in 2017, nearly double the consumption level of Germany. In other EU Member States, Italy, the Netherlands, Luxembourg, and Spain had the greatest resource productivity in 2018, while Bulgaria, Romania, Latvia, and Finland had the lowest. The amount of material used by an economy is unquestionably important in achieving environmental sustainability, from the resource extraction required for consumption and production activities to materials discharged into the atmosphere in the form of toxins.

According to the EU Scoreboard on Resource Efficiency in 2017, our nation has had the greatest increase in natural resource use in Central and Eastern Europe (per capita consumption has climbed by 180% in the last 15 years). Of course, such a proportion, which implies a deficiency in growing resource productivity, necessitates both a decrease in the deficit with other EU countries and a boost to green economy business development. As a result, the problem is represented first by reducing the resource loss that can be returned into the financial circuit, and second, by altering the mentality of individuals who want to promote ecological behavioral thriving economy necessitates resource efficiency and waste, as well as environmental protection and development.

The green economy, a relatively recent idea related to social participation and low carbon dioxide emissions, involves specific types of possibilities. Thus, we differentiate between economic opportunities, such as recycling capacity for specific fields and ecofriendly acquisitions, legislative opportunities, such as the community acquis that must be transposed at the national level, social opportunities, such as job creation, and structural opportunities, such as applied education initiatives. In this regard, we feel compelled to point out that these opportunities are hampered by a number of constraints, including economic constraints (such as a lack of funds for innovation and infrastructure, as well as low purchasing power), legislative constraints (the incomplete transposition of European legislation into national legislation in the Member States), social constraints (poverty and a low level of population awareness), and structural constraints.

Given these realities, specific public policy suggestions are required, particularly for the legislative component, but also for the educational component. In terms of the legislative component, we believe that it is vital to promote a national plan for efficient and sustainable production and consumption, as well as to build a suitable legislative framework for the green economy, which necessitates the development of green economy plans at the regional and local level (this has been done successfully by countries such as Finland, Sweden and Germany, which have adopted national resource efficiency programs). Initiating public debates on the appropriateness of adopting new national standards for resource efficiency, as well as an integrated approach to identifying market opportunities and evaluating legislative proposals, is also required. Similarly, we recognize the need to promote ecological design principles. This can be achieved by encouraging industrial sustainability models associated with current taxation systems, and promoting operators' access to hazardous substance information and establishing criteria for the reduction and prevention of food and home waste. It would also be appropriate to encourage the extension of average product life through consumer protection legislation, as well as update the law on urban green purchasing and waste disposal regulations by promoting the idea of efficient and sustainable resource use.

Sustainable Development Assessment (Guo et al., 2020)

1. Index of Environmental Sustainability (ESI). This measure incorporates 76 variables into environmental sustainability indicators. These indicators include the country's natural resource endowments, environmental management activities, past and present levels of pollution, the country's capacity to increase environmental efficiency, and so on.
2. Index of Environmental Performance (EPI). The EPI index is made up of 16 metrics that track progress toward environmental sustainability. Childhood mortality (deaths per 100 000 children 1-14 years old); air pollution; access to water supply (%); geographic ozone; oxide level in drinking water, water usage; wildlife protection; timber produce rate (%); farm subsidies; overfishing; alternative resources; clean energy; and emissions of carbon dioxide per GDP are among the indicators.

Methods

The figure below is based on the 17 sustainable development goals.

Figure 3. A graphical representation of the process of assessing the relationship between sustainable development and green technology

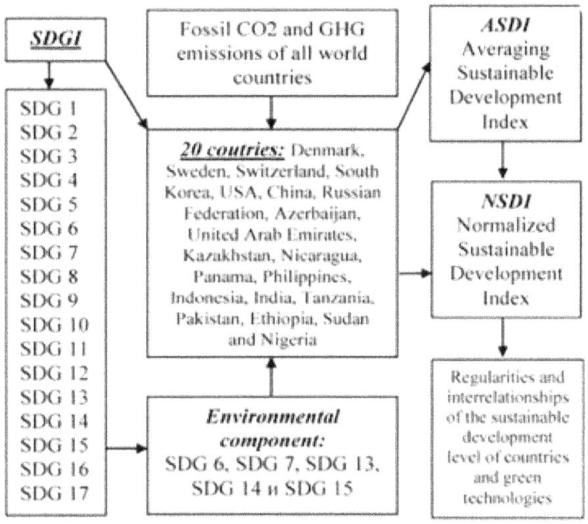

A set of targets relating to environmental sustainability was chosen from among all SDGs: SDG 7, SDG 13, SDG 6, SDG 15, and SDG 14. This set was then combined with the general averaging (ASDI—Averaging Sustainable Development Index) and normalized (NSDI—Normalized Sustainable Development Index) indices to form a fresh methodological approach to assessment. The total index's relative weight varied according to the amount of indicators attributed to one of the core components of environmental sustainability.

Because each index has various units & numbers, all units were normalized to a range of 0 to 1, where 0 represents the least stable aim and 1 represents a most stable objective for each country. Equation (1) is a straightforward equation that is used to normalize each

'I' denotes the sustainability index discovered for a certain aim, and N denotes the normalized value; I denotes the index type; j denotes the country, and n denotes the number of indicators. This study employed five indicators (SDG 7, SDG 6, SDG 13, SDG 15, and SDG 14), so n = 5.

The following phrase was used to normalize ASDI to the range of 0 to 1:

Here Index N denotes the Normalized Sustainable Development Index (NSDI).

The following formula was used to compute the variance between each normalized index and the NSDI:

where D denotes deviation.

To measure the level of sustainable growth, a maximum of 20 countries from the SDG index were chosen., Sweden (85), Denmark (85.2), South Korea (78.3), Switzerland (78.8),the United States (74.5), China (73.2), Azerbaijan (70.5), the Russian Federation (70.9), the, Nicaragua (67.9), Kazakhstan

(68.7), Panama (66.3), the, Indonesia (64.2)Philippines (64.9),, India (61.1),, Pakistan (55.6), Sudan (51.4), Tanzania (55.8)Ethiopia (53.2), United Arab Emirates (69.7)and Nigeria (46.4) are among these countries [35]. The sample includes nations with values ranging from very good to very low in order to find trends and correlations between a country's level of sustainability and green technologies. The country's location was also taken into account.

THEORETICAL ASPECTS OF GREEN ECONOMY DEVELOPMENT (INESA ET AL., 2021)

The "green economy" is defined across the world as a dynamic method of economic transformation toward low-carbon development, boosting resource efficiency and population well-being via the use of technology and innovations that generate new employment while lowering long-term environmental hazards (Frone & Frone, 2015).

Figure 4. Green economy growth prospects

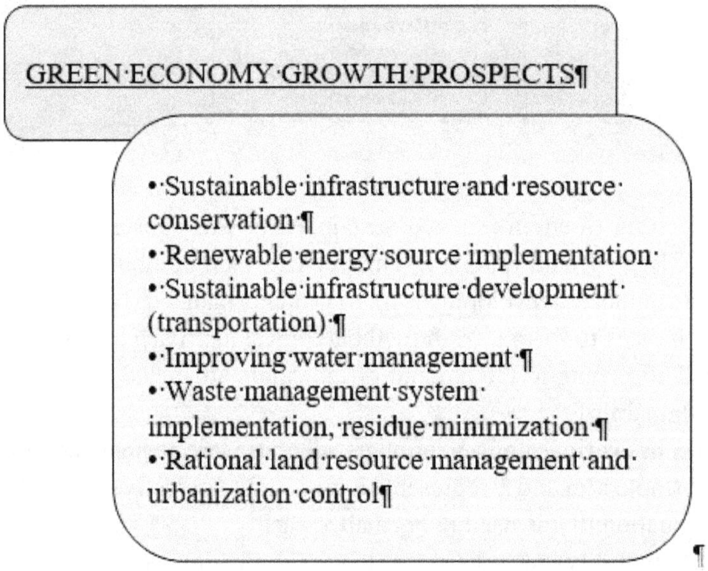

No nation has yet succeeded in turning its economy "green." However, affluent countries have substantially greater levels of environmental technology adoption and continuous monitoring of conformity with already set norms. There are a plethora of government policy instruments available to accelerate the adoption of a green economy, many of which are not solely economic in nature. In a market economy, where profits are the primary sign of productivity, it is the state's responsibility to regulate critical industries in order to implement sustainable growth.

The primary tools for stimulating the "green economy" and leveling the playing field include:

- Subsidies and grants to businesses that have a low environmental effect, as well as a tax increase and penalties for noncompliance with specified criteria.
- Improve control over corporate operations that have an environmental impact, as well as continuous ecosystem diagnostics
- Enhancing the communication and management system among all business entities (population segments), developing online maps in all sectors of "green economy" growth, and forming a fast reaction group to complaints received.
- Any incentive from the state or the public to focus on the ecosystem and raise demand for items produced using environmentally friendly technology.
- Transparency provides data on production methods and the influence of economic entities on the environment, the struggle against market monopolization and the promotion of free market competition, where the aim is to preserve the ecological state, and the adjustment of information policy are all priorities.
- The development of open contests and the use of funding programs to promote the development of a green and circular economy.

The Big Bang vs. the Ramp (Krugman, 2010)

Some major concerns are shared by economists who study climate policies.

There is widespread agreement that we must impose a price on carbon pollution, that this price must ultimately be quite high, but that the adverse economic consequences of this strategy will be bearable. To put it another way, we should indeed take steps to minimize climate change.

However, there is a heated dispute among educated experts concerning time, namely how quickly carbon pricing should climb to major levels. On one hand are economics who have spent years developing so-called integrated evaluation methods, which combine climate change models with projections of both the damage that global warming has caused and the costs of reducing emissions. Thus, Nordhaus' DICE model predicts that the cost of carbon dioxide emissions would eventually reach more than $200 per ton, virtually trebling the price of coal, yet that the majority of that growth will occur later this decade, with a considerably lower starting fee of roughly $30 per ton. Nordhaus refers to this advice for a strategy that progressively increases over time as the "climate-policy ramp."

On the other hand, some newer entrants to the area use comparable models but reach different findings. Most notably, in 2006, Nicholas Stern, an economist at the London School of Economics, pushed for immediate, vigorous action to cut emissions, which would almost certainly result in considerably higher carbon pricing. This alternate viewpoint does not appear to have a recognized name, therefore I will refer to it as the "climate-policy big bang."

I find it easier to understand the arguments if I conceive of carbon-cutting initiatives as a type of public investment: you pay a cost now and benefit later in the shape of a less-damaged earth.

And by later, I meant much afterward; today's emissions will alter the quantity of carbon in the air for decades, if not millennia. So, in order to determine if a given money invested in reducing emissions is worthwhile, you must estimate this same damage that such an additional ton of carbon in the air will cause, not just this year, but for the next century or more; and you must also decide what more weight to give to harm which will take a long time to manifest.

The policy-ramp supporters believe that the damage caused by an extra ton of carbon in the air is quite little at current; the cost will not become significant unless there is much more carbon dioxide within the atmosphere, which will not happen until later this century. And they believe that expenses that are far in the future shouldn't have a big effect on policy now. Big-bang supporters say that the government should have a far longer perspective than private investors. Furthermore, proponents of rapid action argue that the harm from carbon output may be much greater than policy-ramp evaluations suggest, because either global average temperatures are more responsive to greenhouse gasses than previously thought, or because the damage to the economy from a large temperature increase is much larger than the estimates in climate-ramp models.

Green Economy Better Than Brown Economy (Victor and Jacson, 2012)

According to the UNEP analysis, a green economy expands quicker than a brown economy. This conclusion has been contested for three primary reasons.

For starters, the CO2 reduction obtained in the crucial G2 scenario is woefully inadequate in response to the threat of severe climate change. Second, the UNEP model's approach of investment overly favors the green G2 situation since it allows for greater investment than the brown BAU2 situation with which it is contrasted. Furthermore, neither scenario addresses the critical issue of how the increased investment would be funded. Third, the G2 scenario makes implicit assumptions regarding the allocation of global economic production between richer and poorer nations. A fully green economy achieves both social fairness and environmental goals. Different assumptions regarding the wealth divide might have very different consequences for CO2 intensity reductions. The goals of equity and the environment are closely intertwined. Without some regional difference, economic growth, social fairness, and the environment cannot be fully examined in a global paradigm.

To summarize, it seems unlikely that considerable reduction in CO2 emissions (not to include other global environmental challenges) and significant closing of the gap between wealthy and poor (as needed by a truly green economy) can be achieved without some drop in economic development objectives.

Aggregate Supply and Demand, Green Economy (Ayunisari)

Green economy initiatives have a great bond of macroeconomic impacts on aggregate demand and supply. Those that operate on aggregate supply have received a great deal of attention in the current literature, particularly in regard to climate change. Aggregate demand impacts are less widely studied, although they play an important role in Keynesian stimulus packages and demand-driven growth models. The supply impacts may be thought of in two distinct but complementary ways. The first is to incorporate a stock of capital assets that impacts aggregate output alongside other capital stocks such as physical and human capital, as well as more purchases such as social and institutional capital. One issue with this technique is that measurement issues are massive, much more so than those related with assessing other types of capital. The second approach is to see ecological degradation as a limitation on aggregate supply, or, finally, as a loss of productivity or even a rising aggregate coordination costs.

The distinction between both methods is significant in distinguishing two fundamental ways of conceptualizing the relationships between the macroeconomy and ecosystems.

The first, proposed by World Bank (2006), views growth as a "process of asset management" in which resource rent from depletable natural resources may be converted into other resources through investment.

The Bank develops a metric of "adjusted total benefit" from this, which takes into consideration all types of capital investments as well as physical capital depreciation and natural capital depletion. However, it mistakenly suggests that resource scarcity cannot be viewed as a bottleneck since expenditures in human and physical capital may compensate for natural resource depletion - a concept known as "weak sustainability." As a result, this idea is only relevant in a limited sense when it comes to understanding the macroeconomics of a green economy.

The alternative perspective, derived from ecological economics, regards the macroF economy as an open subsystem inside a limited natural environment. This gives rise to the notion of "strong sustainability," which holds that there are environmental constraints to economic expansion.

The new Green Economy Report by UNEP provides a comprehensive study of the macroeconomic ramifications of environmental conservation (UNEP, 2011b, chapter 13).

According to the simulations, investing $1.3 trillion in the green economy, equivalent to 2% of global GDP or one-tenth of overseas investment, may result in slower development for a few years (compared to the situation in which those funds are invested as according past patterns), but will lead in higher growth after 5F10 years. Aside from providing longer-term growth, the green economy reduces the downside risks associated with climate change, energy shocks, water scarcity, and the loss of ecosystem services, raises employment (as green investments are generally more employment intensive), and has immediate benefits in terms of poverty alleviation.

Risks of Misuse of the Green Economy Concept (Khor, 2011)

A One-Dimensional Strategy

The first risk is that the "green economy" is defined or operationalized in a one-dimensional manner, removed from its context within the framework of sustainable development, and promoted in a purely "environmental" manner (without fully considering the advancement and equity aspects) and without regard for the international dimension, particularly its bad impacts on developing countries. In such a case, if the green economy idea gains importance while the sustainability concept recedes, the comprehensive sustainable development approach may be lost, with imbalances across the three pillars.

"One Size Fits All" Strategy

The second concern is that a "one size fits all" strategy is used, in which all nations are treated equally. This would result in failures for the environment, development, or both. Countries' degrees and phases of development must be properly examined, as must the goals and situations of developing countries. The notion of shared but differentiated accountability must be honored and implemented. As a result, while examining various concepts, policies, and objectives, enough flexibility and special treatment for developing nations, such as exclusions, allowing for more lenient responsibilities, and the supply of funding, technology, and capacity building, should be offered.

New Stipulation

Another concern is that the "green economy" may be used to impose additional conditions on developing nations in exchange for aid, loans, debt rescheduling, or debt relief. This may put pressure on impacted developing nations to implement one-dimensional environmental regulations rather than long-term development policies that consider economic, social, and equitable concerns.

Environmental Requirements

Another possible issue is the implementation of environmental laws for products; developing nations that fail to fulfill the criteria risk losing exports. The attitude to developing nations should be one of providing resources and technology to help them improve their environmental technologies and standards, rather than penalizing them. Many important standards are currently "globalized" from those of advanced nations without the concomitant assistance to developing nations to assist them in complying with such standards, necessitating the full and efficient involvement of developing countries in setting global standards.

Subsidies and Their Treatment

Another source of worry for many developing nations is that certain rich countries have provided significant subsidies to their industries for research and development (R&D) of ecologically sound products. This disadvantages poor nations, especially when they have the financial wherewithal to match the affluent countries' subsidies. Given this unjust mismatch in subsidies, developing nations and their businesses would be even more competitive if they had to decrease their tariffs for environmental items.

Trying to get Market Access Under the Pretense of the Environment

Another concern is that nations may utilize the environment to encourage the entry of their products and services into the markets of other countries. There is concern that the Green Economy idea will be utilized to further mercantile interests. For example, poor nations have voiced concerns inside the WTO that some rich countries are seeking to persuade them to reduce tariffs on many of their items, which the proponents argue are "environmental goods." This is in response to a demand in the Doha talks to decrease or remove obstacles to environmental products and services.

Connecting our Green Economy to the Blue Bodies (Steiner, 2014)

The distinction between both methods is significant in distinguishing two fundamental ways of conceptualizing the relationships between the macroeconomy and ecosystems.

The first, proposed by the World Bank (2006), views growth as a "process of asset management" in which asset rents from depletable natural resources may be converted into the other assets through investment. The Bank develops a measurement of "modified net savings" from this, which takes into consideration all types of capital investments as well as physical capital depreciation and natural capital depletion. This approach conveys the proper message: nations, particularly developing ones, should completely conserve natural resource rents.

However, it mistakenly suggests that resource scarcity cannot be viewed as a bottleneck since expenditures in human and physical capital may compensate for natural resource depletion - a concept known as "weak sustainability." As a result, this idea is only relevant in a limited sense when it comes to understanding the macroeconomics of a green economy. The alternative perspective, derived from ecological

Figure 5. A categorization of policy responses to the double crisis
(Bina, 2013)

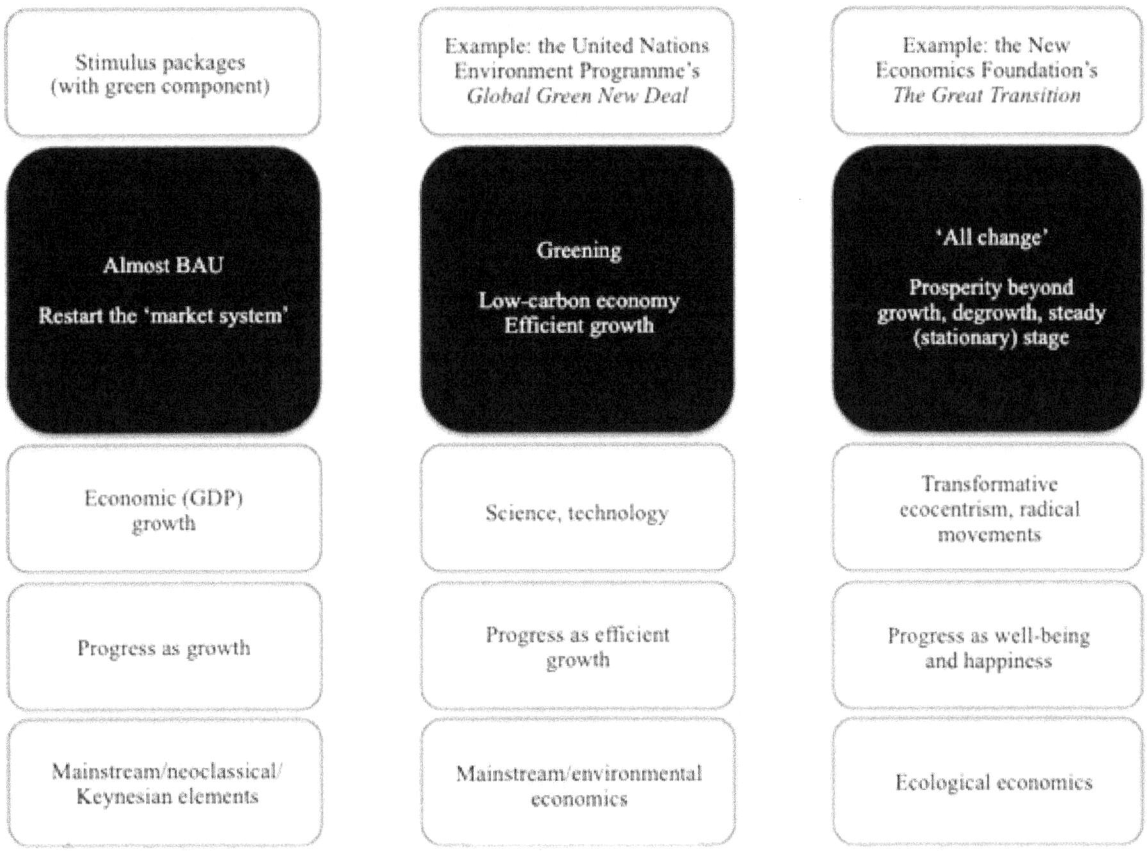

economics, regards the macroF economy as an open subsystem inside a limited natural environment. Its overall conclusion would be that capital cannot replace resources since they serve various roles, some of which cannot be recreated by people. This gives rise to the notion of "strong sustainability," which holds there are ecological constraints to economic expansion.

REFERENCES

Ayunisari, M. K. (2022). *Home*. Video. [Youtube.] https://d1wqtxts1xzle7.cloudfront.net/61020782/UN-DESA__20UNCTAD_20Transition_20GE20191025-7038-1yz04en-with-cover-page-v2.pdf?Expires=1669460288&Signature=LP6jRRpaX2ELVcf-jKZ0qOs6ZmjQo9s0B211~6nV5jnsuScrXsTbS1QhQ~QewQ8sw7KiobHCm0aNLv5O-2EZcQq~xRiOZXFVJvty. Accessed 26 November 2022.

Bina, O. (2013). *Home*. Video. [Youtube.] https://journals.sagepub.com/doi/epdf/10.1068/c1310j..

Collins, P. (2021). Sustainable development: Definition, objectives and examples. *Climate Selectra*. https://climate.selectra.com/en/environment/sustainable-development.

Dogaru, L. (2021). Green Economy and Green Growth—Opportunities for Sustainable Development. *MDPI*. https://www.mdpi.com/2504-3900/63/1/70.

GEC. (2020). The 5 Principles of Green Economy. *Green Economy Coalition*. https://www.greeneconomycoalition.org/news-and-resources/the-5-principles-of-green-economy.

Guo, M. (2020). Green Technology and Sustainable Development: Assessment and Green Growth Frameworks. *MDPI*. https://www.mdpi.com/2071-1050/12/16/6571.

Jenkins, T., & Simms, A. (2020). CHALLENGE PAPERS. *Stakeholder Forum*. https://stakeholderforum.org/wp-content/uploads/2020/06/PAPER-1_Green-Economy_Final_vj.pdf.

Kaushik, V. (2021). What is Green Economy? *Analytics Steps*. https://www.analyticssteps.com/blogs/what-green-economy.

Khor, M. (2011). Risks and uses of the green economy concept in the context of sustainable development, poverty and equity. *EconStor*. https://www.econstor.eu/bitstream/10419/232158/1/south-centre-rp-040.pdf.

Krugman, P. (2010). Climate Change - Building a Green Economy. *NYTimes.com*. https://cobblab.eas.gatech.edu/energy/Readings/envEcon_krugman.pdf.

Kth. (2020). Global objectives for sustainable development. *KTH*. https://www.kth.se/en/om/miljo-hallbar-utveckling/utbildning-miljo-hallbar-utveckling/verktygslada/sustainable-development/fn-s-globala-mal-for-hallbar-utveckling-1.612059.

Steiner, A. (2014). Resilience and Adaption. *The Economist*. https://impact.economist.com/sustainability/resilience-and-adaptation/bringing-the-green-economy-to-the-blue-world?gclid=CjwKCAiAhKycBhAQEiwAgf19ejdQ0-_l8rACjFf57BARdoZRBJG8b0Yf3vqR1K4I2kmMSJOCmjYftxoCREYQAvD_BwE&gclsrc=aw.ds

Stoddart, H. (2022). *earthsummit2012*. Stakeholder Forum. https://stakeholderforum.org/wp-content/uploads/2020/06/Earth-Summit-2012-Principles-for-the-Green-Economy-1.pdf.

UN. (2022). Green economy: Sustainable Development Knowledge Platform. *Sustainable Development Goals*, https://sustainabledevelopment.un.org/index.php?menu=1446.

UNEP. (2022). Green economy. *UNEP*. https://www.unep.org/regions/asia-and-pacific/regional-initiatives/supporting-resource-efficiency/green-economy

UNRIC. (2022). *Green economy: a path towards development and poverty eradication*. UNRIC. https://unric.org/en/green-economy-a-path-towards-sustainable-development-and-poverty-eradication/.

Victor, P. A., & Jacson, T. (2012). *Home*. CloudFront. https://d1wqtxts1xzle7.cloudfront.net/57512350/j.ecolecon.2012.02.02820181005-18531-a8youb-with-cover-page-v2.pdf?Expires=1669460251&Signature=W~mm1Wn175O2ZBMs8yy6KcEQwRpOxMnsJ93yaI~5GGM3lA0uQdoJKrHJlghkjCuXziSAlgUuMePH8PvnlFYVQniNdY6mJsRFMK5KrqGr9QEGUU67S.

Chapter 2
From Stockholm 1972 to Stockholm 2022:
Fifty Years Later

Edwin Vegas
Universidad Peruana de Ciencias e Informática, Peru

Wilfredo Vegas López
Public Prosecutor's Office, Peru

Rui Alexandre Castanho
https://orcid.org/0000-0003-1882-4801
WSB University, Portugal

ABSTRACT

This chapter reflects on the significant developments in environmental awareness and action over five decades. It discusses the evolution of global perspectives on environmental challenges, tracing the journey from the inaugural Earth Summit in Stockholm in 1972 to the present day. This brief chapter highlights the progress, the challenges, and the urgent need for continued international cooperation to address pressing environmental issues. It also explores the role of subsequent summits and initiatives in shaping policies and promoting sustainable practices, ultimately emphasizing the ongoing relevance of the ecological agenda as we mark fifty years since the first Earth Summit.

THE STARTING POINT

Fifty years have passed since the First Earth Summit held by the United Nations in Stockholm, Sweden; in 1972; Conceived on May 29, 1968, in which the Organization approved holding the United Nations Conference on the Human Environment -CNUMH- (Lescano et al., 2013).

Twenty-three years have passed since the official creation of the United Nations or two human generations lost, for the international community to become interested and realize the magnitude of the human damage produced and the capital importance that must be given to the care of the "environment

DOI: 10.4018/979-8-3693-1297-1.ch002

that surrounds the man" (section 1 of the Proclamation of the Stockholm Declaration on the Human Environment, produced as a consequence of the United Nations Conference on the Human Environment (UNCHR), June 16, 1972, also called the United Nations Scientific Conference.

The most remote antecedent of a scientific meeting that dealt with environmental issues was the United Nations Scientific Conference on Conservation and Use of Resources from August 17 to June 6, 1949, held in New York, United States of America.

However, it should be noted that the concern for the rights of Nature dates back to 1836, when Ralph Waldo Emerson published his essay Nature, advocating that "behind nature and in all of nature the spirit is present." That one, he was a pioneering critic of buoyant economic growth, predicting "the dangers of trade, as a threat to the balance of man and nature."

Another predecessor in the thought of the rights of nature is Chief Noath Seattle (1854), of the Suquamish tribe, with his famous letter to the President of the United States Franklin Pierce, who proposed to him to buy the Northwest Territories of the United States, which today they are part of the State of Washington (Vegas, 2000).

There is also Henry David Thoreau (1861), who, with a prophetic vision due to his affection for nature, pointed out: "*Most men, it seems to me, do not care about Nature and would sell their share for a declared sum and even for a glass of rum and it is for the same reason that a son does not care about these things that we must continue to protect everyone from the vandalism of a few*."

We must also mention Aldo Leopold (1996) in his famous essay. Ecological Balance: A Sandy County Almanac, noting *"(...) our best society today acts like a hypochondriac, so obsessed with its own economic health, that it has lost the ability to stay sane and perhaps we can achieve that change in values if we do a reassessment of artificial things, tame them and manage to circumscribe them based on natural, free and wild things.*"

Leopold continues: "*Conservation has gotten nowhere because it is incompatible with our biblical concept of the Earth (with the conservation of matter and energy, our addition) (...) we abuse it because we see it as a consumer product that it belongs...when we see the Earth as something to which we belong, we can begin to use it with love and respect (...) in no other way will it be possible for the Earth to survive the impact of mechanized man, nor will we be able to enjoy the aesthetic harvest it is capable of to offer ourselves, through science, as a contribution to culture*".

With her work Silent Spring, Rachel Carson (1962) brought much to the conservation spirit.

THE STOCKHOLM DECLARATION 1972

The Stockholm Declaration has a proclamation with six recitals and 26 Principles aimed at conserving and improving the human environment. It also has an Action Plan with recommendations for international environmental action.

From the Proclamation, it is noted that the words Science and Technology, mentioned six times, are the axis of the Declaration. Thus, recital 1 of the Proclamation reads: "*With the rapid acceleration of science and technology, man has acquired the power to transform in innumerable ways and on an unprecedented scale, what surrounds him.*" That is to say, the man who transforms and generates environmental damage; is the same man who, with Science and Technology, the call to repair that one, to overcome and improve well-being, including fundamental human rights.

This reference to Science and Technology is explicit in Principle 18 *"(…) to use Science and Technology (…) to solve environmental problems and for the common good of humanity*".

Likewise, Principle 20 refers to the role that: *"(…) scientific research and development regarding the solution of environmental problems*" should have in the countries.

However, this "scientific-technological strategy" of Stockholm 1972 was very far from achieving a preventive environmental policy, which by the way, no country has materialized a strictly preventative ecological approach, not even Japan has completed it (Simonis U.E, 1997), and instead encouraged a curative environmental policy, promoting post-process measures instead of a preventive approach, that was recently given in the Rio Declaration 1992 (Principle 15).

In our opinion, the problem with the "technological solution" is that industrial society does not consider permanent the analysis of the life cycle of the products and runs the risk of the iceberg dilemma: only part of the ice sticks out of the water - and it sometimes remains hidden behind the mist.

The positive thing about Stockholm 1972 is that it outlined an initial level of environmental policy, interrelating three factors of its cycle: ecological damage, scientific-technical knowledge, and environmental awareness. Ideally, to accelerate scientific-technical expertise and improve the threshold of ecological awareness necessary to reduce or mitigate environmental damage.

Point six of the Proclamation reads: "*We have reached a moment in history in which we must guide our actions (…)*"; in an apparent allusion to working for a better quality of life with a PRO TIERRA approach. In fact, this occurred by the fact that in 1972, Meadows's work appeared: The Limits to Growth: Report of the Club of Rome on the predicament of humanity, who argued convincingly "*(…) that if economic growth continued as it had been until then, it would eventually exceed the limits of the Earth's resources and lead to its collapse."*

Also, in 1972 a study conducted by the Massachusetts Institute of Technology (MIT); concluded: "*(…) humanity's quest for economic growth without regard to environmental and social costs would lead to the collapse of society by the middle of the 21st century*" much in line with the COVID 19 pandemic of the recent past.

According to Herrington (2021), this collapse of society would occur in 2040: "*(…) without a drastic change, industrial society is heading towards collapse*." She used the World3 computer model for her predictive analysis, considering ten variables: world population, fertility and mortality rates, industrial production, services, non-renewable resources, persistent pollution, human well-being, and ecological footprint. With all this, she concluded that: *"(…) the consumerist business mentality that emphasizes business above all else will lead to a decline in economic growth in the next decade (2021-2030), followed by total social collapse by 2040."*

However, this terrifying and apocalyptic prognosis "does not mean that humanity will cease to exist," but rather that: "*(…) industrial and economic growth will stop and then slow down, damaging food production and living standards."*

About the 26 UNCHR Principles, what is referred to in the first is fascinating: the achievement of fundamental human rights violated by the liberal market economy development model in its linear sequence. It is evident that the answer involves the ethical challenge of the States; in the search for a development model with welfare and without victims, changing that model of primary export development, dependent on natural resources, in which western naturalism predominates, which considers nature external to humans, without it being a subject of law.

Principles 2 and 3 have to do with the global ecological footprint, in which almost eight billion inhabitants consume much more than the Earth's capacity for food production.

Principle 6 has a thermodynamic approach consistent with the laws of conservation of matter and energy: "avoid materials from releasing heat"; given that unnecessary heat release with linear technologies contributes to entropy with system paralysis.

Although the 1972 Stockholm Action Plan considered climate change, it did not become the conference's central theme. It was there that the issue of climate change was raised for the first time, warning governments that they should take an interest in activities that cause climate change and assess the probability and magnitude of their impact on the climate and commissioned the World Meteorological Organization to understand better the atmosphere and the causes of climate change, either natural or as a result of human activity.

Contextually, Principle 6 should be the basis of public policies in its double meaning: that they do not generate exclusion, much less rivalry. Otherwise, we would face the Tragedy of the Commons (Hardin, 1968).

Principle 10 invokes a bridge between the economy and ecology, having to promote the circular economy as a response to the sustainability model.

Principle 11 introduces the concept of environmental policy in its three stages, discussed above.

Principle 15 calls for "abandoning projects aimed at colonialist and racist domination." This theme is still valid today, and we exemplify it with the "Coltan war" (Columbia and Tantalum) in the Democratic Republic of Congo, in which there were five million deaths. Thereby, this leads to the need to work on Sustainable Development Goals in a new approach to Social ecology.

Principle 22 marks the beginning of international environmental law developing the Polluter-Payer Principle.

Principle 23 introduces considering "value systems." This is the crux of the matter, and as Klisberg (2004) points out: *"(...) more ethics is required to have more development, especially countries, like Peru, dominated by state corruption, drug trafficking, uncontrolled migration, lack of health and education; as well as the illegal international trade in wild flora and fauna*".

Principle 26 related to the latent threat of a Third World Nuclear War, which already produces collateral damage to the environment in general, on the occasion of the Russia-Ukraine War.

In short, the merit of these 26 Principles is that world attention has focused on development with support "intellectually, morally, socially and spiritually."

The United Nations Conference on the Human Environment (1972, Stockholm, Sweden) had the challenge and merit of placing sustainability on the international stage in a context of economic growth and development, included in the Stockholm Declaration Document on the Human Environment 50 years ago (June 16, 1972) (Lescano et al. 2013).

According to Sachs, "sustainable development" was introduced in 1980 in the report "World Conservation Strategy: The conservation of living resources for the achievement of sustainable development."

FIFTY YEARS LATER: FROM STOCKHOLM TO RIO DE JANEIRO TO JOHANNESBURG

In 1992 the Earth Summit was held in Rio de Janeiro, Brazil, which constituted an important milestone that allowed the establishment of a new Plan of Action for Sustainable Development. This happened thirty years after Stockholm.

In Rio 1992, the States agreed "that protecting the environment, social and economic development was essential to achieve sustainable development; based on 27 Rio Principles.

Ten years later, Rio, the World Summit on Sustainable Development takes place in Johannesburg, South Africa (decadal evaluation of the application and execution of Agenda or Program 21), reaffirming the political commitment to the Sustainable Development of humanity from the African continent, the cradle of humankind and reaffirming the "vital role of indigenous problems in development" and noting that "multilateralism is the future" with the need for "international institutions and multilateral organizations that are more effective, democratic and responsible for their actions."

In 2012 in Rio, Brazil, the United Nations Conference on Sustainable Development produced the report: The future we want with 283 policy guidelines for environmental, social, and economic development.

In 2015, the 17 Sustainable Development Goals (SDGs) were formulated in an intellectual project.

Likewise, in recent years, Conferences on Biological Diversity and 26 Conferences of the Parties on Climate Change have been held.

In Vegas (2022), the case of Peru is pointed out in particular, which depicts the paradoxical poverty of the country with its biological wealth, which due to its exceptional location in South America, has high ecological and specific diversity; It is a privileged country due to its natural wealth, with two-thirds of its territory occupied by the Andes Mountains, whose mountain ranges run more or less parallel to the coastal zone.

Vegas (2018) points out that in Peru, biodiversity items can play an essential role in national development, conceived with a modern futuristic vision and taking advantage of little-used or totally untapped comparative benefits until today.

This rich biological heritage of Peruvians is paradoxical if we compare it with their human development, which ranges from medium to low, with 51.3% of Peruvians in poverty and 23.1% in extreme poverty (figures before the pandemic). Peru ranks 123 out of 196 countries in literacy rate and 88 in infant mortality (18.4 deaths per thousand normal births); life expectancy (79.74 years) is in 36th place globally and third regionally.

FINAL THOUGHTS

As a result, we can conclude that imminent climate change, the loss of biodiversity, and pollution; It is the triple threat that humanity faces, added to them the global health crisis of the Covid pandemic and other pandemics to come, which puts us in the challenge to avoid the collapse of society, in the construction of a new paradigm of sustainability in the approach of social ecology and the perspective of human rights, with the understanding of rethinking State policies, aimed at achieving a development model with a new lifestyle and by the consideration of the 2030 Agenda in a post-pandemic world, which needs cooperation, multilateralism and greater productive integration in the vision of environmental policy preventative rather than curative. Thus, this is the current dilemma of humanity.

The dilemma is that we need to consider that the economic subsystem has already reached or exceeded the essential sources of resources, and there is no limit to its growth.

Therefore, the solution to the environmental problems facing humanity and exacerbated since 1970; Innovative policies and management instruments are needed that include:

1. Avoid excess carrying capacity of terrestrial and marine ecosystems;

2. Avoid using technologies that increase entropy (waste heat) as polluting sources;
3. Avoid land conversion that destroys habitat, increases soil erosion, and accelerates the loss of species diversity.

Likewise, it is clear to us that the international framework of environmental policy, in the past fifty years, has been strengthened, with treaties and agreements aimed at countries generating their development strategies to manage their renewable or non-renewable natural resources.

Furthermore, it should also be highlighted that sustainable development involves dispensing with the linear economy with an anthropocentric vision and transitioning into productive activities, bridging the laws of nature, in the conservation of matter and energy, with a picture of the circular economy, and in a strict sense of justice to the protection of human rights.

REFERENCES

Carson, R. (1962). *Silent spring*. Houghton Mifflin.

Costanza, R., Cumberland, J., Daly, H., Goodland, R., & Noorgard, R. (1997). *An Introduction to Ecological Economics. St. Lucie Press*. Florida e ISEE International Society for Ecological Economics. doi:10.1201/9781003040842

Herrington, G. (2021). Update to limits to growth: Comparing the World3 model with empirical data. *Journal of Industrial Ecology*, *25*(3), 614–626. doi:10.1111/jiec.13084

Klisberg, B. (2004). *Más ética más desarrollo*. Temas Grupo Editorial.

Leopold, A. (1996). *Equilibrio Ecológico: Almanaque de un condado arenoso*. Ediciones Gernika.

Lescano, J., Valdéz, L., Vegas, E., Reyes, C., & Belaúnde, M. (2013). *Manual del Desarrollo Sostenible*. Guevara Garay S.A. y Geo Lab SRL.

Meadows, D. H., Meadows, D. L., Randers, J., & Behrens, W. (1972). *The limits to growth*. Universe.

Sachs, J. (2015). *La era del Desarrollo Sostenible*. Ediciones Deusto.

Simonis, U. E. (1997). Reorientación ecológica de la sociedad industrial. In *La protección del medio ambiente, conceptos y políticas. CIEDLA*. Editores Josef Thesing y Wilhelm Hofmeister.

Vegas, E. (2003). *Hacia un Perú sustentable. Colección Perú Sustentable*. Repositorio institucional de la Universidad Peruana de Ciencias e Informática. repositorio.upci.edu.pe

Vegas, E. (2018). *Biodiversidad de la macro región norte del Perú: Estado y estrategia para su conservación y usos sustentable*. Repositorio institucional de la Universidad Nacional de Piura, Perú. https://repositorio.unp.edu.pe/handle/UNP/1580

Vegas, E., & Vegas, W. (2022). *Los Objetivos de Desarrollo Sostenible en tiempo pos-Covid-19 y en la mirada de los derechos humanos. Revista 131: enero-junio 2022. POLÍTICA INTERNACIONAL*. Academia Diplomática del Perú.

Chapter 3
The European Union's Border Carbon Tax Regulation and Its Possible Effects on Turkey's Exports in the Short Term

Şahin Akkaya
Istanbul University, Turkey

ABSTRACT

The European Union's carbon border adjustment mechanism (CBAM) ratified by the European Parliament as a part of the European Green Deal in 2023 will be in effect in the beginning of the year of 2026. But EU's CBAM regulation shows that compensatory carbon tax on imports cannot be applied in a non-discriminatory manner in terms of the destination principle. Therefore, it is seen that the paragraph G of Article 20 of the GATT allowing for the measures to protect the exhaustible natural resources, may constitute a more appropriate justification for the EU's carbon adjustment at the border. The EU's border carbon adjustment mechanism will also have a negative impact on international competition, primarily in terms of carbon-intensive industries in the countries such as Turkey. It is considered reasonable for Turkey to introduce appropriate policy tools to price carbon in a way not being subject to the European Union's carbon tax at the border.

INTRODUCTION

The European Union's the Carbon Border Adjustment Mechanism (CBAM) was ratified by the European Parliament as a part of the European Green Deal and officially entered into force the day after its publication in the Official Journal of the EU on 16 May 2023. But this regulation will be in effect in the beginning of the year of 2026. The Green Deal adopted by the European Union (EU) within the framework of the Paris Climate Agreement is important in terms of reducing carbon dioxide emissions in order to slow down global warming. As known, the use of any policy tool aiming to reduce carbon dioxide emissions by all countries can ensure that carbon leakage doesn't occur. In addition, any carbon-

DOI: 10.4018/979-8-3693-1297-1.ch003

reducing policy tool applied globally would have the function of reducing the existing negative impact on international competition. However, both the Kyoto Protocol and the Paris Climate Agreement mainly focus on reducing the carbon emissions of the developed countries, taking into account the concerns of developing countries. This situation has led the European Union to implement a carbon tax at the border, primarily starting from carbon-intensive industries, in order to address carbon leakage and thus the negative impact on international competition.

Within the framework of the European green deal, the European Union's border carbon adjustment mechanism (CBAM), which is stated to be mainly for carbon leakage, has two important aspects that need to be addressed. The first of these is the issue of whether the carbon regulation at the border complies with the World Trade Organization (WTO)legislation. It should be noted that the issue of carbon adjustment at the border had been addressed in many studies before the EU's regulation. The second important issue regarding this regulation is how the foreign trade of non-union countries with European Union countries will be affected, depending on the effect of the implementation on the international competition of carbon-intensive industries. As of 2026, the European Union will impose carbon tax during imports of carbon-intensive industries' products such as cement, iron-steel, aluminum, fertilizer and electricity in the short term. In the long run, carbon pricing at the border is planned to cover more sectors.

In the second part of this study, it will be focused on whether the European Union's border carbon adjustment mechanism (CBAM) is in compliance with the WTO legislation. The European Union's border carbon adjustment mechanism will also have an impact on international competition, primarily in terms of carbon-intensive industries. This situation will also affect the foreign trade of non-union countries with European Union countries, which cannot take measures in terms of carbon pricing or cannot take adequate measures. Therefore, in the third section, the possible short-term effects of the European Union's border carbon tax implementation on Turkish foreign trade with the Union will be discussed. In the last section, the findings of the study will be presented.

THE EUROPEAN UNION'S BORDER CARBON TAX ADJUSTMENT AND WORLD TRADE LEGISLATION

In a situation where global cooperation cannot be achieved, it is seen that developed countries, especially the European Union countries, have made a certain commitment in terms of reducing greenhouse gases. Because the more industrial goods production in order to get lower production cost gives rise to more carbon emission in developing countries having higher carbon intensive economies than developed ones, global carbon emissions cannot be reduced sufficiently. This situation also causes the complaints by the industries having energy-intensive technology and therefore faced with the disadvantage in international competition in developed countries (see Bullock, 2018, p.610).

It is not possible to say that the border carbon adjustment of the European Union is not related to the competitive disadvantage of the industries with energy-intensive technology in the Union. Due to the production-based determination of the amount of carbon in the carbon reduction policy, some producers moving their production to countries not taking carbon reduction measures can enable developed countries to achieve their emission reduction target. However, in such a case, a harmful dynamic effect known as carbon leakage occurs in terms of reducing the emission of greenhouse gases globally (Dröge, 2011, p.1195).

BORDER CARBON TAX ADJUSTMENT IN TERMS OF DESTINATION PRINCIPLE

The "destination principle" may constitute the basis of the proposals to impose a carbon tax at the border in order to address the competitive disadvantage in the countries taxing carbon and the carbon leakage that may arise in the case of unilateral implementation of a carbon tax. As it is known, the principle of destination requires tax refunds on exports and compensatory tax for import for goods subject to international trade. Since these two practices will ensure that the goods with indirect tax like value added tax subject to international trade are cleared from indirect taxes in the world markets, these taxes will not affect international competition and the allocation of international resources.

The direct carbon leakage that may occur due to the carbon reduction measures taken by the developed countries is especially limited to sectors such as steel, cement, iron, aluminum, chemicals industry and paper production. Therefore, it can be argued that instead of the border carbon regulations within the framework of the destination principle, international sectoral regulations mainly targeting these sectors will be more effective (Eckersley, 2010, pp.375-378). This argument is also related to the question of why the European Union primarily considers energy-intensive industries in terms of border carbon pricing.

On the other hand, carbon leakage mainly due to the measures taken by developed countries originates from both imports and exports. The fact that the goods imported from countries without carbon costs can be sold at lower prices than the goods produced in the country taking the unilateral measure shows the carbon leakage caused by imports. Due to the increase in the prices of the goods exported by the countries using instruments such as carbon tax, carbon leakage arises coming from exports. As a result, the goods of the countries not taking carbon emission reduction measures and therefore producing with lower cost will become exportable to the countries that previously had imported from the countries which today starting to take carbon reduction measures (Dröge, 2011, p.1192).

The border carbon tax adjustment of the European Union does not include carbon tax refunds on exports. Therefore, the issue of carbon tax refunds on exports will not be analyzed in terms of the destination principle.

Article 1 (art.1/1) of the General Agreement on Customs Tariffs and Trade (GATT), referring to Article 3, stipulates that the compensatory duty to be charged on imports on the basis of the destination principle must not be contrary to the clause of the "most favored country". Therefore, within the scope of the EU's carbon tax application at the border, the compensatory carbon tax on imports may be violation the "most favored country" clause (Mc Lure, 2011, p.462). Likewise, the second article of the GATT (art. 2/2a), again referring to the third article, indicates that a fiscal obligation equivalent to the domestic tax may be imposed on like goods during import. In this case, it is not possible to base the compensatory tax at the border of the European Union on the carbon contents of the goods produced in the exporting country (Feaver & Sheehy, 2012, p.813).

The concepts of "product" and "like" in the third article (art. 3/2) of GATT, which states that compensatory tax on imports cannot exceed the tax on comparable products, should also be considered in terms of the European Union's border carbon tax at the border. As per the report of WTO Appellate Body first of all, it is necessary to determine whether the goods produced in the importing country and the goods imported are like products to each other. When the products are like goods to each other, then it will be necessary to consider whether the internal indirect tax on the imported goods is equal to the tax on the goods produced in the importing country (Bullock, 2018, pp.626-627).

As it is known, the carbon tax, which is an emission tax, is not a tax on the product; it can be argued that carbon tax is a third category fiscal obligation such as taxes on machinery, auxiliary materials and energy, therefore, according to the actual carbon emissions coming from imported goods, making carbon adjustments at the border is against world trade legislation (Holzer & Shariff, 2012, p.251). In addition, since the carbon dioxide released into the atmosphere is not included in the product, the application of compensatory carbon tax on imports will be contrary to the provisions of GATT (Mc Lure, 2011, p.460).

There are two aspects of the concept of like. The first is related to the goods produced in the importing country and the exporting country. The second is the like discussion regarding the goods produced in different exporting countries. Since a good produced with the energy obtained from coal is a like when it is produced with electricity obtained from renewable energy sources, a product produced by using renewable energy sources in the importing country will not be subject to carbon tax. In this case, how to apply compensatory tax on the imported goods produced with the energy obtained from fossil fuels without discrimination is an important issue (Metcalf & Weisbach, 2009, p.547). Secondly, because the imported goods coming from two different exporting countries with the same physical properties, used for the same purpose, having the same consumer perception and the same tariff classification are like products, the different production technologies of these goods imported from different exporting countries don't make these two goods different products (Holzer & Shariff, 2012, p.251).

The use of the average of the tax collected from the goods produced in the country in the calculation of the tax to be charged at the border will also lead to the levying of more carbon tax than the imported goods produced as a result of lower carbon emissions. It will be a violation of Art.3 of GATT (Porterfield, 2019, p.40). Likewise, the carbon tax to be collected at the border by using the average of the tax collected from the goods produced in the importing country will not be suitable for the purpose of reducing carbon emissions when the exporting countries cause more carbon emissions while producing the relevant goods. Because this means levying lower carbon tax at the border. Both of these cases show that compensatory carbon tax on imported goods cannot be applied in a non-discriminatory manner.

BORDER CARBON TAX ADJUSTMENT IN TERMS OF GATT ARTICLE 20

The European commission has designed three possible different CBAM policy instruments in 2020. These are 1- carbon tax on selected products imported and produced in the country 2- new carbon customs tax on imported products 3- making the EU ETS system cover also imported goods. Not all of these alternative EU CBAM policy instruments can be justified under the non-discrimination provisions of the GATT, particularly in terms of articles I, III and XI..As can be seen here, none of these policy instruments comply with WTO legislation, except for Article 20 of the GATT, which contains provisions of general exceptions (Englisch & Falcao, 2022-1). The Article 20 of the GATT on exceptions, states that; it has decreed that they can take measures to limit imports without making any distinction between countries, for the reasons listed in ten paragraphs, such as protecting public morals, protecting national historical or archaeological values.

It is possible to see that within the framework of Article 20 of GATT; Paragraphs "b" for the measures necessary to protect the life and health of humans, animals or plants, and "g" for the measures to protect the exhaustible natural resources, are the exceptions that allow discriminatory carbon tax on the imported goods coming from the countries not taking measures to reduce carbon emissions. When the phrase "protection of global natural resources" is taken into account, it can be considered that the exception in clause g will be a more solid basis in terms of damage to the global atmosphere. Therefore, paragraph g of Article 20 of the GATT may constitute a more appropriate justification for the EU's carbon adjustment at the border.

In this respect, it is important that the US argument in the US-Gasoline conflict was accepted by the relevant Panel. In the US-Gasoline dispute, it is noteworthy that the relevant Panel agrees with the US argument, since the US based her argument on that clean air is an exhaustible natural resource and is consumed due to pollutants arising from fuel oil (gasoline) consumption (Englisch & Falcao, 2022-2, p.10939). However, carbon tax adjustment at the border should, above all, be supportive of climate policies, and should not aim to impose sanctions on countries not taking measures for reducing carbon emissions and to protect domestic producers from foreign competition (Dröge, 2011, p.1194).

First of all, as in the chapeau of Article 20, any practice must also comply with the provisions of not making arbitrary or unjustifiable discrimination between countries in the same condition or disguised restriction on international trade (Bullock, 2018, p.634). Secondly, any practice under CBAM of the EU justifiable under Article 20 of the GATT, must be in accordance with paragraphs b and/or g. Therefore, it is necessary to be proven by the EU that the actions to be taken comply with both conditions (Englisch & Falcao, 2022-2, p.10936).

Although levying more carbon tax at the border due to the fact that the imported goods contain more carbon depending on the production process compared to the goods produced in the importing country is a violation the provisions of Article II and III of GATT, it can be argued that it is justified within the framework of the environmental exception provisions of the article XX of the GATT. Here, the important thing in terms of carbon tax at the border is that the rate of the tax to be calculated according to the emission does not exceed the tax rate on domestic products in the importing country (Porterfield, 2019, pp.38-39).

In addition, it should be noted that the exception in paragraph "g" of Article 20 regarding the protection of exhaustible natural resources allows for imposing carbon tax on imported goods, but it is not possible to rebate tax on exports (Mc Lure,2011,pp.462-463).While border carbon adjustment on imports is legitimate/legal within the framework of article XX of GATT, it is likely to be considered by WTO that these applications are giving illegal export subsidy, when exported goods have been excluded from carbon tax or ETS application within the EU, or ETS regulated companies have been rebated according to their exports (Böhringer et al. 2022, p.23).

Based on the Panel report on the United states-Gasoline dispute, the question of whether it is appropriate to levy carbon tax at the border on imported carbon-containing products such as iron and steel used in the production of any final goods is in accordance with the Article 20 should also been answered. In this case, there is no direct or explicit relationship between the goods the carbon tax levied at the border and the clean air. However, because such a measure aims to reduce carbon emissions and therefore contributes to the preservation of clean air, as an exhaustible natural resource, it can be argued that levying carbon tax on imported carbon-containing inputs will comply with b and g paragraphs of article XX of GATT. In this regard, it should be noted that WTO member countries will seek to interpret their trade obligations in light of their environmental commitments (See Englisch & Falcao, 2022-2, p.10939).

On the other hand, it should be noted that the EU's border carbon adjustments will face several implementation difficulties. First of all, it should be kept in mind that the EU cannot demand from foreign ones a restriction that its own producers are not subject to. The second difficulty in implementation is related to the determination of the carbon amount in the imported products. It will be difficult to determine the carbon content of the imported products and to price the carbon accordingly at the border. In this framework, according to the rules of the World Trade Organization, the compensation opportunities provided to the producers in the Union should also be given to the foreign producers. The carbon pricing at the border must be done by taking into account the carbon pricing scheme that offers specific conditions to the industries of EITE (Emissions Intensive and Trade Exposed). Also, if carbon emissions are priced in the exporting country, then carbon pricing at the border by the EU should theoretically be done by taking into account the difference between the taxes in exporting country and the EU. However, factors such as exceptions, exemptions and free emission rights (free allocations) given by the EU member countries make it difficult to determine the mentioned differences (Böhringer et al. 2022, pp.23-24).

About the difficulty how to determine the carbon content of the goods imported, it may also be advisable to reach an international agreement adopting average emission standards determined by the importing countries or "best available technology" for imported goods from all countries (Dröge, 2011, pp.1196-1197). In this context, it can also be argued that, as per the world trade legislation, the least discriminatory practice is essentially the determination of carbon contents according to the best available technology in the importing countries (Holzer & Shariff, 2012, p.252).

However, the important issue in terms of tax adjustment at the border is to determine that the actual carbon tax will levy on the imported goods. In this respect, since the "processes and production methods"(PPMs) is based on the actual carbon emissions of the imported goods, it is the most appropriate method for the carbon tax charged at the border, but this method is difficult to apply (Holzer & Shariff, 2012, p.250). Besides, it can be argued that the PPM-process or production methods (PPMs) will not pose a significant obstacle in the development and implementation of carbon taxes in terms of the WTO legislation. In this regard, the exception provisions in the 20th article of the GATT and the border carbon measures based on the production processes of imported goods, which are flexible enough and do not force exporting countries to adopt certain PPMs (specific PPMs) may be interpreted within this framework (Porterfield, 2019, p.37).

In terms of the justification of the EU's CBAM application within the framework of Article 20(g) of GATT, the fact that the carbon pricing in the EU (for example, the carbon tax) and the carbon pricing at the border for imported goods must be the same in order to ensure competition neutrality between the goods produced in the EU and imported ones. In this regard, the EU must take the necessary measures.

Because EU member states have price carbon in different ways. Therefore, implementing an EU-wide carbon tax would be an important step (Englisch & Falcao, 2022-2, pp.10940-10942). According to the Dispute Settlement Body of GATT (DSB) jurisprudence, a trade-restrictive measure, to be considered appropriate within the framework of Article 20(g), must not force other countries to change their policies. The countries imposing trade restrictions should lift them in the case of the relevant countries change their policies. In this context, it can be argued that the EU's CTA -Carbon tax arrangement) encourages trade partner countries to tax their own carbon emissions but does not have a compelling feature. If exporting countries start pricing carbon by a carbon tax, it is important for these countries to have the flexibility to deduct this tax from the carbon tax at the border (Englisch & Falcao, 2022-2, p.10940).

In addition, it can be mentioned that the implementation of carbon tax at the border, by not taking measures to reduce carbon emissions, will have persuading effect on the countries that cause high carbon emissions to take measures to reduce carbon emissions. It can also be argued that, in terms of convincing other countries, the development and implementation of a border carbon tax in line with the GATT conditions would be supportive of the international climate governance regime created by the Paris Agreement (Bullock, 2018).

POSSIBLE FOREIGN TRADE EFFECTS OF THE EU'S BORDER CARBON TAX ADJUSTMENT ON TURKEY

As mentioned earlier, border carbon tax adjustments in the European Union are primarily recommended against carbon leakage and international competitive disadvantage. In addition, it can be mentioned that the implementation of carbon tax at the border will have persuading effect on the exporting countries that cause high carbon emissions. Because the levying carbon tax at the border on imported goods by importing countries will eliminate the competitive advantage from not collecting taxes by exporting countries, and the potential tax revenues provided by carbon tax will be attractive for tax policy, exporting countries will want to pursuit a policy of pricing their carbon emissions (Metcalf & Weisbach, 2009, pp.545-546). In addition, border carbon adjustments by the importing countries allow these developed countries to obtain additional public revenue, and this additional resource can be used for the projects aimed at reducing carbon emissions in exporting developing countries and therefore this policy will be able to persuade developing countries to contribute to the climate policies (Grubb, 2011, pp.1050-1057).

It is also important how the inputs used in production will been treated in terms of the carbon adjustment of the EU at the border. In order to reduce global carbon emissions by preventing carbon leakage, the carbon emission caused by the inputs used in the production of final goods should also been taken into account. In other words, if the inputs that cause high carbon emissions are used to produce the final product that emits relatively less carbon, making border carbon adjustment only for the final products may not be suitable for the purpose of reducing carbon leakage.

On the other hand, the studies dealing with the possible effects of the European Union's border carbon adjustment mechanism (CBAM) also make scientific contribution in the issue. One of these studies, Eicke et al. (2021), aims to analyze the impact of border carbon adjustment by considering two scenarios. The first is the border carbon pricing to be applied to steel, cement and aluminum imports, which are carbon-intensive industries. The second scenario is the application of border carbon pricing to all importing goods. First of all, it is aimed to understand how the steel, cement and aluminum exports of the some exporting countries to the European Union will be affected by the carbon pricing at the border. In this study, it is found that in terms of both scenarios, because of her high carbon intensities, dependence on trade with the European Union, unsatisfactory surveillance of carbon emissions and low administrative capacities make Morocco the most disadvantageous country. In terms of their insufficient administrative capacities, it is concluded that Bosnia and Herzegovina and Mozambique draw attention.

The second noteworthy study on the effects of the European Union's carbon pricing at the border is Mörsdorf (2022). Starting from the legislative proposal of the European commission on carbon leakage and taking into account only direct emissions, Mörsdorf (2022) which addressed the metals, minerals and chemicals categories shows that carbon leakage could been reduced by around one-third compared to the current situation when a carbon price/tax of $50 per ton at the border on imported products were applied. Secondly, it is concluded that this carbon tax can generate revenue which can reach to 32 billion USD that could be used to support low-carbon innovation and international climate finance.

Cheng (2021) is the third study which shed light on the effects of the European Union's border carbon tax. The effects on carbon emissions are analyzed with a simple two-country model. In this study, two alternatives are presented in terms of tax adjustments at the border. In the first of these, as in the European Union, the country taxing carbon emissions only makes carbon adjustment for the final goods imported. The second alternative is that the country taxing the domestic carbon emissions not only levies the carbon tax on final goods imported but refund the taxes on exported final goods.

In this framework, if the production of final goods is still carried out in the country taxing the carbon despite the carbon adjustments at the border by the importing country, the imported inputs causing high carbon emissions will be taxed at the border as the final goods. Therefore, carbon leakage and global carbon emissions will be reduced by reducing the amounts of imported inputs. However, when producers decide to produce their final goods in the country not taxing carbon, carbon leakage will still be caused if only a border carbon tax is imposed on imported goods. If the carbon tax on the exported goods refunds, this production location change will further increase global carbon emissions.

Huang et al. (2022) elaborates the CBAM issue in terms of China. In this study, it is stated that the reactions of China, which is one of the countries that can be significantly affected by the implementation of the EU's CBAM, will also have an important impact on carbon leakage and global carbon emissions. It is concluded that well-functioning carbon market and lowering the required threshold level to enter this market, ensuring the integration of carbon markets in order to be excluded from the CBAM by the European Union, and the introduction of carbon tax will make the goods exported by China exempt border tax. Second result is that the revenue coming from carbon tax can be used to promote China's development with low-carbon.

Simola (2021) is another study that deals with the effects of the EU's CBAM plan on China, India, Russia, Turkey and Ukraine, from which it imports the most of energy-intensive goods. The EU's 2019 import data shows that the imported energy-intensive goods that would be subject to the EU CBAM are 65% steel and 23% aluminum. It is seen that the shares of imported goods subject to carbon adjustment at the border by the EU in 2019 were 18% from Russia, 12% from China and 11% from Turkey. By assuming that the price of one ton of carbon is 60 Euros, it is estimated that the carbon costs to be incurred in terms of energy-intensive goods exports to the EU are as 2 billion 142 million Euros for Russia, 849 million Euros for Ukraine and 686 million Euros for Turkey.

Acar et al. (2022) is the most comprehensive study on the possible effects of the European Union's border carbon tax adjustment on the Turkish economy. In this study, the potential effects of the border carbon tax adjustments by the EU, on the Turkish economy are analyzed by establishing a dynamic, multi-sectoral applied general equilibrium model. It should be noted that first of all, it is assumed that carbon adjustments at the border will be implemented in a way that will affect all of Turkey's exports. Turkey will face a potential loss of 2.7% of GDP (GDP) if a carbon price per ton is 30 euros until 2030. If the carbon price per ton is 50 euros, this loss is estimated to reach 3.6% of GDP. Accordingly, Turkey's annual carbon bills are been estimated as 1.1 billion (30 Euros) and 1.8 billion (50 Euros) depending on carbon prices in the EU. In addition, it is concluded that the carbon adjustments at the border will affect mostly the cement and electricity sectors. When the carbon price per ton is 30 euros, the cement industry has to give back 13 euros of export revenue of 100 euros, and 22 euros if it is 50 euros. It is estimated that Turkey following a policy of pricing carbon in a way that is not subject to carbon adjustment at the border, may gain the 5.6% of her GDP when carbon price is 30 euros. This gain may be the 6.6% of the GDP when the price is 50 euros.

ANALYSIS OF TURKEY'S CARBON-INTENSIVE GOODS EXPORTS TO THE EUROPEAN UNION

As of 2026, the European Union will switch to border carbon pricing, primarily in terms of carbon-intensive industries such as cement, iron-steel, aluminum, fertilizer and electricity in the short term. In the long run, border carbon pricing is expected to cover more sectors. The European Union's carbon tax at the border will affect third countries that do not price or do price carbon sufficiently, primarily through their exports to the Union.

As can be seen from Table 1, a significant part of Turkey's total exports has been to the European Union countries, although the shares vary over the years. On the other hand, as can be seen from Table 2, between the years 2000-2021, iron and steel exports have the largest share in Turkey's energy-intensive goods exports to the European Union. It is noteworthy that this share is 5.81% in 2021. Aluminum takes the second place in terms of Turkey's export of energy-intensive goods to the European Union. It is seen that aluminum exports to the Union have the highest share of the related period with a rate of 3.17% in 2021. Electricity has the lowest share in Turkey's exports to the European Union. It is noteworthy that since 2003, the share of fertilizer and cement in the exports of energy-intensive industries to the Union is below 1%.

Table 1. Turkey's total and carbon-intensive goods exports to the European Union (in thousand $)

Years	World Total	EU Total	72-Iron and Steel	2523-Portland cement and etc.	7601-Aluminium; unwrought	2716-Electrical energy	31-Fertilizers
1996	23.047.717	11.328.579					
1997	26.244.684	11.959.009					
1998	26.881.362	13.095.387					
1999	26.587.174	13.621.354					
2000	27.485.359	17.241.407	605.117	139.055	20.051		545
2001	31.333.944	19.776.479	712.256	213.238	12.849		6.921
2002	35.761.981	23.284.449	545.627	267.381	6.717		22.003
2003	47.252.836	30.948.311	924.650	263.730	4.659		14.242
2004	63.120.949	40.869.222	1.749.365	258.683	3.031		26.083
2005	73.476.408	44.999.948	1.469.897	271.767	16.043		21.141
2006	85.534.676	52.671.592	2.252.878	174.330	105.822		22.809
2007	107.271.750	65.011.654	3.477.570	195.802	138.942	10.472	29.782
2008	132.027.196	68.214.476	2.931.689	229.567	121.483	-	83.533
2009	102.142.613	50.803.169	1.168.762	302.696	43.448	-	29.087
2010	113.883.219	56.854.480	1.221.367	219.332	166.649	-	80.354
2011	134.906.869	67.824.801	2.288.677	178.223	90.875	20.607	129.991
2012	152.461.737	62.653.218	1.153.743	121.939	118.660	13.591	74.846
2013	161.480.915	67.142.509	1.661.973	98.924	72.503	2.750	39.757
2014	166.504.862	72.081.056	1.620.444	84.152	87.621	16.381	95.112
2015	150.982.114	68.269.267	1.264.457	77.768	75.629	28.763	68.738
2016	149.246.999	73.516.848	1.456.521	70.334	49.482	5.534	18.710
2017	164.494.619	78.461.780	2.734.911	78.997	47.523	53.459	41.649
2018	177.168.756	89.667.316	4.759.902	83.281	79.056	68.117	84.892
2019	180.832.722	89.436.111	4.081.464	127.939	117.725	63.201	95.249
2020	169.657.940	71.039.358	2.695.557	184.196	29.522	50.899	93.378
2021	225.219.237	91.955.365	5.348.682	295.342	315.477	104.949	132.703
2022	254.201.009	103.552.194	5.898.243	343.083	436.272	198.717	399.206

Source: UN, 2023

Table 2. The share of Turkey's carbon-intensive goods exports to the European Union (as percent)

Years	Iron and Steel	Portland cement, and etc.	Aluminium; unwrought	Electrical energy	Fertilizers
2000	3,510	0,807	0,116		0,003
2001	3,602	1,078	0,065		0,035
2002	2,343	1,148	0,029		0,094
2003	2,988	0,852	0,015		0,046
2004	4,280	0,633	0,007		0,064
2005	3,266	0,604	0,036		0,047
2006	4,277	0,331	0,201		0,043
2007	5,349	0,301	0,214	0,016	0,046
2008	4,298	0,337	0,178	-	0,122
2009	2,301	0,596	0,086	-	0,057
2010	2,148	0,386	0,293	-	0,141
2011	3,374	0,263	0,134	0,030	0,192
2012	1,841	0,195	0,189	0,022	0,119
2013	2,475	0,147	0,108	0,004	0,059
2014	2,248	0,117	0,122	0,023	0,132
2015	1,852	0,114	0,111	0,042	0,101
2016	1,981	0,096	0,067	0,008	0,025
2017	3,486	0,101	0,061	0,068	0,053
2018	5,308	0,093	0,088	0,076	0,095
2019	4,564	0,143	0,132	0,071	0,106
2020	3,794	0,259	0,042	0,072	0,131
2021	5,817	0,321	0,343	0,114	0,144
2022	5,696	0,331	0,421	0,331	0,386

Source: Author's own calculations based on data from the sources mentioned in Table 1

POSSIBLE EFFECTS OF THE EUROPEAN UNION'S BORDER CARBON TAX REGULATION ON TURKISH EXPORT IN THE SHORT TERM

The table below shows the direct CO2 emissions and/or CO2 equivalents of five energy-intensive industries. According to Table 3, when the direct CO2 emission amounts of energy-intensive industries in Turkey are examined for the period of 2000-2020, it is seen that the highest emission is caused by electricity generation. The second energy-intensive sector in terms of CO2 emissions is the cement sector. Especially, according to the emission data in recent years, the fertilizer sector ranks third in terms of CO2 emission equivalent. The iron-steel industry, on the other hand, draws attention as the energy-intensive industry, which is the fourth largest emission source. The CO2 amount originating from aluminum production comes in the last place.

It is important to calculate the amount of CO2 contained in energy-intensive goods exported to the European Union, in order to estimate how much carbon tax burdened at the border. Thus, under the assumption that the amount of exports will not change in case of a carbon tax at the border, it will be

Table 3. CO2 emissions from carbon-intensive goods' production in Turkey (kt CO2 eq.)

Years	Iron and steel production	Cement production	Aluminum production	Public electricity and heat production	Fertilizers
1990	6.914	10.445	99,2	32.938	17.314
1991	7.303	12.021	101,7	34.550	17.155
1992	6.355	13.265	97,7	39.186	17.527
1993	6.417	13.049	54,1	38.390	18.078
1994	5.430	13.493	110,3	44.721	15.931
1995	5.793	14.133	114,4	46.020	15.871
1996	5.956	14.662	108,2	49.919	16.391
1997	5.848	15.105	108,2	55.000	16.023
1998	6.175	15.292	115,5	60.544	17.306
1999	5.822	14.590	113,9	65.993	17.643
2000	5.653	15.184	112,7	73.371	16.870
2001	5.704	15.087	111,4	75.586	15.107
2002	5.543	15.513	110,9	69.578	15.103
2003	5.996	16.022	111,3	69.501	16.054
2004	6.663	17.207	111,5	70.485	16.591
2005	6.814	19.117	102,2	85.407	16.880
2006	7.069	20.841	108,0	90.994	17.422
2007	7.634	22.780	117,3	108.595	16.740
2008	7.962	24.850	111,8	113.633	15.250
2009	8.006	27.040	51,2	115.222	16.474
2010	8.779	29.977	96,4	108.892	17.006
2011	9.838	31.454	100,3	120.031	17.421
2012	10.383	31.372	76,4	120.889	19.334
2013	10.468	33.913	55,3	116.110	20.905
2014	10.359	34.498	54,9	127.006	20.764
2015	10.590	34.441	74,7	127.958	21.006
2016	11.572	37.528	117,3	135.554	23.147
2017	11.784	39.469	108,4	146.220	23.607
2018	12.250	39.413	107,3	150.032	23.022
2019	10.214	32.349	112,1	139.116	24.342
2020	10.132	40.813	80,2	131.662	27.389

Source: Turkish Statistical Institute, 2022

possible to estimate the carbon cost that these industries will incur. Assuming that the carbon tax to be charged at the border can be 30 euros or 50 euros per ton (following Acar et al., 2022), table 4 has been prepared by calculating the carbon tax costs of the carbon amounts contained in the goods exported to the European Union by five energy-intensive industries.

As can be seen, Table 4 reveals the high carbon tax costs that will be caused by the EU and thus the competitive disadvantage of the five energy-intensive industries of Turkish economy. When used the export data of the year of 2020 and assumed that the carbon tax is 30 euros per ton, the fertilizer industry would face a carbon tax of 63,800,241 euros, the cement industry 49,396,054 euros, and the iron and steel industry 36,079,152 euros. Besides, when carbon tax amounts calculated by using 50 Euros per ton, carbon tax cost per annum would increase to 106,333,735 euros for the fertilizer industry, 82,326,757 euros for the cement industry and 60,131,920 euros for the iron and steel industry. Naturally, it should be taken into account that this competitive disadvantage may reduce exports to the European Union. It should not be forgotten that this disadvantage will increase even more when the European Union's CBAM regulation covers all imports.

Table 4. Estimated border carbon tax costs to Turkish Economy by industries (in thousand €)

Year	Iron and steel		Cement		Aluminum		Electricity		Fertilizers	
	Carbon price 30€	Carbon price 50€	Carbon price 30€	Carbon price 50€	Carbon price 30€	Carbon price 50€	Carbon price 30€	Carbon price 50€	Carbon price 30€	Carbon price 50€
2000			38.806	64.677	656	1.093			767	1.279
2001			74.305	123.842	417	694			9.735	16.224
2002			90.667	151.112	244	407			23.881	39.801
2003			79.530	132.550	157	262			14.085	23.476
2004	32.600	54.334	62.562	104.270	88	146			18.129	30.215
2005	26.197	43.662	57.965	96.609	379	632			3.391	5.651
2006	34.851	58.084	29.035	48.392	2.152	3.586			17.788	29.647
2007	42.148	70.246	27.870	46.451	2.704	4.507			12.836	21.393
2008	25.424	42.374	29.885	49.808	2.460	4.099			17.413	29.022
2009	17.297	28.828	53.129	88.549	1.228	2.047			16.844	28.073
2010	12.631	21.052	40.894	68.157	3.788	6.314			30.647	51.078
2011	21.610	36.016	31.227	52.045	1.752	2.920	4.037	6.729	39.352	65.587
2012	10.833	18.055	22.201	37.002	2.609	4.349	2.467	4.112	24.650	41.084
2013	19.533	32.555	17.644	29.406	1.647	2.744	614	1.023	15.800	26.333
2014	17.311	28.851	14.872	24.787	1.890	3.151	3.194	5.324	39.032	65.053
2015	18.329	30.548	14.314	23.857	1.648	2.747	9.398	15.663	27.714	46.190
2016	27.149	45.249	12.891	21.484	1.136	1.894	2.211	3.684	11.967	19.945
2017	39.587	65.979	15.049	25.082	929	1.548	15.216	25.360	28.775	47.958
2018	65.592	109.320	15.218	25.363	1.438	2.397	17.370	28.950	53.504	89.174
2019	57.382	95.636	32.434	54.056	2.334	3.890	15.684	26.139	71.341	118.901
2020	36.079	60.132	49.396	82.327	679	1.132	9.537	15.894	63.800	106.334

Source: Author's own calculations based on data from the sources mentioned Table 1 and Table 2

As can be seen from Table 1, a significant part of Turkey's total exports has been to the European Union countries, although the shares vary over the years. On the other hand, as can be seen from Table 2, between the years 2000-2021, iron and steel exports have the largest share in Turkey's energy-intensive goods exports to the European Union. It is noteworthy that this share is 5.81% in 2021. Aluminum takes the second place in terms of Turkey's export of energy-intensive goods to the European Union. It is seen that aluminum exports to the Union have the highest share of the related period with a rate of 3.17% in 2021. Electricity has the lowest share in Turkey's exports to the European Union. It is noteworthy that since 2003, the share of fertilizer and cement in the exports of energy-intensive industries to the Union is below 1%.

CONCLUSION

The Green deal adopted by the European Union within the framework of the Paris Climate Agreement is important in terms of reducing carbon dioxide emissions in order to slow down global warming. As known, the use of any policy tool aimed at reducing carbon dioxide emissions by all countries can ensure that carbon leakages do not occur. In addition, any carbon-reducing policy tool applied globally would have the function of reducing the existing negative impact on international competition.

However, both the Kyoto Protocol and the Paris Climate Agreement taking into account the development of developing countries mainly have focused on reducing the carbon emissions coming from developed countries. This situation has led the European Union's CBAM regulation, primarily starting from carbon-intensive industries, in order to address carbon leakage and thus the negative impact on international competition.

Within the framework of the European green deal, the European Union's regulation about border carbon adjustment mechanism (CBAM), which is stated to be mainly for carbon leakage, has two important aspects that need to be addressed. The first issue is of whether the carbon adjustments at the border complies with the World Trade Organization legislation. The second important issue regarding this regulation is how the foreign trade of non-union countries with European Union countries will be affected, depending on the impacts on the international competition power of carbon-intensive industries. As of 2026, the European Union plans to implement carbon pricing at the border in the short term, primarily within the framework of imports of carbon-intensive industries such as cement, iron-steel, aluminum, fertilizer and electricity. In the long run, border carbon pricing is expected to cover more sectors.

EU CBAM policy instruments cannot be justified under the non-discrimination provisions of the GATT, particularly in terms of articles I, III and XI. In other words, EU's CBAM regulation shows that compensatory carbon tax on imports cannot be applied in a non-discriminatory manner. Therefore, it is seen that the paragraph g of Article 20 of the GATT allowing for the measures to protect the exhaustible natural resources, may constitute a more appropriate justification for the EU's carbon adjustment at the border.

Under the assumption that the amount of exports will not change in case of a carbon tax at the border by the EU, it will be possible to estimate the carbon cost that these industries will incur. Assuming that the carbon tax to be charged at the border can be 30 euros or 50 euros per ton, the calculated carbon tax costs of the carbon amounts contained in energy-intensive goods exported to the European Union shows that Turkish economy will bear relatively heavy burden in the short term.

As seen, high carbon tax costs that will be caused by the EU and thus the competitive disadvantage of the five energy-intensive industries of Turkish economy. When used the export data of the year of 2020 and assumed that the carbon tax is 30 euros per ton, the fertilizer industry would face a carbon tax of 63,800,241 euros, the cement industry 49,396,054 euros, and the iron and steel industry 36,079,152 euros. Besides, when carbon tax amounts calculated by using 50 Euros per ton, carbon tax cost per annum would increase to 106,333,735 euros for the fertilizer industry, 82,326,757 euros for the cement industry and 60,131,920 euros for the iron and steel industry.

Naturally, it should be taken into account that this competitive disadvantage may reduce exports to the European Union. It should not be forgotten that this disadvantage will increase even more when the European Union's CBAM regulation covers all imports. It is considered reasonable for Turkey to introduce appropriate policy tools to price carbon in a way that will not be subject to the European Union's border carbon tax. As it is already known, after Turkey's Paris Climate Agreement was approved by the parliament in 2022, at the United Nations Climate Conference COP 27 meeting in Egypt, it is seen that important steps have been taken in this regard by committing to reduce carbon emissions that are likely to occur in 2030 by 41 percent.

REFERENCES

Acar, S., Aşıcı, A. A., & Yeldan, A. E. (2022). Potential effects of the EU's carbon border adjustment mechanism on the Turkish economy. *Environment, Development and Sustainability*, *24*(6), 8162–8194. doi:10.100710668-021-01779-1 PMID:34483717

Böhringer, C., Fischer, C., Rosendahl, K. E., & Rutherford, T. F. (2022). Potential impacts and challenges of border carbon adjustments. *Nature Climate Change*, *12*(1), 22–29. doi:10.103841558-021-01250-z

Bullock, D. A. C. (2018). Combating climate recalcitrance: Carbon-related border tax adjustments in a new era of global climate governance. *Washington International Law Journal*, *27*(3), 609–644.

Cheng, H. (2021). Border carbon adjustments with endogenous assembly locations. *Economic Modelling*, *105*(105666), 1–15.

Dröge, S. (2011). Using border measures to address carbon flows. *Climate Policy*, *11*(5), 1191–1201. doi:10.1080/14693062.2011.592671

Eckersley, R. (2010). The politics of carbon leakage and the fairness of border measures. *Ethics & International Affairs*, *24*(4), 367–393. doi:10.1111/j.1747-7093.2010.00277.x

Eicke, L., Weko, S., Apergi, M., & Marian, A. (2021). Pulling up the carbon ladder? Decarbonization, dependence, and third-country risks from the European carbon border adjustment mechanism. *Energy Research & Social Science*, *80*(102240), 1–11. doi:10.1016/j.erss.2021.102240

Feaver, D., & Sheehy, B. (2011). Climate policy and border adjustment regulation: Designing a coherent response. *Melbourne Journal of International Law*, *13*, 792–817.

Grubb, M. (2011). International climate finance from border carbon cost levelling. *Climate Policy*, *11*(3), 1050–1057. doi:10.1080/14693062.2011.582285

Holzer, K., & Shariff, N. (2012). The inclusion of border carbon adjustments in preferential trade agreements: Policy implications. *Carbon & Climate Law Review*, *6*(3), 246–260. doi:10.21552/CCLR/2012/3/222

Joachim, E., & Tatiana F. (2021). EU carbon border adjustments and WTO law, part one. *Environmental Law Reporter, 10*, 51 ELR 10857-10882.

Joachim, E., & Tatiana, F. (2022). EU carbon border adjustments and WTO law, part two. *Environmental Law Reporter*, *11*, 51 ELR 10935-10946.

Mc Lure, C. E. (2011). A primer on the legality of border adjustments for carbon prices: Through a GATT darkly. *Carbon & Climate Law Review*, *5*(4), 456–465. doi:10.21552/CCLR/2011/4/193

Metcalf, G. E., & Weisbach, D. A. (2009). The design of a carbon tax. *The Harvard Environmental Law Review*, *33*, 499–556.

Mörsdorf, G. (2022). A simple fix for carbon leakage? Assessing the environmental effectiveness of the EU carbon border adjustment. *Energy Policy*, *161*, 1–13. doi:10.1016/j.enpol.2021.112596

Porterfield, M. C. (2019). Border adjustments for carbon taxes, PPMs, and the WTO. *University of Pennsylvania Journal of International Law*, *41*(1), 1–42.

Simola, H. (2021). *CBAM! Assessing potential costs of the EU carbon border adjustment mechanism for emerging economies*. Bank of Finland, BOFIT - Institute for Emerging Economies.

Tao, H., Zhixin, L., & Tian, Z. (2022). Evolutionary game analysis of responding to the EU's carbon border adjustment mechanism. *Energies*, *15*(2), 1–20.

Turkish Statistical Institute. (2022). *Turkish greenhouse gas inventory 1990-2019*. National Inventory Report for submission under the United Nations Framework Convention on Climate Change, TÜİK.

UN. (2023). *UN comtrade database*. United Nations. https://comtradeplus.un.org/

Chapter 4
A Spatial Econometric Analysis of the Regional Variations of Residential Energy Consumption in Europe

Eda Ustaoglu
Abdullah Gul University, Turkey

ABSTRACT

A residential energy consumption model was estimated by using socio-economic characteristics, economic activities, mobility, land cover, natural hazards, governance, energy, air quality, and green economy variables for the EU-27 and UK. Regional variations of the energy consumption were also investigated through focusing on European regional typologies including urban, intermediate, and rural regions. The residential energy consumption model was estimated by using spatial econometric approaches as well as specific regression models were estimated for the urban, intermediate, and rural regions. The key variables used in regression analysis were selected according to their importance using the Random Forest (RF) classification method. The results from the regressions confirm that socio-economic, environmental, governance, technology, and natural hazards related variables explain residential energy consumption in Europe. The variations of sign and coefficients of the variables according to different regional typologies were also uncovered.

1. INTRODUCTION

The majority of the world's population resides in urban areas and it is anticipated that urban populations will grow in the coming decades (UN, 2018). Cities and urban regions can be thought of as major consumers of energy resources and significant contributors to greenhouse gases emissions due to inefficient structures in the built environment and transportation activities. Cities are responsible for up to 80% of the world's energy consumption (UN, 2020) where in the EU in 2020, the residential sector accounts for about 27% of total energy consumption while it is 26.1% and 28.4% for the industrial and transport

DOI: 10.4018/979-8-3693-1297-1.ch004

sectors, respectively (URL1). As urbanisation continues inducing a large share of energy consumption that in the long run indicates significant negative effects on well-being and sustainability, energy conservation and emissions reduction in residential buildings is playing an increasingly important role in creating sustainable cities and urban regions.

Similar to most of the countries, petroleum products and natural gas account for a large share of total energy supply (58.2%) (URL2) and are the type of fuels most commonly used in the EU member countries. Although carbon-intensive infrastructures are predominant in many European countries, a structural shift is underway towards a shift to renewables be used in different sectors in the economy (EEA, 2017). This is related to the 2005 framework of the United Nations Kyoto Protocol on Climate Change, which came into force in 1997, and aims to reduce CO_2 emissions not only in developing countries but also in developed countries such as the EU. The EU is committed to reducing overall average emissions by 8% between 2008 and 2012 compared to 1990 levels (EC, 1999). This is because the EU's energy market reforms and market liberalisation will give consumers choice of supply and enable citizens to actively participate in the market leading to more efficient use of energy resources (Roggenkamp and Diestelmeier, 2020). The EEA (2022) reported that greenhouse gas emissions in the EU decreased by 32% between 1990 and 2020 indicating a considerable overachievement of the EU's 2020 reduction target of 20%. Due to Covid19 crises effecting the EU economy resulted a decrease in energy consumption in 2020 where the primary energy consumption dropped to 1236 Mtoe which is 5.8% below the EU2020 target level (EC, 2022). In 2018, the amended Energy Efficiency Directive (EU2018/2002) came into force introducing a headline EU Energy Efficiency Target for 2030 of at least 32.5% including a clause for a possible upwards revision by 2023 (EC, 2022). Improving the energy efficiency as well as promoting energy production from renewable energy resources can be essential to achieve a necessary progress. Through adopting energy efficiency measures and the use of renewable energy technologies, households can make a huge contribution in reducing greenhouse gas emissions. Therefore, the determinants of household energy consumption have come to the forefront as this can contribute to our understanding of the factors influencing residential energy consumption and their impacts on the environment and socio-economic well-being.

As the second largest region after Asia with about 447 million people as of 2020 (World Bank, 2022), accounting for 6.4% of the world's population, understanding the ways of energy use and their determinants for urban, peri-urban and rural households in European Union States will be of increasing importance. Accompanying industrial and services growth and energy consumption expansion summarise the development of urbanisation patterns in Europe. It is reported that 39.1% of the European population live in cities, 31.6% live in towns and suburbs and 29.1% live in rural areas (Eurostat, 2022). Urbanisation is linked to the rapid access of production factors such as labour, capital and energy resources but at the same time it has encountered problems such as air pollution, energy shortages, and decline in ecological environmental quality (Tilt, 2019; An et al., 2022, Jamil, 2022). Compared to rural areas, urban areas provide more space for energy saving as these are the core areas for achieving energy conservation goals and constructing resource-saving societies (Hu and Fan, 2020). Nevertheless, an increase in urbanisation rate is not linearly correlated with energy consumption. To benefit from scale economies, technology diffusion and energy efficiency, urban sectors tend to agglomerate in an urban space accompanied by reduction in urban energy consumption. Rural areas, on the other hand, are low density occupied areas, having limited benefits from scale economies and energy conservation as these account for a significant proportion of total energy consumption of a country. Urban-rural typologies are important in targeting socio-economic policies and revealing development patterns (Fertner, 2012) and their linkages with energy consumption and greenhouse gas emissions. The urban-rural typologies developed by the European Commission, Eurostat and DG Regio classified the regions as 'predominantly urban', 'predominantly intermediate' and 'predominantly rural' for each country in Europe[1] (Figure 1) (Dijkstra and Poelman, 2010). The regions are characterised by different climate, natural resources, population density, industrial development and socio-economic status, which means that there are regional variances, and these should be incorporated in the energy consumption studies. Energy consumption data collected at the country level in previous studies may fail to reflect changes in the urban-rural regions and its effects on household energy consumption in recent years. The residential energy consumption patterns across urban, intermediate and rural regions for the years 2002 and 2012 were analysed (Figure 2) and it is noted that energy consumption in urban areas in both years are lower than that of intermediate and rural areas. It is noteworthy to highlight that energy consumptions in all type of areas are lower in 2012 compared to 2002 figures. This may be related to efficiency gains in energy consumption resulting from the reform and liberalisation of the EU energy markets. To reflect regional differences in Europe, this study aims to identify the determinants of energy consumption of the residential sector at the NUTS3[2](nomenclature of terrestrial units for statistics) level for which the energy consumption data is available over the period 2002-2012. It also separates NUTS3 regions into predominantly urban, predominantly intermediate and predominantly rural regions based on the classification introduced by Dijkstra and Poelman (2010) (Figure 1).

Figure 1. Predominantly urban and rural regions in Europe

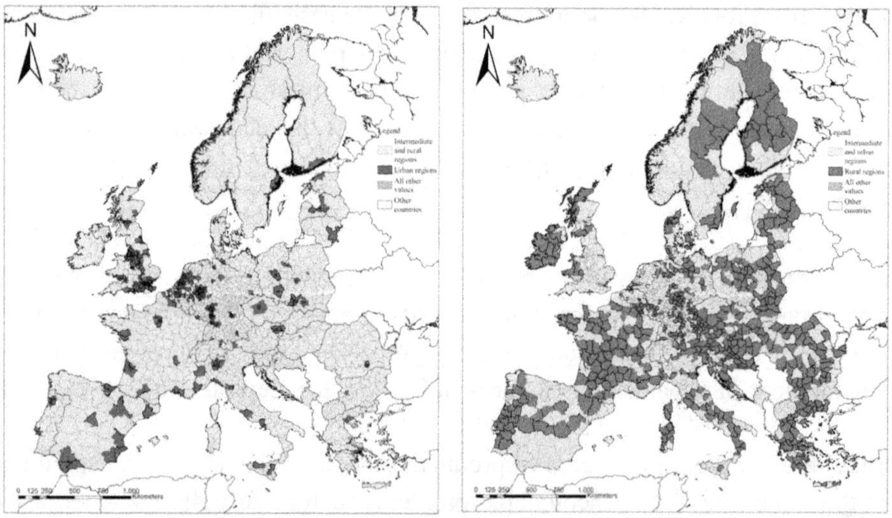

(a) Urban regions (b) Rural regions

An increasing number of studies have focused on energy consumption in Europe. The most recent literature focuses on the determinants of energy consumption at the pan-European level using the country totals as the unit of analysis (Filipovic et al., 2015; Andrei et al., 2017; Popescu et al., 2018). An example is Pais-Magalhaes et al. (2020) which analysed the determinants of household electricity consumption efficiency through using fractional regression models covering the years 2005 and 2016. Tzeiranaki et

Figure 2. Distribution of residential energy demand in Europe regions, 2002, 2012

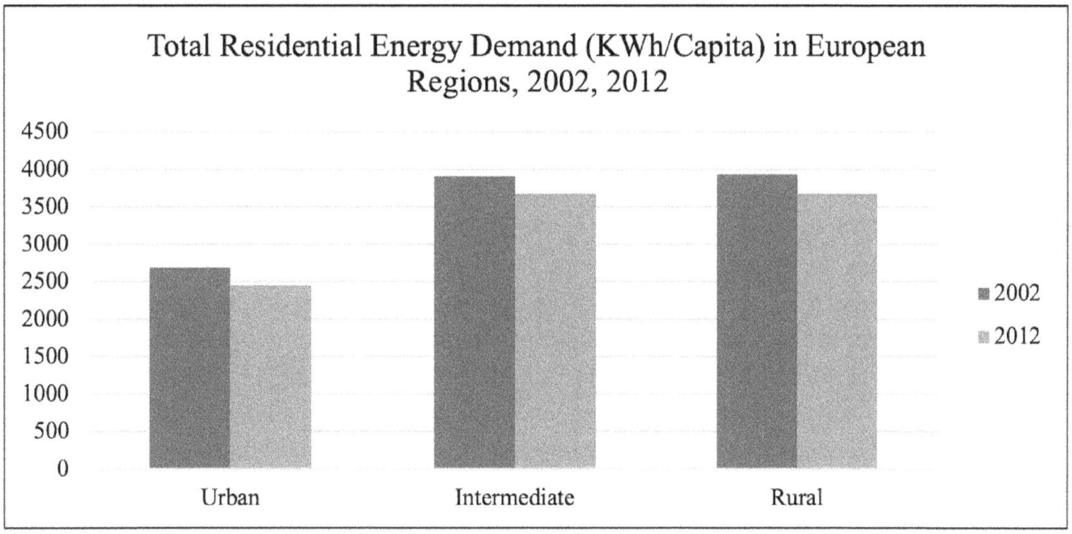

al. (2019) instead undertook a more deterministic study and examined the energy efficiency progress from 2000 to 2016 using the official Eurostat data to explicate its drivers, the impact of current policies, and future policy implications. Karatasou et al. (2018) focused on household socio-demographic and building characteristics to explain high energy consumption for space and water heating in European social housing and found that these characteristics were significant in explaining high energy consumption. On the other side, there are increasing number of studies focusing on the determinants of renewable energy consumption in Europe. Papiez et al. (2018) researched the factors that determines renewable energy use and influences their distribution between 1995 and 2014 using regression models. Akadiri et al. (2019) found a positive significant long-run nexus among environmental sustainability, renewable energy consumption and economic growth over the period 1995-2015 in the 28 EU member countries. Similarly, Usman et al. (2021) showed that CO_2 emissions, clean energy technology, GDP growth and globalisation positively impact clean energy consumption for a panel of EU-28 countries in the period from 1995 to 2017. Other examples on the determinants of renewable energy consumption in Europe are Chen et al. (2021), Yu et al. (2021), and Tu et al. (2022).

There are other studies conducted at the regional or more local levels in Europe aiming to search the determinant factors of energy consumption and energy efficiency. For instance, Sineviciene et al. (2017) adopted a stochastic frontier function approach for the 1996-2013 period to investigate the factors determining energy efficiency and energy consumption for the post-communist countries in Eastern Europe. Navamuel et al. (2018) used regression analysis to examine the impact of urban sprawl on energy consumption in Spain, affirming that single family homes increase electricity consumption and urban agglomeration has the opposite effect. Azam et al. (2016) evaluated the socio-economic factors influencing the energy consumption in Greece over the 1975-2013 period and highlighted urbanisation, infrastructure, trade, income, population growth and foreign direct investment be the most important determinants of energy consumption. The literature in this field is directed towards national research utilising micro level data set to study the energy consumption determinants. For instance, through integrating dwelling characteristics, household attributes, climate and household energy use behaviour,

Belaid (2017) assessed direct and indirect effects of households and dwelling units describing energy use in France. Alternatively, Fuerst et al. (2020) used big data at the household level obtained from the English Housing Survey to explicate the relationship between household and building characteristics and used regression analysis methods to estimate household energy use. Borozan (2018) is another example of a micro-level study which incorporates NUTS2 regions in Europe as the unit of analysis to search for the socio-economic, climate and location factors on the consumption of households' energy.

The covered literature whether it is country level study or micro-level analysis rarely discussed the drivers of energy consumption in Europe from a spatial perspective. These studies are based on a common assumption that regions are spatially independent, however significant spatial dependence and spatial spillover effects are likely to exist in the relationship between energy consumption and its determinants. Few studies have explored the spatial relationships of energy consumption and its socio-economic, location, climate and other determinants (Liu and Lin, 2019; Guo et al., 2021), and to the knowledge of the author, there is no study at the pan-European level which consider spatial dependence and spillover effects in modelling the residential energy consumption. It is on this ground that the current study seeks to contribute to the literature on determinants of energy consumption, using NUTS3 regions of EU-27+UK countries as a case study for the 2002-2012 period. However, unlike existing studies that used non-spatial regression analysis to model energy consumption, this study utilises spatial econometric methods to analyse the impact of selected factors on residential energy consumption.

1.1. Urbanisation and Energy Consumption

Three main theoretical perspectives have been developed to explain the relationship between urbanisation, energy consumption and environmental quality. These include compact city theory (CCT), urban environmental transition theory (UETT) and ecological modernization theory (EMT) (Poumanyvong and Kaneko, 2010; Adams et al., 2020). CCT and UETT mainly focus on the linkages between positive externalities of urbanisation on the environment. It not only suggests that increasing urbanisation results in high densities and rising congestion, which are associated with increased energy consumption and carbon emissions (Burton, 2000); but also proposes that policy makers implement policies to reduce environmental pollution and degradation (Poumanyvong and Kaneko, 2010). Differently, EMT argues that different stages of urban development are associated with different degrees of agglomeration and city size and their impacts on residential energy consumption also vary. In the early stages of urban development, the main goal is to achieve economic growth and sustain income; and therefore, governments relax environmental regulations. In such a case, energy consumption is expanding in accordance with the city size. In the later stages of urban development, governments and different stakeholders pay more attention to clean and efficient production, promoting intensive energy use and emission reduction; therefore, the goal is to maximize economic output with less input (Sadorsky, 2014). At this point, the city's energy consumption decreases thanks to the application of strict environmental regulations. From these theoretical arguments, the net effect of urbanisation on energy consumption cannot be determined as a priori but there is a need for empirical studies. This constructed a framework for the current study which investigates whether there are differences in residential energy consumption across urban, peri-urban and rural regions in Europe and to quantify its determinants.

By using the OECD's territorial classification scheme, Dijkstra et al. (2015) showed that European urban regions performed below the output and labour productivity growth rates of the intermediate and rural regions close to cities. This implies that there are different trajectories in the urbanisation phase of

European regions: During the last decade, "predominantly rural regions have outperformed intermediate regions in GDP per capita growth, and these outperformed that of predominantly urban regions" (Dijkstra et al., 2013: 342). Based on EMT, we can expect that the highly growing rural and intermediate regions lead to higher energy consumption and pollution through increasing production. As the wealth of cities improves as in case of predominantly urban regions, these regions are characterised by more intensive use of energy and diminishing environmental pollution owing to structural change, technological improvement and environmental regulation. Using the data on residential energy consumption for the years 2002 and 2012, Figure 3 shows the relationship between energy consumption in 2002 and that of 2012 for the

Figure 3. Distribution of residential energy consumption (K Wh/capita) in 2002 and 2012 across urban, intermediate, and rural regions

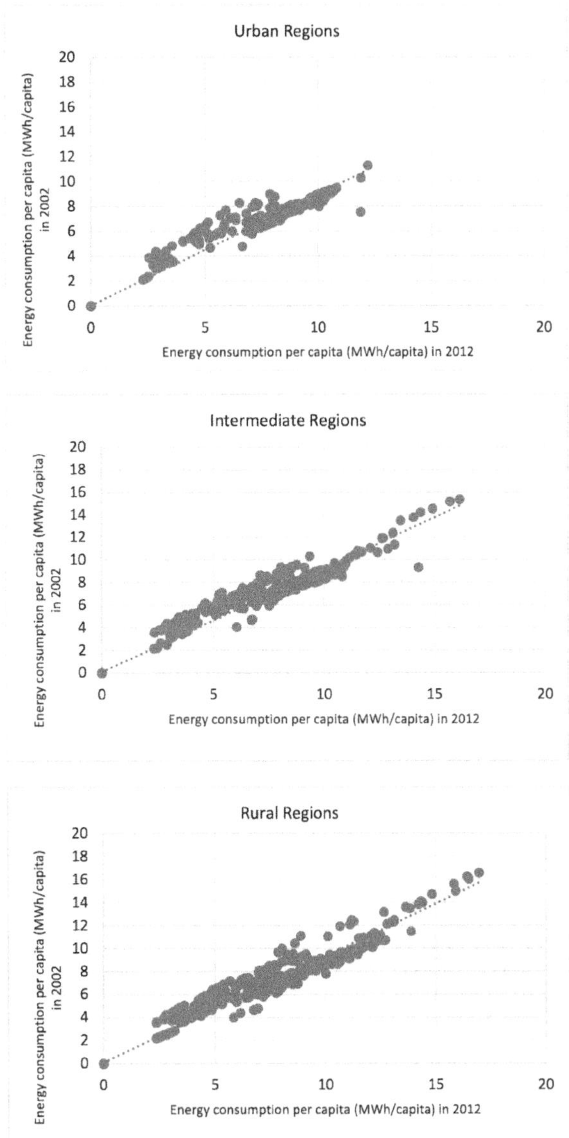

urban, intermediate, and rural regions in Europe. It is clear that the extent of energy consumption is lower in urban regions compared to intermediate and rural regions where the latter regions show similar patterns.

2. DATASET AND VARIABLES

The dataset used was obtained from Eurostat, European Environment Agency (EEA) and European Commission ESPON project databases and other official European sources were used as well. The independent variables relate to a cross-section data whereas the dependent variable represents the change in energy consumption between 2002-2012 period. Besides a range of socio-economic characteristics as well as economic activities, the dataset provides information about mobility, land cover, natural hazards, governance, energy, air quality, green economy, location and regional characteristics. As shown in Table A1 in the appendix, the indicators are from the years 2010, 2011 or 2012 representing cross section data. Because there is no continuous data for the 2002-2012 period, panel data models could not be applied in the study but instead cross-section data was used to construct the spatial regression models. The details of spatial regression models will be elaborated in the methodology section.

2.1. Dependent Variable

The dependent variable was calculated by subtracting the final energy demand for space heating and cooling, water heating, appliances and lighting and gas for cooking in the residential sector of the year 2002 from the final energy demand of the subject uses in the residential sector of the year 2012. The change data is the final energy demand per capita represented by KWh/capita. These indicators for the years 2002 and 2012 were obtained from the database of the ESPON (2018)-LOCATE-Territories and Low Carbon Economy Project. In Figure 4, it can be seen that the highest percentage of energy demand is assigned to space heating and cooling and water heating with more than 80% of the total energy use, followed by electricity for appliances and lighting (more than 10%), and gas for cooking (more than 1%). The distribution of the energy demand for the years 2002 and 2012 is very similar but there are regional

Figure 4. Distribution of energy demands in the residential sector, 2022, 2012

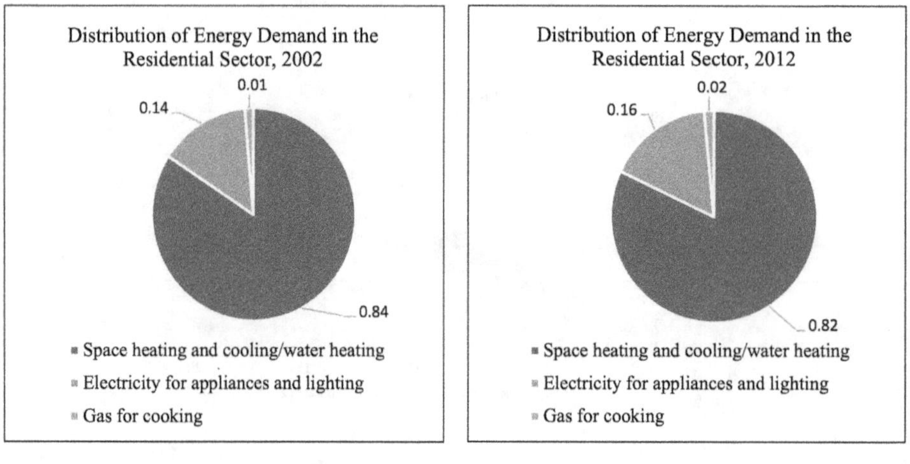

differences in the total energy demand (Figure 5) as of 2012 where the northern regions and central Europe account for the highest energy consumption, Eastern Europe, Spain and Portugal are associated with the lowest energy consumption numbers.

Figure 5. Residential energy consumption per capita (K Wh/capita) in EU27+UK, 2012

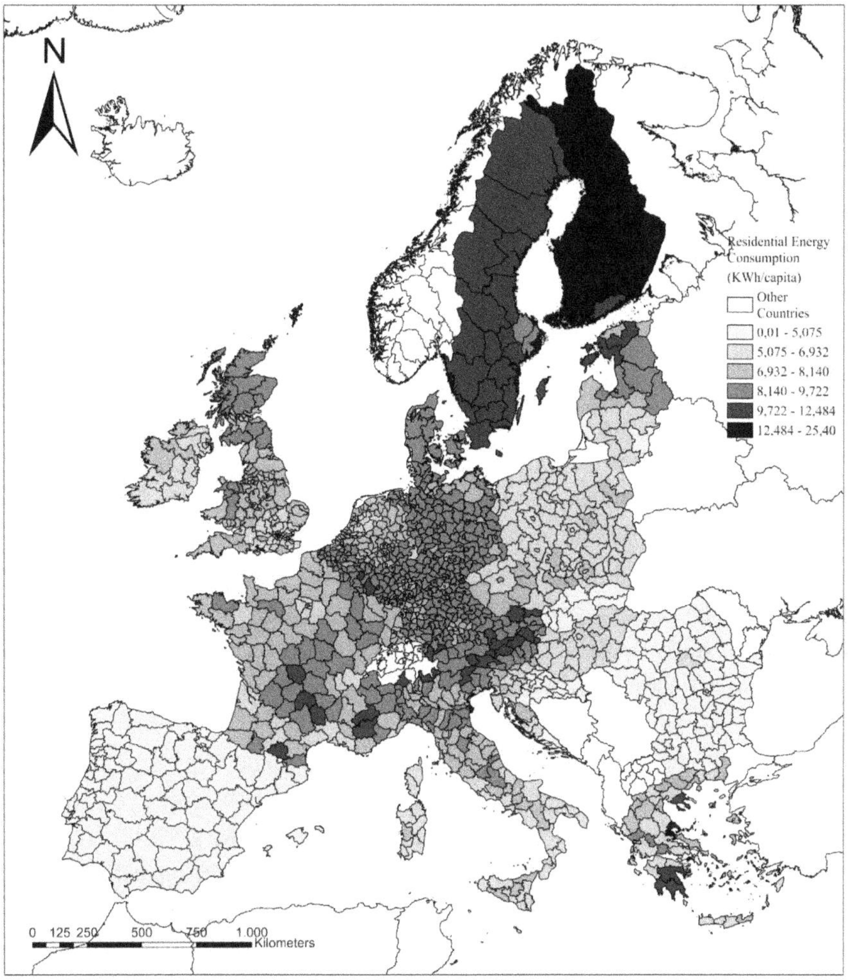

2.2. Energy Demand Determinants

Nine categories of explanatory variables were considered: socio-economic characteristics, economic activities, mobility, land cover, natural hazards, governance, energy, air quality and green economy. In Table A1 in the appendix the variables are listed according to their geographical scales and references. Socio-economic characteristics and economic activities have been repeatedly used as explanatory variables to explain energy demand in different countries (Gyamfi et al., 2013; Salari and Javid, 2016; Kaiser et al., 2020). In these studies, the variation in energy demand is based on socio-economic factors, type of energy and household characteristics (family size, household members' age, level of education, the way people live, race and ethnicity etc.) and others. Energy prices and households' income are the two key drivers of the energy consumption, based on microeconomic theories including utility optimization and consumer rationality (Gyamfi et al., 2013). It is centred on the idea that the consumer weighs expected benefits and costs of various means and chooses the most favourable or cheapest among them (Jackson, 2005). High energy prices lead households to reduce gas and electricity consumption. For this reason, policymakers are interested in how households respond to price changes and how the price changes affect energy consumption decisions. As a contrary example, Reiss and White (2002) found that a significant proportion of households are price insensitive. In other words, as household income in her representative sample of 1300 households in California increases, household responsiveness to price decreases. Another view suggests that higher prices will disproportionately hit low income households unable to take steps to avoid paying high peak hourly rates (Gyamfi et al., 2013).

There is positive association between per capita wealth and per capita energy consumption, which varies by country. Countries with similar economic performance may have different energy consumption due to differences in energy resources, energy prices, climate, population density, land use, technological efficiency, fuel-mix, economic structure, regularity criteria and others (Sineviciene et al., 2017). The low share of energy in total input costs suggests that increased energy consumption could make a modest contribution to economic output growth (Sorrell, 2015). The significant decline in energy demand is due to the weakening of the link between energy flows and economic production as a result of the spread of information and communication technology (ICT) (Kander et al., 2014). Kander et al. (2014) claimed that ICT drives less energy intensive forms of economic development and that Europe's decline in energy intensity in recent decades has been attributed to the spread of ICT rather than to a shift to a service-based economy. Economic growth is a major factor influencing energy efficiency improvement according to the results of study by Zhang (2013). Higher GDP impacts other factors of energy efficiency and provides opportunities for investment in new technologies and increased capital stock. Fan and Xia (2012) analysed the factors behind changes in China's energy intensity and concluded that improvements in industrial structure and technology have a significant impact on energy demand.

Numerous variables and quantitative methodologies have been employed to analyse the causes of energy consumption, among which technical advancement, energy intensity and economic advancement have been identified as the three key elements determining urban energy use. Energy efficiency is more strongly influenced by energy intensity and technical advancement (Esseghir and Khouni, 2014) while economic development is more pronounced in increasing energy demand (Shahbaz et al., 2018). Regarding urbanisation and population, a consensus cannot be reached on their effects as both negative and positive relationships with energy consumption have been described. For instance, Mashhoodi et al. (2020) observed a negative association between population density and energy consumption whereas Fan et al. (2007) estimated a positive association between urbanisation and carbon emissions. Scale effect such as population aggregation reduce energy use in the former case while in the latter urbanisation increases urban energy use and the infrastructure construction. Apergis et al. (2015) investigated energy use in OECD countries from 1985 to 2011 and found a positive relationship between energy consumption and population growth. A positive correlation between energy consumption, urbanisation and energy intensity is supported by various studies such as Ma (2015) and Lin and Zhu (2017).

The central theme of the literature on energy economics, especially in recent decades, is the connection between CO_2 emissions and energy consumption. In a panel of 35 developed countries, Akhmat et al. (2014) studied the demand for nuclear energy and its relationship to climatic conditions and discovered that using nuclear energy considerably reduces air pollution and greenhouse gas emissions. Alkhathlan and Javid (2013) demonstrated that economic development and energy consumption in Saudi Arabia have caused carbon dioxide emissions both in the short and long term. They did this by focusing on the interconnection between economic growth, carbon emissions, and energy use at the aggregate and dis-aggregate levels for Saudi Arabia during the 1980-2011 period. Ajmi et al. (2015) examined the effects of energy use and economic expansion on CO_2 emissions and discovered a bidirectional, time-varying causal relationship between CO_2 emissions and energy demand in the US as well as a causal relationship between energy use and carbon emissions in France. In the current study, air pollutant indicators were included in the model as explanatory variables to understand whether changes in different air pollutants impact on the demand for residential energy consumption or energy consumption is irresponsive to the changing volumes of air pollutants. CO_2 emissions as well as other pollutants were used as determinants in the models estimating energy consumption and energy efficiency such as Sineviciene et al. (2017) and Sarkodie and Adom. (2018a).

According to the literature, good governance and quality institutions are important factors for improved environmental quality and sustainability (İbrahim and Law, 2016; Ali et al., 2019). Quality institutions can be viewed as inputs for developing sound legislation and policies that when implemented effectively can help to reduce environmental degradation and improve environmental quality (Lau et al., 2014). According to some studies, advances in financial growth is beneficial to environmental quality given that well-established financial entities fund renewable energy projects and green technology development which will improve environmental quality by reducing energy use from fossil fuels (Khan et al., 2020). For instance, Ali et al. (2019) investigated the influence of quality institutions on CO_2 emissions in developing countries and discovered that well-established institutions reduce carbon emissions in the sampled countries thereby improving environmental quality. Ibrahim and Law (2015) is the other study that focused on the effect of trade, institutional quality and their effects on carbon dioxide emissions in the Sub-Saharan African countries and found that the effect of trade on the environment was related to the quality of institutions in the subject countries. The impact of political institutional quality on energy consumption and environmental pollution can be found in Bhattacharya et al. (2017), Sarkodie and Adams (2018b), and Nguyen et al. (2022).

The literature searching the connection between natural disasters and energy use is scarce. One example is Lee et al. (2021) who examined the impact of natural disasters on energy consumption for 123 countries and found a significant negative effect for low-income countries and those in the Africa region. Natural disasters have an impact on household consumption instability by reducing people's incomes and expenditures, which increases poverty and inequality, particularly in low-income countries. Kosec and Mo (2017) found evidence of decreased willingness to consume following a natural disaster, much of which is associated with household expenditures, education and wealth. This is also confirmed by Cassar et al. (2017) who indicated that changes in personal preferences discourage people from engaging in consumption. The relationship between natural disasters and energy use varies by level of economic development, geographical location, or types of natural disasters, and this should be considered as a determinant factor in the energy consumption studies, which are often overlooked in many studies.

3. METHODOLOGY

3.1. Variable Selection With Random Forest (RF) Method

RF classification is an ensemble method of machine learning where a set of classification trees are trained using bootstrapped samples from the training data (Breiman, 2001). Within the context of this study, each tree of a RF is composed of energy consumption determinants based on pure mathematics. Bagging is a method used in RF algorithm used to generate a training data set by randomly drawing data from the original dataset or a randomly selected part of training set be used in the construction of individual trees for each feature combination (Breiman, 1996). In each bootstrapped sample, about two-thirds of the training data are used to grow a regression tree and one-third of the sample (the out-of-the-bag samples) is used to estimate the out of bag (OOB) error. Some vectors may be trained more than once in a classifier while other vectors may never be used. Hence it becomes more robust when it comes up with slight changes in input data and increases classification accuracy where the differences in Overall Accuracies between the best configurations and other configurations for RF are small. The number of variables used (n) at each node to generate a tree and the number of trees to be grown (k) are user-defined parameters considered in RF classifications. Therefore, a k number of trees can be set up for k samples and a k number of classification results are obtained. Each tree gives a classification which is validated using the OOB data and the RF predictor is formed by averaging of generalisation error over k trees. RF is accepted for being fast, stable against overfitting and requiring small sample size with high dimensional input (Zafari et al., 2019). It is also shown that RF is more robust than a single decision tree and its generalisation performance is much better than traditional learning algorithms (Schroff et al., 2008).

To estimate the importance of variables, the OOB error of each decision tree in RF needs to be calculated from the OOB data. This is measured by the mean decrease in accuracy (MDA) score, which is calculated randomly by changing the values of the related variable. In addition to the MDA, another method of calculating the importance of the variable is the Gini measure. Gini importance score provides a relative ranking of the features, which is a by-product in the training of the random forest classifier. It is used as one of the important ways for selecting the best split in a RF and measures the impurity of a selected variable. According to this method, the more reduction in Gini index caused by variable changes, the more important the variable is (Foody and Arora, 1997). The RF classification approach applied in this study used the Gini Index as a proxy for measuring the importance of each indicator and based on their importance, the variables were selected accordingly to be included in the regression analysis.

3.2. Moran Index

It is important to distinguish whether there is an adjacency relationship of the geographical areas where households consume energy from residential sources. The spatial statistical methods are used to reveal spatial characteristics of a dataset by reflecting the mean difference between a range of spatial units and their adjacent units (Anselin, 1995). The spatial weight matrix W is used to describe the spatial-geospatial linkages across different data points. As one of the techniques of spatial statistical analysis, the explanatory spatial data analysis (ESDA) is used to analyse spatial autocorrelation by identifying spatial dependence and heterogeneity (Liu et al., 2013). One of the most commonly used ESDA indicators is the Global Moran's I (GMI). In this study, the spatial correlation of residential energy consumption across the NUTS3 regions was calculated using the GMI index as given in Eq. (1) using ArcGIS software.

$$GMI = \frac{n}{\sum_i (x_i - \overline{x})^2} \frac{\sum_i \sum_{j \neq i} W_{ij} (x_i - \overline{x})(x_j - \overline{x})}{\sum_i \sum_{j \neq i} W_{ij}} \tag{1}$$

where n represents the number of spatial units i.e. NUTS3 regions; x_i and x_j are the values of the tested variables; $\overline{x} = (\sum_i x_i) / n$ is the average value of the tested variable; W_{ij} represents the corresponding value in the spatial weight matrix. A GMI index equals to 1 indicates that the variable has completely positive spatial correlation whereas a value of -1 means that the variable has completely negative spatial correlation. GMI equals to 0 shows that there is no spatial correlation in the subject variable.

3.3. Spatial Econometric Models

By taking the spatial correlation and spillover impacts into account, the spatial econometric models can better reflect the spatial impacts of different factors on residential energy consumption. Not considering the spatial impacts may cause the traditional econometric models to fail (Anselin, 1988). For these reasons, spatial econometric models were constructed to improve accuracy and robustness of the results. The common spatial econometric models include a Spatial Auto Regression (SAR) model, a Spatial Error Model (SEM) and a Space Durbin Model (SDM) (Long et al., 2016). Spatial econometric models extend linear regression through allowing outcomes of one area to be influenced by (a) outcomes of nearby areas, (b) covariates from nearby areas and (c) errors from nearby areas. Spatial correlation is reflected in the dependent variable in case of the SAR given by the following formula:

$$Y = \rho WY + X\beta + \varepsilon; \varepsilon \sim N\left(0, \delta^2 I_n\right) \tag{2}$$

where Y represents the dependent variable; W is the normalised spatial weight matrix which characterise the spatial relationships between areas; ρ is the spatial regression coefficient, which reflects the spatial effect of the adjacent area observation value WY on local observation value; X represents the independent variables and β s are their coefficients; and ε is the error term. The Spatial Error Model (SEM) investigates the spatial dependence existing in the error term indicating that spatial spill over effects are present in the error term. The SEM is given by Eq. (3)

$$Y = X\beta + \lambda W\mu + \varepsilon; \varepsilon \sim N\left(0, \delta^2 I_n\right) \tag{3}$$

where ε is the random error term; λ is the space error coefficient of the error term; and μ represents the normally distributed random error term. If both the dependent variable and independent variables reflect the spatial correlation, there is the Spatial Durbin Model (SDM) which is shown in Eq. (4)

$$Y = \rho WY + X\beta + WX\gamma + \varepsilon; \varepsilon \sim N\left(0, \delta^2 I_n\right) \tag{4}$$

where WX represents the spatial lag explanatory variables, which has been introduced to enhance the SAR model; and γ represents the coefficient of spatial lag independent variables.

An important issue of the spatial econometric analysis is to reflect the spatial linkages between data points. One type of spatial weight matrix was constructed i.e. geographical distance. The geographical distance weight matrix is based on the geographical distance between data points. The matrix weight is set according to the geographical distance between the NUTS3 regions of this study. The geographical distance weight matrix is also normalised. The matrix element is represented by Eq. (5) where D_{ij} shows the geographical distance between NUTS3 regions of i and j.

$$W_{ij} = \frac{1/D_{ij}}{\sum_{j=1}^{N}(1/D_{ij})} \tag{5}$$

The goodness of fit for the models of SAR, SEM, and SDM were tested using the AIC and BIC measures where

$$AIC = 2k - 2\ln\left(likelihood\right) \tag{6}$$

$$BIC = kln\left(N\right) - 2\ln\left(likelihoold\right)$$

where k is the number of parameters to be estimated and N is the number of observations. Suppose that there are R candidate models and AIC values of these models are AIC_1, AIC_2,..., AIC_R. Let AIC_{min} is the minimum of those values. Then the quantity $(AIC_{min}-AIC_i)/2$ can be interpreted as being proportional to the probability that the ith model minimizes the estimated information loss. BIC is another criterion for model selection which is closely related to AIC. Models with lower BIC are generally preferred as it is the case of AIC.

4. RESULTS

4.1. Regression Diagnostics

In order to acquire a comprehensive understanding of the factors explaining residential energy consumption in Europe, first, the most important variables were selected using the RF classifier, and the important variables from the RF were included in the spatial regression models i.e. SAR, SEM, and SDM. Regarding the spatial regression analysis, the Wald test indicated that the overall models had statistical significance ($p<0.001$) and the value of the adjusted R-squared ranging from 0.71 to 0.77 showed a relatively high goodness-of-fit. Multicollinearity was controlled with variance inflation factors (VIFs), which did not pose a problem in the current models where all the variables show below 10.0. Prior to the application of the spatial regression models, an OLS model was estimated using the same explanatory variables and the error terms from this model were used to compute the Global Moran's Index (GMI) (Table 1).

Table 1. The results from Global Moran's index

	Method 1	Method 2	Method 3
Moran's Index	0,059422	0,188875	0,014621
Expected Index	-0,001437	-0,001437	-0,001437
Variance	0,000058	0,000300	0,000016
z-score	7,993,795	10,981,421	4,006,568
p-value	0,000000	0,000000	0,000062
Conceptualization:	INVERSE_DISTANCE	K_NEAREST_NEIGHBORS	FIXED_DISTANCE
Distance Method:	EUCLIDEAN	EUCLIDEAN	EUCLIDEAN

Three different methods including inverse distance, K-nearest neighbours and fixed distance were used to compute GMI. The results from these methods indicate that residential energy consumption point to significant agglomeration characteristics. Moran's index is greater than 0, so it can be concluded that energy consumption exhibits positive agglomeration, which means high energy consumption areas are surrounded by regions with high energy consumption values, low energy areas are surrounded by regions with low energy consumption values. Because there is spatial autocorrelation which OLS model does not take into consideration means that findings from OLS model may not be robust. Therefore spatial regression models were utilised to quantify the determinants of residential energy consumption in Europe. For the measurement of goodness of fit and model selection, AIC and BIC were used and their results are provided in Table 2. From the Table, it is clear that SEM has the lowest values regarding AIC and BIC, therefore in can be inferred that the subject model performs better than the other models.

Table 2. Results from AIC and BIC

Model	Observations	ll (model)	df	AIC	BIC
SAR	1399	-22289.96	31	4641.93	4804.48
SEM	1399	-1992.12	30	4044.24	4201.54
SDM	1399	-1991.97	31	4045.94	4208.49

Note: AIC: Akaike Information Criterion; BIC: Bayesian Information Criterion

Because of the possible interdependence between GDP per capita and several other explanatory variables including energy consumption, this interaction can cause reverse causality and result in parameter estimation deviations; thus, instrumental variables must be included in the regression to control possible endogeneity of the parameters of the econometric model. Instrumental variables should be strongly associated with endogenous variables and have adequate exogeneity; thus, share of industrial, commercial and transportation units and long-term development of urban use areas were used as instrumental variables to account for the endogeneity between economic output and energy consumption in the estimation of spatial regression models. These instrumental variables were chosen based on the consideration that industrial and commercial areas are the land uses which contribute to the value of the economic output and the share of urban use areas are also correlated with GDP and can be used as an instrumental variable to capture the endogeneity between GDP and energy consumption.

4.2. Estimation Results

It can be seen that (Tables 3 and 4) GDP per capita is one of the significant factors determining residential energy consumption in Europe. Its coefficient is positive in all regressions indicating that GDP per capita is positively associated with energy consumption levels. This verifies the findings of previous studies performed by Sarkodie and Adom (2018a) for Kenya; Hu and Fan (2020) for China; and Canh et al. (2021 for the selected countries in the world. It contradicts with the findings of Borozan (2018) which found negative relationship with energy consumption and GDP per capita indicating that wealthier regions in Europe have physical access to modern energy, energy efficient products and technologies. The sampled countries in Borozan (2018) is limited and did not cover all the EU countries and the unit of the analysis was NUTS2. These factors may explain the contradictory findings from the current study and Borozan (2018).

Economically active population is negatively associated with energy consumption indicating that the regions with higher population i.e. more urbanised regions economize the energy use. Unemployment rate and poverty rate are also negatively related to energy consumption where the former variable is insignificant in some regressions whereas the latter is significant in all. This implies that if the regions are characterised by income constraints, they have declining energy use at the household level. Due to financial restrictions, long-term unemployed persons and households suffering from poverty cannot afford to use more energy and buy more energy efficient appliances. They are forced to use less energy unless they are supported by the government to afford high energy use (Borozan, 2018). The case where the residents are supported with the government funding is represented by the variable 'Fund_gov_supp', which has an expected positive coefficient indicating that the increase of government support increases energy consumption of the regions. Quality and accountability of government services are expected to decrease energy consumption of the regions and increase environmental quality: Government quality variable has an expected negative sign in some regressions and positive in others showing that it is not a robust variable. Therefore, the models cannot capture the impact of government quality on residential energy consumption. As the government quality variable is insignificant in the regression models verifies the previous findings (Acheampong and Dzator, 2020) that showed that regulations have an insignificant effect on carbon emissions. It contradicts with the findings of Acheampong et al. (2019) and Adams et al. (2020) where institutional quality shows a negative and significant association between regularity quality and environmental quality.

Patent applications and index of access to technology are the two variables that are both significant and negatively related to energy consumption in all regressions given that these represent existence of high technological industries, which are more energy efficient compared to traditional industries. Market demand and share of self-employed people are positively correlated with energy consumption considering that high share of employment and market demand increase energy consumption in the regions. Price of gas for heating and price of Euro-super 95 per 1000L are important drivers of energy consumption. The results show that higher energy prices lead to less energy use in the former case while the reverse occurs in the latter. The price of Euro-super 95 can be considered as a proxy for the unincluded variables in the

Table 3. Estimation results of spatial regression models for all regions in Europe

Variables	SAR		SAR		SEM		SEM		SDM		SDM	
	Coefficient	z	Coefficient	z	Coefficient	z	Coefficient	z	Coefficient	z	Coefficient	z
Constant	0.5517**	3.91	1.1301**	6.32	0.3022**	2.08	0.0935	1.16	0.2851**	3.2	0.9875**	5.82
Eco_act_pop	-0.0003**	-5.75	-0.0003**	-3.06	-0.0001**	-3.15	-0.0001	-1.21	-0.0001	-1.4	-0.0003	-0.48
Unempl_rate	-0.0166	-1.17	-0.0553**	-3.73	-0.0232*	-1.66	-0.0196	-0.85	-0.0181	-0.66	-0.0566**	-3.79
Pov_excl	-0.0418**	-3.8	-0.0231*	-1.88	-0.0299**	-2.72	-0.0118	-0.73	-0.0408**	-2.43	-0.0297**	-2.47
Pat_appl	-0.0076**	-2.21	-0.0006**	-2.59	-0.005*	-1.78	-0.0004**	-2.68	-0.0005**	-2.09	-0.0006**	-2.55
Access_Tech	-0.6167**	-2.53	-0.3516	-1.46	-0.8821**	-3.15	-0.7867**	-2.54	-0.9574**	-2.90	-0.2246	-0.91
Market_dem	4.083**	6.11	4.0908**	4.12	7.132**	9.62	2.6471**	2.70	7.3442**	4.14	6.1271**	5.30
GDP_cap	0.0001**	2.52	0.0001*	1.60	0.0001**	3.42	0.0001*	1.29	0.0001**	2.65	0.0001**	2.67
Prvt_enterpr	0.0753**	7.51	0.0447**	2.61	0.0794**	7.93	0.0554**	2.78	0.0753**	4.35	0.0429**	2.37
Euro-super 95	0.0001**	10.89	0.0001**	8.23	0.0001**	10.4	0.0001**	3.44	0.0001**	7.14	0.0001**	7.77
Gasl_automobile	0.0001	1.21	0.0001	0.99	-0.0001	-0.04	0.0001	1.54	-0.0001	-0.06	0.0001	0.93
Gas oil heating	-0.0002**	-9.82	-0.0001**	-8.32	-0.0001**	-8.23	-0.0001**	-4.09	-0.0001**	-6.99	-0.0001**	-8.21
Forest	0.0201**	7.04	0.0235**	5.16	0.0217**	7.88	0.0121**	2.23	0.0214**	4.93	0.0232**	5.44
Econ_dam_drought	-30.175**	-12.99	-36.3995**	-9.06	-27.3442**	-12.21	-28.0427**	-5.83	-27.2709**	-6.24	-37.0275**	-9.49
Econ_dam_wind	1.0584	0.55	2.4557*	1.60	-0.4905	-0.26	5.7528**	3.17	-0.3764	-0.25	2.1138	1.37
Gov_qual	-0.0076	-0.08	0.2848**	2.95	0.1976**	2.12	0.4874**	3.66	0.1711*	1.62	0.2746**	2.94
Fund_gov_supp	1.6844**	5.97	1.7245**	6.13	1.2453**	4.16	1.3983**	3.97	1.3125**	3.45	1.4259**	4.89
PhElExpT	0.0061**	3.06	0.0061**	3.26	0.0047**	2.44	0.0031*	1.83	0.0050**	2.7	0.0071**	3.90
Cool_days	0.0117**	3.39	0.0071	0.8	0.0156**	4.64	0.0248*	1.69	0.0146	1.29	0.0072	0.77
BioFuPoT	0.0001**	2.47	0.0001	0.80	0.0001	1.09	-0.0001	-0.22	0.0001	0.42	-0.0001	-0.06
NO2_emission	-0.0379**	-2.38	-0.0096	-0.57	-0.0197	-1.19	-0.0258	-1.09	-0.0204	-0.77	-0.0337*	-1.83
Sphere_2	-0.0143**	-4.32	-0.0198**	-4.89	-0.0061*	-1.57	-0.0227**	-5.30	-0.0041	-0.7	-0.0119**	-2.66
Sphere_3	-0.0324**	-6.67	-0.0248**	-4.33	-0.00273**	-5.71	-0.0229**	-3.24	-0.0278**	--4.31	-0.0241**	-4.21
Sphere_4	-0.0021	-0.58	0.0096**	2.05	0.0012	0.33	0.0094**	1.92	0.0017	0.39	0.0109**	2.39
Metropol	-1.1182**	-2.02	-0.2694**	-3.17	-0.1448*	-1.65	-0.1276**	-2.28	-0.1209*	-1.63	-0.2451**	-2.97
Western	-0.6474**	-3.97	-	-	-1.314**	-6.68	-	-	-1.2542**	-3.99	-	-
Eastern	-1.531**	-6.95	-	-	-2.3692**	-8.85	-	-	-2.3729**	-5.49	-	-
Southern	-2.2267**	-7.9	-	-	-2.8419**	-9.55	-	-	-2.7583**	-5.14	-	-
Urban_Region	-0.1926**	-1.69	-	-	-0.2891**	-2.62	-	-	-0.2212**	-2.18	-	-
Rural_Region	0.0734*	1.74	-	-	0.1159*	1.26	-	-	0.1008	0.55	-	-
Western_Urban	-	-	0.118*	1.12	-	-	0.0202	0.23	-	-	0.1442	1.26
Eastern_Urban	-	-	-0.1367	-0.54	-	-	-0.1221	0.52	-	-	-0.2857	-1.15
Southern_Urban	-	-	-1.128**	-2.96	-	-	-0.7175**	-2.92	-	-	-0.9936**	-2.68
Western_Rural	-	-	0.1134	0.72	-	-	-0.0624	-0.45	-	-	0.1732	1.13
Eastern_Rural	-	-	-0.5541**	-2.30	-	-	-0.3886*	-1.43	-	-	-0.6659**	-2.73
Southern_Rural	-	-	-0.5681*	-1.30	-	-	-0.1978	-0.48	-	-	-0.5573	-1.26
No. Observations	1399		1399		1399		1399		1399		1399	
Wald chi2	4558.68		10879.22		4263.73		8214.2		15,405.8		13,557.40	
Prob>chi2	0.000		0.000		0.000		0.000		0.000		0.000	
Pseudo R2	0.76		0.76		0.71		0.72		0.74		0.77	
Wald test of spatial terms	chi2(1)=15.0**		chi2(1)=23.18**		chi2(1)=192.9**		chi2(1)=406.81**		chi2(4)=288.06**		chi2(4)=69.74**	

Table 4. Estimation results of spatial regression models for all regions in Europe (Instrumental variable approach)

Variables	SAR		SAR		SEM		SEM		SDM		SDM	
	Coefficient	z	Coefficient	z	Coefficient	z	Coefficient	z	Coefficient	z	Coefficient	z
Constant	0.5298**	3.73	0.4159**	2.93	0.397**	2.66	0.2231	1.50	0.1941	1.3	0.0963	0.64
Eco_act_pop	-0.0003**	-5.54	-0.0002**	-3.71	-0.0001**	-4.34	-0.0001**	-2.45	-0.0001**	-2.66	-0.0003	-1.43
Unempl_rate	-0.0173	-1.21	-0.0503**	-4.44	-0.0064	-0.40	-0.0341**	-2.60	-0.0149	-0.89	-0.0225*	-1.63
Pov_excl	-0.0456**	-3.99	-0.0175*	-1.65	-0.0461**	-3.58	-0.0151	-1.17	-0.0241*	-1.87	-0.0052	-0.41
Pat_appl	-0.0078**	-2.26	-0.0009**	-2.57	-0.0004	-1.59	-0.0005*	-1.78	-0.0004	-1.57	-0.0005*	-1.91
Access_Tech	-0.6572**	-2.67	-0.4712*	-1.92	0.8331**	3.00	0.6757**	2.40	-1.1109**	-3.79	-0.8006**	-2.73
Market_dem	4.265**	6.22	4.4172**	6.52	3.5528**	4.89	3.2037**	4.46	2.1327**	3.01	2.4244**	3.44
GDP_cap	0.0001**	2.13	0.0001*	1.54	0.0001	0.97	0.0001	0.68	0.0001**	2.09	0.0001	1.30
Prvt_enterpr	0.0755**	7.2	0.0563**	6.24	0.0787**	7.14	0.0561**	5.86	0.0859**	7.65	0.0562**	5.73
Euro-super 95	0.0001**	10.82	0.0001**	9.53	0.0001**	8.85	0.0001**	6.60	0.0001**	6.30	0.0001**	4.93
Gas_automobile	0.0001	0.95	0.0001	0.42	0.0001	1.33	0.0001	1.27	0.0001**	2.51	0.0001*	1.86
Gas oil_heating	-0.0002**	-9.8	-0.0001**	-9.16	-0.0001**	-7.30	-0.0001**	-6.15	-0.0001**	-5.04	-0.0001**	-4.93
Forest	0.0197**	6.88	0.0190**	6.69	0.0181**	6.35	0.0155**	5.52	0.0127**	4.53	0.0118**	4.15
Econ_dam_drought	-29.416**	-12.47	-33.910**	-15.17	-26.705**	-10.60	-30.639**	-12.44	-24.2443**	-9.51	-29.0255**	-11.62
Econ_dam_wind	1.365	0.7	2.986	1.55	2.491	1.19	4.968**	2.39	3.184	1.50	5.448**	2.56
Gov_qual	-0.0259	-0.28	0.2594**	3.23	0.0277	0.27	0.4127**	4.40	0.1443	1.35	0.5073**	5.38
Fund_gov_supp	1.7339**	6.03	1.5094**	5.85	1.8527**	5.70	1.4651**	4.93	1.7788**	5.19	1.343**	4.34
PhElExpT	0.0066**	3.33	0.0053**	2.74	0.0049**	2.56	0.0031*	1.65	0.0043**	2.39	0.0035**	1.94
Cool_days	0.0117**	3.36	0.008**	2.67	0.0184**	5.21	0.0193**	5.58	0.0243**	6.98	0.0229**	6.51
BioFuPoT	0.0004**	0.65	0.0001	0.67	-0.0001	-0.84	-0.0001	-0.22	0.0001	0.93	0.0001	0.61
NO2_emission	-0.0451**	-2.77	-0.0726**	-4.75	-0.0282	-1.59	-0.0364**	-2.07	-0.0037	-0.21	-0.0217	-1.24
Sphere_2	-0.0155**	-4.47	-0.0174**	-5.06	-0.0194**	-4.72	-0.0211**	-5.01	-0.0154**	-3.61	-0.0199**	4.72
Sphere_3	-0.0296**	-5.67	-0.0248**	-4.83	-0.0284**	-4.82	-0.0248**	-4.17	-0.0337**	-5.84	-0.0270**	-4.74
Sphere_4	0.0026	0.71	0.0058	1.57	0.0062	1.55	0.0094**	2.37	0.0041	1.01	0.0083**	-2.10
Metropol	-1.1883**	-2.01	-0.3031**	-3.31	-0.0952	-1.14	-0.1638**	-2.10	-0.111	-1.48	-0.1577**	-2.12
Western	-0.6584**	-4.01	-	-	-0.7622**	-3.90	-	-	-0.866**	-3.95	-	-
Eastern	-1.468**	-6.57	-	-	-1.5485**	-5.88	-	-	-1.905**	-6.61	-	-
Southern	-2.1593**	-7.53	-	-	-2.2968**	-7.13	-	-	-2.691**	-7.92	-	-
Urban_Region	-0.2042*	-1.69	-	-	-0.2242**	-2.10	-	-	-0.1011	-1.03	-	-
Rural_Region	0.0460	0.46	-	-	0.0242	0.27	-	-	-0.0127	-0.16	-	-
Western_Urban	-	-	0.0385	0.27	-	-	-0.0254	-0.17	-	-	0.0921	0.67
Eastern_Urban	-	-	0.1150	0.40	-	-	0.131	0.51	-	-	0.0936	0.38
Southern_Urban	-	-	-1.0132**	-4.18	-	-	-0.8109**	-3.70	-	-	-0.7856**	-3.75
Western_Rural	-	-	-0.0455	-0.36	-	-	-0.0248	-0.22	-	-	-0.056	-0.52
Eastern_Rural	-	-	-0.5534**	-3.41	-	-	-0.3631**	-2.48	-	-	-0.3711**	-2.61
Southern_Rural	-	-	-0.6491**	-3.39	-	-	-0.2605*	-1.61	-	-	-0.2202	-1.42
No. Observations	1399		1399		1399		1399		1399		1399	
Wald chi2	4508.08		4422.98		3428.92		3244.62		3201.52		3,064.46	
Prob>chi2	0.000		0.000		0.000		0.000		0.000		0.000	
Pseudo R2	0.75		0.75		0.74		0.73		0.72		0.72	
Wald test of spatial terms	chi2(1)=21.**		chi2(1)=27.6**		chi2(1)=460.3**		chi2(1)=635.5**		chi2(2)=942.2**		chi2(2)=925.3**	

regressions and the positive coefficient of this variable may reflect the impact of the proxied variables on the dependent variable. The sign and value of the estimated coefficient of price of gas for heating is stable across regressions and is consistent with the findings of the other studies including Blazquez et al. (2013) and Navamuel et al. (2018), which focused on residential electricity demand in Spain.

The next significant factor influencing energy consumption is NO_2 emissions recorded in the regions. This indicator is significant in some regressions and insignificant in others, but its coefficient is negative in all regression models. An increment of NO_2 emissions in a region decreases energy consumption indicating that the more NO_2 emissions are produced, the lower level of residential energy consumption we can report. NO_2 emissions is the consequence of burning fossil fuels; therefore, when energy consumption increases, NO_2 emissions also increase. The results from the regression analysis indicate that there is reverse causality implying that the increase in air pollutants from NO_2, which have negative impacts on the environment, persuade residents to lower their energy consumption. The area of forest in a region is correlated with the typology of the region i.e. whether the region is rural or urban. The area of forest land use in rural regions are comparatively higher than that of urban regions. The coefficient of Forest is positive implying higher energy consumption in rural areas compared to urban areas. This is also verified by the coefficients of Urban_Region and Rural_Region variables, the former has a negative coefficient while the latter has positive coefficient. Building construction practices in urban regions include high density buildings with less heating and cooling requirements than detached or semi-detached houses that are frequently located in rural regions. This is also verified by Wiesmann et al. (2011), Huang (2015), and Xie et al. (2020) which showed that detached or semi-detached houses consume significantly more electricity than flats, apartments and other attached housing. An alternative explanation is the change in life patterns of the residents of the urban space as more time is spent away from home during working, leisure facilities and external services to care for children or dependent members of the family (Navamuel et al., 2018). There are also contrary findings in the literature which claimed that, for instance Romero-Jordan et al. (2016), in lower quantiles of electricity consumption distribution, households consume more in urban areas than in rural areas. By contrast, Labandeira et al. (2006) found that rural households spend more on electricity than households in urban municipalities.

The regional dummies showed that there are regional disparities in residential energy consumption where the energy consumption in western, eastern and southern regions are lower than that of the northern region (i.e. northern region is the base category and the dummy variables of the other regions are equal to 1) as they have all significant and negative coefficients. It is also found that metropolitan regions consume less energy compared to other regions pointing to the agglomeration effects in metropolitan regions that reduce the demand for energy consumption. Northern regions use more energy compared to other regions due to climatic factors, which are characterised by humid, cold winters, and mild, humid summers. The variable Cool_days also verify the impact of climate on energy use indicating that the number of the cool days experienced in a region are positively associated with residential energy consumption. Colder weather will increase energy consumption as the residents are heating indoor spaces and energy consumption in warmer weather would be less (Borozan, 2018). The natural disasters variables are Econ_dam_draught and Econ_dam_wind; the former is significant and negative in all regressions whereas the latter is insignificant with an unexpected positive sign. This showed that natural disasters i.e. draught are affecting energy consumption negatively and wind is not a robust variable. Because natural disasters have a negative impact on the income, this results in lower demand of residential energy consumption compared with the cases where there are no disasters. This coincides with the findings of Doytch and Klein (2018), Otsuka (2019), and Rakshit (2021) which showed that total energy consumption declines with the occurrence of disasters.

The potential for generating energy from renewable sources in the regions indicate a positive relationship with residential energy consumption. This was captured with the use of two variables i.e. exploitation rate of potential electricity generation by solar photovoltaics (PhElExpT) and primary energy potential of forestry products and forestry residues (BioFuPoT), both having significant and positive coefficients. The renewable energy sources are generally located in intermediate and rural regions, which are associated with higher energy consumption compared to urban regions. Green economic performance indices are negatively related to energy consumption. High-income economies allocate more resources to promote green economic growth. The current findings on green economic performance indices verify Fisher-Vanden et al. (2004), which argued that public budget on energy R&D has a positive impact on reducing energy intensity and on the reduction of greenhouse gases emissions. Developed economies replace traditional inefficient technologies with the more efficient ones, therefore enhancing environmental quality (Copeland and Taylor, 2004).

The differences in energy consumption across different regional typologies are presented in Figure 6. It can be observed from the Figure that urban regions are associated with lower values of energy consumption followed by intermediate and then rural regions. In 2002, urban regions indicate some data points that are identified as outliers whereas there are fewer outliers in the intermediate and rural regions for the same year. In 2012, there are no outliers for intermediate regions, but a number of outliers were identified for urban and rural regions. The Figure also indicates that there are variations in energy consumption across eastern, western, southern and northern regions. In 2012, it follows that the energy consumption distribution among the regions are more heterogeneous compared to 2002 figures. In order to assess the correlation of determinant factors with residential energy consumption, region specific regression models were estimated regarding predominantly urban regions, predominantly intermediate

Figure 6. Residential energy consumption of different European regions in 2002 and 2012 (K Wh/capita)

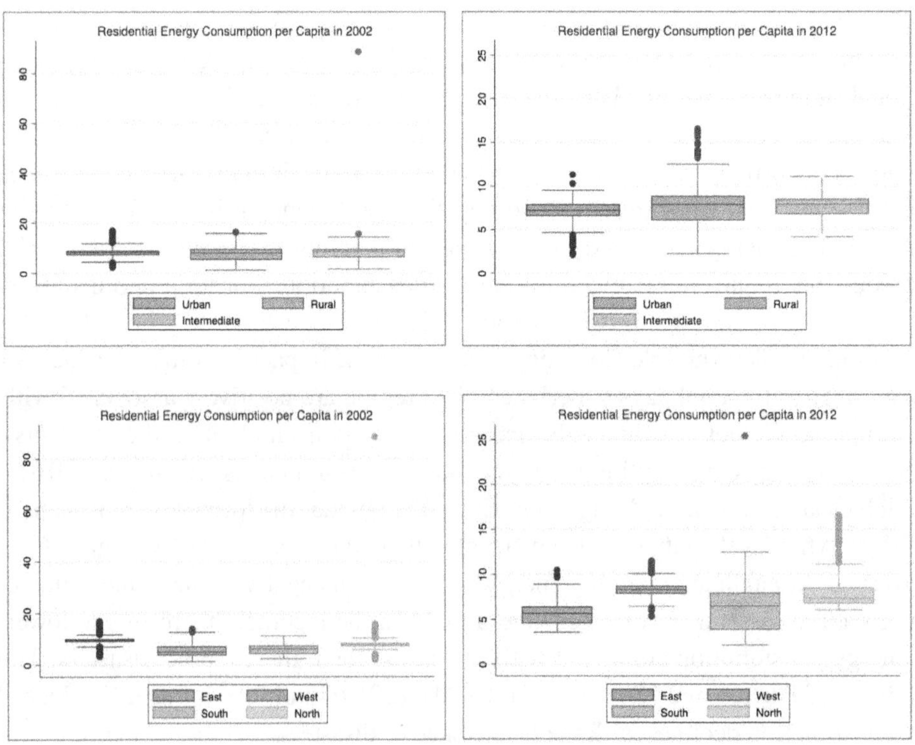

regions, and predominantly rural regions. Estimation results for predominantly urban regions (Table 5) indicate that price of gas oil for automobile, forest, renewable energy potential, GDP growth and western region variables were significant with positive signs. Access to technology, price of gas for heating,

Table 5. Estimation results for predominantly urban regions in Europe

Variables	SAR		SEM		SDM	
	Coefficient	z	Coefficient	z	Coefficient	z
Eco_act_pop	-0.0001	-0.63	-0.0001	-0.61	-0.0001	-0.27
Unempl_rate	-0.0552	-1.46	-0.0541	-1.33	-0.0597*	-1.61
Pov_excl	-0.0173	-0.78	-0.0107	-0.43	-0.0243	-1.16
Pat_appl	0.0001	0.55	0.0002	0.9	0.0001	0.33
Access_Tech	-1.092**	-3.91	-1.0636**	-3.48	-0.8621**	-2.92
Market_dem	-0.0383	-0.07	-0.0169	-0.03	0.3827	0.72
GDP_cap	0.0001	0.13	0.0001	0.12	0.0001	0.48
Prvt_enterpr	0.0437	1.5	0.0524*	1.73	0.0375	1.32
Euro-super 95	0.0001	0.96	0.0001	1.18	0.0001	0.48
Gas oil_automobile	0.0001**	2.49	0.0001**	3.13	0.0001**	2.23
Gas oil_heating	-0.0001*	-1.35	-0.0001*	-1.57	-0.0001	-1.37
Forest	0.0189**	3.61	0.0201**	3.85	0.0191**	3.66
Econ_dam_drought	-15.0912**	-3.46	-17.344**	-3.49	-15.6247**	-3.7
Econ_dam_wind	-2.9813	-1.01	-3.2277	-1.1	-2.722	-0.93
Gov_qual	-0.0515	-0.41	0.1155	0.75	-0.1196	-0.91
Fund_gov_supp	-1.543*	-1.58	-1.9187*	-1.87	-1.3315	-1.37
PhElExpT	0.0062**	2.07	0.0048*	1.49	0.0057*	1.80
Cool_days	-0.0296**	-2.21	-0.0192	-1.42	-0.0278**	-2.12
BioFuPoT	-0.0001	-0.21	0.0001	0.94	-0.0001	-0.74
NO2_emission	0.0002	0.01	-0.0372**	-2.59	-0.0054	-0.35
Sphere_2	-0.0281**	-3.72	-0.0364**	-4.5	-0.0293**	-3.87
Sphere_3	-0.0235*	-1.65	-0.0334**	-2.35	-0.0241*	-1.73
Sphere_4	-0.0121*	-1.89	-0.0141**	-2.15	-0.0124*	-1.96
Western	0.4612*	1.81	0.3617	1.34	0.4465*	1.76
Eastern	-2.8196**	-5.45	-2.2335**	-3.96	-2.9944**	-5.72
Southern	-2.4676**	-3.09	-2.9322**	-3.75	-2.1711**	-2.82
Metropol	-0.0949	-0.93	-0.2062*	-1.69	-0.0411	-0.39
GVA_cap	-0.0001*	-1.47	-0.0001	-1.55	-0.0001	-1.33
GDP_growth	0.0235**	2.67	-0.0093	-0.62	0.0255**	2.91
Constant	11.3015**	10.77	11.668**	10.95	11.1079**	10.0
No. Observations	346		346		346	
Wald chi2	1478.29		1097.69		1532.93	
Prob>chi2	0.000		0.000		0.000	
Pseudo R2	0.75		0.71		0.75	
Wald test of spatial terms	chi2(1)=11.59**		chi2(1)=13.97**		chi2(4)=19.02**	

Note: Instrumental variables were used in the estimation of the spatial regression models

economic damage due to draught, access to funding and government support, number of cool days, GDP per capita, green economic performance, eastern and southern regions were significant with negative signs. Different from urban regions, the estimation results for intermediate regions (Table 6) showed that

Table 6. Estimation results for predominantly intermediate regions in Europe

Variables	SAR		SEM		SDM	
	Coefficient	z	Coefficient	z	Coefficient	z
Eco_act_pop	-0.0003	-0.44	-0.0001	-0.44	0.0001	0.08
Unempl_rate	-0.0224	-1.01	0.0003	0.02	-0.0181	-0.83
Pov_excl	-0.0616**	-3.81	-0.635**	-3.57	-0.0641**	-4.10
Pat_appl	0.0002	0.83	0.0001	0.02	0.0001	0.60
Access_Tech	-1.0198**	-4.73	-0.904**	-4.05	-0.9769**	-4.48
Market_dem	1.0001	1.51	0.7201	0.98	1.7749**	2.90
GDP_cap	0.0001	0.81	0.0001	0.54	0.0001*	1.47
Prvt_enterpr	0.0201	1.24	0.0351**	2.21	0.0244*	1.56
Euro-super 95	0.0001**	7.16	0.0001**	6.17	0.0001**	6.83
Gas oil_automobile	0.0001**	2.32	0.0001**	2.91	0.0001**	2.17
Gas oil_heating	-0.0001**	-6.63	-0.0001**	-5.74	-0.0001**	-6.38
Forest	0.0285**	7.57	0.0265**	7.30	0.0294**	7.97
Econ_dam_drought	-28.8331**	-7.33	-27.3001**	-7.40	-29.4433**	-7.5
Econ_dam_wind	-4.4086**	-2.37	-2.8317	-1.52	-4.7896**	-2.52
Gov_qual	0.3496**	3.18	0.3831**	2.97	0.2881**	2.67
Fund_gov_supp	0.3084	0.73	0.0793	0.18	0.2106	0.49
PhElExpT	0.0049**	2.74	0.0029	1.52	0.0051**	2.66
Cool_days	-0.0008	-0.17	0.0011	0.22	0.0003	0.07
BioFuPoT	-0.0001	-0.73	-0.0001	-0.04	-0.0001	-0.60
NO2_emission	-0.0279	-1.53	-0.0636**	-4.04	-0.0297*	-1.62
Sphere_2	-0.0271**	-4.95	-0.0301**	-5.03	-0.0283**	-4.97
Sphere_3	0.0076	0.97	0.0102	1.21	0.0098	1.26
Sphere_4	0.002	0.44	-0.0015	-0.33	0.0032	0.72
Western	-0.6744**	-3.31	-0.8371**	-3.80	-0.6408**	-3.25
Eastern	-2.6611**	-9.07	-2.7785**	-8.01	-2.8166**	-9.32
Southern	-2.9665**	-5.58	-3.0181**	-5.49	-2.9694**	-5.63
Metropol	-0.5455**	-5.22	-0.5386**	-5.5	-0.5248**	-5.08
GVA_cap	0.0001	1.08	0.0001	0.22	0.0001	0.80
GDP_growth	-0.0121	-1.31	-0.0018	-0.12	-0.0069	-0.83
Constant	11.6872**	16.58	11.2212**	14.11	11.1303**	15.17
No. Observations	834		834		834	
Wald chi2	2643.46		2167.69		2727.03	
Prob>chi2	0.000		0.000		0.000	
Pseudo R2	0.72		0.72		0.73	
Wald test of spatial terms	chi2(1)=12.48**		chi2(1)=73.70**		chi2(4)=24.38**	

Note: Instrumental variables were used in the estimation of the spatial regression models

poverty, economic damage due to wind, western region and metropolitan area are negatively associated with energy consumption while price of gas for automobile and Euro-super 95 and quality of government are negatively related. Rural regions, on the other hand, include economically active population that is negatively related to residential energy consumption and quality of the government that is positively related to energy consumption (Table 7). Differences in model results are highlighted in Table 8.

Table 7. Estimation results for predominantly rural regions in Europe

Variables	SAR		SEM		SDM	
	Coefficient	z	Coefficient	z	Coefficient	z
Eco_act_pop	-0.0043**	-2.94	-0.0015*	-1.81	-0.0044**	-2.94
Unempl_rate	-0.0342	-1.12	-0.0033	-0.11	-0.0342	-1.12
Pov_excl	-0.0271	-1.3	-0.0372**	-1.97	-0.0271	-1.30
Pat_appl	-0.0008	-0.71	-0.0007	-1.20	-0.0008	-0.71
Access_Tech	-1.1675**	-2.83	-0.9428**	-2.95	-1.1675**	-2.83
Market_dem	16.388	1.4	10.6733	1.08	16.3883	1.40
GDP_cap	0.0003	1.56	0.0001	1.42	0.0001	1.56
Prvt_enterpr	0.0209	1.08	0.0292	1.48	0.0209	1.08
Euro-super 95	0.0001**	5.24	0.0001**	4.35	0.0001**	5.24
Gas oil_automobile	-0.0001	-0.95	0.0001	0.78	-0.0001	-0.95
Gas oil_heating	-0.0001**	-3.91	-0.0001**	-3.69	-0.0001**	-3.91
Forest	0.0301**	5.45	0.0291**	6.46	0.0301**	5.45
Econ_dam_drought	-30.9295**	-6.56	-29.5657**	-6.52	-30.9295**	-6.56
Econ_dam_wind	-9.7689**	-3.2	-3.5721	-1.35	-9.7689**	-3.20
Gov_qual	0.2115*	1.39	0.4221**	2.95	0.2115	1.39
Fund_gov_supp	0.7643	1.47	0.2841	0.57	0.7643	1.47
PhElExpT	-0.0069*	-1.77	-0.0041	-1.37	-0.0069*	-1.77
Cool_days	-0.0062	-0.89	-0.0029	-0.48	-0.0062	-0.89
BioFuPoT	0.0008**	2.38	-0.0003	-0.98	0.0008**	2.38
NO2_emission	-0.0288	-0.6	0.0132	0.25	-0.0288	-0.60
Sphere_2	-0.0289**	-3.57	-0.0249**	-3.28	-0.0289**	-3.57
Sphere_3	0.0015	0.18	0.0051	0.63	0.0015	0.18
Sphere_4	0.0063	1.03	0.0018	0.33	0.0063	1.03
Western	-2.5725**	-5.14	-2.0868**	-4.58	-2.5725**	-5.14
Eastern	-5.1646**	-7.03	-3.9512**	-6.37	-5.1646**	-7.03
Southern	-3.8509**	-5.28	-3.2538**	-4.25	-3.8509**	-5.28
Metropol	-0.0572	-0.24	-0.0064	-0.05	-0.0572	-0.24
GVA_cap	-0.0001**	-3.42	-0.0001*	-1.72	-0.0001**	-3.42
GDP_growth	0.0019	0.18	0.0102	0.63	0.0019	0.18
Constant	3.3456	0.57	6.1238	1.21	3.3457	0.57
No. Observations	488		488		488	
Wald chi2	1929.23		1398.14		1929.23	
Prob>chi2	0.000		0.000		0.000	
Pseudo R2	0.72		0.77		0.72	
Wald test of spatial terms	chi2(1)=17.66**		chi2(1)=46.14**		chi2(4)=17.66**	

Note: Instrumental variables were used in the estimation of the spatial regression models

Table 8. Comparison of signs of the significant coefficients from regional models

Significant Variables	Coefficient Signs		
	Urban Regions	**Rural Regions**	**Intermediate Regions**
Eco_act_pop		-	
Pov_excl			-
Access_Tech	-	-	-
Euro-super 95		+	+
Gas oil_automobile	+		+
Gas oil_heating	-	-	-
Forest	+	+	+
Econ_dam_drought	-	-	-
Econ_dam_wind		-	-
Gov_qual			+
Fund_gov_supp	-	-	
PhElExpT	+		+
BioFuPoT		+	
Cool_days	-		
Sphere_2	-	-	-
Sphere_3	+		
Sphere_4	-		
Western	+	-	-
Eastern	-	-	-
Southern	-	-	-
Metropol			-
GVA_cap	-	-	
GDP_growth	+		

5. DISCUSSION

Policymakers and planners argue that simply changing the supply side of markets will not suffice, the demand side must also be changed. Household energy consumption places significant strain on the environment, accounting for roughly 60% of global greenhouse gas emissions (Ivanova et al., 2016). Energy is required for all types consumption including ICT applications, heating and cooling of the space, mobility and transportation and the food system. Efficient energy use benefits countries because it has a considerable impact on national security in terms of energy, social, economic, and environmental factors. In the context of green economy and sustainable development, reduced energy use and increased energy efficiency have been highlighted as priority topics. Many studies have been undertaken to explore the interrelationships between processes and factors affecting energy efficiency, energy use, economic development and environmental pollution. The lack of agreement in the literature complicates the development of definitive guidelines for the application of sustainable energy policies in regions and countries. Problems with the reliance on fossil energy sources and their negative environmental impacts encourage the research on common factors that influence residential sector energy consumption as the foundation for policy improvements both at micro and macro levels.

This has constructed a framework for the current study which focused on a wide range of factors that influence residential energy consumption at the regional level in Europe. By including socio-economic characteristics, economic activities, mobility, land cover, natural hazards, governance, energy, air quality and green economy into the energy demand analysis and selecting the most important determinants to include in the spatial regression models, the study added to the literature in three subjects: First, there are limited number of studies which considered all the variables of socio-economic, and environmental factors, natural hazards and governance into the regression models. Therefore, including these variables in the regression analysis has extended the scope of this research and enabled us to quantify their impacts in explaining residential energy consumption in Europe. Second, there are few relevant studies on energy consumption determinants at the regional scale in the EU. One example is Baranzelli et al. (2016) that focused on energy generation and consumption by the transport sector in Europe and the other one is Borozan (2018) that researched the household energy consumption determinants for the 64 NUTS2 European regions between 2005 and 2013. The former study disaggregated the energy consumption data into regional level through focusing on transport sector. The latter study focused on residential sector but did not cover all the European regions and focused on a limited number of determinant factors due to data availability issues. The current study contributed to this literature through using different variables in various contexts and all the European countries were included in the regressions where the unit of analysis is NUTS3 regions. The use of NUTS 3 regions in the regressions has enabled to better capture the variability of data across regions by contrast to the studies which conducted the regression analysis at the coarser scale (Filipovic et al., 2015; Sineviciene et al. 2017; Popescu et al., 2018). Third, the studies that use regions as the unit of analysis do not consider spatial correlation and spillover impacts (Borozan, 2018; Xie et al., 2020; Hu and Fan, 2020). The majority of studies have relied on conventional regression models, which fail to uncover spatial correlations and therefore may not provide robust estimations. There are only limited studies which applied spatial econometric models for estimating energy demand (Liu and Lin, 2019; Guo et al., 2021) and there are no studies at the pan-European level that utilise spatial econometrics for the energy demand analysis. Forth, to investigate the determinants of energy consumption in residential areas that are located in urban, intermediate and rural regions, region-specific models were additionally investigated. The results showed that the level of urbanisation matters: the level of urban/regional development determines the extent of influence of explanatory variables on residential energy consumption. For instance, energy consumption in rural regions are more than intermediate regions whereas urban regions are less then intermediate regions.

European regions mainly relying on fossil fuel use not only threatens the regions' sustainable development but also influences future climate change. As cities and regions have played a key role in socio-economic development through accumulating different forms of capital and intense economic activities, research into NUTS3 regional level energy demand analysis is of vital importance. The availability of statistics at the NUTS3 level from various European official sources has enabled the author to conduct regional level analysis for estimating the residential energy consumption in European countries. The preliminary findings from traditional OLS regressions showed that there was spatial autocorrelation across the regions and to threat these spatial correlation effects, spatial regression models were utilised including SEM, SAR, and SDM. Based on the results presented in Tables 3 and 4, it can be concluded that economic damage due to draught is the most significant factor of decreasing energy consumption on average in the European regions. An increase in economic damage due to draught by 1% does decrease energy consumption by 24% to 33% (Table 4). Therefore, the author confirms that the more increase in the economic damage caused by draught the less energy is consumed. This can be explained by the fact that natural hazards have reduced the income of individuals and led to poverty in some cases, particularly in low income countries; therefore, people with less income prefer to decrease their energy consumption in the residential sector as they can spend their income on other goods and services.

The second most significant variable is the index of expected market demand having a positive sign. An increase in expected market demand by 1% does increase energy consumption by 2% to 4% (Table 4). The market demand variable is highly correlated with disposable income of households i.e. the higher the income levels of the households, the more is the expected market demand. The market demand variable also indicates the consumption patterns of the individuals towards electronic devices, appliances and high-tech products, which consume energy when they are used. Therefore, an expected increase in market demand is associated with an increase in energy consumption at the regional level in Europe. Other than this, the Southern and Eastern variables are also highly significant with estimated coefficients equal to -2.296 and -1.548 (SEM model estimates), respectively (Table 4). It indicates that the energy consumption in southern regions is 2.3% and eastern regions is 1.5% less than those of the northern regions (i.e. the base category). This is explained by climatic factors where northern regions experience humid, cold winters and mild, humid summers, and contrary to this, southern regions have mediterranean climate, which features cool to mild winters and hot, dry summers. Eastern regions have continental climate which features warm to hot summers and cold winters. It can be noted that energy consumption to heat a space is higher than to cool a space; therefore energy demand is higher in winter season than in summer. Because northern regions have colder winters in comparison to southern regions as well as eastern regions, it is usual to expect that energy demand is higher in northern regions compared to southern and eastern regions. Urban regions and metropolitan regions are the other variables that are significant and having negative signs. A metropolitan region is defined as an area of a densely populated urban agglomeration and surrounding territories sharing industrial, commercial areas, transport network, infrastructures and housing. Urban regions are highly integrated with urban agglomeration and characterised with rural population accounting for <20% of the total population. High densities and agglomeration effects are associated with less energy demand in metropolitan and urban regions compared to peri-urban and rural regions. This is also confirmed by Wang et al. (2019) which found that population density had an effect in reducing direct CO_2 emissions; and Adams et al. (2020) which showed that urbanisation reduces carbon emissions in Sub-Saharan Africa.

Also notable is that there is significant diversification of energy consumption between urban, intermediate and rural regions. It was found that urban regions consume less energy and rural regions consume more energy compared to intermediate regions. This result implies that high density development and agglomeration effects in urban regions are relevant in reducing residential energy demand whereas low density developments as in the case of intermediate or rural regions increase energy demand. Urbanisation has a direct impact on energy use through changing the external environment and indirect effect through changing of the household attributes: Compared to rural households, urban households earn more income, live in smaller spaces and make different choices in consumption and lifestyles. New trends and housing demands in Europe show an increase in low-density sprawled development. For a variety of reasons, the number of cities accompanied by sprawled development patterns is increasing, and the proportion of residents that choose to live in detached houses is also increasing significantly. Sprawl type developments and low densities such as detached housing mean more consumption of fossil fuels that give considerable harm to the environment. Because detached houses are less efficient in terms of electricity consumption, improving energy efficiency in the subject housing units is essential in making progress towards sustainable development. The estimation results suggest that the distribution of urban functions should be concentrated as it is the case of urban regions rather than dispersed. High density urban developments may have lower interzonal interactions, benefit from energy savings of high-density buildings and lower energy consumption patterns of households and thus can reduce more energy consumption. Therefore, it is necessary to reduce energy consumption and promote ecological development through appropriate urban population size and land use planning.

As regions differ in terms of their socio-economic development and natural conditions, policies should be directed to local conditions. First, the findings showed that there is positive correlation between GDP per capita and energy consumption; therefore, majority of regions are experiencing economic growth that rely on increasing energy consumption. To economize energy consumption at the expense of economic growth is not a wise option in any of these regions. Technological innovation should be enhanced and investment on green technologies can be promoted in these regions. Second, it is showed in the findings that natural hazards have significant impact on residential energy consumption. These regions having natural hazards should be identified and mapped and new strategies to cope with natural hazards should be developed. Third, the ratio of new energy sources such as wind and solar energy should be increased in the regions which are characterised by high energy consumption as these regions rely on fossil energy sources which have adverse consequences on environmental quality. This requires an agenda in the diversification of the energy mix through new technologies to promote the use of renewable energy sources that will contribute to the environmental quality. Though renewables more than doubled between 2004 and 2021, its share in electricity production is 37.5% in the EU in 2021 (Eurostat, 2023). While the above suggestions are vital to reducing the extent of environmental degradation, country and region-specific characteristics should be considered when implementing energy-related programs and policies.

6. CONCLUSION

The role of the typology of the regions in contributing to residential energy consumption and carbon emissions cannot be underestimated. Prior research has generally examined the energy consumption based on country level data or household level was also used in micro level studies. However, not much attention was given to the regional variations of residential energy consumption in Europe through application of spatial regression models. This study contributes to the literature through developing a spatial model for the residential energy consumption using social, economic, technology, governance, natural hazards, and environmental variables and including typology of the regions into the regressions. The models were estimated by using European data obtained from various European sources and applying SEM, SAR, and SDM as econometric procedures. Endogeneity problems were corrected through including instrumental variables into the regressions. Based on a global perspective, Moran's Index was found to lie within the range from 0.01 to 0.18 and the existence of positive agglomeration was confirmed. Because OLS model may not be robust in case of spatial autocorrelation, spatial regression models were utilised to quantify the determinants of residential energy consumption in Europe.

There are regional disparities in energy consumption where northern and central European regions consume more energy compared to eastern and southern regions. These regional variations can be explained with climatic and environmental factors as well as household attributes and life styles are influential. The residential energy demand is positively and significantly related to several variables including market demand, GDP per capita, government support, share of self employed persons, share of forest land use, number of cool days, and renewable energy potential. It is significantly and negatively related to gas prices, economically active population, poverty rate, patent applications, access to technology, natural hazards, air pollution, green economy, western, eastern and southern regions. The empirical results also showed that urban and metropolitan regions are negatively associated with energy consumption while rural regions are positively related in comparison to intermediate regions. European economic growth is occurring in intermediate and rural regions where economic growth in these regions promotes energy consumption. Urban and metropolitan regions, on the other hand, have population agglomerations and high-density development and benefit from these in reducing energy consumption. Therefore, more density regions should be developed to promote efficient agglomeration of industries and high-density development of residential land use and thus benefit from energy saving effects.

REFERENCES

Acheampong, A. O., Adams, S., & Boateng, E. (2019). Do globalization and renewable energy contribute to carbon emissions mitigation in Sub-Saharan Africa? *The Science of the Total Environment*, *677*, 436–446. doi:10.1016/j.scitotenv.2019.04.353 PMID:31059886

Acheampong, A. O., & Dzator, J. (2020). Managing environmental quality: does institutional quality matter? In C. M. Hussain (Ed.), *Handbook of environmental materials management* (pp. 1–24). Springer. doi:10.1007/978-3-319-58538-3_215-1

Adams, S., Boateng, E., & Acheampong, A. O. (2020). Transport energy consumption and environmental quality: Does urbanisation matter? *The Science of the Total Environment*, *744*, 140617. doi:10.1016/j.scitotenv.2020.140617 PMID:32712414

Ajmi, A. N., Hammoudeh, S., Nguyen, D. K., & Sato, J. R. (2015). On the relationships between CO2 emissions, energy consumption and income: The importance of time variation. *Energy Economics*, *49*, 629–638. doi:10.1016/j.eneco.2015.02.007

Akadiri, S. S., Alola, A. A., Akadiri, A. C., & Alola, U. V. (2019). Renewable energy consumption in EU-28 countries: Policy toward pollution mitigation and economic sustainability. *Energy Policy*, *132*, 803–810. doi:10.1016/j.enpol.2019.06.040

Akhmat, G., Zaman, K., Shukui, T., Sajjad, F., Khan, M. A., & Khan, M. Z. (2014). The challenges of reducing greenhouse gas emissions and air pollution through energy sources: Evidence from a panel of developed countries. *Environmental Science and Pollution Research International*, *21*(12), 7425–7435. doi:10.100711356-014-2693-2 PMID:24584642

Ali, H. S., Zeqiraj, V., Lin, W. L., Law, S. H., Yusop, Z., Bare, U A A., & Chin, L. (2019). Does quality institutions promote environmental quality? *Environmental Science and Pollution Research International*, *26*(11), 10446–10456. doi:10.100711356-019-04670-9 PMID:30891699

Alkhathlan, K., & Javid, M. (2013). Energy consumption, carbon emissions and economic growth in Saudi Arabia: An aggregate and disaggregate analysis. *Energy Policy*, *62*, 1525–1532. doi:10.1016/j.enpol.2013.07.068

An, M., Xie, P., He, W., Wang, B., Huang, J., & Khanal, R. (2022). Spatiotemporal change of ecologic environmental quality and human interaction factors in three gorges ecologic economic corridor, based on RSEI. *Ecological Indicators*, *141*, 109090. doi:10.1016/j.ecolind.2022.109090

Andrei, J. V., Mieila, M., & Panait, M. (2017). The impact and determinants of the energy paradigm on economic growth in European Union. *PLoS One*, *12*(3), e0173282. doi:10.1371/journal.pone.0173282 PMID:28301505

Anselin, L. (1988). *Spatial econometrics: Methods and models*. Kluwer Academic. doi:10.1007/978-94-015-7799-1

Anselin, L. (1995). Local indicators of spatial association-LISA. *Geographical Analysis*, *2*(2), 93–115. doi:10.1111/j.1538-4632.1995.tb00338.x

Apergis, N., Aye, G. C., Barros, C. P., Gupta, R., & Wanke, P. (2015). Energy efficiency of selected OECD countries: A slacks based model with undesirable outputs. *Energy Economics*, *51*, 45–53. doi:10.1016/j.eneco.2015.05.022

Azam, M., Khan, A. Q., Zafeiriou, E., & Arabatzis, G. (2016). Socio-economic determinants of energy consumption: An empirical survey for Greece. *Renewable & Sustainable Energy Reviews*, *57*, 1556–1567. doi:10.1016/j.rser.2015.12.082

Baranzelli, C., Lavalle, C., Sgobbi, A., Aurambout, J. P., Trombetti, M., & Jacobs-Crisioni, C. (2016) *Regional patterns of energy production and consumption factors in Europe*. [EUR 27697] Exploratory Project EREBILAND2016. . doi:10.2788/357099

Belaid, F. (2017). Untangling the complexity of the direct and indirect determinants of the residential energy consumption in France: Quantitative analysis using a structural equation modelling approach. *Energy Policy*, *110*, 246–256. doi:10.1016/j.enpol.2017.08.027

Bhattacharya, M., Churchill, S. A., & Paramati, S. R. (2017). The dynamic impact of renewable energy and institutions on economic output and CO_2 emissions across regions. *Renewable Energy*, *111*, 157–167. doi:10.1016/j.renene.2017.03.102

Blazquez, L., Boogen, N., & Filippini, N. (2013). Residential electricity demand in Spain: New empirical evidence using aggregate data. *Energy Economics*, *36*, 648–657. doi:10.1016/j.eneco.2012.11.010

Borozan, D. (2018). Regional-level household energy consumption determinants: The European perspective. *Renewable & Sustainable Energy Reviews*, *90*, 347–355. doi:10.1016/j.rser.2018.03.038

Breiman, L. (1996). Bagging predictors. *Machine Learning*, *24*(2), 123–140. doi:10.1007/BF00058655

Breiman, L. (2001). Random forests. *Machine Learning*, *45*(1), 5–32. doi:10.1023/A:1010933404324

Burton, E. (2000). The compact city: Just or just compact? A preliminary analysis. *Urban Studies (Edinburgh, Scotland)*, *37*(11), 1969–2006. doi:10.1080/00420980050162184

Canh, N. P., Schinckıs, C., Thanh, S. D., & Chong, F. H. L. (2021). The determinants of the energy consumption: A shadow economy-based perspective. *Energy*, *225*, 120210. doi:10.1016/j.energy.2021.120210

Cassar, A., Healy, A., & Von Kessler, C. (2017). Trust, risk, and time preferences after a natural disaster: Experimental evidence from Thailand. *World Development*, *94*, 90–105. doi:10.1016/j.worlddev.2016.12.042

Chen, C., Pınar, M., & Stengos, T. (2021). Determinants of renewable energy consumption: Importance of democratic institutions. *Renewable Energy*, *179*, 75–83. doi:10.1016/j.renene.2021.07.030

Copeland, B. R., & Taylor, M. S. (2004). Trade, growth, and the environment. *Journal of Economic Literature*, *42*(1), 7–71. doi:10.1257/.42.1.7

Dijkstra, L., Garcilazo, E., & McCann, P. (2013). The economic performance of European cities and city regions: Myths and realities. *European Planning Studies*, *21*(3), 334–354. doi:10.1080/09654313.2012.716245

Dijkstra, L., Garcilazo, E., & McCann, P. (2015). The effects of the global financial crises on European regions and cities. *Journal of Economic Geography*, *15*(5), 935–949. doi:10.1093/jeg/lbv032

Dijkstra, L., & Poelman, H. (2010). A *revised urban-ruraltypology. In: Feldmann B, Önnerfors A (Eds) Eurostatregional yearbook 2010* (pp. 239–253). Publications Office of the European Union, Luxembourg. https://www.researchgate.net/publication/254266928_Downscaling_

Doytch, N., & Klein, Y. L. (2018). The impact of natural disasters on energy consumption: An analysis of renewable and non-renewable energy demand in the residential and industrial sectors. *Environmental Progress & Sustainable Energy*, *37*(1), 37–45. doi:10.1002/ep.12640

EC. (1999). *The Load Sharing Agreement is Found in the Annex of the Commission Communication to the Council and the European Parliament Preparing for the Application of the Kyoto Protocol COM230 Final of 19.05.1999*. Council and the European Parliament. https://ec.europa.eu/clima/sites/clima/files/ets/ docs/com_1999_230_en.pdf.

EC. (2022) *Energy efficiency targets*. EC. https://energy.ec.europa.eu/topics/energy-efficiency/energy-efficiency-targets-directive-and-rules/energy-efficiency-targets_en

EEA. (2017). *Renewable energy in Europe-2017 update: Recent growth and knock-on effects. European Environment Agency Report no. 23/2017*. Publications Office of the European Union, Luxembourg.

EEA. (2022). *Total greenhouse gas achievement trends and projections in Europe*. EEA. https://www.eea.europa.eu/ims/total-greenhouse-gas-emission-trends.

Esseghir, A., & Khouni, L. H. (2014). Economic growth, energy consumption and sustainable development: The case of the Union for the Mediterranean countries. *Energy*, *71*, 218–225. doi:10.1016/j.energy.2014.04.050

Eurostat. (2022a). *Urban and rural living in the EU*. Brussels. https://ec.europa.eu/eurostat/web/products-eurostat-news/-/edn-20200207-1.

Eurostat. (2023). *Renewable energy statistics*. Brussels. https://ec.europa.eu/eurostat/statistics-explained/index.php?title=Renewable_energy_statistics

European Commission (2022b) *Background*. Brussels. https://ec.europa.eu/eurostat/web/nuts/.

Fan, Y., Liu, L. C., Wu, G., Tang, T. H., & Wei, Y. M. (2007). Changes in carbon intensity in China: Empirical findings from 1980-2003. *Ecological Economics*, *62*(3-4), 683–691. doi:10.1016/j.ecolecon.2006.08.016

Fan, Y., & Xia, Y. (2012). Exploring energy consumption and demand in China. *Energy*, *40*(1), 23–30. doi:10.1016/j.energy.2011.09.049

Fertner, C. (2012). Downscaling European urban-rural typologies. *Geografisk Tidskrift*, *112*(1), 77–83. doi:10.1080/00167223.2012.707805

Filipovic, S., Verbic, M., & Radovanovic, M. (2015). Determinants of energy intensity in the European Union: A panel data analysis. *Energy*, *92*(3), 547–555. doi:10.1016/j.energy.2015.07.011

Fisher-Vanden, K., Jefferson, G., Liu, H., & Tao, Q. (2004). What is driving China's decline in energy intensity? *Resource and Energy Economics*, *26*(1), 77–97. doi:10.1016/j.reseneeco.2003.07.002

Foody, G. M., & Arora, M. K. (1997). An evaluation of some factors affecting the accuracy of classification by an Artificial Neural Network. *International Journal of Remote Sensing*, *18*(4), 799–810. doi:10.1080/014311697218764

Fuerst, F., Kavarnou, D., Singh, R., & Adan, H. (2020). Determinants of energy consumption and exposure to energy price risk: A UK study. *Immobilienökonomie*, *6*(1), 65–80. doi:10.136541056-019-00027-y

Guo, H., Tan, J., Liao, S., & Liang, Z. (2021). Exploring the spatial aggregation and determinants of energy intensity in Guangdong province of China. *Journal of Cleaner Production*, *282*, 124367. doi:10.1016/j.jclepro.2020.124367

Gyamfi, S., Krumdieck, S., & Urmee, T. (2013). Residential peak electricity demand response–highlights of some behavioural issues. *Renewable & Sustainable Energy Reviews*, *25*, 71–77. doi:10.1016/j.rser.2013.04.006

Hu, W., & Fan, Y. (2020). City size and energy conservation: Do large cities in China consume more energy? *Energy Economics*, *92*, 104943. doi:10.1016/j.eneco.2020.104943

Huang, W.-H. (2015). The determinants of household electricity consumption in Taiwan: Evidence from quantile regression. *Energy*, *87*, 120–133. doi:10.1016/j.energy.2015.04.101

İbrahim, M. H., & Law, S. H. (2016). Institutional quality and CO2 emission-trade relations: Evidence from sub-saharan Africa. *The South African Journal of Economics*, *84*(2), 323–340. doi:10.1111aje.12095

Jackson, T. (2005). *Motivating sustainable consumption: A review of evidence of consumer behaviour and behavioural change. Sustainable Development Research Network*. DEFRA.

Jamil, M. N. (2022). Critical analysis of energy consumption and its impact on countries economic growth: An empirical analysis base on countries income level. *J Environ Sci Econ*, *1*(2), 1–12. doi:10.56556/jescae.v1i2.11

Kaiser, M., Bernauer, M., Sunstein, C. R., & Reisch, L. A. (2020). The power of green defaults: The impact of regional variation of opt-out tariffs on green energy demand in Germany. *Ecological Economics*, *174*, 106685. doi:10.1016/j.ecolecon.2020.106685

Kander, A., Malanima, P., & Warde, P. (2014). *Power to the people: energy in Europe over the last five centuries*. Princeton University Press.

Khan, H., Khan, I., & Binh, T. T. (2020). The heterogeneity of renewable energy consumption, carbon emission and financial development in the globe: A panel quantile regression approach. *Energy Reports*, *6*, 859–867. doi:10.1016/j.egyr.2020.04.002

Kosec, K., & Mo, C. H. (2017). Aspirations and the role of social protection: Evidence from a natural disaster in rural Pakistan. *World Development*, *97*, 49–66. doi:10.1016/j.worlddev.2017.03.039

Labandeira, X., Labeaga, J.M., & Rodríguez, M. (2006). A residential energy demand system for Spain. *Energy, 27,* 87e112.

Lau, L. S., Choong, C. K., & Eng, Y. K. (2014). Carbon dioxide emission, institutional quality, and economic growth: Empirical evidence in Malaysia. *Renewable Energy*, *68*, 276–281. doi:10.1016/j.renene.2014.02.013

Lee, C.-C., Wang, C.-W., Ho, S.-J., & Wu, T.-P. (2021). The impact of natural disaster on energy consumption: International evidence. *Energy Economics*, *97*, 105021. doi:10.1016/j.eneco.2020.105021

Liu, K., & Lin, B. (2019). Research on influencing factors of environmental pollution in China: A spatial econometric analysis. *Journal of Cleaner Production*, *206*, 356–364. doi:10.1016/j.jclepro.2018.09.194

Liu, Y., Lu, S., & Chen, Y. (2013). Spatio-temporal change of urban-rural equalized development patterns in China and its driving factors. *Journal of Rural Studies*, *32*, 320–330. doi:10.1016/j.jrurstud.2013.08.004

Long, R., Shao, T., & Chen, H. (2016). Spatial econometric analysis of China's province-level industrial carbon productivity and its influencing factors. *Applied Energy*, *166*, 210–219. doi:10.1016/j.apenergy.2015.09.100

Mashhoodi, B., Stead, D., & van Timmeren, A. (2020). Local and national determinants of household energy consumption in the Netherlands. *GeoJournal*, *85*(2), 393–406. doi:10.100710708-018-09967-9

Navamuel, E. L., Morollon, F. R., & Cuartas, B. M. (2018). Energy consumption and urban sprawl: Evidence for the Spanish case. *Journal of Cleaner Production*, *172*, 3479–3486. doi:10.1016/j.jclepro.2017.08.110

Nguyen, C. P., Schinckus, C., Su, T. D., & Chong, F. H. L. (2022). The energy consumption: The global contributions from financial development and institutions. *Environmental Science and Pollution Research International*, *29*(13), 18721–18740. doi:10.100711356-021-17134-w PMID:34697709

Otsuka, A. (2019). Natural disasters and electricity consumption behaviour: A case study of the 2011 Great East Japan Earthquake. *Asia-Pasific J Region Sci*, *3*(3), 887–910. doi:10.100741685-019-00129-4

Pais-Magalhaes, V., Moutinho, V., & Robaina, M. (2020). Determinants of the household electricity consumption efficiency of an ageing population: Evidence for the EU-28. *Energy Reports*, *6*(8), 415–422. doi:10.1016/j.egyr.2020.11.193

Papiez, M., Smiech, S., & Frodyma, K. (2018). Determinants of renewable energy development in the EU countries. A 20-year perspective. *Renewable & Sustainable Energy Reviews*, *91*, 918–934. doi:10.1016/j.rser.2018.04.075

Popescu, G. H., Mieila, M., Nica, E., & Andrei, J. V. (2018). The emergence of the effects and determinants of the energy paradigm changes on European Union economy. *Renewable & Sustainable Energy Reviews*, *81*(1), 768–774. doi:10.1016/j.rser.2017.08.055

Poumanyvong, P., & Kaneko, S. (2010). Does urbanisation lead to less energy use and lower CO_2 emissions? A cross-country analysis. *Ecological Economics*, *70*(2), 434–444. doi:10.1016/j.ecolecon.2010.09.029

Rakshit, B. (2021). Impact of natural disasters on energy consumption: Evidence from Indian states. *Energy Res Let*, *2*(3). doi:10.46557/001c.27017

Reiss, P. C., & White, M. W. (2002). *Household electricity demand, revisited.* Stanford University Publication.

Roggenkamp, M., & Diestelmeier, L. (2020). Energy market reforms in the EU: A new focus on energy consumers, energy poverty, and energy (in)justice? In I. del Guayo, L. Godden, D. D. Zillman, M. F. Montoya, & J. J. Gonzalez (Eds.), *Energy justice and energy law* (pp. 160–177). Oxford University Press. doi:10.1093/oso/9780198860754.003.0010

Romero-Jordan, D., del Río, P., & Penasco, C. (2014). Analysing the determinants of household electricity demand in Spain. An econometric study. *Int J Electr Power Energy Syst, 63*, 950e961.

Sadorsky, P. (2014). The effect of urbanisation on CO2 emissions in emerging economies. *Energy Economics*, *41*, 147–153. doi:10.1016/j.eneco.2013.11.007

Salari, M., & Javid, R. J. (2016). Residential energy demand in the United States: Analysis using static and dynamic approaches. *Energy Policy*, *98*, 637–649. doi:10.1016/j.enpol.2016.09.041

Sarkodie, S. A., & Adams, S. (2018b). Renewable energy, nuclear energy, and environmental pollution: Accounting for political institutional quality in South Africa. *The Science of the Total Environment*, *643*, 1590–1601. doi:10.1016/j.scitotenv.2018.06.320 PMID:30189575

Sarkodie, S. A., & Adom, P. K. (2018a). Determinants of energy consumption in Kenya: A NIPALS approach. *Energy*, *159*, 696–705. doi:10.1016/j.energy.2018.06.195

Schroff, F., Criminisi, A., & Zisserman, A. (2008). *Object class segmentation using Random Forests.* BMVC. doi:10.5244/C.22.54

Shahbaz, M., Shahzad, S. J. H., Mahalik, M. K., & Sadorsky, P. (2018). How strong is the casual relationship between globalization and energy consumption in developed economies? A country-specific time-series and panel analysis. *Applied Economics*, *50*(13), 1479–1494. doi:10.1080/00036846.2017.1366640

Sineviciene, L., Sotnyk, I., & Kubatko, O. (2017). Determinants of energy efficiency and energy consumption of Eastern Europe post-communist economies. *Energy & Environment*, *28*(8), 870–884. doi:10.1177/0958305X17734386

Sorrell, S. (2015). Reducing energy demand: A review of issues, challenges and approaches. *Renewable & Sustainable Energy Reviews*, *47*, 74–82. doi:10.1016/j.rser.2015.03.002

Tilt, B. (2019). China's air pollution crisis: Science and policy perspectives. *Environmental Science & Policy*, *92*, 275–280. doi:10.1016/j.envsci.2018.11.020

Tu, Y.-X., Kubatko, O., Piven, V., Sotnyk, I., & Kurbatova, T. (2022). Determinants of renewable energy development: Evidence from the EU countries. *Energies*, *15*(19), 7093. doi:10.3390/en15197093

Tzeiranaki, S. T., Bertoldi, P., Diluiso, F., Castellazzi, L., Economidou, M., Labanca, N., Serrenho, T. R., & Zangheri, P. (2019). Analysis of the EU residential energy consumption: Trends and determinants. *Energies*, *12*(6), 1065. doi:10.3390/en12061065

UN-HABITAT. (2020). *The Strategic Plan 2020-2023*. UN. https://unhabitat.org/sites/default/files/documents/2019-09/strategic_plan_2020-2023.pdf.

United Nations, Department of Economic and Social Affairs, Population Division. (2018). *World urbanization prospects: The 2018 revision*. UN, New York. https://ec.europa.eu/eurostat/web/products-eurostat-news/-/ddn-20220617-1.

Usman, M., Ma, Z., Zafar, M. W., Waheed, A., & Li, M. (2021). Analyzing the determinants of clean energy consumption in a sustainability strategy: Evidence from EU-28 countries. *Environmental Science and Pollution Research International*, *28*(39), 54551–54564. doi:10.100711356-021-14473-6 PMID:34018103

Wiesmann, D., Lima Azevedo, I., Ferrao, P., & Fernandez, J. E. (2011). Residential electricity consumption in Portugal: Findings from top-down and bottom-up models. *Energy Policy*, *39*(5), 2772–2779. doi:10.1016/j.enpol.2011.02.047

World Bank. (2022). *Population total-European Union*. World Bank. https://data.worldbank.org/indicator/.

Yu, B., Fang, D., Yu, H., & Zhao, C. (2021). Temporal-spatial determinants of renewable energy penetration in electricity production: Evidence from EU countries. *Renewable Energy*, *180*, 438–451. doi:10.1016/j.renene.2021.08.079

Zafari, A., Zurita-Milla, R., & Izquierdo-Verdiguier, E. (2019). Evaluating the performance of a Random Forest kernel for land cover classification. *Remote Sensing (Basel)*, *11*(5), 575. doi:10.3390/rs11050575

Zhang, F. (2013). The energy transition of the transition economies: An empirical analysis. *Energy Economics*, *40*, 679–686. doi:10.1016/j.eneco.2013.09.001

ENDNOTES

1 The EU's classification of regions is based on the shares of a region's rural and urban population. A region is classified as urban if the rural population accounts for <20% of the total population, intermediate if the rural population is between 20% and 50% of the total population, and rural if the rural population is >50% of the total population.

2 The NUTS represent administrative divisions of countries for statistical purposes. There are three levels of NUTS representing different levels of local and regional administrative units. NUTS1 refers to major socio-economic region; NUTS2 corresponds to basic regions for the application of regional policies and NUTS3 is the smallest regional level applicable for specific diagnoses (Eurostat, 2022b).

APPENDIX

Table 9. Variable list and data sources

Dimension	Variable	Explanation	Scale	Source
Socio-economic characteristics	Eco_act_pop	Economically active population per km2	NUTS3	Eurostat (2016)
	Sh_pop_urban	Share of population living in urban areas	NUTS3	
	Sh_pop_mountain	Share of population living in mountainous areas	NUTS3	
	Sh_pop_rural	Share of population living in rural areas	NUTS3	
	Sh_mount_total	Share of mountain area in total area	NUTS3	
	Sh_pop_border	Share of population living in a 25 km corridor along the border	NUTS3	
	Old_depend	Old age dependency ratio: Ratio of economically inactive persons to the persons of working age	NUTS3	
	Young_depend	Young age dependency ratio: Ratio of persons of 0-14 aged to the persons of working age	NUTS3	
	Net_migr	Net migration	NUTS3	Eurostat (2015)
	Doc_inh	Medical doctors per hundred thousand inhabitants	NUTS0, NUTS1, NUTS2	Eurostat (2014)
	Hbeds_inh	Hospital beds per hundred thousand inhabitants	NUTS0, NUTS1, NUTS3	
	Unempl_rate	Unemployment rate	NUTS2	
	Disp_inc	Disposable income (Euro per inhabitant)	NUTS2	
	Tert_educ	Share of population aged 30-34 with tertiary education	NUTS2	Eurostat (2015)
	Life_expct	Life expectancy	NUTS2	
	Pov_excl	People at risk of poverty or social exclusion	NUTS2	
Economic activities	Empl_agri	Ratio of employment in agriculture, forestry, fishing in total employment	NUTS3	Eurostat (2013)
	Empl_ind_const	Ratio of industrial and construction employment in total employment	NUTS3	
	Empl_services	Ratio of services employment in total employment	NUTS3	
	Pat_appl	Number of patent applications per million inhabitants	NUTS3	Eurostat (2012)

continued on following page

Table 9. Continued

Dimension	Variable	Explanation	Scale	Source
	Access_Tech	Index of access to technology	NUTS2	ESPON GREECO Project (2013) (https://database.espon.eu/project-data-package/968/)
	Market_dem	Index of expected market demand	NUTS2	
	Human_res	Index of human resources, knowledge and skills	NUTS2	
	GDP_cap	Gross Domestic Production (GDP) at current market prices in Euro per capita	NUTS3	Eurostat (2014)
	GVA_cap	Gross Value Added (GVA) at basic prices in Euro per capita	NUTS3	Eurostat (2014)
	GDP_growth	GDP growth rate based on GDP from 2009 and 2014 market prices	NUTS3	ESPON LinkPA's Project (2017) (https://www.espon.eu/protected-areas)
	Prvt_enterpr	Share of self-employed persons on total employed persons	NUTS2	Eurostat (2014)
	HiTech_empl	Share of employment in technology and knowledge intensive sectors	NUTS2	Eurostat (2015)
	R&D empl	Share of R&D personnel and researchers on active population	NUTS2	Eurostat (2013)
	Ft_empl	Share of full time employments on total employment	NUTS2	Eurostat (2014; 2016)
	Pt_empl	Share of part-time employment on total employment	NUTS2	
	F_empl	Female employment ratio	NUTS2	
	Euro-super 95	Price of Euro-super 95 per 1000L	NUTS0	EC Weekly Oil Bulletin (2022) (https://energy.ec.europa.eu/data-and-analysis/weekly-oil-bul letin_en)
	Gas oil_automobile	Price of gas oil for automobile per 1000L	NUTS0	
	Gas oil_heating	Price of gas oil for heating per 1000L	NUTS0	
Mobility	Accs_road	Potential accessibility by road transport	NUTS3	ESPON-TIA (2014)
	Accs_rail	Potential accessibility by rail transport	NUTS3	
	Accs_air	Potential accessibility by air transport	NUTS3	
	Accs_multimodal	Potential accessibility by multimodal transport	NUTS3	
	Accs_primary_sc	Share of regions that have poor access to primary schools	NUTS3	ESPON PROFECY Project (https://database.espon.eu/project-archives/#/archives)

continued on following page

Table 9. Continued

Dimension	Variable	Explanation	Scale	Source
	Accs_second_sc	Share of regions that have poor access to secondary schools	NUTS3	
	Accs_hospital	Share of regions that have poor access to hospitals	NUTS3	
	Accs_close_doctor	Share of regions that have poor access to closest doctors	NUTS3	
	Accs_pharmacy	Share of regions that have poor access to pharmacies	NUTS3	
	Accs_bank	Share of regions that have poor access to bank offices	NUTS3	
	Accs_train_stat	Share of regions that have poor access to train stations	NUTS3	
	Accs_urb_morph	Share of regions that have poor access to urban morphological zone	NUTS3	
	Accs_cinema	Share of regions that have poor access to cinemas	NUTS3	
	Accs_shop	Share of regions that have poor access to shops	NUTS3	
	Accs_reg_centre	Share of regions that have poor access to regional centres	NUTS3	
Land Cover	Agri_land	Share of agricultural land including arable land, permanent crops and pastures	NUTS3	EEA (2021) Ecosystem Extent Accounts, CLC (2012)
	Nat_veg	Share of scrub and/or herbaceous vegetation associations	NUTS3	
	Forest	Share of forest land	NUTS3	
	Urban_fabric	Share of residential land	NUTS3	
	Ind_com_trans	Share of industrial, commercial and transport units	NUTS3	
	Protect_area	Protected areas (total surface)	NUTS3	ESPON LinkPA Project (2017) (https://www.espon.eu/protected-areas)
	Protect_area_sh	Share of protected areas	NUTS3	
	Municip	Number of municipalities in a region	NUTS3	
	Dens_pop	Inhabitants per km2	NUTS3	Eurostat (2015)
	uu_dev	Long term development of urban use areas 2000-2018	NUTS3	ESPON SUPER Project (https://database.espon.eu/project-data-package/2104/)
	pa_uu	Share of urban use in protected areas	NUTS3	
	Env_GI	Spatial distribution of green infrastructure	NUTS2	ESPON TITAN Project (2018) (https://www.espon.eu/natural-disasters)

continued on following page

Table 9. Continued

Dimension	Variable	Explanation	Scale	Source
Natural hazards	Wind_haz	Windstorm hazard (maximum wind speed for three-second gusts)	NUTS3	
	Flood_haz	100-year river flood (Flooded area in percentage of NUTS3 area)	NUTS3	
	Aggreg_nat_haz	Aggregated values for all natural hazards	NUTS3	
	Susc_nat_haz	Territorial susceptibility to natural hazards	NUTS3	
	Cop_nat_haz	Territorial coping capasity to natural hazards	NUTS3	
	Vul_nat_haz	Territorial vulnerability to natural hazards	NUTS3	
	Econ_dam_flood	Economic damage due to floods, average of yearly impacts	NUTS3	
	Econ_dam_drought	Economic damage due to droughts, average of yearly impacts	NUTS3	
	Econ_dam_earth	Economic damage due to earthquakes, average of yearly impacts	NUTS3	
	Econ_dam_wind	Economic damage due to windstorms, average of yearly impacts	NUTS3	
Governance	Gov_qgi	Quality of government index	NUTS2	
	Gov_corrupt	Corruption in the government services, health care, education and law enforcement	NUTS2	World Bank (2013)
	Gov_qual	Quality and accountability of government services, health care, education and law enforcement	NUTS2	
	Gov_impart	Impartiality of government services, health care, education and law enforcement	NUTS2	
	Good_gov	Index of good governance	NUTS2	ESPON GREECO Project (2013) (https://database.espon.eu/project-data-package/968/)
	Ter_assets	Index of territorial assets and physical conditions	NUTS2	
	Fund_gov_supp	Index of access to funding and financial support	NUTS2	
	LE_quality	Quality of law enforcement	NUTS1, NUTS2	European Quality of Government Index (2013)

continued on following page

Table 9. Continued

Dimension	Variable	Explanation	Scale	Source
	Polit_trust	Trust in the political system	NUTS0, NUTS1, NUTS1	SPI(2016)
	Legal_trust	Trust in the legal system	NUTS0, NUTS1, NUTS2	
Energy	Res_RnEnc	Change in share of renewable energy sources for space heating cooling, and water heating in residential building sector	NUTS3	ESPON LOCATE Project (2018) (https://www.espon.eu/low-carbon-economy)
	WiElExpT	Exploitation rate of potential electricity generation by wind onshore	NUTS3	
	PhElExpT	Exploitation rate of potential electricity generation by solar photovoltaics	NUTS3	
	En_cap	Final energy demand per capita for space heating, cooling, water heating, appliances, lighting, and cooking in the residential sector (MWh/capita)	NUTS3	
	Heat_days	Distribution of heating degree days between 2002 and 2012	NUTS3	
	Cool_days	Distribution of cooling degree days between 2002 and 2012	NUTS3	
	BioWaPoT	Primary energy potential of biodegradable wastes and biogas	NUTS3	
	BioFuPoT	Primary energy potential of biofuels from agricultural products	NUTS3	
	BioFpPoT	Primary energy potential of forestry products and forestry residues	NUTS3	
	GeoThPoT	Primary energy potential of geothermal heating	NUTS3	
Air Quality	CO2_emission	CO2 emissions (thousand tonnes) from non-transport territorial fossil fuel combustion	NUTS3	ESPON GREECO Project (2013) (https://database.espon.eu/project-data-package/968/)
	NO2_emission	Average NO2 concentration in a region	NUTS2	European Environment Agency (2013) (https://www.eea.europa.eu/data-and-maps/data/interpolated-air-quality-data-2)
	Ozone3_emission	Average Ozone3 concentration in a region	NUTS2	
	PM2.5_emission	Average PM2.5 concentration in a region	NUTS2	

continued on following page

Table 9. Continued

Dimension	Variable	Explanation	Scale	Source
	PM10_emission	Average PM10 concentration in a region	NUTS2	
Green Economy	CLUS_CAP	Number of greentech clusters per million of inhabitants	NUTS2	ESPON GREECO Project (2013) (https://database.espon.eu/project-data-package/968/)
	IGETP	Index of green economy theoretical potentials	NUTS2	
	Sphere_1	Regional green economic performance index for environmental sphere	NUTS2	
	Sphere_2	Regional green economic performance index for social sphere	NUTS2	
	Sphere_3	Regional green economic performance index for territorial sphere	NUTS2	
	Sphere_4	Regional green economic performance index for economic sphere	NUTS2	
	Sphere_5	Regional green economic performance index for econosphere sphere	NUTS2	
Location	Western	Regions in Western Europe	NUTS3	Ustaoglu and Williams (2017)
	Eastern	Regions in Eastern Europe	NUTS3	
	Southern	Regions in Southern Europe	NUTS3	
	Northern	Regions in Northern Europe (base category)	NUTS3	
Regional characteristics	Metropol	Regions classified as metropolitan regions	NUTS3	Dijkstra and Poelman (2011)
	Urban_Region	Regions classified as predominantly urban regions	NUTS3	
	Rural_Region	Regions classified as predominantly rural regions	NUTS3	
	Intermediate_Region	Regions classified as predominantly intermediate regions (base category)	NUTS3	

Chapter 5
Energy Security Dilemma in OECD Countries:
The COVID-19 Pandemic, Russia-Ukraine War, and Energy Issues

Seda Yildirim
https://orcid.org/0000-0003-4367-6652
Tekirdag Namık Kemal University, Turkey

Durmus Cagri Yildirim
Tekirdag Namık Kemal University, Turkey

Seyfettin Erdogan
Istanbul Medeniyet University, Turkey

ABSTRACT

The pursuit of sustainability, initiated by the United Nations' adoption of the 2030 Sustainable Development Goals, has prompted developed and developing countries to adopt alternative policies. To address energy security concerns, countries have begun implementing strategies and practices to reduce carbon emissions and limit the use of environmentally harmful energy sources. However, unexpected crises like the COVID-19 pandemic and the Russia-Ukraine conflict have brought energy availability to the forefront as a major challenge. This study aims to examine the issue of energy security in the context of these two crises. By utilizing OECD indicators and current reports, the study will provide an overview of the energy security dilemma.

INTRODUCTION

Throughout history, societies have taken steps toward development that have had a negative impact on environmental sustainability. The industrial revolution was a significant milestone in advancing society, but the damage caused by the era's industrialization has made it necessary to reverse that progress. Natural resources have been excessively consumed due to the desire for rapid industrial development,

DOI: 10.4018/979-8-3693-1297-1.ch005

resulting in irreversible damage to the environment. For instance, climate change, a natural phenomenon, has accelerated in recent years, and scientists attribute most of it to human activities. (NASA Global Climate Change website, n.d). According to "Limits to Growth (Meadows et al., 1972)" in literature, an unsustainable future is imminent. The concept of sustainability became a prominent topic in the 21st century, with the United Nations introducing the phenomenon of "sustainable development" to the world (Yıldırım and Yıldırım, 2020) (Yıldırım, 2023). Economic growth alone is not enough for development. Societies should also strive to achieve positive levels of social welfare and environmental quality in conjunction with economic development. Sustainable development aims to achieve economic growth that is in sync with social welfare and environmental quality (Munasinghe, 2002). In 2015, member countries of the United Nations committed themselves to transform according to new sustainable policies and strategies with the 2030 Sustainable Development Goals. The 17 main targets aimed at achieving a sustainable future. These targets are related to basic topics such as health, education, energy, water, food, and equality. Every country has a rational roadmap for achieving these targets by 2030. While there have been positive developments on some targets, not every target has been equally successful. The Covid-19 pandemic and the Russia-Ukraine conflict particularly halted progress towards sustainable development (Bin-Nashman et al., 2022; United Nations Sustainable Development Group, 2022; Pereira et al., 2022; Chopra et al., 2022; Srivastava et al., 2020; The Lancet Public Health, 2020).

The COVID-19 pandemic has been recorded in the literature as a global epidemic with very serious effects (Aydın et al., 2023). The disease, which started in Wuhan, China, spread to all countries over time and was declared an epidemic by the WTO in March 2020 (AA,2023). The Covid-19 pandemic has had a lasting impact on various aspects of life, particularly on health. Additionally, the Russia-Ukraine conflict has brought about changes in energy and trade policies between nations, similar to the effects of the COVID-19 pandemic. This highlights that policymakers are not always equipped to deal with unexpected crises in the long run. With the shift towards virtual and digital platforms in the economy and social life, energy and the internet have become crucial and primary sources for humanity in the long term.

Increasing green energy investments are promising for sustainability. However, it is important for countries to ensure energy security in terms of balanced economic growth and social welfare. In this study, energy indicators in OECD countries will be examined and whether energy is consistent in terms of the balance between economic growth, social welfare and environmental quality. In the study, the effects of the Covid-19 pandemic and the Russia-Ukraine war will also be discussed in terms of increasing the energy crisis.

ENERGY INDICATORS IN OECD COUNTRIES

OECD data web site gives some indicators for energy in OECD and the world statistics. Indicators including titles as "Primary energy supply; Crude oil production; Electricity generation; Renewable energy; Nuclear power plants" are given in the context of energy statistic. Some energy indicators will be given for OECD countries as below:

In Table 1, data of primary energy supply is given for European Union (27 countries and 28 countries), OECD-Europe, OECD-Total and World between 2019 and 2022.

Table 2 shows crude oil production's statistics between 2018 and 2021. It is seen that crude oil production has a downtrend from 2018 to 2021 in the world.

Table 1. Primary energy supply 2019-2022 (toe/1000 US Dollars)

	2019	2020	2021	2022
European Union (27 countries, 2020)	0.076	0.075	0.075	0.068
European Union (28 countries)	0.073	0.072	0.072	0.066
OECD - Europe	0.071	0.071	0.070	0.064
OECD - Total	0.092	0.089	0.089	0.085
World	0.114	0.113	0.112	
Data is based on OECD (2023a)				

Source: adapted by the authors

Table 2. Crude oil production 2018-2021

	2018	2019	2020	2021
European Union (27 countries, 2020)	21 388.43	19 797.01	18 784.95	17 624.09
European Union (28 countries)	70 646.32	70 912.92	66 082.47	57 235.64
G20	2 399 311.52	2 445 586.55	2 317 574.77	2 323 115.75
OECD - Europe	144 881.14	141 310.38	152 017.51	146 686.33
World	4 032 035.39	3 998 728.49	3 675 341.46	3 717 528.66
Data is based on OECD (2023b)				

Source: adapted by the authors

As seen in Table 3, Electricity generation decreased in 2019 and 2020 comparing with 2018. By 2021, electricity generation increased in OECD-Total and also OECD-EU.

Table 3. Electricity generation 2018-2021

	2018	2019	2020	2021
OECD - Europe	3 519 908	3 487 440	3 394 725	3 522 548
OECD - Total	10 860 101	10 747 327	10 490 220	10 843 111
Data is based on OECD (2023c)				

Source: adapted by the authors

Table 4 shows renewable energy (Total, % of primary energy supply) statistics for OECD in 2021.

Table 5 shows the number of nuclear power plants in the world. In OECD-EU region, there are 127 nuclear power plants and OECD-Total region has 308 nuclear power plants.

In Table 6, renewable energy feed-in-tariffs are shown for OECD countries. There are data for 2000, 2010 and 2019.

Table 4. Renewable energy (Total, % of primary energy supply)

Country	Total, % of primary energy supply, 2021	Country	Total, % of primary energy supply, 2021
Albania	33.880	Malaysia	3.890
Algeria	0.120	Malta	6.210
Angola	58.070	Mauritius	14.040
Argentina	8.100	Mexico	9.220
Armenia	7.090	Moldova	17.620
Australia	8.350	Mongolia	3.760
Austria	30.800	Montenegro	29.470
Azerbaijan	1.130	Morocco	9.420
Bahrain	0.000	Mozambique	83.600
Bangladesh	18.030	Myanmar	51.730
Belarus	7.190	Namibia	28.790
Belgium	8.860	Netherlands	10.630
Benin	53.430	New Zealand	39.650
Bolivia	17.730	Nicaragua	58.370
Bosnia and Herzegovina	24.380	Niger	76.660
Botswana	21.000	Nigeria	76.110
Brazil	44.170	North Macedonia	14.070
Brunei Darussalam	0.000	Norway	50.940
Bulgaria	13.970	OECD - Europe	17.300
Cambodia	44.870	OECD - Total	11.560
Cameroon	75.020	Oman	0.040
Canada	16.110	Pakistan	37.900
Chile	24.580	Panama	25.720
China (People's Republic of)	10.010	Paraguay	99.140
Colombia	29.060	Peru	28.760
Congo	53.300	Philippines	35.770
Costa Rica	51.500	Poland	11.800
Côte d'Ivoire	63.570	Portugal	29.430
Croatia	26.440	Qatar	0.020
Cuba	17.490	Romania	18.630
Cyprus	10.760	Russia	2.690
Czech Republic	12.040	Rwanda	90.930
Democratic Republic of the Congo	97.420	Saudi Arabia	0.030
Denmark	40.410	Senegal	43.530
Dominican Republic	13.700	Serbia	15.820

continued on following page

Table 4. Continued

Country	Total, % of primary energy supply, 2021	Country	Total, % of primary energy supply, 2021
Ecuador	19.560	**Singapore**	1.220
Egypt	6.210	**Slovak Republic**	11.690
El Salvador	50.320	**Slovenia**	17.510
Equatorial Guinea	3.990	**South Africa**	6.210
Eritrea	78.850	**Spain**	16.670
Estonia	30.590	**Sri Lanka**	40.380
Eswatini	63.000	**Sudan**	67.260
Ethiopia	90.270	**Sweden**	45.900
Euro area (19 countries)	16.410	**Switzerland**	24.360
European Union (27 countries, 2020)	17.280	**Syrian Arab Republic**	0.830
European Union (28 countries)	16.900	**Tajikistan**	42.560
Finland	38.840	**Tanzania**	83.170
France	11.640	**Thailand**	18.120
G20	12.470	**Togo**	83.280
G7	10.020	**Trinidad and Tobago**	0.090
Gabon	76.080	**Tunisia**	11.520
Georgia	19.500	**Turkmenistan**	0.040
Germany	15.640	**Türkiye**	15.240
Ghana	40.840	**Uganda**	90.270
Greece	16.550	**Ukraine**	5.640
Guatemala	65.530	**United Arab Emirates**	0.680
Haiti	79.980	**United Kingdom**	12.590
Honduras	49.690	**United States**	8.000
Hungary	11.320	**Uruguay**	59.560
Iceland	88.890	**Uzbekistan**	0.960
India	25.400	**Venezuela**	23.000
Indonesia	26.750	**Viet Nam**	15.090
Iran	0.750	**World**	14.710
Iraq	1.040	**Yemen**	6.050
Ireland	11.500	**Zambia**	81.800
Israel	5.070	**Zimbabwe**	77.330

continued on following page

Table 4. Continued

Country	Total, % of primary energy supply, 2021	Country	Total, % of primary energy supply, 2021
Italy	18.520		
Jamaica	10.050		
Japan	7.070		
Jordan	8.040		
Kazakhstan	1.680		
Kenya	81.240		
Korea	2.130		
Kuwait	0.120		
Kyrgyzstan	31.830		
Lao People's Democratic Republic	75.640		
Latvia	42.460		
Lebanon	4.270		
Libya	3.730		
Lithuania	23.370		
Luxembourg	11.390		
Madagascar	89.960		
Data is based on OECD (2023d)			

Source: adapted by the authors

THE COVID-19 PANDEMIC, RUSSIA-UKRAINE WAR AND ENERGY ISSUES

The policymakers usually take cares of risks and threats when developing strategies in the long term. When considering and making a long-term planning for energy sector, some expected risks will be always determined as an expected threat. In Figure 1, we summarized expected risk factors causing energy crisis based on info and data from Coldwellsolar (n.d.)'s web site. Rising population, limited non-renewable resources, poor organization, old infrastructure and waste problems are general risk factors causing energy crisis in the world (Coldwellsolar, n.d.). On the other side, the world also sees unexpected factors can cause bigger risk for energy crisis in the long term such as pandemic and war.

The Covid-19 pandemic has highlighted the possibility of long-term energy shortages caused by sudden energy crises. The changes in energy supply and demand during the pandemic have underscored the importance of emergency planning for how countries should manage energy security stresses (United Nations Economic and Social Council, 2021).

Energy saving is crucial to the well-being of society and the economy. Access to energy is essential for people to maintain a certain standard of living. In 2020, the Covid-19 pandemic brought significant changes to energy access in Europe. The pandemic highlighted the importance of energy security in light of health concerns. Investing in backup energy sources, rather than relying on non-renewable resources, is imperative. For instance, during the Covid-19 outbreak, power outages resulted in a reduction in electricity flow (European Commission, 2020).

Table 5. Nuclear power plants 2019

Country	Number
Belgium	7
Canada	19
Czech Republic	6
Finland	4
France	58
Germany	7
Hungary	4
Japan	38
Korea	24
Mexico	2
Netherlands	1
OECD - Europe	127
OECD - Total	308
Russia	35
Slovak Republic	4
Slovenia	1
Spain	7
Sweden	8
Switzerland	5
United Kingdom	15
United States	98
Data is based on OECD (2023e)	

European Commission (2020) determined risks and challenges for energy security as below:

The conflict between Russia and Ukraine has brought the issue of the sustainability of an economy reliant on fossil fuels to the forefront. The security of energy is becoming increasingly problematic, with issues such as changes in energy prices, access to energy, and sustainable energy security needing to be addressed in long-term policy. The need for a shift in Europe's energy resources has become apparent, as Russian gas is heavily involved in imports. Although Europe experienced a milder winter and lower energy demand during the conflict, there will likely be issues with Europe's gas supply in the future. To reduce threats to energy security, Europe needs to invest in renewable energy sources and pursue policies based on its own energy. The Covid-19 pandemic and the Russia-Ukraine conflict have caused high inflation and disruptions in the energy supply chain. Most countries are now accelerating their transition strategies to clean energy, and there is a trend towards improving economic conditions. Renewable electricity capacity in European Union countries is expected to increase further by 2027 (IEA, n.d.). EU countries experienced energy and inflation crises together in 2022. European countries, which for many years turned to environmentally friendly policies focused on environmental transformation against climate change instead of energy supply security, had to change their attitude this year. Some closed coal mines and power plants started to come into operation. This has increased the share of coal in the electricity

Table 6. Renewable energy feed-in tariffs (2020)

Year		2000	2010	2019
Country	**Source**			
Australia	Solar PV(S.PV)	-	0,346	0,211
	Wind(W.)	-	-	-
	Small Hydro(S.H.)	-	-	-
	Biomass(B.)	-	-	-
	Waste(W.)	-	-	-
	Geothermal(G.)	-	-	-
	Marine(M.)	-	-	-
Austria	S.PV	0,042	0,434	0,000
	W.	0,042	0,129	0,091
	S.H.	0,000	0,000	0,071
	B.	0,041	0,166	0,177
	W.	0,041	0,066	0,057
	G.	-	0,099	0,081
	M.	-	-	-
Belgium	S.PV	-	-	-
	W.	-	-	-
	S.H.	-	-	-
	B.	-	-	-
	W.	-	-	-
	G.	-	-	-
	M.	-	-	-
Canada	S.PV	-	0,402	-
	W.	-	0,156	-
	S.H.	-	0,124	-
	B.	-	0,129	-
	W.	-	0,096	-
	G.	-	0,000	-
	M.	-	0,042	-
Chile	S.PV	-	0,000	-
	W.	-	-	-
	S.H.	-	-	-
	B.	-	-	-
	W.	-	-	-
	G.	-	-	-
	M.	-	-	-

continued on following page

Table 6. Continued

Year		2000	2010	2019
Country	Source			
Czech Republic	S.PV	-	0,639	-
	W.	-	0,117	-
	S.H.	-	0,157	-
	B.	-	0,189	-
	W.	-	-	-
	G.	-	0,236	-
	M.	-	-	-
Denmark	S.PV	0,037	0,107	-
	W.	0,066	0,074	-
	S.H.	-	0,124	-
	B.	0,037	0,186	-
	W.	0,037	0,132	0,086
	G.	0,037	-	-
	M.	0,037	0,124	-
Estonia	S.PV	-	0,097	0,060
	W.	-	0,097	0,060
	S.H.	-	0,097	0,060
	B.	-	0,097	0,036
	W.	-	0,097	0,060
	G.	-	0,097	0,060
	M.	-	0,097	0,060
Finland	S.PV	-	-	-
	W.	-	-	0,094
	S.H.	-	-	0,000
	B.	-	-	0,000
	W.	-	-	0,094
	G.	-	-	-
	M.	-	-	-
France	S.PV	-	0,601	-
	W.	0,054	0,109	-
	S.H.	-	0,077	0,094
	B.	-	0,199	-
	W.	-	0,063	0,165
	G.	-	0,265	-
	M.	-	0,199	0,142

continued on following page

Table 6. Continued

Year		2000	2010	2019
Country	Source			
Germany	S.PV	0,076	0,448	-
	W.	0,076	0,109	0,108
	S.H.	0,061	0,107	0,089
	B.	0,061	0,128	0,106
	W.	-	0,000	0,115
	G.	-	0,174	0,282
	M.	-	-	-
Greece	S.PV	0,064	0,729	-
	W.	0,064	0,116	-
	S.H.	-	0,116	-
	B.	0,064	0,232	-
	W.	-	0,199	-
	G.	-	0,199	-
	M.	-	-	-
Hungary	S.PV	-	-	0,109
	W.	-	-	-
	S.H.	-	-	0,109
	B.	-	-	0,109
	W.	-	-	0,109
	G.	-	-	0,109
	M.	-	-	-
Iceland	S.PV	-	-	-
	W.	-	-	-
	S.H.	-	-	-
	B.	-	-	-
	W.	-	-	-
	G.	-	-	-
	M.	-	-	-
Ireland	S.PV	-	-	-
	W.	-	0,087	-
	S.H.	-	0,108	-
	B.	-	0,156	-
	W.	-	0,153	-
	G.	-	0,000	-
	M.	-	0,292	-

continued on following page

Table 6. Continued

Year		2000	2010	2019
Country	Source			
Israel	S.PV	-	0,473	-
	W.	-	0,381	-
	S.H.	-	-	-
	B.	-	-	-
	W.	-	-	-
	G.	-	-	-
	M.	-	-	-
Italy	S.PV	-	0,506	-
	W.	0,111	-	0,056
	S.H.	0,092	-	-
	B.	-	-	-
	W.	-	-	-
	G.	0,157	-	-
	M.	-	-	-
Japan	S.PV	-	0,410	-
	W.	-	-	0,252
	S.H.	-	-	0,216
	B.	-	-	0,280
	W.	-	-	0,238
	G.	-	-	0,303
	M.	-	-	-
Korea	S.PV	-	0,423	-
	W.	-	0,093	-
	S.H.	-	0,070	-
	B.	-	0,060	-
	W.	-	0,062	-
	G.	-	0,000	-
	M.	-	0,060	-
Latvia	S.PV	-	0,189	-
	W.	-	0,159	-
	S.H.	-	0,189	-
	B.	-	0,000	-
	W.	-	0,223	-
	G.	-	-	-
	M.	-	-	-

continued on following page

Table 6. Continued

Year		2000	2010	2019
Country	Source			
Lithuania	S.PV	-	-	-
	W.	-	-	-
	S.H.	-	-	-
	B.	-	-	-
	W.	-	-	-
	G.	-	-	-
	M.	-	-	-
Luxembourg	S.PV	-	0,520	-
	W.	0,088	0,109	0,102
	S.H.	-	0,125	0,139
	B.	-	0,178	0,145
	W.	-	0,158	0,169
	G.	0,088	-	-
	M.	-	-	-
Mexico	S.PV	-	-	-
	W.	-	-	-
	S.H.	-	-	-
	B.	-	-	-
	W.	-	-	-
	G.	-	-	-
	M.	-	-	-
Netherlands	S.PV	-	0,599	0,110
	W.	-	0,127	0,078
	S.H.	-	0,129	0,123
	B.	-	0,199	0,096
	W.	-	0,082	0,077
	G.	-	-	0,055
	M.	-	-	0,123
New Zealand	S.PV	-	-	-
	W.	-	-	-
	S.H.	-	-	-
	B.	-	-	-
	W.	-	-	-
	G.	-	-	-
	M.	-	-	-

continued on following page

Table 6. Continued

Year		2000	2010	2019
Country	Source			
Norway	S.PV	-	-	-
	W.	-	-	-
	S.H.	-	-	-
	B.	-	-	-
	W.	-	-	-
	G.	-	-	-
	M.	-	-	-
Poland	S.PV	-	-	-
	W.	-	-	-
	S.H.	-	-	-
	B.	-	-	-
	W.	-	-	-
	G.	-	-	-
	M.	-	-	-
Portugal	S.PV	0,053	0,504	-
	W.	0,053	0,099	-
	S.H.	0,053	0,101	-
	B.	0,053	0,140	-
	W.	0,053	1,023	-
	G.	0,053	0,000	-
	M.	0,053	0,259	-
Slovak Republic	S.PV	-	0,511	-
	W.	-	0,107	-
	S.H.	-	0,113	-
	B.	-	0,171	-
	W.	-	0,167	-
	G.	-	0,260	-
	M.	-	0,000	-
Slovenia	S.PV	-	0,261	-
	W.	-	0,121	-
	S.H.	-	1,053	-
	B.	-	0,243	-
	W.	-	0,154	-
	G.	-	0,202	-
	M.	-	-	-

continued on following page

Table 6. Continued

Year		2000	2010	2019
Country	**Source**			
Spain	S.PV	0,369	0,328	-
	W.	0,061	0,103	-
	S.H.	0,030	0,103	-
	B.	0,060	0,211	-
	W.	0,058	0,153	-
	G.	0,062	0,091	-
	M.	0,000	0,091	-
Sweden	S.PV	0,032	-	-
	W.	0,032	-	-
	S.H.	0,032	-	-
	B.	0,032	-	-
	W.	0,032	-	-
	G.	0,032	-	-
	M.	0,032	-	-
Switzerland	S.PV	-	0,422	0,111
	W.	-	0,122	0,231
	S.H.	-	0,084	0,066
	B.	-	0,112	0,181
	W.	-	0,097	0,267
	G.	-	0,159	0,353
	M.	-	0,000	0,000
Türkiye	S.PV	-	0,072	0,133
	W.	-	0,728	0,073
	S.H.	-	-	0,073
	B.	-	-	0,133
	W.	-	-	0,133
	G.	-	-	0,105
	M.	-	-	0,073
United Kingdom	S.PV	-	0,555	0,001
	W.	-	0,084	0,056
	S.H.	-	0,084	0,071
	B.	-	0,000	-
	W.	-	0,171	0,020
	G.	-	-	-
	M.	-	-	-

continued on following page

Table 6. Continued

Year		2000	2010	2019
Country	**Source**			
United States	S.PV	-	0,098	..
	W.	-	0,085	..
	S.H.	-	0,037	..
	B.	-	0,079	..
	W.	-	0,078	..
	G.	-	0,068	..
	M.	-	0,068	..
Data is based on OECD.Stat, (2020)				

Source: adapted by the authors

Figure 1. Expected risks causing energy crisis
(created by the authors based on data from Coldwellsolar, n.d.)

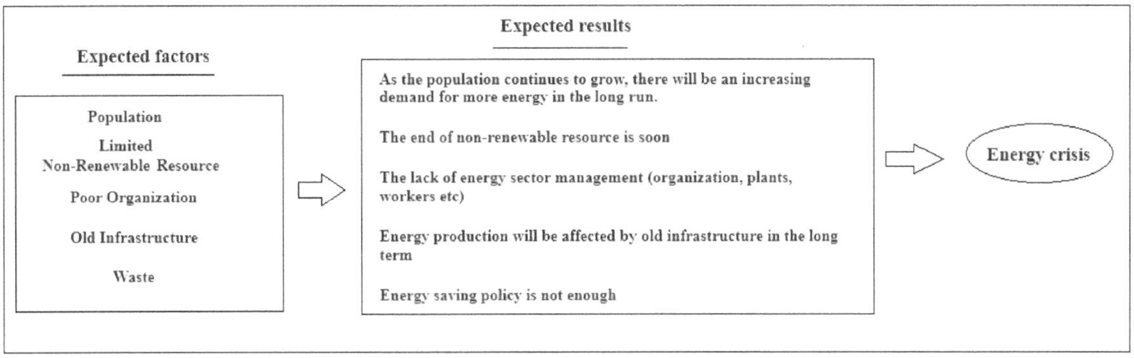

Figure 2. Risks and challenges in energy sector during the COVID-19
(created by the authors based on data from European Commission, 2020)

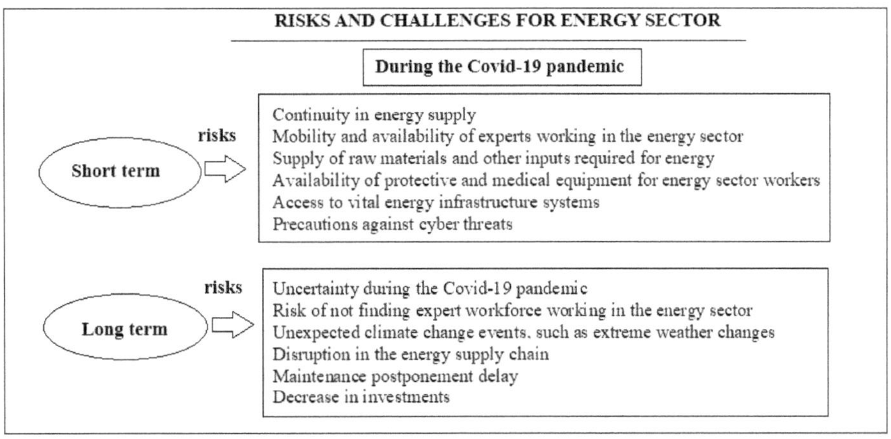

generation of European countries. The energy crisis also caused changes in plans and programs to exit nuclear energy. Due to the energy crisis, many European countries have started to extend the operating periods of their nuclear power plants and prepare new nuclear energy investment plans (AA, 2022).

Russia's fossil fuel resources have led many countries to rely heavily on Russia for energy. For instance, in 2021, the European Union sourced 45% of its coal imports and 36% of its natural gas from Russia according to Eurostat. This has made natural gas, coal, and oil resources a security concern for Europe. The conflict between Russia and Ukraine has caused energy prices to increase globally. Consequently, Europe has made decisions to reduce its energy dependence on Russia, as stated by the European Commission in 2023 (European Commission, 2023). Due to the ongoing war in Ukraine, the sanctions imposed on Russia significantly reduced natural gas supply to European countries. Furthermore, Russia's natural gas rate had already fallen by 80% prior to the war. As a result of the decrease in supply volume, the energy costs of European countries have increased (Altun and Tarhan, 2022).

Developed countries place great importance on managing energy demand in the long term, in order to maintain their current social welfare and ensure economic stability. Encouraging sustainable energy consumption practices will also lead to more efficient use of energy. Implementing insulation in buildings, reducing air travel, and using temperature-controlled operation in devices such as air conditioners are all recommended applications. (United Nations, 2022).

The COVID-19 pandemic has brought global energy access to the forefront. Despite ongoing efforts, a significant portion of the world's population still lacks access to energy, and many continue to rely on environmentally harmful fuels. It's estimated that by 2030, 670 million people may still be without electricity. The energy crisis, which was exacerbated by the Russia-Ukraine war, has further complicated matters (Departmental news, 2022). In terms of SDG7, the key energy-related points are summarized in Table 7.

Table 7. Progress in SDG-7 and Covid-19 pandemic

Sub-goals for SDG-7*	Progress*
Access to electricity	While there was 83% access to electricity in 2010; It was 91% in 2020. The proportion of people without access to electricity has decreased. The Covid-19 pandemic has caused an interruption in this positive progress. It seems difficult to achieve this goal with full success until 2030.
Clean cooking	Access to clean cooking fuels was 69% in 2020. Access to 100% clean cooking fuels by 2030 does not seem possible globally.
Renewable resources	Investments in renewable energy sources have increased. Countries have accelerated their transition to green energy.
Energy efficiency	Energy efficiency policies need to be further developed.
International Financial Flows	Funds and investment instruments supporting clean energy should be increased, and developing countries should be supported. However, the Covid-19 pandemic has caused a decrease in financial support packages.
*The data is based on Departmental news, (2022).	

Source: adapted by the authors

The Covid-19 pandemic has triggered an energy crisis, revealing that relying on fossil fuels for energy security is not sustainable in the long term. As a result, the use of renewable energy sources may be a more effective energy policy in the long run. According to a study by Hoang et al. (2021), the Covid-19 epidemic led to an increase in the percentage of renewable energy usage. Conversely, there has been a decrease in the demand for energy derived from fossil fuels (Hoang et al., 2021).

The Covid-19 pandemic has caused crises in fundamental areas such as health, education, economy, employment, and energy. Countries have undergone significant changes to adapt to the new era. For instance, there has been a rise in digital transformations such as distance education models and an increase in home-office working models in the education sector. However, while the decrease in physical mobility has resulted in a drop in carbon emissions in some countries, it has increased in others (Siksnelyte-Butkiene, 2021).

Gas export from Russia to the Eurozone hit historical lows at the end of 2022, dropping down to 20 percent from the previous rate of about 50 percent. While Europe had a 'mild' winter and benefited from LNG markets, it still faces risks in the years 2023-2024, according to Fatih Birol, President of the International Energy Agency. Europe prepared for winter with savings measures, as the decrease in supply from Russia led to an increase of 60 percent in LNG imports in 2022 compared to the previous year. The oil and gas industry is expected to generate a profit of $4 trillion in 2022, according to Birol. The majority of the LNG imports to Europe came from the USA, Qatar and Russia, as per the Global LNG Outlook report by the Institute for Energy Economics and Financial Analysis (IEEFA). In 2022, the highest LNG importers were France, Spain, the United Kingdom, the Netherlands, Italy, Turkey, and Belgium. France, Spain, Belgium and the Netherlands were the largest importers of Russian LNG in 2022. The total import of Russian LNG by France, Spain and Belgium increased significantly by 55 percent. In contrast, Croatia, Lithuania, Portugal, Sweden, and the United Kingdom considerably reduced their Russian LNG imports in 2022.

Europe may face challenges in its energy policy due to unforeseen circumstances such as accidents or technical problems at major pipelines or LNG export terminals. Extreme weather conditions, low wind or hydroelectric power levels are also likely to add to these challenges. It has been indicated that as China relaxes Covid-19 restrictions, the demand for liquefied gas by ships may increase later this year. This situation could be costly for Europe, which is a major buyer of gas. Poorer countries in Asia and Africa, who cannot afford to compete, are expected to suffer even more. The International Energy Agency has warned Europe that a scenario in which Russia reduces its supply and China's demand increases may cause a gas shortage next winter. Russia still holds some energy cards to play, being a major oil supplier and still sending some gas to Europe. According to Loskot-Strachota of the Center for Oriental Studies, "The energy crisis has not disappeared. We are not experiencing the worst scenario, but the uncertainty factors have not disappeared either" (Euronews, 2023).

The already strained relationship between Russia and Western countries due to the Russia-Ukraine war has worsened the energy crisis caused by COVID-19. The European Union (EU), which is particularly concerned about energy security. With the decrease in supply, energy costs for European countries have increased. The rapid increase in natural gas and electricity prices, particularly since the beginning of 2022, has impacted the entire world, particularly Europe. Unfortunately, a significant decrease in gas prices is not expected in the near future (TRT Haber, 2023).

SOLUTIONS AND RECOMMENDATIONS

Energy security will be a matter of primary importance for developed countries planning a transition to industry 5.0 for sustainable and resilient cities and countries. Energy will be a greater need in the future as smart societies will be supported by smart technologies. Sustainability and digitalization are rising in parallel. Smart technologies, robots and artificial intelligence technologies will support societies to become more resilient and sustainable. Therefore, energy continuity is essential to prevent the loss of these technologies.

While creating management strategies for the energy crisis against ordinary or expected risks; Current strategies are inadequate against the unexpected crises of the future period. Therefore, it can be said that the Covid-19 pandemic and the Russia-Ukraine war give policy makers an idea as a preview of the sudden and unexpected crises of the future. This book chapter offers some suggestions, such as:

- Policy makers should create alternative policies for energy security against sudden crises and unexpected events that may occur in the future.
- Foreign dependency on energy should be as minimal as possible.
- Research on green and clean energy sources should continue
- More incentives and financial support should be given to green and clean energy investments.
- Every country should pursue a sustainable energy policy within its borders.

FUTURE RESEARCH DIRECTIONS

It is recommended that future studies focus on projection studies against crises with the help of statistics specific to OECD countries. Because projection studies for measures against crises can be useful for predictions.

CONCLUSION

The issue of energy security is one of the essential elements for the future to be sustainable for both developed and developing countries in the 21st century. As stated in the 2030 SDGs, clean and accessible energy is essential for all people. Development policies supported by sustainable and green economy models began to be adopted in the 21st century instead of traditional growth theories for economic growth. Thanks to the green economy approach, sustainable policies are followed for economic progress and the damage to the environment is minimized (Yildirim et al., 2023). For example; In energy policies, priority has begun to be given to the use of green-renewable energy sources instead of non-renewable -fossil-based energy sources. Many countries have transferred large funds to green energy systems in energy investment. According to the IEA (2020) report, it can be said that investments in electrical energy continue in the world within the scope of clean and sustainable energy policy. There is a decline in traditional energy systems such as coal, nuclear and hydroelectric energy systems (IEA, 2020).

The Covid-19 pandemic has brought about unexpected consequences and changes for both developed and developing OECD countries. As a result of the global pandemic, they realized that more work was needed for a sustainable future. Under current conditions, it seems impossible for countries to achieve the 2030 SDGs, which are expected to be achieved by 2030. While the Covid-19 pandemic accelerates the digital transformation of countries, the need for energy has increased. While energy consumption decreases in industrial areas; Energy needs in homes and residences have increased. Even though people's energy needs change location, energy demand must be ensured sustainably. It can be said that the amount of energy individuals need while meeting their basic needs has increased even more with digitalization and technology. Internet and electricity have been essential needs in most OECD countries during

Covid-19 pandemic. While individuals provided remote - online education, home-office work, remote health and some remote public services, internet and energy had to be continuous. On the other hand, the Russia-Ukraine war has once again shown how problematic being dependent on foreign energy is in terms of energy security. Foreign dependency on energy is one of the biggest challenges for a sustainable future. Digitalized countries are in search of policies based on continuity in energy.

However, today there are still people who have limited or even no access to energy. While struggling with expected crises, events such as the Covid-19 pandemic and the Russia-Ukraine War have shown that countries still have deficiencies in energy security.

In the case of a new epidemic brought on by health concerns, such as a pandemic, it has become apparent that countries must ensure their energy security in accordance with the new conditions that will arise due to reduced physical mobility and changes in economic conditions. While war was once considered an unexpected situation in the 21st century, it is now evident that developed countries must also be prepared to face this crisis. Consequently, with the possibility of war in the 21st century, developed and developing countries must take necessary precautions in their relations with countries from which they obtain energy supplies. As a result, creating an economic system based on renewable energy sources is viewed as a more reasonable strategy for achieving sustainable economic growth.

ACKNOWLEDGMENT

Turkish references are translated into English. The author(s) gives keywords and definitions based on this study as a result of the review.

REFERENCES

AA. (2022). *Avrupa Birliği 2022'de savaş, enerji krizi ve enflasyonun etkileriyle mücadele etti (European Union grapples with effects of war, energy crisis and inflation in 2022).* Terhaber. https://www.trthaber.com/haber/dunya/avrupa-birligi-2022de-savas-enerji-krizi-ve-enflasyonun-etkileriyle-mucadele-etti-732611.html

AA. (2023). *COVID-19, salgın ilan edilişinin 3. yılında da "küresel acil durum" olarak nitelendiriliyor (COVID-19 is described as a "global emergency" in the 3rd year since it was declared an epidemic).* Terhaber. https://www.trthaber.com/haber/dunya/covid-19-salgin-ilan-edilisinin-3-yilinda-da-kuresel-acil-durum-olarak-nitelendiriliyor-752265.html

Altun, T., & Tarhan, M. (2022). *2023'te dünyayı Rusya-Ukrayna krizinin etkileri ve enerji krizi riski bekliyor (The effects of the Russia-Ukraine crisis and the risk of energy crisis await the world in 2023).* AA. https://www.aa.com.tr/tr/ekonomi/2023te-dunyayi-rusya-ukrayna-krizinin-etkileri-ve-enerji-krizi-riski-bekliyor/2776757

Aydın, K., Yıldırım, S., & Çizer, E. Ö. (2023). Big dilemma in face mask consumption: Environmental sensitivity versus the fear of COVID-19 [IJGW]. *International Journal of Global Warming*, *29*(3), 207–226. doi:10.1504/IJGW.2023.129490

Bin-Nashwan, S.A., Hassan, M.K. & Muneeza, A. (2022), Russia–Ukraine conflict: 2030 Agenda for SDGs hangs in the balance. *International Journal of Ethics and Systems*. doi:10.1108/IJOES-06-2022-0136

Chopra, M., Singh, S. K., Gupta, A., Aggarwal, K., Gupta, B. B., & Colace, F. (2022). Analysis & prognosis of sustainable development goals using big data-based approach during COVID-19 pandemic. *Sustainable Technology and Entrepreneurship*, *1*(2), 100012. doi:10.1016/j.stae.2022.100012

Coldwellsolar, (n.d.). *Causes, Effects, and Solutions to the Global Energy Crisis*. Coldwellsolar. https://coldwellsolar.com/commercial-solar-blog/causes-effects-and-solutions-to-the-global-energy-crisis/

Departmental news. (2022). *Report: COVID-19 slows progress towards universal energy Access*. WHO. https://www.who.int/news/item/01-06-2022-report--covid-19-slows-progress-towards-universal-energy-access

Euronews, (2023). *Avrupa, Rusya'ya karşı enerji savaşını kazandı mı? [Has Europe won the energy war against Russia?]*. Euronews. https://tr.euronews.com/2023/01/11/avrupada-rusyanin-ukrayna-isgaliyle-baslayan-enerji-krizi-sona-erdi-mi

European Commission. (2023). *EU energy security and the war inUkraine: From sprint to marathon, BRIEFING*. European Commission. https://www.europarl.europa.eu/RegData/etudes/BRIE/2023/739362/EPRS_BRI(2023)739362_EN.p df

Haber, T. R. T. (2023). *Rusya-Ukrayna Savaşı küresel ekonomiyi nasıl etkiledi? (How did the Russia-Ukraine War affect the global economy?)*. Terhaber. https://www.trthaber.com/haber/dunya/rusya-ukrayna-savasi-kuresel-ekonomiyi-nasil-etkiledi-752972.html

Hoang, A. T., Sandro Nižetić, Olcer, A. I., Ong, H. C., Chen, W.-H., Chong, C. T., Thomas, S., Bandh, S. A., & Nguyen, X. P. (2021, July). Impacts of COVID-19 pandemic on the global energy system and the shift progress to renewable energy: Opportunities, challenges, and policy implications. *Energy Policy*, *154*, 112322. doi:10.1016/j.enpol.2021.112322 PMID:34566236

IEA. (2020). *Power systems in transition: Challenges and opportunities ahead for electricity security*. IEA. https://iea.blob.core.windows.net/assets/cd69028a-da78-4b47-b1bf-7520cdb20d70/Power_systems_in_transition.pdf

IEA. (n.d.). *Russia's War on Ukraine Analysing the impacts of Russia's invasion of Ukraine on global energy markets and international energy security*. IEA. https://www.iea.org/topics/russias-war-on-ukraine

Kılıçay, İ. (2023). *Rusya-Ukrayna savaşı enerji piyasalarına nasıl yansıdı?(How did the Russia-Ukraine war affect the energy markets?)*. Bloomberght. https://www.bloomberght.com/rusya-ukrayna-savasi-enerji-piyasalarina-nasil-yansidi-2325960

Meadows, D. H., Meadows, D. L., Randers, J., & Behren, W. W., III. (1972). *The Limits to Growth, A reportfor the club of Rome's Project on the predicament of mankind*. Donella Meadows. https://www.donellameadows.org/wp-content/userfiles/Limits-to-Growth-digital-scan-version.pdf

Munasinghe, M. (2002). The Sustainomics Trans-disciplinary Meta-framework for making Development more Sustainable: Applications to energy issues. *International Journal of Sustainable Development*, *4*(2), 6–54. doi:10.1504/IJSD.2002.002563

NASA Global Climate Change web site. (n.d.). *The Causes of Climate Change, Vital Signs of the Planet*. NASA. https://climate.nasa.gov/causes/

OECD. (2020). *Renewable energy feed-in tariffs*. OECD. https://stats.oecd.org/Index.aspx?DataSetCode=RE_FIT

OECD. (2023a), *Primary energy supply (indicator)*. OECD. doi:10.1787/1b33c15a-en

OECD. (2023b). *Crude oil production (indicator)*. OECD. doi:10.1787/4747b431-en

OECD (2023c), *Electricity generation (indicator)*. (Accessed on 09 November 2023) doi:10.1787/c6e6caa2-en

OECD. (2023d). *Renewable Energy*. OECD. doi:10.1787/aac7c3f1-en

OECD. (2023e). *Nuclear power plants (indicator)*. OECD. doi:10.1787/3cc1191d-en

Pereira, P., Zhao, W., Symochko, L., Inacio, M., Bogunovic, I., & Barcelo, D. (2022). The Russian-Ukrainian armed conflict will push back the sustainable development goals. *Geography and Sustainability*, *3*(3), 277–287. doi:10.1016/j.geosus.2022.09.003

Siksnelyte-Butkiene, I. (2021). Impact of the COVID-19 Pandemic to the Sustainability of the Energy Sector. *Sustainability (Basel)*, *13*(23), 12973. doi:10.3390u132312973

Srivastava, A., Sharma, R. K., & Suresh, A. (2020). Impact of Covid-19 on Sustainable Development Goals. *International Journal of Advanced Science and Technology*, *29*(No. 9s), 4968–4972.

The Lancet Public Health. (2020, September). The Lancet Public Health. (2020). Will the COVID-19 pandemic threaten the SDGs? *The Lancet. Public Health*, *5*(9), e460. doi:10.1016/S2468-2667(20)30189-4 PMID:32888438

United Nations. (2015). *Transformıng Our World: The 2030 Agenda For Sustaınable Development*, A/RES/70/1. UN. https://sustainabledevelopment.un.org/content/documents/21252030%20Agenda%20for%20Sustainable%20Development%20web.pdf

United Nations. (2022). *Global impact of war in Ukraine: Energy crisis UN GLOBAL CRISIS RESPONSE GROUP ON FOOD, ENERGY AND FINANCE AUGUST 2022*. UN. https://unsdg.un.org/sites/default/files/2022-08/GCRG_3rd-Brief_Aug3_2022_.pdf

United Nations Economic and Social Council. (2021). *Enhancing energy security in the context of the coronavirus disease pandemic for a greener, more resilient and inclusive energy future in the region*, ESCAP/77/17. UN. https://www.unescap.org/sites/default/d8files/event-documents/ESCAP_77_17_E.pdf

United Nations Sustainable Development Group. (2022). *Global Impact of war in Ukraine on food, energy and finance systems - BRIEF NO.2*. UN. https://unsdg.un.org/resources/global-impact-war-ukraine-food-energy-and-finance-systems-brief-no2

UNPD. (2022). *The impact of the war in Ukraine on sustainable development in Africa, Rapid Assessment by the Regional Bureau for Africa*. UNDP. file:///C:/Users/hp/Downloads/UNDP%20RBA%20-%20IMpact%20of%20the%20war%20%20in%20Ukraine%20on%20Africa%20-%2024%20May%202022%20(1).pdf

Yildirim, S. (2020). The consumer role for sustainable development: how consumers contribute sustainable development goals. In V. Chkoniya, A. O. Madsen, & P. Bukhrashvili (Eds.), *Anthropological Approaches to Understanding Consumption Patterns and Consumer Behavior* (pp. 325–341). IGI Global. doi:10.4018/978-1-7998-3115-0.ch018

Yıldırım, S. (2021). Do green women influencers spur sustainable consumption patterns? Descriptive evidences from social media influencers. *Ecofeminism and Climate Change*, *2*(4), 198–210. doi:10.1108/EFCC-02-2021-0003

Yildirim, S. (2023). Greenwashing: A rapid escape from sustainability or a slow transition*? LBS Journal of Management & Research*, *21*(1), 53–63. doi:10.1108/LBSJMR-11-2022-0077

Yıldırım, S., & Candan, B. (2015). Segmentation of Green Product Buyers Based on Their Personal Values and Consumption Values, *Environmental Values* [October.]. *White Horse Press*, *24*(5), 641–661.

Yildirim, S., Demirtas, I., & Yildirim, D. C. (2022). A Review of Alternative Economic Approaches to Achieve Sustainable Development: The Rising Digitalization and Degrowth Post COVID-19. In R. Castanho (Ed.), *Handbook of Research on Sustainable Development Goals, Climate Change, and Digitalization* (pp. 288–307). IGI Global. doi:10.4018/978-1-7998-8482-8.ch018

Yildirim, S., Kaplan, M., & Yildirim, D. C. (2023). Climate Change and the Ocean Economy: A Review on OECD's Ocean Economy. In A. Pego (Ed.), *Handbook of Research on Bioeconomy and Economic Ecosystems* (pp. 212–232). IGI Global. doi:10.4018/978-1-6684-8879-9.ch012

Yıldırım, S., & Yıldırım, D. Ç. (2020). Achieving Sustainable Development Through a Green Economy Approach. In S. Patti & G. Trizzino (Eds.), *Advanced Integrated Approaches to Environmental Economics and Policy: Emerging Research and Opportunities* (pp. 1–22). IGI Global. doi:10.4018/978-1-5225-9562-5.ch001

Yıldırım, S., Yıldırım, D. Ç., & Gedikli, A. (2016). Sustainable Consumption Trends in the World in the Context of Green Economy and Sustainability. In M. Erdoğdu, T. Arun, & I. Ahmad (Eds.), *Handbook of Research on Green Economic Development Initiatives and Strategies* (pp. 65–84). IGI Global. doi:10.4018/978-1-5225-0440-5.ch004

ADDITIONAL READING

Sevik, N., & Yıldırım, S. (2023). Sustainable Enterprises Post COVID-19 Pandemic: The Rise of Sustainable Fashion Enterprises. In R. Castanho (Ed.), *Handbook of Research on Current Advances and Challenges of Borderlands, Migration, and Geopolitics* (pp. 343–359). IGI Global. doi:10.4018/978-1-6684-7020-6.ch017

Yildirim, S. (2020). The consumer role for sustainable development: how consumers contribute sustainable development goals. In V. Chkoniya, A. O. Madsen, & P. Bukhrashvili (Eds.), *Anthropological Approaches to Understanding Consumption Patterns and Consumer Behavior* (pp. 325–341). IGI Global. doi:10.4018/978-1-7998-3115-0.ch018

Yıldırım, S. (2021). Do green women influencers spur sustainable consumption patterns? Descriptive evidences from social media influencers. *Ecofeminism and Climate Change*, *2*(4), 198–210. doi:10.1108/EFCC-02-2021-0003

Yildirim, S. (2021). 3R Principle in Household Energy Consumption Patterns: A Case of Turkish Households. In M. Danish & T. Senjyu (Eds.), *Eco-Friendly Energy Processes and Technologies for Achieving Sustainable Development* (pp. 88–107). IGI Global. doi:10.4018/978-1-7998-4915-5.ch005

Yildirim, S. (2021), 3R principle in household energy consumption patterns: a case of Turkish households, in Danish, M. and Senjyu, T. (Eds), Eco-Friendly Energy Processes and Technologies for Achieving Sustainable Development. IGI Global. doi:10.4018/978-1-7998-4915-5.ch005

Yıldırım, S., & Bostancı, S. H. (2021). The efficiency of e-government portal management from a citizen perspective: Evidences from Turkey, *World Journal of Science. Technology and Sustainable Development*, *18*(3), 259–273. doi:10.1108/WJSTSD-04-2021-0049

Yıldırım, S., & Candan, B. (2015). Segmentation of green product buyers based on their personal values and consumption values. *Environmental Values*, *24*(5), 641–661. doi:10.3197/096327115X14384223590212

Yildirim, S., Demirtas, I., & Yildirim, D. C. (2022). A Review of Alternative Economic Approaches to Achieve Sustainable Development: The Rising Digitalization and Degrowth Post COVID-19. In R. Castanho (Ed.), *Handbook of Research on Sustainable Development Goals, Climate Change, and Digitalization* (pp. 288–307). IGI Global. doi:10.4018/978-1-7998-8482-8.ch018

Yıldırım, S., & Kantarcı, T. (2022). A Review on Sustainability Policies of Businesses: Recycling and Waste Reduction. *Journal of Recycling Economy & Sustainability Policy*, *1*(1), 1–9. https://respjournal.com/index.php/pub/article/view/1

Yıldırım, S., & Yıldırım, D. Ç. (2020). Achieving Sustainable Development Through a Green Economy Approach. In S. Patti & G. Trizzino (Eds.), *Advanced Integrated Approaches to Environmental Economics and Policy: Emerging Research and Opportunities* (pp. 1–22). IGI Global. doi:10.4018/978-1-5225-9562-5.ch001

KEY WORDS AND DEFINITIONS

2030 SDGs: A guide including 17 main goals to be achieved by 2030.

COVID-19 pandemic: A pandemic which is introduced by the World Health Organization in 2020.

Energy Security: Ensuring sustainable energy policies (including affordable, access and clean energy policies) in general.

OECD: Organisation for Economic Co-operation and Development

Chapter 6
Economy, Environment, and Sustainable Development:
A Conceptual Evaluation

Recep Ulucak
Erciyes University, Turkey

ABSTRACT

Economics, traditionally centered on the production of goods and utility maximization, has often undervalued the pivotal role of the environment in shaping societal welfare. The environment, as a provider of myriad resources, from non-renewable to renewable, and as a sanctuary for relaxation and natural beauty, is intrinsically linked to our economic processes. However, economic activities have progressively degraded this invaluable asset. The emergent focus on sustainability, with its dual lenses of weak and strong sustainability, offers a nuanced understanding of resource interrelations. Disciplines such as environmental economics offer market-based environmental solutions, while ecological economics posits the economy within the broader ecosystem, highlighting an inextricable bond. This chapter focuses on the harmonization of economic endeavors with ecological preservation to pave the way for genuine sustainable development.

INTRODUCTION

Economics is defined as the scientific discipline that strives to meet unlimited human needs with limited resources, aiming to maximize individual utility, firm profits, and ultimately societal welfare. Since the time of Adam Smith, the production of goods and services has been considered a sufficient indicator of welfare, with the belief that societies will be happier when producing more goods. However, the fact that quality environment is an essential prerequisite for true welfare has been overlooked. A high-quality environment is necessary because it provides essential goods and services that sustain life. The potential benefits offered by a high-quality environment can be roughly listed as follows (Pearce and Barbier, 2000):

DOI: 10.4018/979-8-3693-1297-1.ch006

- Non-renewable natural resources such as coal, oil, natural gas, iron, copper,
- Renewable natural resources such as water, fish, timber, wind, sunlight,
- A waste pool where solid, liquid, and gaseous waste resulting from economic activities can be disposed of,
- Natural beauties that offer opportunities for relaxation, healing, and pleasant leisure time,
- Biogeochemical cycles that provide plant and animal food, as well as the purification of water and air, and the stabilization of climates,
- Genetic plans and vital information based on behavioral observations.

Undoubtedly, the importance of the environment is not limited to the items listed above; however, even these factors necessitate a limitation on the boundless pursuit of economic growth and prosperity by humankind. The main reason for this necessity is undoubtedly the economic system that does not take into account the opportunities offered by the environment (Pearce and Barbier, 2000, p. 2). Almost all environmental degradation results from production and consumption activities. As the use of resources for production increases, on the one hand, natural resources decrease, and on the other hand, pollution, and thus environmental costs increase due to the waste generated as a result of production and consumption (Pearce and Turner, 1990.

As seen in Figure 1, both the environment and the economic system are intertwined in terms of both production and consumption activities. The environment supports production and consumption by providing necessary raw materials and other inputs for economic activities to be sustainable. However, these production and consumption processes create pollutants that deteriorate environmental quality. Some of the waste can be transformed back into raw materials thanks to technological possibilities, but in some cases, the return of waste to the environmental system without being transformed brings us back to the beginning of the process and negatively affects economic activities. The mutual dependency between the environment and the economy is derived from the fact that the environment provides raw materials for economic activities and, directly, is the creator of welfare. Therefore, the environmental destruction caused by economic activities will ultimately affect welfare and the performance of the economy (Engin, 2007). To establish economic efficiency, which is defined as the realization of efficiency in production, distribution, and consumption, we must perceive it in a composition that now includes not polluting this composition and/or cleaning it (Güney, 2004).

Figure 1. Environment—Economy relationship

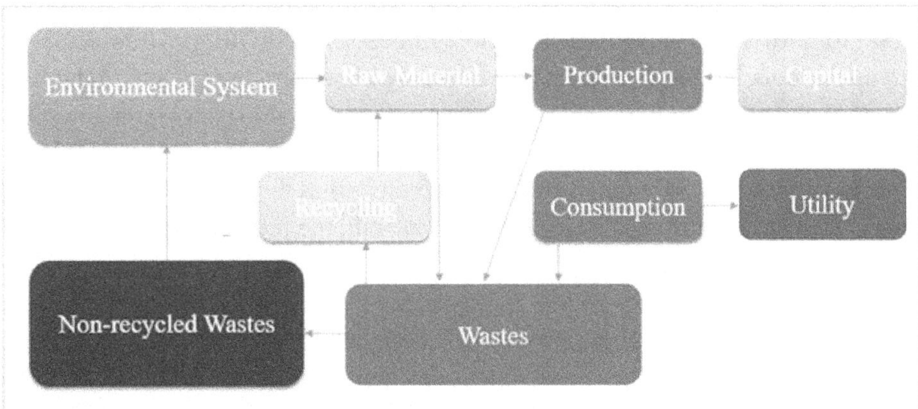

The relationship between economics and the environment has dimensions that go beyond the approach of the mainstream economics and requires further examination and discussion. This is because the deterioration of environmental quality is directly linked to economic activities, and achieving the ultimate goal of economics becomes more difficult due to erroneous strategies pursued without considering the opportunity cost to fulfill these objectives. Therefore, the long-term effects of the strategies to be pursued should be taken into account, and the trap of creating an uninhabitable environment for society while striving to achieve the goal should be avoided. For this reason, it is essential to discuss how economic activities undertaken to increase societal welfare affect the crucially important healthy and high-quality environment for the well-being and even the survival of society, and to establish a sustainable solution. Particularly, the relationship between growth and the environment is an important subject to explore, given that many societies primarily focus on economic growth as a welfare indicator and expect other macroeconomic goals to be achieved along with it. As a result, the relationship between growth and the environment needs to be examined closely.

Claiming that environmental issues have only recently gained sensitivity and that there have been no efforts or approaches prior to that is not entirely accurate. When looking at the environmental threats that emerged in the context of the conditions of the time, it is natural for environmental sensitivity to receive more attention recently. In fact, the environment has been a subject of discussion since the Physiocrats, who economically linked the source of wealth to productive lands, which were the natural resources of their time (Hussen, 2004, p. 246). François Quesnay, a prominent representative of the Physiocrats, presented the first systematic and quantitative approaches to the power of nature in his work "Tableau Économique," which also reflected ideas of sustainability in the relationship between society and the economy, and in the production process (Bartelmus, 2008, p. 20). However, it is still more accurate to consider the views on the environment in the context of economics from the 18th-century Industrial Revolution and Adam Smith's work "An Inquiry into the Nature and Causes of the Wealth of Nations," as economics became a systematic reality during this period.

CLASSICAL ECONOMIC PERSPECTIVE

The relationship between economics and the environment has dimensions that go beyond the approach of the mainstream economics and requires further examination and discussion. This is because the deterioration of environmental quality is directly linked to economic activities, and achieving the ultimate goal of economics becomes more difficult due to erroneous strategies pursued without considering the opportunity cost to fulfill these objectives. Therefore, it is essential to discuss how economic activities undertaken to increase societal welfare affect the crucially important healthy and high-quality environment for the well-being and even the survival of society, and to establish a sustainable solution.

Particularly, the relationship between growth and the environment is an important subject to explore, given that many societies primarily focus on economic growth as a welfare indicator and expect other macroeconomic goals to be achieved along with it. As a result, the relationship between growth and the environment needs to be examined closely.

During the period when the foundations of classical economic thought were laid, the absence of any constraints related to natural resources has pushed the adoption of a system that does not focus on natural resources or the environment into the background. For example, in Adam Smith's work "An Inquiry into the Nature and Causes of the Wealth of Nations," personal interest and rational behavior are seen as the fundamental keys to economic growth and increasing welfare. According to Smith, gains in agriculture are less risky compared to industry because it is the field in which people have the best knowledge at that time. However, as the population increases and land becomes scarce, the profit margin in the agricultural sector will relatively decrease compared to the manufacturing sector (Kula, 1998, p. 15). From Smith's perspective, as the manufacturing sector expands, the importance of labor and capital increases relative to natural resources (land). Of course, initially, the progress in the manufacturing sector will depend on the progress in the agricultural sector because as the agricultural sector progresses, the labor force in this sector will move to the manufacturing sector without any decline in agricultural product supply. As the weight of the agricultural sector decreases in the economy and structural changes occur in the economy due to the expanding manufacturing sector and trade, the development achieved in agriculture will feed other sectors. As a result, while the capacity to consume the food provided by the agricultural sector is limited to people's stomachs, there is no limit to the desire to have other things. Therefore, Smith is optimistic about the future level of welfare based on the principles of a free market and self-interest (Kula, 1998, p. 15).

After Adam Smith, leading classical economists started to change their optimistic views about the future. Especially in terms of food products and natural resources, the value of land and nature has become important for the future well-being. Particularly, Thomas Malthus's population theory is a significant rebellion against the optimistic view. In his theory, Malthus points out that while the population increases geometrically, food supply increases arithmetically due to the limited availability of arable land, and he emphasizes that growth is far from being sustainable.

His statement about the exponential growth of living beings due to the constraints of natural and environmental resources and particularly his emphasis on the scarcity of agricultural land and food production capacity in his time due to rapidly increasing population makes Malthus an essential figure to mention in environmental economics. On the other hand, those who argue that growth cannot be sustainable in the long term based on Malthus's warnings have been called "prophets of doom" (Hussen, 2004, p. 217).

The law of diminishing returns in agriculture, which forms the basis of David Ricardo's land-rent theory, is also a noteworthy development concerning the environment. Ricardo's approach modified the Malthusian approach (Asafu-Adjaye, 2000, p. 219). In other words, as the population increases, people are forced to exploit the existing land more and expand production to less fertile lands. Therefore, total output may increase, but in the absence of technological progress, this process will continue at a decreasing rate. However, the Ricardian approach adopts the idea that resource constraints (especially in agricultural areas) will arise not from population explosion like in the Malthusian approach, but from the decrease in the quality and quantity of resources, namely the law of diminishing returns (Hussen, 2004, p. 205). From this perspective, the Ricardian approach is more optimistic than the Malthusian approach (Asafu-Adjaye, 2000, p. 219).

Leading classical economists such as William Stanley Jevons and John Stuart Mill also highlighted the depletion of resources and growth, but generally did not emphasize that natural resources constituted a limit for growth (Asafu-Adjaye, 2000, p. 219). Unlike Mill, Malthus, and Ricardo, Mill believed that humanity would control population growth, reach a certain standard of living, and then focus on issues such as social justice (Czech, 2009, p. 3). He also believed that natural resource constraints could be somewhat relaxed thanks to technological development (Van Den Bergh, 1996, p. 12). Jevons, although a pioneer of neoclassical economics, focused on the coal mines, the most important energy input during the period dominated by classical thought, and emphasized that the growth of England was constrained by them, indicating that rapid industrialization depletes resources, and extracting increasingly difficult resources will increase costs over time and make the industrial sector difficult (Kula, 1998, p. 45).

In general, considering the conditions prevailing during the dominance of classical economic thought, the scarcity of natural resources and environmental problems did not become significant enough to be the main subjects of concern for classical economists beyond their importance.

NEOCLASSICAL ECONOMIC PERSPECTIVE

In the late 19th century, classical economic thought was revised from various angles, such as replacing the labor theory of value with the utility theory and adopting the marginal approach. This revised school of thought is known as neoclassical economics, which laid a more solid foundation for economic analysis based on marginal values and has remained the most popular among economists until today. However, the neoclassical economic thought naturally prioritized issues such as free-market economy, utility, and profit maximization, while it placed the internalization of problems like the environment and natural resources in the background.

Within neoclassical economics, environmental issues have primarily been highlighted in the context of externalities, investigating problems arising from negative externalities caused by producers and consumers that lead to environmental degradation and the need for corrective mechanisms. The concept of externality was initially addressed by Alfred Marshall but later reinterpreted and associated with welfare economics and external economies by A. C. Pigou in the 1910s (Sönmez, 1987, p. 124). Environmental pollution and degradation have been considered as negative externalities because they cause adverse effects on individuals and society (Colander, 1993, p. 336). To prevent the welfare loss caused by externalities, Pigou proposed applying a tax to the activity causing the externality, equalizing its private cost with its social cost. This kind of taxation is known as Pigouvian taxation in the literature (Pearce and Turner, 1990, p. 84).

Another area in which environmental issues gained prominence in neoclassical economics was the topic of public goods, notably contributed by Paul Samuelson. Public goods, also known as common goods, encompass services such as national defense, justice, and environmental conservation (Hyman, 1999, p. 134). Therefore, a quality environment is considered a public good, and ensuring and preserving this quality cannot be left solely to the private sector's initiative and market solutions. Furthermore, due to environmental pollution crossing national boundaries and negatively impacting transnational regions and even global issues like the destruction of the ozone layer leading to global warming, the environment needs to be evaluated from a global public good perspective, and this aspect must be considered in finding solutions (Nordhaus, 2007, p. 28).

Generally, until the 1960s, neoclassical economists mainly modeled economic individuals (homo economicus) driven by self-interest, emphasizing that increasing consumption of goods and services would raise utility levels, and maximizing utility was their approach. They considered that through economic growth, living standards would improve, and poverty would be eliminated. Growth became the central goal in their models (Common and Stagl, 2005, pp. 3-4). The general views of neoclassical economics on the scarcity, allocation, and measurement of natural resources can be summarized as follows (Hussen, 2004, pp. 221-239):

- Nothing is an alternative to the market mechanism for resource allocation. The efficiency of the market mechanism signals the emergence of resource scarcity and compensates for price distortions resulting from externalities.
- The value of resources depends on individual preferences and the initial stock of resources.
- For privately-owned resources, the market price is the accurate measure of resource scarcity.
- Price distortions caused by externalities can be corrected through appropriate institutional arrangements.
- Scarce resources can be increased through technology.
- Human-made capital such as machinery, buildings, and roads can be substituted for natural capital such as forests, mines, and water bodies.

In the 1970s, neoclassical economics began to focus more on environmental issues by giving rise to disciplines directly addressing the environment, such as environmental economics and natural resource economics. Environmental economics highlights environmental costs internalization and environmental cost-benefit analyses as solutions to market failures in their studies (Bartelmus, 2008, p. 39).

In general, neoclassical economists have neglected to explore the interconnection between the economy and the environment and neglected to prioritize the consideration of environmental constraints. They also believed that economic growth and technological development would solve all social and environmental problems, including pollution (Czech, 2009, p. 2).

In the 1980s, the Ecological Economics approach, which offered a more comprehensive and sensitive approach to the environment, began to develop and gain more supporters. Unlike environmental economics, Ecological Economics does not fit into any economic stream like Keynesian, Post-Keynesian, or institutional economics; it is not only limited to environmental issues but also encompasses natural and social sciences, making it a multidisciplinary approach beyond just economists and ecologists (Stern, 1997, p. 1906). This approach considers nature and the environment as the most crucial issues to be addressed and encompasses long-term technological change and economic growth perspectives, involving natural and social scientists as well.

In summary, while neoclassical economists have explored environmental issues primarily in terms of externalities and public goods, the Ecological Economics approach has gone beyond and emphasizes the interdependence of economics and the environment, focusing on broader and more comprehensive ecological and social perspectives.

ECONOMIC GROWTH AND ENVIRONMENT

Economic growth is one of the primary macroeconomic objectives of both developed and developing countries. To achieve this goal, efforts are made to achieve full employment, where all available production factors participate in production, and to produce goods and services that best meet society's needs (efficient utilization). Essentially, the aim of pursuing economic growth by resolving issues of full and efficient utilization is to increase the well-being of society. As a result of increased investments and production, an important indicator of welfare, per capita consumption, will increase, leading to a reduction in poverty, a significant cause of social unrest. Additionally, economic growth has significant contributions to sociological development. According to Friedman (2005), economic growth leads to increased opportunities, tolerance, economic and social mobility, peace, democracy, intellectual development, and enlightenment, making it crucial for prosperity, especially in low-income countries.

According to the traditional economic understanding, the level of welfare increases for rational individuals and societies as consumption of goods and services increases. As a result, a country's Gross Domestic Product (GDP) and its per capita income, obtained by dividing GDP by the population, are important indicators of national welfare and economic success, and GDP growth signifies the economy's progress (Hueting, 1991, p. 194). The idea that increasing production is necessary to finance the protection of the environment also reflects this belief (Hueting, 1991, p. 195). Similarly, according to Beckerman (1992b), although economic growth may cause environmental deterioration in the early stages of development, countries need to be wealthy to have a high-quality environment.

The thesis that limited environmental factors will constrain economic growth can be examined in three groups (Hepburn and Bowen 2012, p. 2):

The first view argues that environmental factors do not cause any limitation on economic growth. For example, Lomborg (2001) claims that resources are becoming more abundant. Simon (1980) believes that the term "constraint" is entirely misapplied to natural resources. Simon (1981) also argues that there is no real constraint on growth because many resources are being used more economically and are increasing in quantity compared to 10-20 years ago. These views are in line with labor, capital, and human capital-focused neoclassical economic growth and endogenous growth models, which suggest that growth is sustainable as long as technological progress continues. As a result of technological advancement, markets will expand and specialize, leading to increased returns due to economies of scale, as hypothesized by Adam Smith on division of labor and specialization.

The second view argues that the limitation of natural resources will create a constraint (drag) on growth. This environmental constraint arises from the scarcity of natural resources and the effects of various negative impacts of pollution on production and human beings. Nordhaus (1992) and Bruvoll et al. (1999) have attempted to calculate the past and future effects of this environmental constraint. However, these calculations are relatively small.

The third view is based on Tinbergen and Hueting (1992). According to this view, the scarcity of natural resources is of such importance that it prevents sustainability in consumption and production. This view is based on Malthus's (1798) view that the standard of living will be at subsistence level and Mill's (1848) view that the economy will eventually reach a steady state. This view also includes the views of John Maynard Keynes, John Hicks, and Nicholas Georgescu-Roegen on this subject.

Gross Domestic Product (GDP), as an indicator of economic growth in an economy, is a quantitative measure consisting of measurable elements. However, the well-being of a society, which includes intangible elements such as a high-quality environment, vital for the well-being and continuity of life and generations, is also a function of goods and services that are not bought and sold (Ertürk, 1998, p. 100). Nevertheless, all growing economies face the problem of deteriorating environmental quality, and countries must realize that economic growth is not costless, as it comes at the expense of harming the natural environment (Barkley and Seckler 1972, p. 11).

Optimistic Approaches

It is indisputable that economic activities have led to many environmental issues mentioned earlier. However, despite all these, there are optimistic approaches in the literature. The most accepted among these approaches is the income elasticity approach proposed by Beckerman (1992a) and Baldwin (1995).

According to this approach, a high-quality environment is a luxury good, and income elasticity is greater than one. Therefore, as people's income increases, their demand for a high-quality environment will increase proportionally more than the increase in income. In other words, as economic growth occurs, the desire to live in a quality environment will increase, and policies aimed at protecting the environment will prevent environmental damage. The underlying logic of this mechanism assumes that as income rises, people become more educated and cultured, becoming aware of environmental disasters and behaving more sensitively in this regard. This approach parallels the Environmental Kuznets Curve hypothesis, which claims an inverted U-shaped relationship between environmental pollution and income level, suggesting that pollution initially increases with income but decreases after reaching a certain income level. Grossman and Krueger first introduced this approach into the literature in 1992 and later reshaped it in 1995 (Grossman and Krueger, 1995, p. 354).

The second view supports the first view. According to this perspective, the wealth of countries allows for the complete implementation of social, legal, and financial infrastructures for environmental regulations (Baldwin, 1995, p. 61).

The third approach claims that economic growth enables the acquisition of more modern machinery and equipment, which in turn will pollute the environment less (Grossman, 1995, p. 21). This view is also expressed as the concept of Ecological Modernization. The concept of Ecological Modernization entered the literature with the European Union Fourth Environmental Action Program and is a version of the sustainable development approach (Pepper, 1998, p. 2). This approach represents environmentally friendly technological development that does not pollute, reduces emission rates, increases efficiency by using fewer resources, and recycles waste (Christoff, 1996, p. 480). Ecological Modernization also involves producers who aim to maintain or improve their positions in the competitive environment of the free market and prefer environmentally friendly technologies. They produce products that are recycled and meet ISO 14000 quality standards to leave a more positive impression on consumers and increase sales for export while reducing input and operating costs by working more efficiently, contributing to production growth and economic expansion without polluting the environment.

The fourth view is based on structural transformation. According to this view, as the income level increases in a country, the share of the industrial sector in total production decreases, and the share of the service sector increases. The service sector is less polluting than the industrial sector. Therefore, it will be less polluted as a result (Janicke, Binder, and Mönch, 1997, p. 474).

The fifth view is based on the thesis that economic growth or income increase does not only mean a quantitative increase but also signifies an increase in the value of the output. According to this perspective, economic growth is not solely about an increase in output quantity. Thus, economic growth does not always consume natural resources and pollute the environment. The purpose of economic activities is not to do so. Resource utilization and pollution are the undesirable side effects of production. Additionally, as the cost of pollution per unit increases with growth, the value of pollution-intensive production will decrease. This process will also be supported by reuse, restoration, renovation, improvement, and recycling of goods, for which there is no definite upper limit (Ayres, 1997, p. 286).

The sixth view focuses on the environmental consequences of poverty. Discussions about environmental deterioration on developed countries in the 1987 Brundland report have shifted to factors such as poverty and population density in other countries. The report emphasizes that poverty is a significant cause of environmental degradation, but in a world where poverty is widespread, environmental disasters will always be a concern (Finco, 2009, p. 2–4). Particularly in poor countries, the limited availability of alternative resources to meet the needs of their citizens leads to excessive exploitation of natural resources and the environment, exceeding the capacity of nature to renew itself (Arief, 2004, p. 2). While poverty increases environmental degradation, environmental degradation also exacerbates poverty, and there is a mutually reinforcing mechanism between these two phenomena (Duraiappah, 1996, p. 6). In poor countries, people rely more on natural resources for their livelihoods and, as a result, cause more environmental damage. Consequently, the environmental deterioration resulting from this process leads to rapid depletion of these already scarce resources, causing droughts, scarcity, reduction of forest areas, etc., directly or indirectly, leading poverty to undesirable levels. Thus, "for many countries, being rich is the best and probably the only way to have a clean environment" (Beckerman, 1992a, p. 482).

The seventh view takes into account the pressure of increasing population on the environment and argues that environmental problems will ease with a decrease in population growth rate. Especially, the decline in population growth rate in developed countries is the main factor behind this idea.

Pessimistic Approaches

There are various perspectives that do not accept the views that economic growth will improve environmental quality through various mechanisms and criticize them. These perspectives, which are more critical of optimistic views, include the following:

The first view criticizes the claim that the income elasticity of the environment is greater than one, suggesting that as countries become richer, their sensitivity to the environment will increase further. Empirical results do not confirm these claims (Kriström and Riera, 1996, p. 45), and there are countries with low income that have a higher environmental sensitivity (Broad, 1996, p. 811). While it is true that environmental sensitivity may increase proportionally more as income rises, the increase in income leads to an increase in the demand for everything. The cyclical nature of renewing products and the phenomenon of fashion turn satisfied needs into a repeating cycle of demand for many goods, and as a result, the production of these goods continues to grow dynamically, causing pollution and resource waste.

The second view argues that even if pollution per unit output decreases, if the growth rate is still higher than the rate of decline in pollution per unit output, total pollution will increase. The impact of technological change on pollution is essentially uncertain and has two effects (Lopez, 1992, p. 154): the first effect increases the efficiency of traditional production factors, and the second effect creates a deviation towards less environmentally intensive technology. The first effect is equivalent to the accumulation of traditional production factors and has a negative impact on the environment. The second effect depends on whether technological change is environmentally friendly or not, as environmentally friendly technological change reduces environmental pollution. If research and development efforts focus on technological changes that increase production factor efficiency rather than environmental technologies, the second effect will be suppressed. In this case, growth, even if it is solely due to technological change, will still pollute the environment.

The third view criticizes the optimistic view that with structural transformation in the economy, the share of the industrial sector will decrease, and the share of the service sector will increase, leading to less pollution. According to this perspective, it is not a certainty that this mechanism will work in favor of the environment. Because in low-income countries, when income increases, the share of the agricultural sector decreases first, and the share of the industrial sector increases. If strict environmental policies are not implemented, the industrial sector in low-income countries will experience growth, especially with pollution-intensive firms such as chemicals, cement, and iron and steel. Since most countries today are low-income countries, the shift from industry to the service sector in these countries will take many years. Therefore, being optimistic about this process seems unreasonable.

The fourth view emphasizes that instead of improving the sectors that heavily pollute the environment, high-income countries tend to transfer these sectors to low-income countries rather than reforming them. This situation is explained in the literature as the pollution haven hypothesis or, in some sources, as the pollution refuge hypothesis. According to the pollution haven hypothesis, under free trade, multinational companies will transfer pollution-intensive production processes to developing countries where environmental regulations are weak. These countries will become a "paradise" for pollution-intensive sectors, and developed countries will benefit from environmental quality while developing countries will lose (Temurshoev, 2006, p. 2).

Those who strongly oppose globalization argue that the increasing volume of production, consumption, and transportation will further exacerbate environmental degradation, and if stricter environmental measures are taken, it will raise concerns for governments about competitiveness and prevent the adoption of strict measures (Sturm and Ulph, 2002, p. 2).

The fifth view opposes the idea that economic growth will reduce the population growth rate and, therefore, reduce population pressure on the environment. Especially in developed countries, as the level of education and employment of women increases, fertility is directly related to these factors, which leads to a reduction in population growth rate. However, this hypothesis is not valid for all wealthy countries. For example, according to World Bank data, Uruguay has a per capita income of around 7800 dollars in 2013 and falls into the category of a poor country with a population growth rate of 0.35%. Qatar, on the other hand, is a wealthy country with a per capita income of around 60,000 dollars, but its population growth rate is around 5.6%. The increase in population rate in Uruguay is approximately 16 times that of Qatar. Therefore, the hypothesis that wealth will always reduce the population growth rate and its pressure on the environment is not always applicable.

SUSTAINABLE DEVELOPMENT AND THE ENVIRONMENT

The concept of development is much broader than just economic growth; it is not merely an economic phenomenon. Development involves the reorganization and harmonization of the entire economic and social system, encompassing improvements in income and production, as well as changes and improvements in institutional, social, managerial structures, and even traditions and customs. Todaro and Smith (2009) have identified at least three objectives that economic and social development should carry for all societies:

- Increasing existing opportunities and expanding basic needs such as food, shelter, health, and protection.
- Enhancing the quality of life through safer jobs and the development of cultural and human values.
- Liberating individuals and nations from dependence on others and from ignorance and poverty, thus expanding current social choices and economic limitations.

Starting from the second half of the 20th century, economists, realizing the drawbacks of pursuing growth as the sole objective and the policies based on this pursuit, have begun to adopt an approach that considers the costs of growth as well. The concept of economic development has become more critical than economic growth, and the issue of sustainability in development has gained priority. During this process, in 1962, Rachel Louise Carson focused on environmental pollution in her work titled "Silent Spring," drawing attention to the damages to the environment caused by existing industrial practices. In 1972, the "Limits to Growth" report, published by the Club of Rome, brought the relationship between economic development and the environment into sharp focus, emphasizing that humanity would face significant threats due to scarcity and pollution if current development policies continued. Similarly, in 1973, E. F. Schumacher highlighted the problems caused by the prevailing thought structure, stating in his work "Small is Beautiful" that natural resources form a significant part of the capital used in the economy but are not considered as a cost factor, and he emphasized the concept of economic continuity. Later, with the report known as the Brundtland Report titled "Our Common Future," the old traditional concept of growth was abandoned, and the discussion of sustainable economic growth and development became more widespread (Bozloğan, 2005, p. 1015).

Sustainable development, as viewed from different perspectives and indicators of human well-being, includes the Economic Dimension (Economic Sustainability) which concerns health, the availability of natural resources, quality environment, biological diversity, and more. The Environmental Dimension (Environmental Sustainability) is related to the availability of resources and the quality of the environment. The Social Dimension (Social Sustainability) involves human capital, cultural capital, social peace, the existence of socio-political institutions, equality, justice, and more (Munasinghe, 2007). These three fundamental dimensions of sustainable development are illustrated in Figure 2.

As shown in Figure 2, the composition of the social, economic, and environmental dimensions leads to sustainability. There are various definitions of sustainable development, but the most common one is from the report "Our Common Future". According to this definition, sustainable development is the ability to meet the needs of the present without compromising the ability of future generations to meet their own needs. With this definition, sustainable development implies meeting the various activities that enhance the quality of life and well-being of living beings, including humans, without endangering the limited resources of the world. It also involves understanding that the universe consists of interconnected and interdependent living and non-living objects, making it a multidimensional perspective that requires efforts to maintain and not disrupt this system.

Figure 2. three pillars of sustainable development

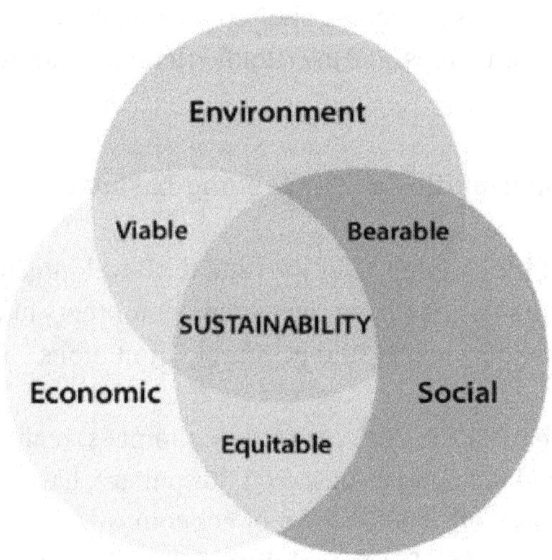

From an economic perspective, sustainable development aims to continue the production of goods and services without causing financial constraints on the country, such as administrative and external debt, and without causing sectoral imbalances that could harm the agriculture and/or industrial sectors. From an environmental standpoint, it aims to preserve biodiversity, maintain the current state of the atmosphere, and avoid excessive use of resources, while respecting the ideal values of the ecosystem components and not causing harm by exceeding reasonable limits when necessary. Social sustainability, on the other hand, aims to improve aspects such as social equality, democracy, political accountability, access to adequate health and education services, and raise them to better standards (Harris, 2000, p. 5-6).

Sustainability encompasses two main approaches in its context. The first approach is ***the Weak Sustainability***, which assumes that resources can be substituted for one another, and it considers to what extent the society preserves its stock of resources. The second approach is ***the Strong Sustainability***, which acknowledges a complementary relationship between natural resources and other resources and focuses on the composition of the preserved resource stock (Cole, 1999, p. 90).

If the concept of sustainable development implies a state of benefit that does not diminish over time, it needs to be examined in both contexts. Since benefits are associated with consumption, Weak Sustainability implies a constant level of consumption or utility over time, whereas Strong Sustainability implies an increasing level of benefit over time (Hamilton, 1995, p. 393). This distinction is particularly applicable when categorizing resources into Natural Capital, Human Capital, and Manufactured Capital. The Weak Sustainability approach is based on the substitutability feature, suggesting that a decrease in natural capital can be compensated by an increase in manufactured or human capital. On the other hand, the Strong Sustainability approach is built on the belief that there is no such compensatory mechanism among resources. Especially for natural resources, which lack substitutability, irreparable losses may occur, so natural resources need to be preserved (Pearce and Barbier, 2000, p. 21).

Regarding the relationship between economic growth and the environment, the Weak Sustainability perspective implies that economic growth and a quality environment can coexist. The Strong Sustainability approach advocates for a reduction in the volume of economic output for the sake of a healthy environment. This is because supporters of this approach doubt the idea that growth can initially pollute the environment and then reverse the process (Cole, 1999, p. 91). For example, Rees (1990) states that the sustainable development approach has been assimilated into the mainstream politics and has drifted away from its primary aim of environmental sustainability.

Hartwick-Solow Approach

The issue of natural resources, which sustainable development emphasizes with great sensitivity, has not been given much attention in the Neoclassical economic approach. In the Neoclassical economic approach, there is no special reason to preserve natural resources. The best-known principle in this regard is derived from the works of Solow (1974, 1986) and Hartwick (1977, 1978a), and it is referred to as the Hartwick-Solow approach. In fact, during those years, the concept of sustainability did not exist, and the attempt of the Neoclassical growth theory to explain non-renewable natural resources as a production factor aligns this concept with Neoclassical economics (Dietz and Neumayer, 2007, p. 621).

The Hartwick rule, also known as this approach, assumes that consumption can remain constant or increase with the depletion of non-renewable resources. However, for this to happen, the income generated from these resources needs to be reinvested in renewable resources (Harris, 2000, p. 9). For example, if forests are cut down, and factories are built in their place, and this process increases economic value, there is no problem as long as social welfare does not decrease over time. In the common definition, welfare level is associated with consumption, so intergenerational sustainability means maintaining the total capital stock with the potential to produce economic goods (Gowdy, 2005, p. 212).

The prominent feature of the Hartwick-Solow approach is its focus on the total capital stock and its assumption of substitutability between natural capital (natural resources) and human-made capital. According to this view, sustainable development is concerned with maintaining the total capital stock. It does not concern itself with the conditions of natural capital, human capital, and human-made capital, which are all measurable components of the total capital. By deducting depreciation or capital consumption from the total gross value of all measured capital types, the total net capital investment is calculated, and this calculation can be generalized as a weak sustainability rule (Dietz and Neumayer, 2007, p. 623). This approach is also referred to as weak sustainability (Hussen, 2004, p. 272).

In the Hartwick-Solow approach, not only is substitutability between resources not allowed, but also transferring natural capital to human-made capital results in a net value greater than the previous state; it becomes an ethical obligation to do so. Otherwise, capital will be used inefficiently, and the well-being of future generations will be needlessly worsened (Gowdy, 2005, p. 212).

Solow (1974) demonstrated that with limited resources, a constant level of consumption could be sustained. However, for this to hold true, the elasticity of substitution between other factors should be greater than that of natural resources, and the production function should be Cobb-Douglas (Hamilton, 1995, p. 394). Hamilton (1995) showed that the Hartwick rule is not applicable in cases where the elasticity of substitution between natural and other resources is very low. In such cases, ultimately, consumption will have to be reduced, and sustainability will not be possible under this rule (Lopez, 2006, p. 65).

For the Hartwick rule to operate beyond the elasticity of substitution, there must be an abundance of natural resources, and the increase in technological development in natural capital productivity must exceed the rate of depletion of these resources (Dietz and Neumayer, 2007, p. 623). Additionally, the derivation of the rule involves serious assumptions. Considering that preferences and resource ownership are determined externally, market prices accurately reflect the social values of resources over time, and a perpetually competitive market prevails, it is more appropriate to consider this rule as an intergenerational efficiency condition rather than a sustainability rule (Hussen, 2004, p. 273).

In the intergenerational efficiency approach, the discount rate plays a crucial role as intergenerational welfare levels are compared. For example, a positive discount rate reflects a preference for consuming in the present rather than the future. In this context, the consumption decisions of the current generation can create an ethical problem, as they will affect the welfare of future generations. However, in the Hartwick-Solow approach, the impact of a positive discount rate is balanced by technological advancements, making it not appear as a significant problem and not considered unethical. Some economists and ecologists argue against the validity of a positive discount rate and advocate questioning the Hartwick-Solow approach concerning the welfare of future generations and its ethical implications (Hussen, 2004, p. 274).

Ecological Economics Approach

Ecological economics is an interdisciplinary field that began to gain prominence in the 1980s, exploring the mutual dependence and interaction between ecosystems and the economy. It offers an integrated perspective on the environment-economy interaction by examining economic activities, ecology, ethics, social sciences, and other natural resources as a whole.

With the increasing awareness and threat posed by environmental problems, Rachel Carson's (1962) work on environmental pollution titled 'Silent Spring' and Barry Commoner's (1971) work, 'The Closing Circle,' which focused on the environmental damages caused by current industrial practices, along with the publication of 'Limits to Growth' by the Club of Rome in 1972, showing how population growth, agricultural activities, depletion of natural resources, industrial activities, and pollution would limit economic growth and negatively impact the world (Kula, 1999, p. 136), are considered fundamental pillars in the emergence of the ecological economics approach (Czech, 2009, p. 2).

Kenneth Boulding's (1966) work, 'The Economics of the Coming Spaceship Earth,' is also one of the significant milestones of the ecological economics approach (Hussen, 2004, p. 249). In his work, Boulding emphasized that with increasing population, there is a limited space in nature for natural resources, industrial and agricultural wastes, and he explained why the economic goal of continuous growth should not be pursued. Boulding metaphorically defined the world as a spaceship with four sectors: producers, consumers, natural resources, and waste, and highlighted that while natural resources are diminishing, waste is becoming an increasing threat. He argued that survival depends on managing natural resources and waste (Kula, 1998, p. 130-131). Boulding also described the economic system of that time as a 'cowboy economy' which exploits the environment without facing any scarcity issue regarding natural resources, and he criticized the belief that production and consumption are good things in this period as long as natural resources' destruction and pollution are not considered. Moreover, he questioned the measurement of economic success solely based on the quantity of goods and services produced, without considering the depletion of natural resources and pollution (Hussen, 2004, p. 250).

Another significant figure in the ecological economics approach is Nicholas Georgescu-Roegen, who tried to explain economic growth through the lens of physics, particularly thermodynamics. Georgescu-Roegen's (1971) book, 'The Entropy Law and the Economic Process,' provides a strong, logical, and critical assessment of traditional economic views on scarcity and growth based on the laws of thermodynamics (Hussen, 2004, p. 251). Georgescu-Roegen strengthens his arguments with the laws of thermodynamics.

Thermodynamics deals with heat and energy and has two main laws. The first law states that matter and energy cannot be created or destroyed; thus, in a closed system, the total quantity of matter and energy remains constant. The second law, known as the entropy law, states that the entropy of a system will not decrease, but rather increase or remain constant during any thermodynamic process. Entropy can be defined as the energy that cannot be transformed or as a measure of disorder. In this context, an increase in entropy reflects an increase in disorder. The first law essentially implies that economic activities cannot harm the energy stock, but the second law shows that energy will not undergo a quantitative change but will undergo a qualitative change. Therefore, economic activities do not destroy available energy in nature; they transform it into unusable energy. For example, a piece of coal in nature has usable energy and thus has low entropy. However, when coal is burned, it turns into smoke, heat, and ash, becoming unusable energy. Hence, the second law signifies a limit in nature's resources for the economy (Cole, 1999, p. 89). Georgescu-Roegen's view that economic activities transform natural resources into unusable energy is a critique of the notion of unlimited substitution between human-made capital and natural capital based on the neoclassical growth paradigm (Hussen, 2004, p. 252).

Ecological economics differs from traditional environmental economics, which is based on neoclassical welfare theory and microeconomics, as it considers the economy as an integral part of the ecosystem. While traditional environmental economics focuses on the economic impacts of national or regional environmental policies and includes cost-benefit analyses of alternative environmental policies addressing air pollution, water pollution, hazardous waste, solid waste, and global warming, ecological economics treats the economy as an integral part of the ecosystem (Van Den Bergh, 2001, p. 15).

In conclusion, the Hartwick-Solow approach emphasizes maintaining the total capital stock to achieve sustainability, with a focus on substitutability between natural and human-made capital. On the other hand, the ecological economics approach offers a more comprehensive examination of the interaction between the economy and the ecosystem, considering natural resources and ecological balance in the broader context of the economic system.

Ecological economics is a much more comprehensive and realistic field of study. Therefore, it is clear that ecological economics and environmental economics are different areas within economics, with ecological economics embracing the concept of strong sustainability, which means that natural capital (resources) cannot be fully substituted with human-made capital.

Environmental economics focuses more on macro and micro analyses, studying the monetary effects of resource scarcity and environmental degradation on welfare. On the other hand, ecological economics is an approach that analyzes the carrying capacity and self-renewal capacity of ecosystems, considering threshold values and encompassing everything related to life beyond environmental economics. It can be seen as a pioneer of the sustainability approach.

The ecological perspective argues that the quality of life depends on the quality of the environment, and thus preserving the quality of the environment and its assimilative capacity are vital. Any deterioration in these aspects directly affects society's level of well-being. Therefore, for ecological economics, sustainable development means achieving maximum consumption without reducing net welfare, environmental quality, and natural resource stock. However, this condition requires control over consumption and population (Harris, 2000, p. 12).

The sustainability approach of ecological economics aims to dematerialize the economy, reducing pressure on the carrying capacity of the natural system to preserve nature. Consequently, ecological sustainability is less concerned with other socio-economic issues (Bartelmus, 2008, p. 29). This sets it apart from the traditional approach, which is based on consumption-based primitive sustainability and has definite boundaries (Harris, 2000, p. 13). Moreover, the ecological economics approach differs from the traditional one in the following principles:

- Ecological economics sees the economy as a subset of the natural ecosystem and is interested in the nature of matter and energy transformation between the ecosystem and the economy.
- Production, which is based on the transformation of matter and energy, is considered an economic issue. The natural ecosystem is the ultimate source of all inputs to the economic system.
- Ecological economics uses ecological principles and thermodynamics to emphasize the critical role of natural resources in the economic process, focusing on production that involves the transformation of matter and energy.
- All inputs in the production process are complements rather than substitutes. Natural resources cannot be replaced by physical capital and/or labor, making the depletion of natural resources irreparable. Together with the laws of thermodynamics, this is an objection to the neoclassical economic argument of optimistic technology.
- Under current conditions, the volume of economic activities puts excessive pressure on relatively limited natural resources in the global ecosystem.

The ecological economic approach embraces a set of thoughts and actions beyond the traditional economic understanding. The idea that the market can solve everything may be valid only for market goods, but the presence of non-market goods and services that enhance human well-being renders this approach ineffective. For instance, the market cannot determine how much clean air, water, wetlands, or healthy forests we need. Therefore, certain principles should be considered in formulating general policies. Daly and Farley (2004) list these principles as follows:

- Economic policy should always have multiple objectives, and each independent policy goal should have an independent instrument.
- Policies should strive to achieve the required degree of control with minimal sacrifice of freedom and change at the micro level.
- Policies concerning biophysical environments can have a margin of error.
- Policies should always consider that we are facing data starting conditions throughout history.
- Policies should be adaptable to changing conditions.
- The scope of the policy-making institution should be consistent with the scope of the causes and effects of the problem the policy addresses.
- Each of these principles has a different level of importance and priority in achieving sustainability, equitable distribution, and efficient allocation goals (Czech, 2009, 11). Daly and Farley (2004) explain the priority of which policy to adopt as follows:

Ecological economics has three main goals, and therefore it needs three basic instruments. The efficient allocation goal requires the market instrument, at least for private goods. The market does not work for public goods. Sustainable scale requires putting a social or collective constraint on total output to preserve the ecosystem's absorptive and regenerative capacity. The equitable distribution goal requires putting some social constraints on market-generated inequality. It is evident that the market cannot achieve sustainable scale and equitable distribution. Moreover, without achieving these, the market cannot ensure efficient allocation either. Therefore, in the ranking of policy instruments, the market comes in third place. Regarding the priority of the scale and distribution problems, it makes sense to place sustainability in the first place. This is because a constraining scale usually means that freely available natural resources and services must be treated as scarce economic goods.

In conclusion, ecological economics provides a more holistic perspective and approach beyond the traditional economic framework. It recognizes the limitations of the market and focuses on achieving sustainability, equitable distribution, and efficient allocation by employing various principles and instruments.

CONCLUSION

A high-quality environment provides non-renewable natural resources such as coal, oil, natural gas, iron, and copper, as well as renewable natural resources like water, fish, timber, wind, and sunlight. It also includes a waste pool where solid, liquid, and gaseous waste generated from economic activities can be disposed of. Additionally, the environment offers opportunities for relaxation, healing, and pleasant experiences through natural beauty. It provides vital information within the framework of genetic plans and behavioral observations for both plant and animal life. Biogeochemical cycles help in cleaning water and air, and they play a crucial role in maintaining climate stability. However, the relentless pursuit of unlimited economic growth and wealth has started to limit these opportunities. The main reason for this limitation is undoubtedly the economic system that fails to consider the opportunities provided by the environment.

The environment supports economic activities by providing necessary raw materials and other inputs for production and consumption. However, these production and consumption processes also lead to the generation of waste that negatively affects the environment's quality. The relationship between economics and the environment goes beyond the approach of the main economic currents. The degradation of the environment is directly linked to economic activities, and achieving the ultimate goal of economics becomes difficult due to misguided strategies that do not take into account the opportunity cost of achieving these goals. Nevertheless, within the mainstream classical and neoclassical economic currents, the environment has not been adequately considered.

Starting from the second half of the 20th century, economists who realized the drawbacks caused and to be caused by the sole pursuit of growth and the policies carried out in that direction began to adopt an approach that takes into account the costs of growth. Instead of focusing solely on economic growth, the concept of economic development took priority, and the sustainability of development became a major concern. Economic Dimension (Economic Sustainability) focuses on human welfare in terms of various conditions and indicators, Environmental Dimension (Environmental Sustainability) focuses on aspects such as health, non-depletion of natural resources, quality environment, biological diversity, etc., and Social Dimension (Social Sustainability) focuses on human capital, cultural capital, social peace and harmony, the existence of socio-political institutions, equality, justice, etc. These three dimensions form the three fundamental elements of sustainable development. In the context of sustainability, two types of approaches are noteworthy. The first one, Weak Sustainability, takes into account to what extent the society preserves its stock of resources based on the assumption that resources can be substituted for each other. The second one, Strong Sustainability, highlights the composition of the preserved stock of resources based on the understanding that there is a complementary relationship between natural resources and other resources.

By the 1970s, neoclassical economic thought gave birth to disciplines directly focusing on the environment, such as environmental economics and natural resource economics, which increased sensitivity towards the environment. However, these disciplines mainly dealt with market-based solutions and internalization of environmental costs. Thus, they did not make the mutual dependency of the environment and economics a priority and placed it in the background. In the 1980s, the Ecological Economics approach emerged as a more comprehensive and environmentally sensitive approach. Environmental economics investigates the economic effects of national or regional environmental policies and includes benefit-cost analyses of alternative environmental policies against air pollution, water pollution, toxic wastes, solid wastes, and global warming. While environmental economics is a subfield that deals with economic environmental issues, ecological economics considers the economy as a sub-component of the ecosystem. In this regard, ecological economics and environmental economics represent different fields of economics, and ecological economics rejects the proposition that natural capital (resources) can be replaced with human-made capital.

In summary, the relationship between the environment and the economy is more comprehensively addressed through the approach of sustainable development. The contributions of the environment to economic activities and human welfare should be considered, and efforts should be made to manage natural resources sustainably. The ecological economics approach, which emphasizes the inseparable connection between the environment and the economy, should be embraced to protect the environment and achieve sustainable development.

REFERENCES

Arief, A. Y. (2004). *Poverty and Environmental Degradation: Searching for Theoretical Linkages*. (Working Paper in Economics and Development Studies). Equitable Policy. http://www.equitablepolicy.org/

Asafu-Adjaye, J. (2000). Environmental Economics for Non-Economists. World Scientific Publishing Co. Pte. Ltd. Singapore.

Asafu-Adjaye, J. (2000). The Relationship Between Energy Consumption, Energy Prices and Economic Growth: Time Series Evidence From Asian Developing Countries. *Energy Economics*, *22*(6), 615–625. doi:10.1016/S0140-9883(00)00050-5

Ayres, R. (1997). Comments on Georgescu-Roegen. *Ecological Economics*, *22*(3), 285–287. doi:10.1016/S0921-8009(97)00082-7

Ayres, R. (2000). Commentary on the Utility of the Ecological Footprint Concept. *Ecological Economics*, *32*, 347–349.

Ayres, R. U., Van Den Berg, J. C. J. M., Lindenberger, D., & Warr, B. (2013). The Underestimated Contribution of Energy to Economic Growth. *Structural Change and Economic Dynamics*, *27*, 79–88. doi:10.1016/j.strueco.2013.07.004

Baldwin, R. (1995). Does sustainability require growth? In I. Goldin & L. Alan Winters (Eds.), *Economics Of Sustainable Growth* (pp. 51–77). Cambridge University Press.

Barkley, P. W., & David, W. S. (1972). *Economic Growth and Environmental Decay: The Solution Becomes The Problem*. Harcourt Brace Jovanovich.

Bartelmus, P. (2008). *Quantitative Eco-nomics: How Sustainable Are Our Economies?* Springer. doi:10.1007/978-1-4020-6966-6

Beckerman, W. (1992a). *Economic Development and the Environment — Conflict or Complementarity?* (Working Paper No. 961). World Bank.

Beckerman, W. (1992b). Economic Growth and the Environment: Whose Growth? Whose Environment? *World Development*, *20*(4), 481–496. doi:10.1016/0305-750X(92)90038-W

Bozlağan, R. (2005). Sürdürülebilir Gelişme Düşüncesinin Tarihsel Arka Planı. *Sosyal Siyaset Konferansları Dergisi*, (50), 1012–1028.

Broad, R. (1994). The Poor and Environment: Friends or Foes? *World Development*, *22*(6), 811–822. doi:10.1016/0305-750X(94)90055-8

Christoff, P. (1996). Ecological Modernisation, Ecological Modernities. *Environmental Politics*, *5*(3), 476–500. doi:10.1080/09644019608414283

Colander, D. C. (1993). *Microeconomics*. Irwin Publishes.

Cole, M. A. (1999). Limits to Growth, Sustainable Development and Environmental Kuznets Curves: An Examination of the Environmental Impact of Economic Development. *Sustainable Development (Bradford)*, *7*(2), 87–97. doi:10.1002/(SICI)1099-1719(199905)7:2<87::AID-SD102>3.0.CO;2-5

Common, M., & Stagl, S. (2005). *Ecological Economics: An Introduction*. Cambridge University Press. doi:10.1017/CBO9780511805547

Czech, B. (2009). *Ecological Economics*. Center for the Advancement of Steady State Economy. http://steadystate.org/wp-content/uploads/Czech_ Ecological_Economics.pdf

Daly, H. (1990). Towards Some Operational Principles of Sustainable Development. *Ecological Economics*, *2*(1), 1–6. doi:10.1016/0921-8009(90)90010-R

Daly, H. (2007). *Ecological Economics and Sustainable Development: Selected Essays of Herman Daly*. Edward Elgar. doi:10.4337/9781847206947

Daly, H. E., & Farley, J. (2004). *Ecological Economics: Principles and Applications*. Island Press.

Dietz, S., & Neumayer, E. (2007). Weak and Strong Sustainability in the SEEA: Concepts and Measurements. *Ecological Economics*, *61*(4), 617–626. doi:10.1016/j.ecolecon.2006.09.007

Dietz, T. E. A. R., & York, R. (2007). Driving the Human Ecological Footprint. *Frontiers in Ecology and the Environment*, *5*(1), 13–18. doi:10.1890/1540-9295(2007)5[13:DTHEF]2.0.CO;2

Duraiappah, A. (1996). *Poverty and Environmental Degradation: a Literature Review and Analysis*. (CREED Working Paper Series No: 8). CREED. http://www.ce.cmu. edu

Enders, W. (2009). *Applied econometric Time Series* (3rd ed.). Wiley.

Engin, B. (2007). *Avrupa Birliği Özelinde Çevre Politikalarının Etkinliği*. İstanbul Üniversitesi Sosyal Bilimler Enstitüsü İktisat Ana Bilim Dalı. Yayımlanmamış Doktora Tezi.

Ertürk, H. (1998). Çevre Bilimlerine Giriş (3. Baskı). Bursa:Vipaş Yayınları

Finco, M. V. A. (2009). Poverty and Environment Linkages: A Vicious Circle Hypothesis Analysis in the Brazilian Amazon Region. *International Science Conference on the Human Dimensions of Global environmental Change*. Bonn.

Friedman, B. (2005). *The Moral Consequences of Economic Growth*. Alfred A. Knopf.

Gowdy, J. M. (2004). Toward a New Welfare foundation for Sustainability. *Ecological Economics*, *55*, 211–222.

Grossman, G. M., & Helpman, E. (1994). Endogenous Innovation in the Theory of Growth. *The Journal of Economic Perspectives*, *8*(1), 23–44. doi:10.1257/jep.8.1.23

Grossman, M., & Krueger, A. B. (1995). Economic Growth and the Environment. *The Quarterly Journal of Economics*, *110*(2), 353–377. doi:10.2307/2118443

Güney, E. (2004). *Çevre Sorunları*. Ankara: Nobel yayıncılık.

Hamilton, K. (1995). Sustainable Development, the Hartwick Rule and Optimal Growth. *Environmental and Resource Economics*, *5*(4), 393–411. doi:10.1007/BF00691576

Harris, M. (2000). *Basic Principles of Sustainable Development*. (Working Paper). Global Development and Environment Institute. https://notendur.hi.is/bdavids/UAU101/Readings/Harris_2000_Sustainable_development.pdf.

Hartwick, J. M. (1977). Intergenerational Equity and the Investing of Rents from Exhaustible Resources. *The American Economic Review*, *67*(5), 972–974.

Hartwick, J. M. (1978a). Substitution Among Exhaustible Resources and Intergenerational Equity. *The Review of Economic Studies*, *45*(2), 347–354. doi:10.2307/2297349

Hartwick, J. M. (1978b). Investing Returns From Depleting Renewable Resource Stocks and Intergenerational Equity. *Economics Letters*, *1*(1), 85–88. doi:10.1016/0165-1765(78)90102-7

Hepburn, C. & Bowen, A. (2012). *Prosperity With Growth: Economic Growth, Climate Change and Environmental Limits*, (Working Paper No: 109). Centre For Climate Change Economics and Policy. http://www.lse.ac.uk/ GranthamInstitute/wp-content/uploads/2014/02/WP93-prosperity-with-growth-climate-change.pdf

Hueting, R. (1991). Correcting National Income For Environmental Losses: A Practical Solution For A Theoretical Dilemma. In R. Costanza (Ed.), *Ecological Economics: The Science and Management of Sustainability*. Colombia University Pres.

Hussen, A. M. (2004). *Principles of Environmental Economics* (2nd ed.). Routledge. doi:10.4324/9780203507421

Hyman, D. N. (1999). *Public Finance: A Contemporary Application of Theory To Policy* (6th ed.). The Dryden Press.

Janicke, M., Binder, M., & Mönch, H. (1997). Dirty Industries: Patterns of Change in Industrial Countries. *Environmental and Resource Economics*, *9*(4), 467–491. doi:10.1007/BF02441762

Kriström, B., & Riera, P. (1996). Is The Income Elasticity of Environmental Improvements Less Than One? *Environmental and Resource Economics*, *7*(1), 45–55. doi:10.1007/BF00420426

Kula, E. (1998). *History of Environmental Economic Thought*. Routledge.

Lomborg, B. (2001). *The Skeptical Environmentalist: Measuring the Real State of the World*. Cambridge University Press. doi:10.1017/CBO9781139626378

Lopez, R. (1992). The Environment As A Factor of Production: The Economic Growth and Trade Policy Linkages. In P. Low (ed.): *International Trade and Environmet*, World Bank.

Lopez, R. (1994). The Environment as a Factor of Production: The Effects of Economic Growth and Trade Liberalization. *Journal of Environmental Economics and Management*, *27*(2), 163–184. doi:10.1006/jeem.1994.1032

Lopez, R., & Toman, M. A. (2006). *Economic Development and Environmental Sustainability*. Oxford University Press. doi:10.1093/0199298009.001.0001

Malthus, T. (1798). An Essay on the Principle of Population, London, UK.

Mill, J. S. (1848). *Principles of Political Economy with some of their Applications to Social Philosophy*. Oxford University Press.

Munasinghe, M. (2007). *Making Development More Sustainable*. http://www.eoearth.org/article/Sustainable_development_triangle

Nordhaus, W. (2007b). To Tax or Not to Tax: Alternative Approaches to Slowing Global Warming. *Review of Environmental Economics and Policy*, *1*(1), 26–45. doi:10.1093/reep/rem008

Nordhaus, W., Stavins, R. N., & Weitzman, M. L. (1992). Lethal Model 2: The Limits to Growth Revisited. *Brookings Papers on Economic Activity*, *23*(2), 1–60. doi:10.2307/2534581 PMID:12287537

Pearce, D., & Barbier, E. (2000). *Blueprint for a Sustainable Economy*. Earthscan Publications. doi:10.4324/9781849774239

Pearce, D. W. And R. K. Turner. (1990). Economics of Natural Resources And The Environment, Hertfordshire: Harvester Wheatseaf Publishes.

Pepper, D. (1998). Sustainable Development and Ecological Modernization: A Radical Homocentric Perspective. *Sustainable Development (Bradford)*, *6*(1), 1–7. doi:10.1002/(SICI)1099-1719(199803)6:1<1::AID-SD83>3.0.CO;2-8

Rees, W. E. (1990). The Ecology of Eustainable Development. *The Ecologist*, *20*(1), 18–23.

Rees, W. E. (1992). Ecological Footprints and Appropriated Carrying Capacity: What Urban Economics Leaves Out. *Environment and Urbanization*, *4*(2), 121–130. doi:10.1177/095624789200400212

Reyes, R. C. (2011). The Green Solow Model with Natural Resources Constraint: A Theoretical Note. *DLSU Business and Economics Review*, *21*(1), 111–116.

Simon, J. (1980). Resources, Population, Environment: An Oversupply of False Bad News. *Science*, *208*(4451), 1431–1437. doi:10.1126cience.7384784 PMID:7384784

Simon, J. (1981). *The Ultimate Resource*. Robertson.

Solow, R. (1956). A Contribution to the Theory of Economic Growth. *The Quarterly Journal of Economics*, *70*(1), 65–94. doi:10.2307/1884513

Solow, R. M. (1974). Intergenerational equity and exhaustible resources. *The Review of Economic Studies*, *14*, 29–45. doi:10.2307/2296370

Solow, R. M. (1986). On the Intergenerational Allocation of Natural Resources. *The Scandinavian Journal of Economics*, *88*(1), 141–149. doi:10.2307/3440280

Sönmez, S. (1987). *Kamu Ekonomisi Teorisi: Kamu Harcamalarında Etkinlik Arayışı*. Teori Yayınları.

Stern, D. (1997). Van Den Berg: Ecological Economics. *Economic Journal (London)*, *107*(445), 1905–1907.

Sturm, D., & Ulph, A. (2002). "Environment, Trade, Political Economy And Imperfect Information – A Survey". Discussion Papers in Economics and Econometrics, http://www.soton.ac.uk/ (23.02.2015).

Temurshoev, U. (2006). "Pollution Haven Hypothesis or Factor Endownment Hypothesis: Theory and Empirical Examination for US and China". Charles University Center for Economic Research and Graduate Education, Working paper series. http://iweb.cerge-ei.cz/pdf/wp/Wp292.pdf (23.02.2015).

Tinbergen, J., & Hueting, R. (1992). GNP and Market Prices. In R. Goodland, H. Daly, & S. El Serafy (Eds.), *Population, Technology and Lifestyle: the Transition to Sustainability* (pp. 52–62). Island Press.

Todaro, M. P., & Smith, S. C. (2009). *Economic Development* (10th ed.). Addison-Wesley.

Van Den Bergh, J. C. J. M. (1996). *Ecological Economics and Sustainable Development: Theory, Methods and Applications*. Edward Elgar.

Van Den Bergh, J. C. J. M. (2001). Ecological Economics: Themes, Approaches, and Differences with Environmental Economics. *Regional Environmental Change*, *2*(1), 13–23. doi:10.1007101130000020

Van den Bergh, J. C. J. M., & Grazi, F. (2010). On the Policy Relevance Of Ecological Footprints. *Environmental Science & Technology*, *44*(13), 4843–4844. doi:10.1021/es1003582 PMID:20441197

Van den Bergh, J. C. J. M., & Grazi, F. (2014). Ecological Footprint Policy: Land Use as an Environmental Indicator. *Journal of Industrial Ecology*, *18*(1), 10–19. doi:10.1111/jiec.12045

Van den Bergh, J. C. J. M., & Verbruggen, H. (1999). Spatial Sustainability, Trade And Indicators: An Evaluation of the Ecological Footprint. *Ecological Economics*, *29*(1), 61–72. doi:10.1016/S0921-8009(99)00032-4

William, N. (2007a). *The Challenge of Global Warming: Economic Models and Environmental Policy. Yale*. Yale University.

ENDNOTE

1 This work was derived from the PhD dissertation entitled "The Environment in Economic Growth Models: An Application Based on Ecological Footprint," under the supervision of Professor Ekrem Erdem at Erciyes University Institute of Social Science.

Chapter 7
The Contribution of Waste Management Social Enterprises to the SDGs:
Exploring Case Study Organisations From the Global South

Sara Calvo
Open University, UK

ABSTRACT

Waste management is a global challenge that demands innovative solutions for its effective and sustainable resolution. In recent years, the emergence of waste management social enterprises has garnered significant attention. This chapter explores how effective waste management social enterprises (WAMSEs) align with and support the SDGs, emphasizing the importance of responsible waste management in fostering sustainable development using case study examples from the Global South. Six case study organisations from Asia, Africa, and Latin America have been selected to explore the impact of these initiatives in the SDGs. What emerged from the findings is that WAMSEs' motivations, operations, and organisational strategies contribute to the SDGs in the Global South.

INTRODUCTION

Waste management is a global challenge that demands innovative solutions for its effective and sustainable resolution (Sanchez-Molina and Iniesta-Bonillo, 2020). In recent years, the emergence of waste management social enterprises (WAMSEs) has garnered significant attention (Hermann and Oels, 2020; Mirkhani et al, 2020). These enterprises combine the principles of environmental responsibility with a strong commitment to social impact, presenting a promising avenue for addressing both waste issues and societal challenges (Khalili and Yusoff, 2020). The Sustainable Development Goals (SDGs), established by the United Nations, represent a global agenda to address pressing social, economic, and

DOI: 10.4018/979-8-3693-1297-1.ch007

environmental challenges by 2030. Social enterprises, entities that blend business approaches with social and environmental objectives, have gained prominence for their unique ability to contribute to the SDGs (Meadows and Bruijn, 2020).

Waste management is a critical aspect of modern society that plays a pivotal role in achieving the Sustainable Development Goals (SDGs) set forth by the United Nations. SDGs are a comprehensive global framework designed to address various social, economic, and environmental challenges and create a more sustainable and equitable world by 2030. Waste management, as a cross-cutting issue, intersects with multiple SDGs and significantly contributes to their achievement.

WAMSEs in the Global South are pivotal in addressing the multifaceted challenges of waste management while making substantial contributions to the Sustainable Development Goals. These enterprises not only promote responsible consumption and production but also create job opportunities, enhance access to clean water and sanitation, and foster social inclusion. As urbanization and environmental concerns continue to grow in the Global South, the role of waste management social enterprises becomes increasingly significant. By combining economic viability with social and environmental responsibility, these enterprises serve as exemplars of how innovative solutions can drive sustainable development in regions facing complex challenges. To further advance these efforts, it is essential for governments, NGOs, and the private sector to collaborate in supporting and scaling WAMSEs, ultimately contributing to a more equitable and sustainable future for the Global South and the world.

This chapter explores how effective WAMSEs align with and support the SDGs, emphasising the importance of responsible waste management in fostering sustainable development using case study examples from the Global South. Six case study organisations from Asia, Africa and Latin America have been selected to explore the impact of these initiatives in the Agenda 2030 and the SDGs.

THE RISE OF WASTE MANAGEMENT SOCIAL ENTERPRISES

WAMSEs are organisations that prioritize both environmental sustainability and social welfare as core elements of their mission. They operate at the intersection of environmental stewardship, economic development, and community engagement (Cohen, 2019). WAMSEs represent a promising pathway toward addressing the global waste crisis while concurrently advancing social well-being. Their holistic approach to environmental sustainability and social impact demonstrates the potential for businesses to be agents of positive change. As these enterprises continue to innovate and expand, they inspire a shift in societal values towards responsible consumption, waste reduction, and community empowerment (Bull, 2007). To fully realize their potential, it is crucial for governments, investors, and consumers to support and collaborate with these enterprises, creating a more sustainable and equitable world for all (Chiu and Wuepper, 2021). These enterprises have gained prominence due to several factors:

Sustainability Concerns: Growing environmental concerns, such as climate change, pollution, and resource depletion, have elevated the importance of responsible waste management. Social enterprises have emerged as proactive agents of change by integrating sustainable waste practices into their operations.

Social Impact: Addressing social issues, including poverty, unemployment, and community well-being, is a fundamental aspect of social enterprises. By creating job opportunities, empowering marginalized communities, and improving local living conditions, waste management social enterprises contribute to broader social development goals.

Innovation: Social enterprises often bring fresh perspectives and innovative approaches to waste management. They leverage technology, creative recycling solutions, and community-driven initiatives to optimize waste collection, processing, and disposal.

WAMSEs hold several key significances including local economic development as these enterprises create job opportunities, particularly in economically disadvantaged areas, by establishing waste collection and processing centers (De Araujo et al, 2020). They empower individuals with employment, training, and income-generation opportunities. WAMSEs also foster community involvement by encouraging responsible waste disposal and recycling. Through educational programs and outreach, they promote environmental awareness and behaviour change. By implementing sustainable practices like recycling and waste-to-energy technologies, these enterprises reduce the burden on landfills and limit resource depletion. This contributes to the conservation of natural resources and minimizes environmental degradation. Moreover, many WAMSEs prioritize hiring from marginalized or vulnerable populations, including individuals with disabilities or those who face discrimination in the job market (Duflo, 2012). This promotes social inclusion and diversity. These enterprises often pioneer sustainable waste management practices, setting examples for both the public and private sectors. They encourage responsible consumption and production, aligning with global sustainability goals (De Araujo et al, 2020).

Social Enterprises and the SDGs

Social enterprises play a significant role in contributing to the Sustainable Development Goals (SDGs) set forth by the United Nations. Their unique business models prioritize both profit and social or environmental impact, making them effective agents for addressing a wide range of global challenges (Becchetti et al, 2020). Here are several ways in which social enterprises contribute to the achievement of the SDGs:

Eradicating Poverty (SDG 1): Social enterprises often operate in marginalized or economically disadvantaged communities, providing job opportunities, skills development, and income generation. By doing so, they directly contribute to poverty alleviation and economic empowerment.

Zero Hunger (SDG 2): Social enterprises engaged in agriculture, food distribution, and food rescue initiatives work to reduce food waste and improve food access for vulnerable populations. They help ensure that food reaches those in need, thus supporting efforts to eliminate hunger.

Good Health and Well-being (SDG 3): Social enterprises in the healthcare sector focus on improving healthcare access and quality, especially in underserved areas. They provide affordable healthcare services, medical supplies, and health education, thus promoting well-being and reducing health inequalities.

Quality Education (SDG 4): Social enterprises often offer educational programs and resources, such as vocational training, mentorship, and affordable educational materials. These initiatives enhance access to quality education, especially in areas with limited educational opportunities.

Gender Equality (SDG 5): Many social enterprises prioritize gender equality by empowering women economically, providing training and employment opportunities, and addressing gender-based discrimination and violence. These efforts contribute to achieving gender parity.

Clean Water and Sanitation (SDG 6): Social enterprises often work on water purification, sanitation, and hygiene projects in communities lacking access to clean water and proper sanitation facilities. Their initiatives directly align with SDG 6 goals.

Affordable and Clean Energy (SDG 7): Some social enterprises focus on renewable energy solutions, such as solar power or biogas, in underserved areas. They help increase access to clean and sustainable energy sources.

Decent Work and Economic Growth (SDG 8): Social enterprises create jobs and promote inclusive economic growth, particularly in regions facing high unemployment rates. They often emphasize fair labor practices, worker empowerment, and income security.

Industry, Innovation, and Infrastructure (SDG 9): Social enterprises are known for their innovative approaches to addressing social and environmental challenges. They contribute to technological advancements, infrastructure development, and sustainable industry practices.

Reduced Inequalities (SDG 10): Social enterprises contribute to reducing inequalities by prioritizing inclusive hiring practices, empowering marginalized groups, and providing economic opportunities to disadvantaged communities. For instance, organizations like Greyston Bakery in the United States practice an open-hiring model, providing jobs to individuals regardless of their background, including those with a criminal record (Hamilton, 2016). This approach fosters social inclusion and addresses inequalities by breaking down barriers to employment.

Sustainable Cities and Communities (SDG 11): Social enterprises are instrumental in promoting sustainable cities and communities by addressing urban challenges, such as housing, transportation, and waste management. Affordable housing social enterprises like Habitat for Humanity provide housing solutions for low-income families, contributing to sustainable urban development (Maginn, 2016). Furthermore, social enterprises focusing on sustainable transportation, such as bike-sharing programs, offer eco-friendly mobility options, reducing the environmental footprint of urban areas (Larsen et al., 2019).

Responsible Consumption and Production (SDG 12): The promotion of responsible consumption and production is at the core of many social enterprises. These enterprises emphasize sustainable and ethical practices throughout their value chains. For example, Fair Trade organizations like Fair Trade USA and Fairtrade International promote responsible consumption by ensuring fair compensation for producers in developing countries (Becchetti et al., 2020). These initiatives encourage consumers to make informed, ethical choices.

Climate Action (SDG 13): Social enterprises play a pivotal role in addressing climate change through innovative and eco-friendly solutions. Renewable energy social enterprises, like Solar Sister in Africa, empower women to distribute solar products, expanding access to clean energy and mitigating the impact of carbon emissions (Barnes et al., 2017). By fostering the transition to sustainable energy sources, they contribute to climate action efforts.

Life Below Water (SDG 14) and Life on Land (SDG 15): Social enterprises also contribute to the preservation of life below water and life on land by addressing issues related to conservation and biodiversity. For instance, Wildlife Works in Kenya combines wildlife conservation with community development. By employing local residents as "wildlife rangers," they protect endangered species and ecosystems while promoting social and economic well-being (Lee, 2018). Such enterprises promote the coexistence of communities and nature.

Peace, Justice, and Strong Institutions (SDG 16): Social enterprises foster peace, justice, and strong institutions by addressing issues related to conflict resolution, access to justice, and community development. Peace Direct, for example, supports local peacebuilders in conflict-affected regions, empowering communities to resolve conflicts peacefully and rebuild (Smith, 2020). This approach contributes to building more just and peaceful societies.

Partnerships for the Goals (SDG 17): Social enterprises frequently form partnerships with governments, NGOs, and the private sector to leverage resources and expertise. The social enterprise Yunus Social Business, founded by Nobel laureate Muhammad Yunus, collaborates with multinational corporations to develop sustainable social business ventures (Ghosh, 2016). These partnerships exemplify the cross-sector collaborations crucial for achieving the SDGs.

Waste Management and the SDGs

Waste management is an essential component of sustainable development that significantly contributes to achieving the SDGs (Khalili, and Yusoff, 2019). By addressing environmental, economic, and social aspects, responsible waste handling promotes cleaner cities, resource efficiency, public health, climate action, and the preservation of ecosystems. Governments, businesses, and individuals must work together to implement sustainable waste management practices and ensure a better future for all while striving to meet the SDGs' ambitious targets by 2030 (Sanchez-Molina and Iniesta-Bonillo, 2020).

SDG 11: Sustainable Cities and Communities

SDG 11 aims to make cities and human settlements inclusive, safe, resilient, and sustainable. Waste management is an integral component of urban sustainability. Proper waste disposal and recycling reduces environmental pollution, enhances public health, and contributes to creating clean and liveable cities. Sustainable waste management practices, such as waste segregation, recycling programs, and the reduction of landfill waste, align directly with the objectives of SDG 11.

SDG 12: Responsible Consumption and Production

SDG 12 calls for responsible consumption and production patterns. Effective waste management encourages resource efficiency and sustainable consumption. Recycling and waste reduction initiatives can help minimize resource depletion, reduce energy consumption, and limit the environmental impact of manufacturing processes. Waste-to-energy technologies also play a role in promoting sustainable production.

SDG 3: Good Health and Well-being

Health and well-being are closely linked to waste management. Inadequate waste disposal can lead to the spread of diseases and pose serious health risks. Proper waste management prevents the contamination of soil and water sources, safeguarding public health. Access to safe sanitation facilities, a component of SDG 6 (Clean Water and Sanitation), is intertwined with effective waste management.

SDG 13: Climate Action

SDG 13 addresses climate change mitigation and adaptation. The management of organic waste through composting or anaerobic digestion reduces methane emissions from landfills. Additionally, recycling and waste-to-energy technologies can help lower greenhouse gas emissions, contributing to the global effort to combat climate change.

SDG 14: Life Below Water and SDG 15: Life on Land

Waste mismanagement has devastating effects on marine and terrestrial ecosystems. Pollution from plastic waste, for instance, harms marine life and disrupts ecosystems. Sustainable waste management practices, including plastic recycling and reduction of single-use plastics, directly support SDG 14 and SDG 15 by protecting biodiversity and preserving the integrity of our oceans and ecosystems.

SDG 8: Decent Work and Economic Growth

Waste management systems create job opportunities across the waste value chain, from collection and sorting to recycling and waste-to-energy operations. Sustainable waste management can stimulate economic growth, particularly in low and middle-income countries, by fostering the development of a green economy and promoting decent work.

SDG 1: No Poverty and SDG 2: Zero Hunger

Waste reduction and food recovery initiatives can address poverty and hunger concerns. By reducing food waste, surplus food can be redistributed to those in need, contributing to SDG 1 and SDG 2 by improving food security and alleviating poverty.

Waste Management Social Enterprises and the SDGs

This section explains the role of WAMSEs in the context of the SDGs, with a focus on their contributions to environmental sustainability, economic development, and social well-being, supported by academic references.

Environmental Sustainability and Responsible Consumption (SDG 12)

WAMSEs are at the forefront of promoting responsible consumption and production, a core element of SDG 12 (United Nations, 2015). These enterprises employ sustainable waste management practices, such as recycling, composting, and waste-to-energy technologies, to reduce the environmental impact of waste disposal (Sanchez-Molina & Iniesta-Bonillo, 2020; Bryceson and Jonsson, 2019). For instance, TerraCycle, a renowned social enterprise, focuses on recycling traditionally non-recyclable items, diverting waste from landfills and incineration (Sanchez-Molina & Iniesta-Bonillo, 2020). By doing so, they contribute directly to SDG 12's objective of ensuring sustainable consumption and production patterns.

Decent Work and Economic Growth (SDG 8)

WAMSEs create job opportunities and promote economic growth, aligning with the goals of SDG 8 (United Nations, 2015). These enterprises often operate in economically disadvantaged communities, providing employment and income-generation opportunities to marginalized populations (Meadows & Bruijn, 2020). For example, Waste Ventures in India empowers waste pickers by offering safer working conditions and better livelihoods through waste segregation and recycling initiatives (Khalili & Yusoff, 2019). Their efforts contribute to SDG 8's aim of promoting sustained, inclusive, and sustainable economic growth.

Clean Water and Sanitation (SDG 6)

WAMSEs play a crucial role in addressing clean water and sanitation challenges, in alignment with SDG 6 (United Nations, 2015). By implementing innovative waste management solutions, they reduce pollution risks and protect water sources from contamination (Hermann & Oels, 2020). Sarvajal, an Indian social enterprise, provides affordable, community-level water purification systems as part of their integrated approach to waste and water management (Khosla et al., 2018). Their initiatives directly contribute to SDG 6's objective of ensuring access to clean water and sanitation for all.

Social Inclusion and Reduced Inequalities (SDG 10)

WAMSEs promote social inclusion and contribute to reducing inequalities, which are central themes of SDG 10 (United Nations, 2015). Many of these enterprises prioritize hiring individuals from marginalized or vulnerable populations, providing them with opportunities for decent work (Chen et al., 2019). In India, SEWA offers financial services, skill development, and employment to women in the informal sector, addressing gender disparities (Chen et al., 2019). Their efforts align with SDG 10's goal of reducing inequality within and among countries.

WAMSEs represent a powerful force in addressing the global waste crisis while concurrently advancing the Sustainable Development Goals. With their dual focus on environmental sustainability and social impact, they contribute significantly to SDGs related to responsible consumption, economic growth, clean water, and social inclusion. These enterprises exemplify the potential of businesses to be agents of positive change, creating a more equitable and sustainable future for all.

WAMSEs and the SDGs in the Global South

Waste management is a pressing issue in the Global South, where rapid urbanization, population growth, and limited infrastructure have led to significant challenges in waste collection, disposal, and environmental sustainability. In this context, waste management social enterprises have emerged as innovative and socially conscious solutions to address the dual challenges of waste management and sustainable development. Drawing upon academic references, in this section we present examples of how these enterprises make a significant impact on environmental sustainability, economic development, and social well-being in the region.

I. Environmental Sustainability and Responsible Consumption (SDG 12)

Waste management social enterprises in the Global South are at the forefront of promoting responsible consumption and production, a key component of SDG 12 (United Nations, 2015). The proliferation of such enterprises in the region has led to innovative waste management practices that prioritize resource efficiency and environmental conservation. One notable example is the Recicla Electronic Waste in Mexico, which focuses on recycling electronic waste (e-waste). E-waste poses significant environmental risks when not properly managed, as it contains hazardous materials. Recicla addresses this challenge by collecting, refurbishing, and recycling electronic devices, diverting them from landfills and incineration (López et al., 2020). By doing so, they align with SDG 12's objective of ensuring sustainable consumption and production patterns.

II. Decent Work and Economic Growth (SDG 8)

Waste management social enterprises create job opportunities and contribute to economic growth, a pivotal goal under SDG 8 (United Nations, 2015). The Global South often faces high unemployment rates and informal labor markets. Waste management enterprises, however, offer a pathway to decent work and economic development. Wecyclers, a Nigerian social enterprise, exemplifies this impact. Operating in Lagos, one of Africa's most populous and rapidly growing cities, Wecyclers engages local communities in the collection of recyclable materials, which are then sold to recycling companies. This model not only promotes waste recycling but also generates income for participants (Agbiboa et al., 2019). By creating jobs and promoting economic growth, Wecyclers contributes significantly to SDG 8's aim of promoting sustained, inclusive, and sustainable economic growth.

III. Clean Water and Sanitation (SDG 6)

Access to clean water and sanitation is a fundamental issue in many parts of the Global South. Inadequate waste management practices can lead to water pollution and poor sanitation conditions. Waste management social enterprises play a vital role in addressing this challenge, aligning with SDG 6 (United Nations, 2015). Sarvajal, an Indian social enterprise, focuses on decentralized community-level water purification systems as part of its integrated approach to waste and water management (Khosla et al., 2018). By providing access to clean drinking water, they not only improve public health but also alleviate the burden on overburdened water resources. Their initiatives directly contribute to SDG 6's objective of ensuring access to clean water and sanitation for all.

IV. Social Inclusion and Reduced Inequalities (SDG 10)

Waste management social enterprises in the Global South promote social inclusion and contribute to reducing inequalities, which are central themes of SDG 10 (United Nations, 2015). Many of these enterprises prioritize hiring individuals from marginalized or vulnerable populations, providing them with opportunities for decent work and economic empowerment. Hasiru Dala, based in Bengaluru, India, is a prime example of such an initiative. It empowers waste pickers, who are often part of the urban informal sector and face discrimination, by offering them safer working conditions and better livelihoods through waste segregation and recycling initiatives (Murali et al., 2020). Their efforts align with SDG 10's goal of reducing inequality within and among countries.

METHODOLOGY

This study employs a multiple case study design, which allows for an in-depth exploration of WAMSEs and their contributions to the Sustainable Development Goals (SDGs) in the Global South. Multiple case studies are a robust qualitative research method that enables the examination of complex phenomena within their real-world context (Yin, 2014).

The selection of case study organizations was guided by purposive sampling to ensure diversity in terms of geographical location, waste management practices, and socio-economic contexts within the

Global South. This approach enhances the external validity of the findings (Patton, 2002). Table 1 shows the characteristics of the six WAMSEs selected for this study.

Table 1. Characteristics of the WASMSEs selected for the study

Name	Sustainable impact	Socio-economic impact	Link to website and video case studies
Case 1. **Sealand (South Africa)**	**Fashion Design.** A company that produces bags out of plastic collected from the sea.	Employed poor people from Cape Town.	https://www.youtube.com/watch?v=AASEOi3FYJs https://sealandgear.com_
Case 2. **Hands of Honour (South Africa)**	**Industrial Design.** A company that upcycle obsolete stock and recyclable items.	Employed homeless men.	http://handsofhonour.co.za https://www.youtube.com/watch?v=oLFlJuS3sA8
Case 3. **H18 (South Africa)**	**Fashion Design.** A company that focused on the production of cotton crochet products.	Employed disadvantaged women (Refugees).	https://www.youtube.com/watch?v=JqEl07_VaLs&t=129s https://h18.co.za
Case 4. **La Da Favelinha (Brazil)**	**Fashion Design.** A company that supports young people with fashion, culture and arts in the slums of Brazil.	Provides employment opportunities as well as creative activities for young people living in slums.	https://www.youtube.com/watch?v=yHD5EDUcSeo
Case 5. **Biji-Biji Initiative (Malaysia)**	**Industrial and Fashion Design.** A company that champions sustainable living, reuse waste creatively and loves collaborative production.	Offers volunteering and job opportunities for young people.	https://www.youtube.com/watch?v=H2ziVcW82s4 https://www.biji-biji.com
Case 6. **Eco-Maximus (Sri Lanka)**	**Industrial Design.** A company that used the elephant dung to enhance the animal's habitat self-sustainably.	Employed rural women.	https://www.youtube.com/watch?v=u5TbaOPHEns https://www.ecomaximus.com

Data collection involves a combination of methods, including semi-structured interviews, document analysis, and direct observations. Semi-structured interviews were conducted with key stakeholders within each organisation, including founders, employees, and beneficiaries (4 with each organisation). These interviews provided valuable insights into the organizations' missions, strategies, and impacts (Yin, 2014). Document analysis included the examination of reports, publications, and organizational documents to gather historical and contextual data (Merriam, 2009). Direct observations were conducted to gain a firsthand understanding of the daily operations and practices of each organization (Stake, 1995). Informed consent was obtained from all participants, and their anonymity and confidentiality was preserved. The study was adhered to ethical guidelines and principles of research involving human subjects, as outlined by relevant institutional review boards and ethical committees.

Data Analysis

Data analysis follows a thematic approach, which involves coding and categorizing qualitative data to identify recurring themes and patterns (Braun & Clarke, 2006). Initially, data was organized according to the SDGs and specific goals relevant to each case. This thematic coding was performed using NVIVO (Miles et al., 2014). Following the individual case analyses, as seen in Table 2, a cross-case analysis was conducted to identify commonalities and differences among the cases (Yin, 2014). This step enabled the extraction of overarching themes related to the contributions of waste management social enterprises

Table 2. Stages of data analysis

Stages	Description of the Process
1. Familiarisation of the data	Watching videos from the semi-structured interviews and other relevant materials (documentary sources, observations and field notes) for each case study.
2. Transcriptions	Creating transcriptions and noting down initial ideas.
3. Identifying and refining nodes in NVivo12.	Identifying and refining nodes by looking at words that were repeated by participants in the word cloud.
4. Themes and Subthemes	The development of themes and subthemes (within case and cross case analysis) to connect this with research objectives and questions.

Source: Compiled by the authors

to the SDGs in the Global South. It also facilitated the development of a comprehensive understanding of the role of these enterprises in sustainable development. To ensure the validity and reliability of the study, multiple data sources, including interviews, documents, and observations were triangulated. Member checking, where participants reviewed and validate the findings were also employed to enhance the study's trustworthiness (Creswell & Miller, 2000). Additionally, the research team engaged in continuous discussions and peer debriefing to minimize bias and enhance the credibility of the analysis (Lincoln & Guba, 1985).

PRESENTATION OF FINDINGS

The findings emerge from the collected data and seek to respond to the research question highlighted in the introduction: What is the contribution of WAMSEs to the SDGs in the Global South? The themes that are identified are the result of the in-depth-triangulated data analysis, using the cross-case study. These are: (i) mot*ivations*, (ii) operations and (iii) strategy.

Given this context, the findings show that WAMSEs addresses most of the SDGs spite the unfamiliarity and unawareness of the SDGs. Tables 4 and 5 depict how WAMSEs' practices are shaped by sustainable values and are driven by the willingness to tackle community needs. As can be seen in Tables 4 and 5 these organisations are created to meet socio-economic needs (e.g., SDG1, SDG2, SDG3 and SDG8), but their practices are bounded by concious values such as the protection of their environment for the sake of the current and future generations (e.g., SDG6, SDG12, SDG13, SDG14 and SDG15), distributing evenly their surplus (e.g., SDG4, SDG10 and SDG16) and respecting every staff member indifferent from gender and age (e.g., SDG5).

There are many factors that demonstrate how WAMSEs' characteristics and practices inform the SDGs. The current pandemic has halted or reversed progress amongst these organisations in many factors such as reduction of poverty, hunger, education, job opportunities, individual security, reducing inequalities and safeguard key biodiversity areas. All the WAMSEs' members mentioned that they have been addressing societal issues for some time now, that include: protection of the environment (SDG13-SDG15), reduction of poverty (SDG1), tackle societal exclusion and misrepresentation (SDG3 and SDG10) and improve education (SDG4) among others. This is exemplified below where participants highlight their role in meeting societal needs through their formal practices.

Motivations

Findings indicated the motivations to develop a WAMSE were mainly (1) providing employment opportunities for the locals, (2) environmental consciousness, preserving cultural values and (4) ensuring inclusion of disadvantaged groups in society.

One of the fundamental motivations behind the establishment of a WAMSE is the desire to provide employment opportunities for local communities. In a world marked by economic disparities, these enterprises recognize their potential to create meaningful jobs. As one interviewee explained:

"We wanted to make a tangible difference in our local community. By setting up our enterprise, we not only reduced waste but also provided job opportunities for many who were struggling to find employment" (Founder,CS1).

Therefore, the emphasis on local employment helps foster economic stability within the community and can be instrumental in addressing unemployment challenges.

Environmental consciousness is a central driver of WAMSEs. These enterprises view themselves powerful to reduce waste, conserve resources, and mitigate the environmental impacts of rampant consumerism. As one respondent succinctly put it:

"We were appalled by the volume of waste generated every day. Our project allows us to take a stand against this wastefulness. Our motivation is clear: we want to reduce our environmental footprint." (Founder,CS3).

By recycling and repurposing materials, these enterprises actively contribute to the preservation of our planet and the mitigation of climate change (Sung et al., 2014; Wilson, 2016), which is aligned with SDG13, SDG14, and SDG15.

WAMSEs often play a vital role in preserving cultural values and traditions. These enterprises recognize the significance of heritage and cultural identity, seeking to infuse these values into their products. As one interviewee shared:

"Our culture is woven into every piece we create. It's not just about upcycling materials; it's about upcycling our heritage. We want to ensure that our traditions and values are passed down through our creations." (Founder,CS5).

Through this approach, these enterprises become a medium through which culture is celebrated and sustained.

The final motivation highlighted by our findings pertains to social inclusion. WAMSEs often make it a mission to include and empower disadvantaged groups in society. Their products are a testament to the belief that every individual, regardless of their background, has the potential to contribute. A respondent articulated this beautifully:

"We work with individuals who have faced numerous challenges in life. Through our enterprise, we aim to provide them with the opportunity to rebuild their lives, regain their confidence, and contribute positively to society." (Founder,CS6).

In this way, these enterprises become a force for social inclusion and rehabilitation.

Operations

Our findings indicate that these operations can be primarily categorized into four distinct areas: (1) leadership roles in their organisations for disadvantaged groups mainly women, (2) Goods and products are produced sustainably, (3) their operations are 100% environmentally friendly and (4) transparency in their operations.

One of the distinguishing features of WAMSEs is their emphasis on providing leadership opportunities to disadvantaged groups, with a particular focus on women. These enterprises recognize the potential within these individuals and actively work to empower them. As one interviewee stated:

"Our leadership team is composed primarily of women who have faced adversity. We believe in their capabilities and are committed to creating an environment where they can lead and inspire others." (Founder,CS4).

This approach not only fosters inclusivity but also leverages the diverse perspectives and talents of these leaders. Sustainability is at the heart of the operations of WAMSEs. These enterprises prioritize the production of goods and products in a manner that minimizes waste and environmental impact. As one respondent emphasized:

"Our commitment to sustainability guides every step of our production process. We use reclaimed materials to create products that are both eco-friendly and beautiful." (staff,CS1).

By repurposing discarded materials, they reduce the strain on natural resources and reduce waste. The commitment to environmental friendliness is a hallmark of WAMSEs. Their operations aim for minimal environmental impact, striving for practices that are not just sustainable but actively restorative. One interviewee articulated this commitment:

"We leave no room for compromise when it comes to being environmentally friendly. Our goal is not just to reduce harm but to actively restore the environment through our operations." (staff,CS3).

This unwavering commitment to eco-friendliness is a defining feature of these enterprises. Transparency is another essential aspect of the operations of WAMSEs. They are open and honest about their processes, materials, and the impact they make. As a responder explained:

"Transparency is vital for building trust with our customers. We want them to know exactly how we operate and the positive impact their choices make on the environment and society." (staff,CS5).

Through this transparency, they foster a sense of accountability and encourage conscious consumer choices.

Strategy

Findings indicated the strategy to develop a waste management social enterprise were mainly (1) Professionalization of the members to enhance the capacity building, (2) Widening networking by using marketing strategies and local communication skills, (3) Educates their employees to enhance their products, (4) Diversification strategies,(5) secure partnerships with external entities to blend local and external knowledges and (6) developing a green agenda and a green road.

WAMSEs prioritize the professionalization of their members to enhance capacity building. They recognize the need for skilled individuals who can effectively manage waste, ensure the safety of workers, and employ efficient methods. One interviewee emphasized this approach:

"Professionalization is our foundation. We invest in training and equipping our team with the necessary skills and knowledge to handle waste effectively and safely."

This emphasis on capacity building is integral to ensuring the enterprise's effectiveness. Networking plays a crucial role in the development of waste management social enterprises. These enterprises employ marketing strategies and local communication skills to engage with the community, local businesses, and other stakeholders. As one respondent stated:

"Our success depends on our ability to connect with the local community and businesses. We use marketing strategies and local communication skills to foster partnerships and increase our reach."

By widening their network, these enterprises can collect waste efficiently and expand their impact. The commitment to education is another key strategy for these enterprises. They invest in educating their employees to enhance the quality of their products. As one interviewee explained:

"We believe in continuous improvement. By educating our employees, we not only enhance our products but also empower our team."

This focus on education ensures that the products and services offered are of the highest standard. Diversification is a strategic approach used by waste management social enterprises. They seek to diversify their services and product offerings to cater to a broad range of waste management needs. One respondent stated:

"We constantly explore new opportunities in waste management. Diversifying our services allows us to address a wider spectrum of waste-related challenges."

Diversification helps them stay adaptable and meet the evolving needs of their community. Waste management social enterprises recognize the importance of external knowledge and expertise. They seek partnerships with external entities to blend local and external knowledge. As one interviewee emphasized:

"Collaboration with external partners brings new ideas and insights. We blend these with our local knowledge to create effective waste management solutions."

Partnerships facilitate innovation and holistic problem-solving. A green agenda is at the core of waste management social enterprises. They develop a green roadmap to guide their operations, ensuring a focus on environmentally friendly practices. As one respondent put it:

"Our commitment to a green agenda is non-negotiable. We believe that a sustainable future depends on responsible waste management, and we're dedicated to that path."

The green agenda is not only a strategy but a fundamental ethos.

5. DISCUSSION AND CONCLUSION

This chapter set out to explore the contribution of WAMSEs to the SDGs in the Global. This work addresses a research gap that points to the lack of studies that explore this phenomenon in such contexts. Further, this work shed light on the role of WAMSEs and the SDGs in developing countries and how they play a key role in the quest for communities to achieve sustainability and well-being.

Lessons can be learnt about this work on WAMSEs from four different Global South countries. The motivations driving WAMSEs encompass a broad spectrum of values and goals. These enterprises are not merely businesses; they are agents of positive change. Whether it be through the provision of employment opportunities for locals, environmental consciousness, cultural preservation, or the inclusion of disadvantaged groups in society, these enterprises are instrumental in crafting a more sustainable and equitable future. In a world where the urgency of sustainable and inclusive development is increasingly recognized, the waste management movement represents a beacon of hope. The motivations behind these enterprises reveal the power of individuals and communities to shape a more environmentally conscious, culturally rich, and socially inclusive world. As we reflect on these motivations, we are reminded that the impact of WAMSEs goes far beyond the creation of beautiful, upcycled products; it extends to the transformation of lives and the betterment of our global community.

The operations of WAMSEs are not merely business strategies; they are powerful mechanisms for societal and environmental change. Whether it's providing leadership opportunities for disadvantaged groups, producing goods sustainably, maintaining 100% environmental friendliness, or being transparent in their operations, these enterprises demonstrate a profound commitment to a better world. In a time when sustainability and social inclusion are paramount concerns, the operations of these enterprises serve as a blueprint for conscious business practices. They embody the idea that business can be a force for good, simultaneously promoting the well-being of individuals and the planet. As we delve into the operational aspects of WAMSEs, we are reminded that their impact transcends economic success—it extends to the empowerment of individuals, the preservation of the environment, and the cultivation of a more ethical and inclusive global community.

The strategies used in the development of waste management social enterprises exemplify a holistic approach to addressing waste challenges, promoting sustainability, and fostering economic development. These strategies, including professionalization of members, networking, education, diversification, partnerships, and a green agenda, underscore the enterprise's commitment to creating a positive impact on both the environment and the communities they serve.

In a world where responsible waste management is paramount, waste management social enterprises stand as beacons of change, demonstrating how innovative strategies can not only tackle waste issues but also create a sustainable, inclusive, and environmentally conscious future. As we explore these strategies, we are reminded that the success of these enterprises goes beyond financial returns; it encompasses the transformation of waste into valuable resources, the upliftment of communities, and the preservation of our planet.

This study has limitations that suggest a cautious interpretation of the results, including the limited number of case study organizations and the inherent subjectivity in qualitative research. Generalizability to other contexts can be constrained due to the specific focus on the Global South and the unique characteristics of each case. However, the use of multiple case study organizations in this research allows for a comprehensive examination of waste management social enterprises and their contributions to the SDGs in the Global South. This approach facilitates the exploration of various dimensions of these enterprises' roles in sustainable development, providing valuable insights for policymakers, practitioners, and academics alike. Thus, further research is also needed to explore this phenomenon using more case study organisations from different regions and compare Global North and South context.

REFERENCES

Agbiboa, D. E., Mignouna, H. D., & Diallo, M. (2019). The "waste" perspective on social enterprise in Africa: The Wecyclers example. In T. Koh & G. M. Idowu (Eds.), *Social Responsibility and Sustainability in Africa* (pp. 221–243). Springer.

Becchetti, L., Castriota, S., & Pelligra, V. (2020). Social cooperatives, a niche or a viable model for future food provision? Evidence from Italy. *Sustainability*, *12*(19), 8066.

Braun, V., & Clarke, V. (2006). Using thematic analysis in psychology. *Qualitative Research in Psychology*, *3*(2), 77–101. doi:10.1191/1478088706qp063oa

Bryceson, D. F., & Jonsson, J. B. (2019). Can Social Enterprises Create Sustainable Livelihoods in Sub-Saharan Africa? Evidence from Zambia. *Sustainability*, *11*(19), 5305.

Bull, M. (2007). Fair Trade labeling: The globalization of social entrepreneurship. In *Social entrepreneurship* (pp. 121–135). Palgrave Macmillan.

Chiu, Y. J., & Wuepper, D. (2021). Harnessing clean energy for all: Social enterprises in off-grid renewable energy. *Energy Policy*, *149*, 112111.

Cohen, B. (2019). *Social and sustainable enterprise: Changing the nature of business*. Routledge.

Creswell, J. W., & Miller, D. L. (2000). Determining validity in qualitative inquiry. *Theory into Practice*, *39*(3), 124–130. doi:10.120715430421tip3903_2

De Araujo, G. T., Ribeiro, L. C., & Fernandes, A. M. (2020). Innovation processes in social enterprises for sustainable development: A multiple case study in Brazil. *Sustainability*, *12*(17), 7086.

Duflo, E. (2012). Women's empowerment and economic development. *Journal of Economic Literature, 50*(4), 1051–1079. doi:10.1257/jel.50.4.1051

Hamilton, N. (2016). The impact of open hiring on employers. *Journal of Occupational Rehabilitation, 26*(2), 217–232.

Hermann, B. G., & Oels, A. (2020). From waste to value—A systematic review on social business models for the circular economy. *Sustainability, 12*(14), 5545.

Khalili, S. J., & Yusoff, R. B. (2019). Role of social enterprises in waste management: An empirical investigation. *Resources, Conservation and Recycling, 141*, 66–74.

Khosla, R., Urmila, T., Gupta, T., Goyal, V., & Verma, A. (2018). Sarvajal: Water for all in Rural India. *Case Research Journal, 38*(2), 140–162.

Larsen, J., Bojö, J., Larsson, J., & Lindgren, M. (2019). Business models for sustainable urban mobility: A literature review. *Sustainability*, 11.

López, J. A., Mireles, A. I., & Jaramillo, A. C. (2020). E-waste management in Mexico: Current situation, policies, and prospects. *Sustainability, 12*(3), 1024.

Maginn, P. J. (2016). Affordable housing, social enterprise, and the elusive logic of scale. *Housing Studies, 31*(1), 1–18.

Meadows, K., & Bruijn, E. J. D. (2020). Measuring the impact of social enterprises on sustainable development goals: A study of 60 social enterprises in 9 European countries. *Sustainability, 12*(9), 3613.

Merriam, S. B. (2009). *Qualitative research: A guide to design and implementation*. Jossey-Bass.

Miles, M. B., Huberman, A. M., & Saldana, J. (2014). *Qualitative data analysis: A methods sourcebook*. Sage Publications.

Mirkhani, S., Abdolshah, M., & Rashidi, K. (2020). The role of social entrepreneurship in solving environmental problems: A case study of a recycling social enterprise in Iran. *Sustainability, 12*(6), 2404.

Murali, D., Morisetty, S., & Sengupta, S. (2020). *Hasiru Dala: Transforming the lives of waste pickers through social entrepreneurship*. Ivey Publishing.

Patton, M. Q. (2002). *Qualitative research and evaluation methods* (3rd ed.). Sage Publications.

Sanchez-Molina, R., & Iniesta-Bonillo, M. A. (2020). Sustainable waste management practices and social entrepreneurship: A systematic literature review. *Journal of Cleaner Production, 246*, 119029.

Stake, R. E. (1995). *The art of case study research*. Sage Publications.

United Nations. (2015). *Transforming our world: The 2030 Agenda for Sustainable Development*. United Nations.

Yin, R. K. (2014). *Case study research: Design and methods* (5th ed.). Sage Publications.

Chapter 8
Systems Engineering:
Driving Green Economy and Renewable Energy Transitions

Alex Zárate
https://orcid.org/0000-0001-6440-0108
Universidad Peruana de Ciencias Aplicadas, Perú

Analy Huanco
Universidad Peruana de Ciencias Aplicadas, Perú

ABSTRACT

This chapter provides a synthesis of the key issues related to systems engineering and its contribution to the green economy and energy sustainability. It explores essential concepts in sustainable energy systems, renewable technologies, energy efficiency, and highlights global challenges in cooperation, emerging technologies, education, policy and regulations, and investment in sustainable infrastructure. Systems engineering consolidates its position as a fundamental pillar.

1. SUSTAINABLE ENERGY SYSTEMS

This first section lays the groundwork for understanding the importance of systems engineering in the context of the transition to a green economy and the use of renewable energy. Sustainable energy systems engineering is essential to address today's challenges related to sustainability and climate change. In this section, the fundamental concepts related to sustainable energy systems engineering, design and optimization will be explored and concrete examples of successful projects will be provided.

1.1. Sustainable Energy Systems Engineering

Sustainable energy systems engineering is a multidisciplinary field that focuses on designing, developing and managing energy systems that are environmentally friendly, economically viable and socially

DOI: 10.4018/979-8-3693-1297-1.ch008

acceptable. This area of study is critical to addressing global challenges related to sustainability and climate change by ensuring a reliable and clean energy supply for present and future generations.

1.1.1 Definition and Scope

Sustainable energy systems engineering encompasses a wide range of aspects, from energy generation and distribution to final energy consumption, and can be defined as the design, development, implementation and management of energy systems that minimize their environmental impact, optimize efficiency and ensure equitable and affordable access to energy.

1.1.2 Importance of Sustainability

Sustainability is a fundamental principle in sustainable energy systems engineering, involving the ability to meet current needs without compromising the ability of future generations to meet their own needs. This requires a balanced approach that takes into account the economic, environmental and social aspects of energy production and use.

1.1.3 Multidisciplinary Approach

Sustainable energy systems engineering is inherently multidisciplinary. Drawing on knowledge and techniques from diverse disciplines, including electrical engineering, mechanical engineering, civil engineering, economics, environmental science and public policy, this multidisciplinarity is essential to address the complexity of energy challenges and develop effective solutions.

1.1.4 Objectives of Sustainable Energy Systems Engineering

Key objectives of sustainable energy systems engineering include:

Reduce greenhouse gas emissions: A primary objective is to reduce greenhouse gas emissions associated with power generation. This is achieved by transitioning to renewable energy sources, such as solar and wind, and implementing carbon capture and storage technologies.

Promote energy efficiency: Improving efficiency at all stages of the energy chain, from production to consumption, is essential. This involves the development of efficient technologies and the adoption of appropriate energy management practices.

Ensure energy security: Ensuring a reliable and stable energy supply is fundamental. This implies diversifying energy sources and strengthening energy infrastructure.

Promote equity and universal access to energy: It is essential that all people have access to affordable and reliable energy services. This implies addressing the access gap in rural and disadvantaged areas.

1.2. Design and Optimization of Energy Systems

The design and optimization of energy systems are fundamental elements of sustainable energy systems engineering. These processes enable the creation of systems that are efficient in energy production and utilization, thereby reducing environmental impact and promoting long-term sustainability. In this section, the fundamentals of these two key areas will be explored.

1.2.1 Design of Energy Systems

Energy system design involves planning and creating systems that can generate, store, distribute and use energy efficiently and sustainably. It is essential to consider a variety of factors when designing energy systems, including energy demand, natural resource availability, and environmental constraints.

One of the key concepts in the design of energy systems is the selection of appropriate energy sources. It is important to use renewable energy sources, such as solar and wind energy, which are abundant and have a reduced environmental impact compared to fossil fuels.

In addition, the design should consider the integration of carbon capture and storage (CCS) technologies to reduce greenhouse gas emissions in systems that still rely on fossil fuels.

1.2.2 Optimization of Energy Systems

The optimization of energy systems is a continuous process that seeks to maximize efficiency and minimize costs and environmental impact. It is based on modeling and analysis techniques that allow informed decisions to be made about the configuration and operation of energy systems.

One technique commonly used in energy system optimization is multiobjective optimization, which seeks to find solutions that balance multiple objectives, such as energy efficiency and cost-effectiveness. Another important technique is optimization under uncertainty, which takes into account variability in power generation from renewable sources.

In addition, energy system optimization can consider energy demand management, which involves encouraging efficient energy use and reducing demand at times of high load.

1.2.3 Application Examples

An example of the successful application of energy system optimization is the design of intelligent power distribution networks, known as "smart grids," which use optimization to coordinate power generation and distribution efficiently, reducing energy losses and improving supply reliability.

Another example is the optimization of energy systems in commercial and residential buildings. The optimization of heating, ventilation and air conditioning systems can significantly reduce energy consumption in buildings, which has a positive impact on both the environment and operating costs.

1.3. Greenhouse Gas Emissions

Improving efficiency and reducing greenhouse gas (GHG) emissions are critical objectives in sustainable energy systems engineering. In this section, we will explore key approaches that enable progress toward more efficient and environmentally friendly energy systems.

1.3.1. Transition to Renewable Energy Sources

A fundamental approach to reducing GHG emissions is the transition to renewable energy sources. An energy system based on renewable sources, such as solar, wind and hydropower, can drastically reduce GHG emissions and provide a long-term sustainable energy source.

Solar energy, in particular, has experienced rapid growth due to its availability and low environmental impact. Technological advances in solar cell efficiency and cost reduction, it is becoming increasingly competitive compared to conventional energy sources.

1.3.2. Energy Efficiency in Generation and Consumption

Improving energy efficiency is essential in both energy generation and consumption. In generation, the implementation of more efficient energy conversion technologies, such as combined cycle gas turbines, can reduce energy losses and reduce GHG emissions.

In consumption, energy efficiency in buildings and industrial processes is crucial. The implementation of energy management practices and the adoption of efficient technologies, such as LED lighting systems and high-efficiency heating and cooling systems, can lead to significant energy savings and emissions reductions.

1.3.3 Carbon Capture and Storage

For systems that still rely on fossil fuels, carbon capture and storage (CCS) technology plays an important role in reducing GHG emissions. CCS enables the capture of CO2 from industrial sources and its safe long-term storage, preventing CO2 from reaching the atmosphere.

CCS is particularly relevant in the coal and natural gas power generation industry.

1.3.4. Environmental Policies and Regulations

Effective implementation of environmental policies and regulations is essential to promote energy efficiency and reduce GHG emissions. Governments play an important role in setting energy efficiency standards and implementing economic instruments, such as carbon taxes and emissions trading systems.

Environmental regulation can also influence investment in clean technologies and the adoption of renewable energy. Policies that encourage research and development of clean technologies can accelerate the transition to a low-carbon economy.

1.4. Engineering Of Sustainable Energy Systems

In this section, specific examples of sustainable energy systems engineering projects that have proven effective in promoting sustainability and reducing greenhouse gas emissions will be presented. These projects illustrate how the principles and approaches discussed above are applied in practice.

1.4.1. Block Island Offshore Wind Farm

The Block Island Offshore Wind Farm, located off the coast of Rhode Island in the United States, is an outstanding example of a renewable energy project in which sustainable energy systems engineering has been applied. This wind farm, which began operating in 2016, consists of five wind turbines generating a total of 30 megawatts of electrical power.

The project has been praised for its ability to significantly reduce GHG emissions by replacing fossil fuel-based power generation. In addition, it has served as a model for offshore wind farm development in other coastal regions of the United States.

1.4.2. Noor Ouarzazate Photovoltaic Solar Power Plant

The Noor Ouarzazate Photovoltaic Solar Power Plant in Morocco is an impressive example of the adoption of solar energy on a large scale. This facility consists of four phases and is expected to reach a total capacity of 580 megawatts upon completion. The first phase, Noor I, was completed in 2016 and has a capacity of 160 megawatts.

This project highlights the importance of using solar energy in regions with abundant solar radiation, such as North Africa, to generate electricity sustainably and reduce GHG emissions. It also serves as an example of how investment in renewable energy can foster economic development in emerging regions.

1.4.3. Rural Electrification Plan in India

The Deen Dayal Upadhyaya Gram Jyoti Yojana (DDUGJY) Program in India is a project that focuses on bringing electricity to rural villages. This program aims to improve the quality of life of rural residents by providing them with access to reliable and affordable energy services.

The DDUGJY is an example of how sustainable energy systems engineering can address the energy access gap in disadvantaged areas and contribute to emissions reductions by using renewable energy sources where possible.

1.4.4 Hornsdale Power Reserve Project

The Hornsdale Power Reserve Energy Storage project in Australia, developed by Tesla, is a leading example of large-scale energy storage. This project uses lithium-ion batteries to store energy generated by wind and solar farms.

The Hornsdale Power Reserve has proven to be crucial in stabilizing the Australian power grid by providing storage capacity and rapid response to energy demand. This contributes to the successful integration of intermittent renewables into the grid and the reduction of GHG emissions.

2. DEVELOPMENT OF RENEWABLE ENERGY TECHNOLOGIES

2.1. Renewable Energy Technologies

Renewable energy technologies play a crucial role in the transition to more sustainable and environmentally friendly energy systems. In this section, the most relevant renewable energy technologies and their impact on sustainable energy systems engineering will be examined.

2.1.1. Solar Photovoltaic Energy

Solar photovoltaics (PV) is one of the most prominent and widely adopted renewable energy technologies. It involves the conversion of solar radiation into electricity using solar panels. Solar PV has experienced a rapid decrease in cost and increase in efficiency, making it increasingly competitive with conventional energy sources.

Solar photovoltaic systems are used in applications ranging from residential and commercial installations to large-scale solar plants. Its ability to generate electricity in a clean and sustainable manner makes it a key technology in reducing GHG emissions.

2.1.2. Wind Energy

Wind energy harnesses the kinetic energy of the wind to generate electricity using wind turbines. Wind energy is an abundant and sustainable source of renewable energy, especially in regions with consistent winds.

Onshore and offshore wind farms are examples of large-scale wind energy applications. Wind energy has proven to be an efficient technology for electricity generation and is fundamental for the diversification of the energy matrix and the reduction of GHG emissions.

2.1.3. Hydroelectric Power

Hydropower uses the force of moving water to generate electricity. Hydropower plants are a stable and reliable source of renewable energy and account for a significant portion of the world's generating capacity.

There are different types of hydropower plants, including storage (dams) and free-flow (river turbines). Large-scale hydropower can provide a substantial amount of electricity and contribute to grid stability.

2.1.4. Geothermal Energy

Geothermal energy harnesses the Earth's natural heat to generate electricity and heat. This technology is based on the exploitation of hot springs, geysers and subway geothermal reservoirs.

Geothermal energy is especially relevant in regions with geothermal activity, such as Iceland and New Zealand. It can provide a steady source of energy with low GHG emissions, making it a sustainable option for electricity generation and heating.

2.1.5. Biomass and Biogas

Biomass includes the conversion of organic matter into energy, whether in the form of solid, liquid or gaseous biomass. Biomass and biogas are used in applications ranging from electricity generation to biofuel production and heating.

Biomass and biogas are particularly relevant in waste management and energy production from agricultural and forestry resources. These technologies can contribute to the mitigation of GHG emissions by replacing fossil fuels in industrial and heating applications.

2.1.6. Wave and Tidal Energy

Wave and tidal power harness the movement of waves and tides to generate electricity. These technologies are under development and have the potential to provide a steady and predictable source of energy.

Although not yet used on a large scale, wave and tidal energy can be relevant in coastal regions with adequate resources. These technologies can contribute to the diversification of the energy matrix and reduce GHG emissions in near-shore areas.

2.2. Renewable Energy Technologies: Innovations

This section focuses on recent innovations and advances in renewable energy technologies, highlighting how these improvements are shaping the landscape of sustainable power generation.

2.2.1. Solar Energy

In the field of solar energy, recent innovations have focused on improving the efficiency and reducing the cost of solar cells. Multi-junction solar cells are available, which take advantage of different wavelengths of sunlight to achieve higher efficiency. These cells can overcome the efficiency barriers of conventional silicon cells.

In addition, thin-film technology, such as perovskite solar cells, has advanced rapidly in recent years. These cells promise to be more economical to manufacture and more versatile in their application.

2.2.2. Wind Energy

In the field of wind energy, recent advances have focused on the design of larger, more efficient turbines. Wind turbines can harness winds at higher altitudes, where the wind speed is more constant and stronger.

Offshore wind turbine technology has also advanced significantly. Offshore wind turbines can take advantage of stronger and more constant winds at sea, and floating systems have been designed that allow the installation of turbines in deeper waters.

2.2.3. Hydroelectric Power

In hydropower, innovations have focused on reducing environmental impacts and improving turbine efficiency. Low-pressure axial flow turbine systems can reduce fish mortality and improve generation efficiency.

In addition, more efficient and flexible pumped hydro storage systems have been developed. These systems allow energy to be stored during periods of low demand and released when needed.

2.2.4. Geothermal Energy

Geothermal energy has seen advances in drilling technologies and fluid circulation systems to enhance geothermal heat recovery. In addition, binary geothermal systems, which can operate at lower temperatures and in a variety of geographic locations, have been investigated.

2.2.5. Other Renewable Energy Sources

In the area of other renewable energy sources, such as biomass and biogas, advances have focused on conversion efficiency and emissions reduction. Pyrolysis and gasification of biomass produce cleaner and more efficient biofuels.

Wave and tidal energy technology has also advanced in recent years. Wave energy conversion systems using floating and oscillating devices generate electricity more efficiently.

3. PLANNING AND DESIGN OF SUSTAINABLE CITIES

3.1. Concepts in Sustainable Urban Planning

Sustainable urban planning is a crucial approach to the design and development of cities that are socially, economically and environmentally viable over the long term. In this section, we will explore the key concepts that underpin sustainable urban planning.

3.1.1 Sustainable Urban Density

One of the key concepts in sustainable urban planning is adequate urban density. Density is essential to reduce reliance on automobiles and promote public transportation, bicycling, and walking. Higher density can also foster the creation of more vibrant communities and access to services and jobs without the need for long commutes.

However, it is important to note that density does not necessarily imply skyscrapers and tall buildings everywhere. A varied density includes denser areas in the city center and transitions gradually to less dense areas on the outskirts, promoting a more balanced urban design.

3.1.2 Sustainable Mobility

Sustainable mobility is another pillar of sustainable urban planning. It is important to develop efficient and accessible public transport systems, as well as pedestrian- and bicycle-friendly infrastructure. This not only reduces traffic congestion and greenhouse gas emissions, but also improves the quality of life for urban residents by providing healthier mobility options.

3.1.3 Efficient Land Use

Efficient land management is a crucial concept in sustainable urban planning. It is important to avoid unplanned urban sprawl and to promote the revitalization of existing urban areas. This not only preserves natural and agricultural areas, but also reduces the need for costly and extensive infrastructure.

Sustainable urban planning also advocates mixed land use, where housing, commercial and green spaces are combined in the same neighborhood. This mix of uses can improve accessibility to services and reduce the need for long commutes.

3.1.4 Community Involvement and People-Centered Design

Community participation and people-centered design are essential elements of sustainable urban planning. It is important to involve residents in the urban design and decision-making process. This ensures that solutions are tailored to the needs and desires of the community, promoting greater acceptance and long-term sustainability.

3.2. Efficient Design, Sustainable Mobility

In this section, we will explore in detail design approaches that promote energy efficiency and sustainable mobility in the context of sustainable urban planning.

3.2.1 Public Transport-Oriented Design

A fundamental approach to promoting sustainable mobility is public transport-oriented design. It is important to create an urban environment that facilitates the efficient use of public transport. This involves the strategic location of bus stops and train stations, as well as the creation of dedicated public transport corridors.

The promotion of accessible and reliable public transportation is essential.

3.2.2 Pedestrian and Cycling Infrastructure Design

The creation of pedestrian and bicycle friendly infrastructure is essential to promote sustainable mobility. The construction of wide, safe sidewalks, separated bike lanes, and pedestrian walkways improve the safety and comfort of those who choose to walk or bike.

In addition, sustainable urban planning includes creating urban designs that reduce the need for long trips. Proximity to housing, workplaces and services is a key approach that decreases the demand for motorized transport.

3.2.3 Sustainable Building Design

Energy efficiency in the built environment is a crucial component of sustainable urban planning. There are design strategies that reduce energy consumption in buildings, such as proper orientation of buildings to maximize natural light and minimize sun exposure.

The promotion of certified sustainable buildings, such as LEED (Leadership in Energy and Environmental Design) or BREEAM (Building Research Establishment Environmental Assessment Method), is another important approach. Certification of sustainable buildings, including the reduction of GHG emissions and the efficient use of resources, is beneficial.

3.2.4 Compact Urban Design

Compact urban design is an approach that promotes energy efficiency and sustainable mobility by reducing distances between homes, workplaces and services. Compactly planned communities facilitate walking and biking access to daily needs.

The compact urban design also supports efficient land use by minimizing urban sprawl.

3.3. Sustainable Cities: Examples

In this section, we will explore successful cases of cities that have implemented sustainable practices in their urban planning and design. These examples illustrate how the adoption of sustainability strategies can have a positive impact on the quality of life of citizens and the mitigation of environmental impacts.

3.3.1 Copenhagen, Denmark

Copenhagen is widely recognized as a model sustainable city. The city has invested in an extensive network of bicycle lanes, bicycle rental stations, and pedestrian facilities, which has led to more than half of the population using bicycles as a means of transportation.

In addition, Copenhagen has implemented an ambitious climate action plan with the goal of becoming carbon neutral by 2025. This includes investing in offshore wind energy and promoting sustainable buildings. The city has demonstrated that it is possible to combine a high quality of life with sustainable practices.

3.3.2 Bogotá, Colombia

Bogota is another example of a city that has adopted sustainable practices in its urban planning. We have the success of Bogotá's public transportation system, TransMilenio, which combines exclusive bus lanes with high-capacity stations. This system has improved mobility and reduced traffic congestion.

Bogotá has also prioritized the creation of green areas and the promotion of cycling. The city has developed an extensive network of bicycle lanes and has implemented the Ciclovía program, which temporarily closes some streets on Sundays and holidays so that cyclists and pedestrians can enjoy safe spaces.

3.3.3 Curitiba, Brazil

Curitiba has been a pioneer in sustainable urban planning in Latin America. There is an efficient public transportation system known as BRT (Bus Rapid Transit). This system has reduced dependence on automobiles and improved accessibility in the city.

Curitiba has also invested in green areas and parks, which has improved the quality of life of its inhabitants. The city has demonstrated that it is possible to strike a balance between urban growth and environmental preservation.

3.3.4 Portland, United States

Portland, Oregon, is a benchmark for sustainable practices in the United States. Urban planning focused on public transportation, the promotion of cycling and the creation of sustainable neighborhoods.

Portland has adopted land use policies that encourage urban density and proximity to services, thereby reducing the need for long commutes. In addition, the city has invested in an extensive public transportation network and bicycle lanes, which has led to a decrease in traffic congestion.

4. LIFE CYCLE AND ENVIRONMENTAL IMPACT ASSESSMENT

4.1. Life Cycle in Technology Assessment

In this section, the importance of life cycle assessment (LCA) in the evaluation of technologies and projects will be discussed, highlighting its usefulness in understanding environmental impacts and making informed decisions.

4.1.1 Concept of Life Cycle Assessment

LCA is a methodology that assesses the environmental impacts of a product or system throughout all stages of its life cycle, from raw material extraction to final disposal. International Organization for Standardization (ISO, 2006) has developed standards that establish guidelines and procedures for conducting a systematic and comprehensive LCA.

4.1.2 Identification of Environmental Impacts Throughout Life Cycle Assessment

LCA makes it possible to identify environmental impacts at all stages of the life cycle of a product or project. The importance of considering not only direct impacts, such as greenhouse gas emissions, but also indirect impacts and displacements, which can be equally significant.

For example, in the evaluation of an electric car, not only emissions during use must be considered, but also those related to the manufacture of the battery and the generation of electricity used to charge it.

4.1.3 Informed Decision Making

One of the key benefits of LCA is that it provides sound information for informed decision making. LCA allows comparing different options and assessing the environmental performance of products or projects, which helps to identify opportunities for improvement and impact reduction.

For example, in the design of a solar power plant, LCA can help select materials and manufacturing processes that minimize environmental impacts compared to other power generation technologies.

4.1.4 Fulfillment of Sustainability Objectives

The integration of LCA in the evaluation of technologies and projects contributes to meeting sustainability objectives. LCA can be a valuable tool for assessing the environmental performance of technologies and products in line with greenhouse gas emission reduction targets and sustainable resource use.

In a world where sustainability is a growing concern, LCA enables companies and governments to take concrete steps to reduce their environmental footprint.

4.2. Environmental Impact Assessment: Methods

In this section, we will explore the key methods used to conduct a proper environmental impact assessment (EIA) in the context of projects and technologies related to sustainable energy systems engineering.

4.2.1 Environmental Impact Assessment (EIA) Methods

The EIA is a fundamental process in the evaluation of sustainable energy technologies and projects, since it allows identifying, predicting and evaluating the environmental impacts that may arise throughout the life cycle of a project, and includes the following stages:

Identification of impacts: In this stage, potential environmental impacts that could arise as a result of the project are identified. Aspects such as air quality, water, biodiversity, among others, are analyzed.

Impact prediction: Here the impacts identified in the previous stage are quantified and predicted. Mathematical models and simulation tools can be useful to estimate impacts accurately.

Impact assessment: In this stage, impacts are evaluated in terms of their magnitude, scope and significance. It is determined whether an impact is adverse and requires mitigation measures.

Mitigation of impacts: If adverse impacts are identified, strategies are developed to mitigate them and minimize their negative effect. A balance is sought between project development and environmental preservation.

4.2.2 Life Cycle Assessment (LCA)

LCA is an essential method for environmental impact assessment, as it allows the quantification and evaluation of impacts throughout the entire life cycle of a product or project. The general LCA process includes the following steps:

Definition of objectives and scope: The objectives of the assessment are determined and the scope of the analysis is established, identifying the stages of the life cycle to be included.

Data collection: Relevant data is collected for each stage of the life cycle, from raw material extraction to final disposal. This data may include resource consumption, emissions and energy used.

Inventory analysis: Environmental impacts are quantified at each stage of the life cycle using collected data. This allows the identification of "hot spots" where the greatest impacts are generated.

Impact assessment: Quantified impacts are assessed in terms of environmental impact categories such as climate change, acidification, eutrophication, among others.

Interpretation of results: LCA results are interpreted to make informed decisions about sustainability and opportunities for improvement are identified.

4.2.3 Comparison of Alternatives

A fundamental aspect of EIA is the comparison of alternatives. The importance of evaluating different options and technologies serves to determine which has the least environmental impact and meets sustainability objectives.

For example, when evaluating renewable energy generation projects, different technologies, such as solar and wind power, can be compared to determine which is more suitable in a specific environment in terms of their environmental impact and cost.

4.3. LCA Applications in Energy Projects

In this section, we will examine specific examples of how LCA is applied in energy projects, highlighting its usefulness in assessing sustainability and environmental impacts.

4.3.1 Life Cycle Assessment of Solar Energy Technologies

An outstanding example of the application of LCA is the life cycle assessment of solar energy technologies. An LCA of solar photovoltaic energy systems, including solar panel production, installation and lifetime use, was conducted and found that, despite the energy required to manufacture the panels, the energy generated during their lifetime largely offset these impacts, resulting in a positive balance from an environmental point of view.

This type of assessment is critical to understanding the environmental and economic implications of solar energy and making informed decisions about its implementation.

4.3.2 Comparison of Life Cycle Assessment Among Energy Sources

Another example is the comparison of life cycle assessment between different energy sources. In a study of the comparative life cycle assessment of various energy sources, including solar, wind, nuclear and natural gas revealed that renewable energy sources, such as solar and wind, generally have a lower environmental impact compared to conventional and nuclear energy sources, especially in terms of greenhouse gas emissions.

This comparison is essential to guide public policy decisions and investment strategies towards more sustainable energy sources.

4.3.3 Life Cycle Assessment of Offshore Wind Energy Projects

Offshore wind energy is a growing technology for renewable energy generation. An LCA of an offshore wind farm was conducted to assess its environmental impacts and compare them with fossil fuel power generation, in which offshore wind energy was shown to have a lower environmental impact, especially in terms of greenhouse gas emissions.

This type of assessment is essential to support the expansion of offshore wind energy as a sustainable energy source.

5. PROMOTION OF ENERGY EFFICIENCY PRACTICES

5.1. Energy Efficiency in Various Sectors

This section focuses on exploring key strategies to promote energy efficiency in a variety of sectors, from industry to transportation to housing. Energy efficiency is essential for reducing energy consumption and environmental impacts.

5.1.1 Multisectoral Approach to Energy Efficiency

Energy efficiency is not a single approach; it is a combination of strategies that are applied across multiple sectors. The importance of a multi-sectoral approach lies in addressing energy efficiency effectively, as various sectors face unique challenges and opportunities. This involves adopting efficiency measures in industry, improving the efficiency of buildings, promoting the use of efficient vehicles, and developing sustainable agricultural practices.

5.1.2 Energy Efficiency in Industry

In the industrial sector, energy efficiency is essential to reduce energy consumption and operating costs. The importance of implementing energy management systems, conducting energy audits and promoting the use of energy-saving technologies lies in the optimization and sustainability of our energy consumption, thus contributing to efficiency and cost reduction. Investing in more efficient technologies, such as high-performance electric motors, can also lead to significant energy savings.

5.1.3 Energy Efficiency in Transportation

The transportation sector is one of the largest consumers of energy and emitters of greenhouse gases. The need to promote sustainable mobility and encourage the use of efficient vehicles is essential to reduce the environmental footprint and improve air quality, in addition to optimizing transportation efficiency. This includes the expansion of public transport systems, the promotion of ridesharing, and the promotion of electric vehicles. In addition, urban planning can play a key role in designing cities that reduce the need to travel long distances.

5.1.4 Energy Efficiency in Housing

In the housing sector, energy efficiency is achieved through improvements in construction and the adoption of efficient technologies. The importance of thermal insulation, the choice of efficient materials, and the implementation of efficient heating and cooling systems lies in the ability to improve the energy efficiency of a building or space, thereby reducing energy consumption and associated costs, while contributing to a more sustainable and comfortable environment. LED lighting and home energy management are also effective strategies.

5.2. Reduction of Energy Consumption

In this section, we will address the implementation of technologies and policies as key strategies to reduce energy consumption. These actions are essential to promote energy efficiency and mitigate environmental impacts.

5.2.1 Energy Saving Technologies

The implementation of energy saving technologies is essential to reduce energy consumption in various sectors. The role of technologies such as LED lighting systems, efficient appliances and advanced heating and cooling systems is essential to improve energy efficiency in our homes and environments, which in turn contributes to reducing energy consumption, lowering costs and minimizing environmental impact. Investing in these technologies not only reduces energy consumption, but can also generate significant savings in operating costs over time.

5.2.2 Energy Efficiency Policies

Government policies play a crucial role in promoting energy efficiency. The effectiveness of policies, such as energy efficiency standards for appliances and vehicles, is critical in promoting the adoption of more efficient technologies, reducing energy consumption and mitigating environmental impacts, while incentivizing innovation in the industry and contributing to a more sustainable use of energy resources. These policies establish minimum efficiency requirements that manufacturers must meet, which encourages the adoption of more efficient technologies in the market.

5.2.3 Certifications and Energy Labeling

Energy certifications and labeling are tools that help consumers make informed decisions about more efficient products and buildings. Energy labels, which indicate the efficiency of a product or building, can have a significant impact on purchasing decisions by providing valuable information to consumers and potential buyers, making it easier to choose more efficient and sustainable options. These labels provide information on energy consumption and operating costs, which can motivate consumers to opt for more efficient products and buildings.

5.2.4 Investment in Energy Infrastructure

Investment in energy infrastructure is also crucial to reduce energy consumption. The effectiveness of investments in public transportation systems and the expansion of electric vehicle charging infrastructure is crucial to fostering more sustainable mobility and reducing dependence on fossil fuels, while contributing to the mitigation of air pollution and climate change. These investments not only improve accessibility and convenience, but also promote sustainable mobility and the adoption of more efficient transportation technologies.

5.3. Energy Efficiency: Benefits

This section focuses on the economic and environmental benefits derived from energy efficiency. The implementation of efficiency measures not only reduces operating costs, but also contributes to climate change mitigation and air quality improvement.

5.3.1 Reduced Operating Costs and Economic Savings

One of the most obvious economic benefits of energy efficiency is the reduction of operating costs. Companies can reap economic benefits by investing in more efficient technologies and practices, as these investments often lead to reduced operating costs, increased productivity and greater competitiveness in the marketplace. They also contribute to the responsible use of resources and the reduction of environmental impacts. Reduced energy consumption translates into lower energy bills and greater long-term profitability.

5.3.2 Employment Generation and Economic Development

The implementation of energy efficiency projects can also generate employment and contribute to local economic development. Energy efficiency investments can generate employment in sectors such as construction and manufacturing of efficient technologies. These investments not only contribute to the reduction of energy consumption and operating costs, but also stimulate the economy by boosting job creation in areas related to energy efficiency and sustainability.

5.3.3 Reduction of Greenhouse Gas Emissions

Energy efficiency plays a crucial role in reducing greenhouse gas emissions. The adoption of more efficient technologies and practices plays a key role in achieving emission reduction targets. These measures help to reduce the carbon footprint by reducing energy consumption and optimizing processes, which in turn supports efforts to combat climate change and promote environmental sustainability. Reduced energy consumption leads to less burning of fossil fuels and, therefore, less release of carbon dioxide and other pollutants.

5.3.4 Improved Air Quality

Energy efficiency not only benefits the climate, but also improves air quality. Reduced energy consumption leads to reduced air pollution, which in turn has beneficial effects on public health. By reducing the emission of air pollutants, such as greenhouse gases and harmful particulates, air quality is improved and the risk of respiratory diseases and other health problems in the population is reduced.

5.3.5 Energy Resilience and Security

Energy efficiency also improves energy resilience and security of supply. The adoption of energy efficiency technologies can reduce dependence on imported fossil fuels, which strengthens a country's energy security. By reducing the need to import energy resources, a country becomes more self-sufficient and less vulnerable to fluctuations in international prices and disruptions in energy supply. In addition, energy efficiency can help avoid blackouts by reducing peak energy demand.

6. ADVANCED ENERGY STORAGE

6.1. Renewable Energies: Storage Technologies

Section 7.1 focuses on the development of energy storage technologies specifically designed to integrate renewable energy sources into energy systems. These technologies are essential to overcome the intermittency and variability of renewable sources and ensure a constant and reliable energy supply.

6.1.1 Need for Storage for Renewable Sources

The growth of renewable energies, such as solar and wind, has highlighted the critical need for energy storage solutions. Renewable sources are intermittent in nature, which means that they do not always produce energy when it is required. Energy storage acts as a bridge, capturing excess energy at times of excess production and releasing it when demand is high.

6.1.2 Storage Technologies for Renewable Energy

Different storage technologies are best suited to different renewable energy applications. Available storage options include lithium-ion batteries, thermal storage systems, pumped storage and hydrogen storage systems. These technologies play a key role in managing energy generated from renewable sources, allowing it to be used when it is needed most, even at times when renewable energy sources are not generating electricity. Each of these technologies has its own advantages in terms of efficiency, capacity and applicability.

6.1.3 Advances in Solar Energy Storage

Solar energy storage is particularly important due to the variability of solar radiation. The development of specific storage technologies for solar systems, such as solar battery systems and molten salt thermal storage systems, is essential to maximize the efficiency and availability of energy generated from solar radiation. These solutions make it possible to harness solar energy during periods of lower irradiation, ensuring a constant and reliable energy supply and allowing greater penetration of solar energy into the power grid.

6.1.4 Wind Energy Storage

Wind power also benefits from energy storage to address fluctuations in wind speed. The use of batteries and hydro storage systems is essential to optimize wind energy production and ensure a constant delivery of energy to the grid. These technologies allow the energy generated by wind turbines to be stored during times of abundant wind and released when demand is high or when wind conditions are less favorable, helping to maintain the stability and reliability of the electricity supply.

6.1.5 Large-Scale and Home Energy Storage

Energy storage is not limited to large installations; it is also relevant in residential and small-scale applications. The implementation of home storage systems allows homeowners to take full advantage of locally generated solar energy. These systems store excess solar energy produced during the day for later use, giving homeowners greater energy independence and the ability to use their solar energy even when the sun is not present, such as at night or on cloudy days. These systems provide energy autonomy and reduce dependence on the grid.

6.2. Storage Systems: Application

This section focuses on providing an overview of energy storage systems and how they are applied in various scenarios. These systems play a key role in energy management, from load leveling in power grids to supporting critical applications in isolated environments.

6.2.1 Energy Storage Systems: An Overview

Energy storage systems can take various forms and technologies, including batteries of various types (such as lithium-ion batteries, flow batteries and lead-acid batteries), thermal storage (using latent or sensible heat), pumped storage, hydrogen storage systems and supercapacitors. Each technology has its own advantages and limitations, allowing its application in different situations.

6.2.2 Electrical Network Applications

Energy storage systems play a key role in power grid management. The application of storage systems plays an essential role in several areas, such as load leveling, frequency regulation, peak demand management and the integration of intermittent renewable energies. These technologies allow smoothing the variability of demand and generation, ensuring the stability and reliability of the electricity supply, as well as facilitating the incorporation of renewable energy sources that are not always constantly available, such as solar and wind. In this context, lithium-ion batteries have proven to be particularly effective due to their rapid response capacity.

6.2.3 Storage in Decentralized Renewable Energy Systems

Storage systems are also essential in decentralized renewable energy systems, such as residential solar installations. Storage systems allow homeowners to take full advantage of locally generated solar energy. These systems store excess solar energy produced during the day, giving homeowners the ability to use their solar energy even when the sun is not present, such as at night or on cloudy days, which in turn reduces their dependence on the conventional power grid and their energy costs.

6.2.4 Microgrid and Isolated Network Applications

In microgrids and isolated grids, storage systems are essential to ensure a constant and reliable power supply. Storage systems, such as batteries and thermal storage systems, are used in microgrids to balance energy supply and demand, as well as to support critical applications such as hospitals and data centers. These technologies help maintain grid stability, manage generation variability, and ensure the continuous supply of electricity to sensitive facilities, even in emergency situations.

6.2.5 Storage for Electric Mobility

Storage systems also play an important role in electric mobility. The incorporation of storage systems in electric vehicles plays an essential role in extending the range of these vehicles and allowing them to be charged quickly and efficiently. These storage systems, mostly based on advanced high-capacity batteries, accumulate the energy needed to power the electric vehicle. High-performance batteries are essential in this context.

6.3. Energy Storage and Emerging Solutions

Section 7.3 focuses on large-scale energy storage research and emerging solutions that are transforming the energy landscape. This research is crucial for improving the efficiency and reliability of energy storage in critical applications and large-scale power systems.

6.3.1 Research in Advanced Storage Systems

Research in advanced storage systems is essential to overcome current challenges and improve the efficiency of existing technologies. Progress in the development of advanced storage systems, such as solid-state batteries and energy storage systems based on nanostructured materials, represents a significant milestone in energy storage technology. These advances have the potential to increase the energy density and lifetime of batteries, which is critical for large-scale applications.

6.3.2 Large-Scale Power Grid Applications

Large-scale energy storage plays a key role in the stability and reliability of power grids. Large-scale energy storage systems are used to manage the intermittency of renewable energy sources and ensure a constant and reliable power supply. These systems play a crucial role in the effective integration of renewable energy sources, such as solar and wind, which can vary in their availability throughout the day and depending on weather conditions. By storing excess energy produced when these sources are abundant, storage systems allow it to be released when demand is high or when renewable sources are not generating electricity, thus helping to maintain grid stability and ensure a constant supply of energy. Solutions such as compressed air storage systems and large-scale battery storage systems are key in this area.

6.3.3 Advanced Thermal Energy Storage

Thermal energy storage is an important technology for large-scale applications such as concentrated solar power generation and industrial heating. The advancement in the development of advanced thermal energy storage systems, including phase change materials and molten salt thermal energy storage systems, represents an important milestone in energy storage technology. These systems enable high-density energy storage and controlled release.

6.3.4 Emerging Solutions in Energy Storage

In addition to existing technologies, emerging energy storage solutions are being developed. The use of hydrogen-based energy storage systems and zinc-air flow batteries is critical to managing energy more efficiently and sustainably. These technologies provide flexibility, durability and the ability to harness intermittent renewable energy sources, which is essential for moving towards a cleaner and more reliable energy system. These emerging solutions offer advantages in terms of energy density and cost.

6.3.5 Impact on the Energy Transition

Research in large-scale energy storage and emerging solutions is playing a critical role in the transition to a cleaner and more sustainable energy matrix. Energy storage is essential to optimize the use of renewable energy sources and reduce dependence on fossil fuels. This technology plays a fundamental role in allowing energy generated from renewable sources, such as solar and wind, to be stored and used when it is most needed, even at times when these sources are not generating electricity on a consistent basis. This helps stabilize the energy supply, ensures a constant supply and reduces the need to resort to fossil fuels, which in turn reduces greenhouse gas emissions and promotes a transition to a cleaner, more sustainable energy system.

7. INTERNET OF THINGS (IOT) - ENERGY EFFICIENCY

7.1. IoT in the Context of Energy Efficiency

Section 8.1 provides a key introduction to the concept of the Internet of Things (IoT) in the context of energy efficiency. IoT is a disruptive technology that has transformed the way we collect, manage and use energy-related data.

7.1.1 Definition of IoT and Its Relevance to Energy Efficiency

IoT refers to the interconnection of physical devices via the Internet, which can collect and share data in real time. In the context of energy efficiency, this means that devices such as sensors, smart meters and control devices can communicate with each other and with management systems to optimize energy use. IoT has the potential to transform energy efficiency in a variety of applications.

7.1.2 IoT in Intelligent Buildings

One of the most prominent areas of IoT application in energy efficiency is in smart buildings. The Internet of Things (IoT) is used to monitor and control systems such as lighting, HVAC and energy management in real time. This technology enables the interconnection of devices and sensors that collect data in real time, making it possible to optimize and automate systems, as well as make informed decisions to improve efficiency and sustainability in environments such as buildings and energy systems.

7.1.3 IoT in Industry and Manufacturing

IoT also has a significant impact on energy efficiency in industry and manufacturing. The Internet of Things (IoT) is used for machinery monitoring, supply chain optimization and real-time energy management. This technology enables the interconnection of devices and sensors that collect data in real time, enabling more accurate machinery monitoring, greater supply chain efficiency and more effective energy management in various industrial and commercial sectors. This has led to reduced costs and a smaller carbon footprint in industrial production.

7.1.4 IoT in Mobility

IoT plays an important role in energy efficiency in transportation. The Internet of Things (IoT) is used in traffic management, vehicle monitoring and electric vehicle charging. This technology enables the interconnection of devices and sensors that collect data in real time, making it possible to optimize traffic flow, track vehicles and efficiently manage electric vehicle charging, thus contributing to smarter and more sustainable mobility by reducing fossil fuel consumption and greenhouse gas emissions.

7.1.5 Challenges and Considerations

Despite its benefits, implementing IoT in energy efficiency also presents challenges. Addressing privacy and data security concerns, as well as ensuring the interoperability of Internet of Things (IoT) devices, is critical. Protecting data privacy and security is essential to ensure that information collected and shared by IoT devices is safeguarded against potential threats and unauthorized access. At the same time, interoperability between devices allows them to communicate and work together effectively, which is essential to realize the full potential of the IoT and ensure a smooth user experience and widespread adoption of this technology.

7.2. IoT Use Cases: Monitoring and Control

Section 8.2 focuses on presenting concrete use cases of the Internet of Things (IoT) for monitoring and control of energy systems. These examples illustrate how IoT is transforming energy management in various applications.

7.2.1 Smart Grids

One of the most prominent IoT use cases is in smart grids. The Internet of Things (IoT) enables real-time monitoring of the power grid, including fault detection and load management. This technology enables the interconnection of devices and sensors that collect data in real time, resulting in a smarter and more efficient power grid. The ability to detect faults instantly and manage load dynamically is essential to improving grid reliability and management, which benefits utilities and consumers. Smart meters, equipped with IoT sensors, collect data on users' energy consumption and send this information to utilities. This enables more efficient grid management, early detection of problems and the ability to adjust power distribution in real time.

7.2.2 Smart Buildings and Energy Management

In the field of smart buildings, IoT is used for monitoring and controlling energy systems. Internet of Things (IoT) sensors in buildings can detect room occupancy and automatically adjust lighting, HVAC and other systems to optimize energy consumption. This technology enables smarter and more efficient management of resources in buildings by adapting the environment to the actual needs of the occupants, resulting in less energy waste and greater comfort.

7.2.3 Precision Agriculture and Energy Efficiency

Precision agriculture is another area where IoT has revolutionized energy efficiency. Internet of Things (IoT) sensors are used to monitor weather conditions, soil moisture and other agricultural parameters. This technology allows farmers to collect real-time data on environmental conditions, which helps them make informed decisions in managing their crops. The information gathered through IoT sensors is valuable for optimizing irrigation, preventing plant diseases and improving farming efficiency.

7.2.4 Sustainable Mobility and Intelligent Transportation

IoT also plays an important role in promoting sustainable mobility and intelligent transportation. Internet of Things (IoT) sensors in vehicles and road infrastructure can provide real-time data on traffic and road conditions. This technology enables more effective traffic management by providing up-to-date information on congestion, accidents and road conditions, which can improve road safety and facilitate more efficient navigation for drivers. In addition, this data is valuable to transportation planning and mobility management authorities. This enables more efficient traffic management, reduces congestion and ultimately lowers fuel consumption and greenhouse gas emissions.

7.2.5 Industry and Equipment Monitoring

In industry, IoT is used for equipment monitoring and energy management. Internet of Things (IoT) sensors on industrial machines have the ability to detect problems and maintenance needs early. This prevents unplanned downtime and reduces energy consumption associated with inefficient production. These sensors collect real-time data on machine performance and health, allowing operators and maintenance teams to take preventive action before serious problems occur. Ultimately, this anticipation contributes to more continuous and efficient production while minimizing wasted energy and resources, which is essential for competitiveness and sustainability in the industry.

7.3 IoT Implementation: Energy Efficiency

Section 8.3 addresses a critical aspect of implementing the Internet of Things (IoT) for energy efficiency: security challenges and considerations. As IoT becomes more ubiquitous in energy management, it is essential to understand and address the risks associated with the collection, processing, and transmission of energy data.

7.3.1 Data Privacy

One of the main challenges in implementing IoT in energy efficiency is data privacy. IoT devices collect a large amount of information, including energy consumption and user behavior data. This raises concerns about the privacy of individuals. It is essential to establish robust privacy policies and ensure that data is handled securely and users' identities are protected.

7.3.2 IoT Device Security

Another major challenge is the security of IoT devices themselves. IoT devices often have limitations in terms of processing and storage capacity, which makes them vulnerable to attacks. It is critical to emphasize the importance of securing IoT devices through measures such as strong authentication, data encryption and secure firmware updates. Security in IoT devices is essential to safeguard privacy and data integrity, as well as to prevent potential cyber threats. Authentication ensures that only authorized users have access to devices, while encryption protects the confidentiality of transmitted information. Secure firmware updates help to correct vulnerabilities and maintain device security over time. These measures are essential to ensure trust in IoT systems and to maintain the integrity and security of data and connected infrastructure.

7.3.3 Network Vulnerabilities

Communication between IoT devices and energy management systems takes place over networks, which can be a point of vulnerability. Implementing network security measures, such as firewalls and intrusion detection systems, is essential to mitigate these risks.

7.3.4 Interoperability and Standards

Interoperability between IoT devices and energy management systems is critical to their effective operation. However, the lack of common standards and protocols can hinder the integration of different devices and systems. It is essential to emphasize the need to develop standards that promote interoperability and facilitate security in the Internet of Things (IoT). These standards are essential to ensure that IoT devices from different manufacturers can communicate with each other efficiently and securely. Interoperability enables the creation of broader and more diversified ecosystems, which drives IoT adoption and utility. In addition, security standards establish common guidelines that help protect devices and data from potential cyber threats. By adhering to these standards, sound security practices are established that protect the privacy and integrity of information, which is essential in an environment where connectivity and data collection are increasingly common.

7.3.5 Upgrades and Maintenance

IoT devices require regular firmware updates and maintenance to address emerging vulnerabilities. However, managing updates can be a challenge in distributed IoT environments.

8. ENVIRONMENTAL EDUCATION AND AWARENESS

8.1. Environmental Education: Sustainability

Section 10.1 focuses on the fundamental importance of environmental education in moving toward sustainability. Environmental education is an essential component in developing a sound understanding of environmental issues and in promoting a pro-environmental attitude. Authors and studies support the relevance of environmental education in promoting sustainability and will be discussed below.

8.1.1 Fundamentals of Environmental Education

Environmental education is based on the idea that in order to address current and future environmental challenges, it is crucial that people understand environmental issues and adopt more environmentally friendly behavior. Environmental education is not only about transmitting knowledge, but also about developing skills and attitudes that foster active engagement with the environment.

8.1.2 Promoting Awareness and Understanding

Environmental education plays a key role in promoting awareness and understanding of environmental issues. This education helps people understand the interconnectedness between natural and human systems, allowing for a more holistic view of environmental challenges. It also promotes appreciation of biological and cultural diversity.

8.1.3 Promotion of Active Citizenship

United Nations Educational, Scientific and Cultural Organization (UNESCO, 2014) emphasizes that environmental education is essential for the development of engaged and active citizens. It helps people understand their role in society and their ability to influence policies and practices that affect the environment. This aligns with the notion of environmental citizenship, which involves participating in decision-making and acting to address environmental problems.

8.1.4 Application in Different Contexts

Environmental education is not limited to the classroom; it can be applied in a variety of contexts, from schools and universities to community organizations and public outreach programs. This makes it possible to reach diverse audiences and tailor environmental education to the needs and characteristics of each group.

8.1.5 Contribution to Sustainability

Environmental education is an essential component of the transition to sustainability. Environmental education is fundamental to changing mindsets toward a culture of sustainability. It helps people understand the urgency of environmental problems and take concrete steps to address them, whether at the individual, community or global level.

8.2. Awareness of Renewable Energy

This section focuses on identifying and discussing effective strategies to promote awareness of renewable energy. Promoting public awareness of the importance of renewable energy sources is crucial for the transition to a more sustainable energy matrix.

8.2.1 Awareness and Communication Campaigns

Awareness campaigns are effective tools for disseminating information about renewable energy. It is critical to highlight the importance of effectively communicating the benefits of renewable energy, such as carbon emission reductions and energy independence. Efficient communication plays a crucial role in raising public awareness and acceptance of clean energy sources. By clearly communicating the benefits of renewables, such as reduced carbon emissions that contribute to climate change, and energy independence that decreases dependence on non-renewable and often imported energy sources, greater support and adoption of these sustainable energy sources can be encouraged. This, in turn, can accelerate the transition to a cleaner, more sustainable energy system, with both environmental and economic benefits.

8.2.2 Education in Schools

Renewable energy education in schools is critical to raise awareness from an early age. Including renewable energy in the school curriculum can inspire younger generations and foster interest in careers in sustainable energy. Educational programs can include visits to wind or solar farms and hands-on energy-related projects.

8.2.3 Community Participation

Active community participation is essential to promote awareness of renewable energy. The importance of involving communities in decision making about renewable energy projects. Public consultation and participation in open discussions can help address concerns and build consensus around the implementation of renewable technologies.

8.2.4 Incentives and Grants

The implementation of government incentives and subsidies can stimulate the adoption of renewable energy. Financial incentives, such as tax credits and feed-in tariffs, can reduce costs for consumers and businesses investing in renewable energy. Thcsc policies can be a strong motivator for the transition to cleaner energy sources.

8.2.5 Citizen Mobilization Campaigns

Citizen mobilization campaigns, such as those organized by environmental groups and NGOs, can generate public support for renewable energy. These actions can raise the visibility of energy-related issues and pressure policy makers to take action.

8.3. Systems Engineering and Environmental Disclosure

Section 10.3 focuses on the role of systems engineering in the dissemination of environmental knowledge. Systems engineering plays a crucial role in the planning and execution of projects related to renewable energy and sustainability. Through the dissemination of environmental knowledge, systems engineers can promote the adoption of more sustainable practices.

8.3.1 Interdisciplinary Nature of Systems Engineering

Systems engineering is an interdisciplinary discipline based on the integration of knowledge from various areas to address complex problems. Systems engineers focus on the management of complex systems and their operational efficiency. This ability to approach problems from a holistic perspective is essential for the transition to sustainability.

8.3.2 Development of Integrated Solutions

Systems engineering focuses on the development of integrated solutions that consider multiple aspects, including environmental aspects. Systems engineers can design energy systems that optimize efficiency and minimize environmental impact. This is achieved by identifying synergies between technologies and considering complete life cycles.

8.3.3 Effective Communication of Environmental Data

Systems engineers are responsible for communicating environmental data effectively to stakeholders, including the community, decision makers and businesses. t is crucial to emphasize the importance of data visualization and clear communication to convey environmental information in an understandable manner. Effective data visualization, through graphs, maps and visual representations, allows environmental information to be presented in a way that is more accessible and easier to understand for the general public. Clear communication, together with these visual representations, facilitates the transmission of environment-related data, such as air quality, biodiversity, climate change or natural resource management.

Understanding environmental issues is essential for making informed decisions, influencing policy and encouraging more sustainable practices in society. Therefore, data visualization and effective communication play a key role in environmental awareness and action by enabling people to assimilate and act on information presented in a clear and accessible manner.

8.3.4 Incorporation of Sustainability Principles

Systems engineers can integrate sustainability principles into energy system design and operation decision making. This involves considering not only technical efficiency, but also environmental and social impacts throughout the life cycle of a project.

8.3.5 Participation in Research and Development

Systems engineering plays an active role in the research and development of sustainable technologies and practices. Systems engineering research can drive innovation in renewable energy and more efficient energy storage systems. This research contributes to the advancement of sustainability.

REFERENCES

International Organization for Standardization. (2006). *Environmental management - Life cycle assessment - Principles and framework*. ISO.

United Nations Educational, Scientific and Cultural Organization. (2014). *Roadmap for implementing the Global Action Programme on Education for Sustainable Development*. UNESCO.

KEY TERMS AND DEFINITIONS

Energy Efficiency: The ability to use the least amount of energy to carry out a specific task or process without sacrificing quality or the desired result. Energy efficiency seeks to optimize the use of energy resources to reduce energy consumption and minimize waste.

Environmental Education: A process that aims to create awareness and understanding of environmental issues, foster responsible attitudes towards the environment, and enable people to take actions and make informed decisions that contribute to the conservation and protection of the natural environment.

Environmental Impact Assessment: A systematic process that evaluates the potential environmental effects of a project, plan or program prior to its implementation. It aims to identify, predict and assess impacts on the environment and propose measures to prevent, minimize or compensate for negative impacts. In other words, it seeks to ensure that development decisions are sustainable and respectful of the natural environment and nearby communities.

Green Economy: An economic approach that focuses on sustainable development, environmental conservation and responsible management of natural resources, with the aim of achieving equitable and sustainable economic growth.

Renewable Energy: Energy that comes from natural sources that are inexhaustible or constantly renewable, such as solar radiation, wind, water flow and geothermal heat. These natural sources are used to generate electricity, heat and other types of energy without depleting the underlying resources and with reduced environmental impact.

Sustainability: The ability to maintain a long-term balance between economic prosperity, social well-being and environmental health, so that the needs of the present generation are met without compromising the opportunities and resources of future generations.

Sustainable Cities: Cities that are designed and planned to be socially, economically and environmentally sustainable in the long term. These cities seek to balance urban growth with environmental conservation, the quality of life of their inhabitants, and efficiency in the use of resources.

Sustainable Development: A comprehensive approach that seeks a balance between economic growth, social equity and environmental conservation to ensure a better future for present and future generations.

Chapter 9
Tax Carbon Policy:
Momentum to Accelerate Indonesia's Sustainable Economic Growth Towards Green Economy

I. Made Laut Mertha Jaya
https://orcid.org/0000-0001-9722-7217
Universitas Mahakarya Asia, Indonesia

Miguel Angel Esquivias Padilla
https://orcid.org/0000-0002-1282-6163
Universitas Airlangga, Indonesia

ABSTRACT

The transition to a green economy has been widely discussed around the world as a response to the worsening climate change crisis. Carbon tax is predicted to be a significant first step. The authors conducted in-depth interviews related to the carbon tax policy as a momentum to accelerate the sustainability of Indonesia's economic growth that is in accordance with the concept of green economy or not. Therefore, the new hypothesis that emerges later can show the true purpose and role of the carbon tax policy for Indonesia's future. It is concluded that, similar to other countries in the world, Indonesia has the potential to implement a carbon tax policy in order to reduce and control carbon emissions. The sectors that can be directly burdened by carbon tax are power generation, transportation, building industry, pulp and paper industry, cement, and petrochemicals. Although not perfect, this carbon tax should be implemented immediately.

INTRODUCTION

"It also seems irrelevant if efforts to boost the economy are still sacrificing environmental interests. The reason is, in the midst of environmental crises, one of which is the climate crisis, which is increasingly worrying, moving from an extractive economy to a green economy, which is of course environmentally friendly and sustainable, is a necessity."

DOI: 10.4018/979-8-3693-1297-1.ch009

Climate change has started to become a concern for many people recently (Ojha & Schofield, 2022). This cannot be separated from the impact that is directly felt by humans. This is because the climate plays an important role in many aspects of earth's life including food security, health, and energy (Bayhaqi, 2019; Yildirim, 2020). If climatic conditions gradually worsen over time, humans will feel the negative impact. Although, generally these changes take place over a long period of time with slow changes.

Indonesia actually has an important role in climate control efforts (Bappenas, 2021). The country that is called the lungs of the world has vast forests to be able to maintain the earth's temperature. As is well known that forests can be effective carbon sinks (Sukma Aisya, 2019). Unfortunately, the land area in Indonesia is decreasing rapidly. However, in the last 6 years the deforestation rate in Indonesia has reached 2.1 million hectares. This will have a bad impact, considering that deforestation is one of the triggers for the big impacts of climate change (Hermanto Sirait, 2019). As a country with a very large population, Indonesia contributes quite a large amount of carbon emissions, which accounts for 2% of the world's total carbon emissions. This resulted in Indonesia being included in the 10 largest emitting countries in the world (Nurdiawansyah et al., 2018).

This climate problem will also affect the increase in temperature and change the pattern and distribution of rainfall, so that the effect is the preservation of water resources, crop productivity, and community activities will be disrupted (Ojha & Schofield, 2022). Unwise exploitation and use of natural resources leads to excessive energy consumption and environmental damage (Qadir et al., 2021). Greenhouse gas emissions have also threatened the living space of all human beings. Therefore, in order to reduce the impact of global climate change and achieve sustainable development, countries around the world are starting to prioritize green development (He et al., 2022). The impact of climate change felt by the people of Indonesia has encouraged the government to implement sustainable development by implementing one of the economic transformation strategies in the medium to long term, namely the green economy policy (Bappenas, 2014; Hidayattuloh et al., 2020).

Green Economy is an economic system that aims to improve human welfare without compromising the rights of future generations to enjoy natural resources (Rounaghi, 2019). In addition, a green economy can also be defined as an economy that is low carbon, resource efficient, and socially inclusive (Kasztelan, 2017). Based on these definitions, it can be concluded that a green economy is a form of concern for future generations. This concern can be started by reducing carbon emissions. The government's next plan is to set tariffs on carbon emissions through the imposition of a carbon tax which is seen as one of the progressive steps in supporting efforts to tackle the global climate crisis (Kumala et al., 2021; Saputra, 2021). In general, carbon taxes themselves are imposed for various forms of gas emissions that cause the greenhouse effect, such as carbon dioxide (CO2), nitrous oxide (N2O), and methane (CH4) at rates that are adjusted to the needs and conditions of a country (Brandl & Zielinska, 2020). The Indonesian government has set a planned carbon tax rate of at least IDR 75 per kilogram (kg) of carbon dioxide equivalent (CO2e) or an equivalent unit. Even though it is far from the recommendation of the World Bank and IMF, the tariff set by the Government of Indonesia is still tolerable as a good first step, and in accordance with current conditions.

Implementing a carbon tax can be a good start in encouraging efforts to reduce emissions (Selvi et al., 2020; Yunis & Aliakbari, 2020). The carbon tax will mainly be contributed from the power, transportation and industrial sectors as Indonesia's largest emitters in the energy sector (Ratnawati, 2016). Not only is it present as a new tax source that is predicted to be able to boost state revenues, carbon taxes are also very useful in efforts to reduce carbon foot prints dangerous for the world's climate (Carattini et al., 2018; OEC, 2019).The acceleration of carbon tax implementation will also put pressure on polluters to

Figure 1. Appearance of mean annual temperatures above 29°C in Indonesia by 2070. Points indicate large agglomerations
Map by Simon Papai

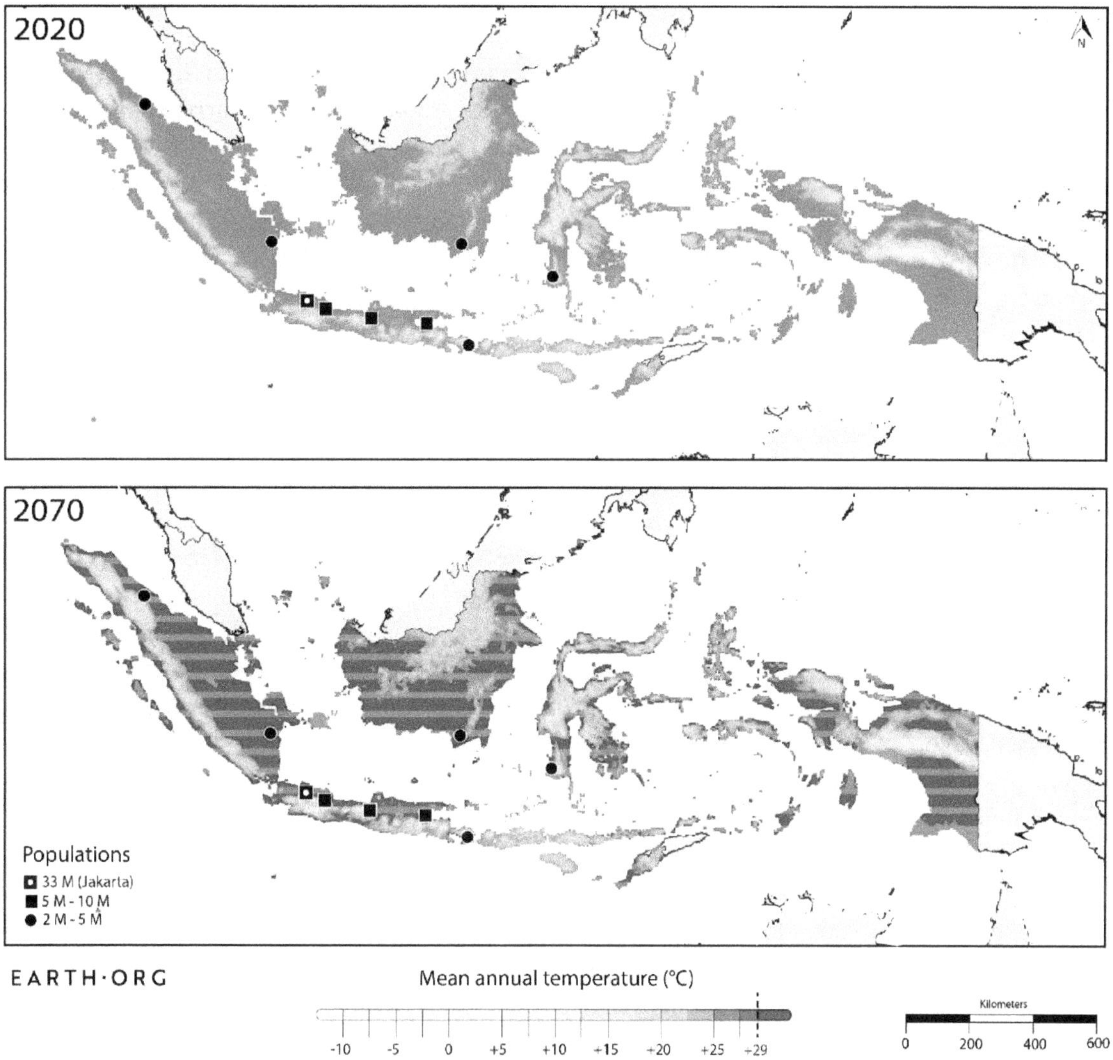

control the production of carbon emissions, so that the emission reduction target in accordance with Law Number 16 of 2016 can be achieved (Selvi et al., 2020). In other words, a carbon tax is a government measure to make business actors significantly responsible for the carbon produced from their production systems. The application of a carbon tax will encourage the public and business actors to reduce or even switch from fossil fuels to clean energy or new renewable energy (Al-Shetwi, 2022; Arimura & Matsumoto, 2020). This step can be a stimulus in starting the implementation of a sustainable green economy (Kasztelan, 2017).

It seems that the implementation of a carbon tax will not be as smooth as imagined and the imposition of a carbon tax will basically raise various polemics because it has the potential to reduce economic growth, reduce social welfare, and can even damage industrial competitiveness (Lin & Li, 2011). Like the chaos that occurred in Paris in 2018 where Prime Minister Macron unilaterally raised the carbon tax rate without considering the situation of the people so that the price of gasoline and diesel oil soared, this could become a reference for the government. How decisions that are not thought through carefully have a negative impact, especially for the wider community. Therefore, policies issued by the government regarding carbon taxes must be wise and pay attention to all aspects. Research covering the Asia and Pacific region also suggests that the implementation of carbon taxes can be carried out in stages and adapted to the conditions of each country (Ferdian, 2021). The challenges for the Government of Indonesia in implementing carbon taxes are of course more severe than that because this policy will directly impact the people's economy which is sluggish due to the ongoing pandemic. When a country that is used to extractive energy, such as fossil fuels, tries to leave it all behind through the implementation of a carbon tax, it is clear that turmoil will occur, inflation will increase, the price of goods may skyrocket, and those who are not ready will be affected. Nevertheless, this is of course only temporary because in fact the economy will continue to find its balance, however, not in a climate where, if it is already in a deep crisis, it seems impossible to recover quickly.

The legal umbrella for the carbon tax was born through the Tax Regulation Harmonization Act. As an initial stage, a carbon tax will be implemented in the Coal-fired Power Plant sector on April 1, 2022 using a tax mechanism based on emission limits. A tariff of IDR 30 per kilogram of carbon dioxide equivalent is applied to emission amounts that exceed a set cap (Ratnawati, 2016). This figure is relatively low when compared to carbon tax rates in developed countries. However, this cannot be compared with the economic strength of developing countries, such as Indonesia (Saputra, 2021). The inclusion of a carbon tax in the Law on the Harmonization of Tax Regulations is a progressive step in reducing emissions as well as the start of low-carbon development. In addition, the carbon tax revenue generated can later be used for low-carbon development, for example for renewable energy subsidies, green technology research, green industry incentives, and others.(Marron & Morris, 2016). This is certainly very much in line with Indonesia's Nationally Determined Contribution (NDC) target of reducing emissions by 29% on its own and 41% with international support by 2030.

In considering the implementation of a carbon tax, the government must also look at the opportunities and challenges ahead, because don't let good intentions to patch up the economy and save the environment instead become an additional burden that is difficult to accommodate (Bappenas, 2021). Because the carbon tax has the probability to generate debate or even opposition from society and the business sector. However, carbon taxes remain one effective mechanism for limiting higher emissions (Khastar et al., 2020). Even though at the beginning of its implementation it may cause turmoil, inflation, and skyrocketing prices of goods, this will only last temporarily because the true economy will continue to find its balance. Meanwhile, if the climate is already in a deep crisis, it will be difficult to restore it quickly (Bappenas, 2021)The government is demanded to be active in socializing the carbon tax to the public, especially the industrial world and business actors before it is officially implemented in 2022. Clear and transparent information might have been able to minimize the rejection that occurred in the early days of implementing the carbon tax (Kumala et al., 2021). The seriousness of the government and the ability of the community to execute this policy will be the key to implementing a carbon tax to achieve a green economy (Bappenas, 2021). Based on the description of these issues and phenomena, we will conduct in-depth interviews regarding tax carbon policies as a momentum for accelerating the sustainability of Indonesia's economic growth whether or not it is in accordance with the green economy concept. For this reason, new hypotheses that emerge can later show the true purpose and role of tax carbon policies for Indonesia's future.

WHY TAX CARBON?

The industrial revolution that started at the end of the 18th century was a turning point in world history. Over the past two hundred years population growth and sustained average incomes have increased dramatically and have never happened before. Growing population and production require more energy than energy produced from burning wood and animal power. Answering this problem, came the innovation of alternative energy use of coal and oil-based production (Al-Shetwi, 2022; Qadir et al., 2021). The consequence of burning coal and oil is that a lot of carbon dioxide (CO2) is released into the atmosphere and accumulatively collects in the air which in turn creates negative externalities of air pollution and global warming (Ratnawati, 2016). Air pollution is a negative externality that deserves common attention considering the importance of air as the main support for human, animal and plant life and its characteristics which are public goods. Referring to the results of a 1996 United Nation Environment Programme, it was found that air pollution in Jakarta is the third worst in the world after Mexico City and Bangkok. In 2011, data from the World Resources Institute stated that Indonesia was ranked 6th out of the top 10 carbon emitting countries in the world. This is very ironic considering the importance of air as the main supporting element in the life of living things.

The Copenhagen Climate Change Conference, Indonesia is committed to reducing carbon emission levels by 26% by 2020, for this reason a policy is needed that can facilitate the target of reducing these carbon emission levels. Carbon tax is one of the effective instruments available to achieve this goal. Several developed countries such as Sweden, Finland and Denmark have been able to reduce negative externalities due to carbon emissions by 7-15% by using carbon taxes (International Energy Agency, 2013). Based on research and the success of other countries in implementing the carbon tax, it is concluded that carbon tax is the right policy in overcoming the negative externalities of carbon emissions towards the current and future implementation of a green economy.

TAX CARBON AND SUSTAINABLE ECONOMIC GROWTH

Carbon tax is a type of pollution tax levied on the use of fossil fuels to remedy market failures (Rabe & Borick, 2012). The main failure of the market for fossil fuel products is the emergence of negative externalities, such as climate change and air pollution (Ratnawati, 2016). In the absence of a carbon tax, consumers do not bear the full cost of using the product, which is the sum of production, distribution costs and social costs, such as economic losses from climate change and air pollution. In theory, increased costs due to taxation will reduce the demand for fossil fuels.

Based on these reasons, the absence of a carbon tax will lead to excessive fuel consumption, and the carbon tax aims to correct this market failure by incorporating the social costs of the resulting negative externalities into the selling price of fuel. The inclusion of social costs then causes the selling price of fossil fuels to be higher, and is expected to reduce the amount of demand for fossil fuels by consumers. On the other hand, the impact of climate change which has become a global challenge also needs to be addressed together. As a country that is classified as vulnerable to the threat of climate change, Indonesia ratified the Paris Agreement which included a Nationally Determined Contribution (NDC) commitment in 2016, and make tackling climate change one of the national priority agendas in the 2020-2024 development planning and implementation (**Figure 2**). In the NDC document, Indonesia is committed to reducing greenhouse gas emissions that are harmful to the environment, with a reduction of 29% with

Figure 2. Indonesia ratified the Paris Agreement which included an NDC commitment in 2016

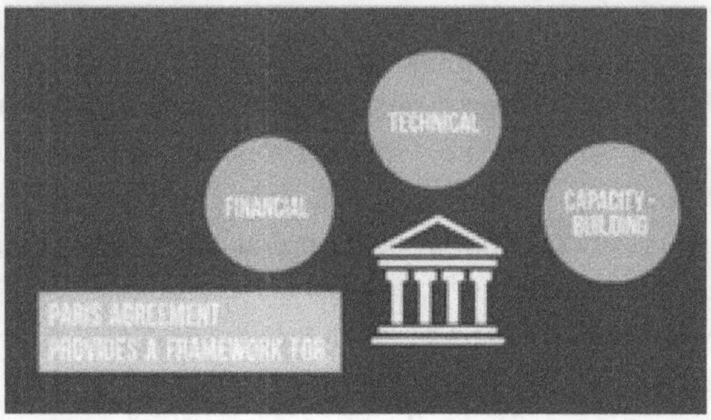

its own capabilities and 41% with international support in 2030. The main priority for reducing greenhouse gas emissions is in the forestry sector, as well as the energy and transportation sectors which have covered 97% of Indonesia's total NDC emission reduction target. Furthermore, with the increasingly strong global trend towards the issue of climate change, Indonesia has also targeted to achieve Net Zero Emissions in 2060 or earlier. In order to achieve this target.

On October 7, 2021, a carbon tax was born through the Law on the Harmonization of Tax Regulations and added to a series of fiscal policies used as instruments to control climate change. Indonesia is the first mover of carbon taxes in the world, especially for emerging economies. This is evidence of the consistent commitment of the Government of Indonesia in realizing a strong, just and sustainable economy. As a very strategic policy in tackling climate change, the imposition of a carbon tax provides a strong signal that will encourage the development of carbon markets, technological innovation, and investments that are more efficient, low carbon and environmentally friendly. In the context of development, state revenues from carbon taxes can be used to increase development funds, invest in environmentally friendly technologies.

Another main goal of imposing a carbon tax is changing the behavior of economic actors to switch to green, low-carbon economic activities. This is in line with various government efforts to achieve the target of reducing greenhouse gas emissions in the medium and long term. In its implementation, the government will also make the right transition so that the imposition of a carbon tax can be consistent with the momentum of post-Covid-19 economic recovery (Sevik & Yildirim, 2023). The implementation of carbon taxes and the development of carbon markets are important milestones towards a sustainable Indonesian economy, as well as proof of Indonesia's seriousness in the climate change control agenda at the global level. This momentum is a valuable opportunity for Indonesia to gain first mover advantage. Indonesia is a global policy determinant, not a follower, in making the transition towards sustainable development. Indonesia will become a reference and destination for low-carbon investment in various development sectors, both in the energy, transportation and manufacturing industries.

TAX CARBON AND GREEN ECONOMY

The application of a carbon tax is a form of Indonesia's commitment to implementing a green economy or green economy (Bappenas, 2021). Green economy is an economy that can create increased human welfare and social equity in line with efforts to reduce environmental risks and ecological scarcity (Papaspyropoulos et al., 2016). Changes towards a green economy have been considered as one of the important issues for the world community as a form of concern over climate change that is getting worse. Most countries in the world including Indonesia are also starting to rush towards the green economy (Bappenas, 2014). The implementation of a carbon tax is predicted to be a significant first step towards a green economy. The carbon tax policy is one of the initial stages in the road map towards a green economy (Ratnawati, 2016). The application of carbon taxes is carried out in stages and aligned with carbon trading as part of the green economy roadmap to minimize its impact on the business world while continuing to play a role in reducing carbon emissions (Arimura & Matsumoto, 2020; Busch et al., 2020; Yunis & Aliakbari, 2020).

The application of a carbon tax can directly or indirectly reduce economic activities that pollute the environment, and prevent environmental damage by encouraging environmentally friendly production/consumption methods. Implementation of a carbon tax also serves to initiate a green economy transformation and more quickly reduce emissions in the future. In addition, a carbon tax is needed to maintain environmental quality for sustainable economic development, in accordance with the concept of sustainable development that future generations must have at least provided economic opportunities for the present generation in order to create their own economic prosperity (Kasztelan, 2017). Green economy transformation means that the economy is not aimed at continuously growing and developing but an economy with steady-state conditions, and society (humans) being hospitable does not threaten other species or the planet itself (Yildirim & Yildirim, 2020). The green economy itself is called a system of economic activities related to the distribution, production and consumption of goods and services that result in an increase in people's welfare in the long term, while not causing future generations to face significant environmental risks or ecological scarcity. In theory, one would use less fossil fuels when their prices rise. In other words, the government can save the environment by implementing the carbon tax feature.

SUSTAINABLE DEVELOPMENT AND GREEN ECONOMY

The main reason for the emergence of the concept of green economy and green growth is the movement towards a more integrated and comprehensive approach to incorporate social and environmental factors in economic processes, in order to achieve sustainable development (Yildirim & Yildirim, 2020). Meanwhile, green growth is economic growth that contributes to the responsible use of natural capital, prevents and reduces pollution, and creates opportunities to increase social welfare as a whole by building a green economy, and ultimately enables the achievement of sustainable development goals. Thus, these three terms cannot be separated: green growth, green economy, and sustainable development (He et al., 2022; Hidayattuloh et al., 2020).

The importance of green growth arises from concerns about the unintended social, environmental and economic consequences of rapid population growth, economic growth and consumption of natural resources (He et al., 2022). This issue has led to the development of various approaches and mechanisms based on science and technology, to achieve strong economic growth, but is environmentally friendly and socially inclusive. This program focuses on three sectors, namely energy, landscape, and infrastructure. These three priority sectors were chosen to reflect and ensure alignment with the Nawa Cita, as well as Indonesia's global commitment to the Paris Agreement—as stated in the Nationally Determined Contributions/NDC and Sustainable Development Goals/SDGs (Boyces, 2018).

This green culture has also developed in the last few decades due to increasing shared awareness of the urgency of the benefits of sustainable practices, taking into account environmental aspects which are increasingly experiencing degradation of functions (Paul et al., 2014). The importance of growth in the economic sector, which is one of the pulses of the country's sustainability, of course, must pay attention to harmony with the environment, and social aspects due to rapid population growth and the increasing intensity of consumption of natural resources (OECD, 2023). The process of sustainable development through green economic growth is a commitment to protect human life and the environment in the future through various approaches and mechanisms to achieve strong, environmentally friendly and socially inclusive economic growth (Edwards, 2021). The program also acts as a facilitator that brings together the various needs of stakeholders, including governments, national and international investors, as well as project developers, so that green capital can flow (Yildirim et al., 2022).

THEORITICAL FINDINGS

We have made various efforts in summarizing the results of the review of various views from the key informants of this study, and presenting them in a theoretical hypothesis and discussing them with various perspectives from previous research. From the activities that have been carried out (interviews), it is concluded that similar to other countries in the world, Indonesia has the potential to implement carbon tax policies in order to reduce and control carbon emissions.

However, there are several things that must be considered before implementing a carbon tax, such as the scope, tax points, tax rates, and the allocation of tax revenues. The scope and points of taxation that are possible in implementing a carbon tax in Indonesia, lie in the energy sector, starting from the upstream to midstream and even hybrid levels. However, implementation at the downstream level is of course quite difficult to implement in Indonesia, due to the increasing number of entities to be taxed, resulting in a high cost of taxation. The following is a statement from our source, a public policy practitioner in the field of taxation in Indonesia.

"It is very important to ensure that carbon tax collection regulations are more targeted, so that apart from being an additional state revenue, the implementation of carbon taxes can carry out its important function, namely as a control tool to change behavior that encourages innovation and changes in the way company management works, especially companies that contribute high carbon emissions."

The revenue allocation mechanism is also an important consideration, both when using an earmarking mechanism to encourage environmental investment and/or carrying out tax burden shifting to mitigate impacts on society. In the following, we present a statement from a key informant, an expert practitioner in the field of sustainable economic development in Indonesia.

"The implementation of carbon taxes is expected to contribute to the achievement of climate change mitigation and adaptation goals while increasing economic growth, reducing poverty, and concurrently preserving the environment,"

On the other hand, it is also suspected that the carbon tax policy cannot work alone, so it needs to be balanced with the development of renewable energy investments, maximizing the use of alternative energy, as well as complementary policies that are in line with carbon taxes. Thus, people are encouraged to reduce the use of fossil fuels and have the option to switch to using energy that is more environmentally friendly, so that carbon emissions can be reduced. The following is a statement from one of our sources, a senior researcher in the field of green economy and sustainable development in Indonesia.

"In summary, the process of efforts to reduce CO2 emissions in Indonesia must pay attention to the economic aspect, so that the application of a carbon tax does not have an impact on reducing economic performance in Indonesia. The application of a carbon tax in Sweden has proven to be able to reduce emissions and increase economic growth simultaneously where companies in Sweden are competing to create more efficient technologies so that energy use can be reduced."

Based on all the presentations from the sources of this research, it can be seen that the concept put forward from carbon tax revenues can basically be allocated to provide incentives or subsidies to other very urgent sectors, such as education, health, public transportation, and green industry. Therefore, the implementation of a carbon tax is expected to be a solution to environmental problems, as well as one of the bases for state revenues in the future. The benefits of carbon taxes apart from reducing greenhouse gas emissions, can also improve the country's economy and increase people's welfare. Indeed, to support the implementation of a carbon tax, several considerations are needed. First, the government needs to design and map appropriately to target sectors, activities, and or goods that clearly cause pollution. Because it is this sector that will be responsible for environmental pollution, so that it is burdened with carbon tax levies. The carbon tax is also oriented towards mitigating climate change and becomes an instrument to protect the environment. Its nature that reduces negative externalities, it will be in line with the principles of sustainable development.

CONCLUSION

Conceptually, the sectors that can be directly burdened with a carbon tax are power plants, transportation, the building industry, the pulp and paper industry, cement, petrochemicals and others. Usually, this industry uses a lot of brown energy in the form of petroleum, gas or coal burning which causes a lot of pollution. However, with the implementation of the carbon tax, it is hoped that the industry will change the use of equipment and machinery that are environmentally friendly or as a green industry. The second consideration is what kind of fee scheme will be imposed on these sectors. Is it a new type of tax or refers to existing tax collections, such as excise, income tax, value added tax, luxury goods sales tax or other tax collections. Likewise, the basis for imposition of taxes or rates. For example, whether based on estimates of carbon emissions generated, fuel consumption, or others. Examples that have been successful in implementing a carbon tax, namely Finland which is currently implemented at US$ 24.39 per tons of CO2 emissions or Japan at 289 (IDR 38,000) per tons of CO2 emissions.

The third consideration, this carbon levy is implemented based on the principle of justice. Carbon taxes have been proven to reduce pollution and emissions in several countries that implement them, and increase state revenues. Carbon tax revenues can be used to finance pollution-affected workers and others. Currently, there are around 25 countries that have implemented carbon levies, such as China, Singapore, Canada, Ukraine, Japan, France, Chile, and others. The implementation of this carbon tax has succeeded in reducing carbon emissions. Finland implemented a carbon tax since 1990. Sweden and Norway since 1991 and succeeded in reducing carbon emission levels by 25%. Likewise, Australia and Japan have implemented it since 2012. Followed by China in 2017 and Singapore in 2019, while Indonesia is targeting 2022.

The fourth consideration, how is the regulation of implementation of carbon tax. This is important because it involves preparation, verification and target measurement of the object to be targeted. Implementation of carbon tax can be carried out while continuing the tax reform agenda. Reform can be in the form of simplification of carbon tax administration itself. It is also possible that the carbon tax collection mechanism is made like the existing tax collection. Another hope of implementing a carbon tax in Indonesia is that it does not reduce the competitiveness of a number of goods or products. Therefore, the imposition of this carbon tax requires an in-depth study of its effect on the elasticity or price sensitivity of goods that are urgently needed by the public as a result of the imposition of a carbon tax. On the other hand, the implementation of carbon taxes in Indonesia is also expected to be carried out smoothly by stakeholders, so that all sectors are supportive and there is no ego centricity. Therefore, strong leadership is needed to become a reliable conductor and communicator for the harmonious implementation of carbon tax.

In the future, it is hoped that no one will feel disadvantaged and all will benefit, so that a balance is created in the form of a society that cares about the environment, especially exhaust gases (emissions), and creates a green industry. Challenges ahead will also create carbon trade. Mainly, namely the implementation of this carbon tax requires communication between the government and the community. The government needs to open space and public opinion about this policy in order to educate and change the mindset and behavior of people and entities to achieve certain targets. Likewise, so that implementation can be carried out in stages as was done by China, starting from the local government. While not perfect, this carbon tax should start being implemented soon.

REFERENCES

Al-Shetwi, A. Q. (2022). Sustainable development of renewable energy integrated power sector: Trends, environmental impacts, and recent challenges. *The Science of the Total Environment*, *822*, 153645. doi:10.1016/j.scitotenv.2022.153645 PMID:35124039

Arimura, T. H., & Matsumoto, S. (2020). *Carbon Pricing in Japan*. Springer. https://link.springer.com/book/10.1007/978-981-15-6964-7

Bappenas. (2014). *Model Ekonomi Hijau Provinsi Kalimantan Tengah (KT-GEM) Model Ekonomi Hijau Provinsi Kalimantan Tengah (KT-GEM)*. Bappenas.

Bappenas. (2021). A GREEN ECONOMY FOR A NET-ZERO FUTURE: How Indonesia can build back better after COVID-19 with the Low Carbon Development Initiative (LCDI). In *Ministry of National Development Planning, 12*(4).

Bayhaqi, A. (2019). Ketidakpastian Dalam Pemodelan Perubahan Iklim. *Oseana*, *44*(1), 38–53. doi:10.14203/oseana.2019.Vol.44No.1.30

Boyce, J. K. (2018). Carbon Pricing: Effectiveness and Equity. *Ecological Economics, 150*(November 2017), 52–61. doi:10.1016/j.ecolecon.2018.03.030

Brandl, J., & Zielinska, I. (2020). Reviewing the smart city Vienna framework strategy's potential as an eco-social policy in the context of quality of work and socio-ecological transformation. *Sustainability (Basel)*, *12*(3), 1–17. doi:10.3390u12030859

Busch, T., Bassen, A., Lewandowski, S., & Sump, F. (2020). Corporate Carbon and Financial Performance Revisited. *Organization & Environment*. doi:10.1177/1086026620935638

Carattini, S., Carvalho, M., & Fankhauser, S. (2018). Overcoming public resistance to carbon taxes. *Wiley Interdisciplinary Reviews: Climate Change*, *9*(5), 1–26. doi:10.1002/wcc.531 PMID:31031823

Edwards, M. G. (2021). The growth paradox, sustainable development, and business strategy. *Business Strategy and the Environment*, *30*(7), 3079–3094. doi:10.1002/bse.2790

Ferdian, D. (2021). *Mencermati Peluang dan Tantangan Pajak Karbon di Indonesia*. Www.Mongabay.Co.Id. https://www.mongabay.co.id/2021/07/24/mencermati-peluang-dan-tantangan-pajak-karbon-di-indonesia/

He, R., Baležentis, T., Štreimikienė, D., & Shen, Z. (2022). Sustainable green growth in developing economies: An empirical analysis on the belt and road countries. *Journal of Global Information Management*, *30*(6), 1–15. doi:10.4018/JGIM.20221101.oa1

Hermanto Sirait, Y. (2019). Komitmen Terkait Deforestasi Dan Perubahan Iklim: Perspektif Dari Doktrin Parens Patriae. *Jurnal Jatiswara*, *34*(1), 1. doi:10.29303/jatiswara.v34i1.196

Hidayattuloh, M. H., Bambang, A. N., & Amirudin, A. (2020). The Green Economy Concept as Development Strategy of Cempaka Tourism Village toward Sustainable Tourism Development. *The Indonesian Journal of Planning and Development*, *5*(1), 30–37. doi:10.14710/ijpd.5.1.30-37

Kasztelan, A. (2017). Green growth, green economy and sustainable development: Terminological and relational discourse. *Prague Economic Papers*, *26*(4), 487–499. doi:10.18267/j.pep.626

Khastar, M., Aslani, A., & Nejati, M. (2020). How does carbon tax affect social welfare and emission reduction in Finland? *Energy Reports*, *6*, 736–744. doi:10.1016/j.egyr.2020.03.001

Kumala, R., Ulpa, R., Rahayu, A., & Martinah. (2021). Pajak Karbon: Perbaiki Ekonomi dan Solusi Lindungi Bumi. *Prosiding Seminar Stiami,* *8*(1), 66–73. https://ojs.stiami.ac.id/index.php/PS/article/view/1370

Lin, B., & Li, X. (2011). The effect of carbon tax on per capita CO2 emissions. *Energy Policy*, *39*(9), 5137–5146. doi:10.1016/j.enpol.2011.05.050

Marron, D. B., & Morris, A. C. (2016). How to Use Carbon Tax Revenues. SSRN *Electronic Journal*. doi:10.2139/ssrn.2737990

Nurdiawansyah, Lindrianasari, & Komalasari, A. (2018). Carbon Emission Issues in Indonesia. *Review of Integrative Business and Economics Research,* *7*(3), 20–33. http://repository.lppm.unila.ac.id/7178/1/RIBER 2018%28a%29.pdf

OEC. (2019). Taxing Energy Use 2019: Country Note - Colombia. X, 1–8. https://www.oecd.org/tax/tax-policy/taxing-energy-use-colombia.pdf

OECD. (2023). *Economic Outlook for Southeast Asia, China and India 2023 Reviving Tourism Post-Pandemic*.

Ojha, H., & Schofield, N. (2022). *Climate change and water security in the Indo-Pacific region: risks, responses, and a framework for action*.

Papaspyropoulos, K. G., Karamanolis, D., Sokos, C. K., & Birtsas, P. K. (2016). Enhancing Sustainability in Forestry Using Material Flow Cost Accounting. *Open Journal of Forestry*, *06*(05), 324–336. doi:10.4236/ojf.2016.65026

Paul, I. D., Bhole, G. P., & Chaudhari, J. R. (2014). A Review on Green Manufacturing: It's Important, Methodology and its Application. *Procedia Materials Science, 6*(Icmpc), 1644–1649. doi:10.1016/j.mspro.2014.07.149

Qadir, S. A., Al-Motairi, H., Tahir, F., & Al-Fagih, L. (2021). Incentives and strategies for financing the renewable energy transition: A review. *Energy Reports*, *7*, 3590–3606. doi:10.1016/j.egyr.2021.06.041

Rabe, B. G., & Borick, C. P. (2012). Carbon Taxation and Policy Labeling: Experience from American States and Canadian Provinces. *The Review of Policy Research*, *29*(3), 358–382. doi:10.1111/j.1541-1338.2012.00564.x

Ratnawati, D. (2016). Carbon Tax Sebagai Alternatif Kebijakan Untuk Mengatasi Eksternalitas Negatif Emisi Karbon di Indonesia. *Indonesian Treasury Review Jurnal Perbendaharaan Keuangan Negara Dan Kebijakan Publik*, *1*(2), 53–67. doi:10.33105/itrev.v1i2.51

Rounaghi, M. M. (2019). Economic analysis of using green accounting and environmental accounting to identify environmental costs and sustainability indicators. *International Journal of Ethics and Systems*, *35*(4), 504–512. doi:10.1108/IJOES-03-2019-0056

Saputra, A. I. (2021). Pajak Karbon Sebagai Sumber Penerimaan Negara Dan Sistem Pemungutannya. [AKURASI]. *Jurnal Anggaran Dan Keuangan Negara Indonesia*, *3*(1), 56–71. doi:10.33827/akurasi2021.vol3.iss1.art96

Selvi, R. N., & Rachmatulloh, I. (2020). Urgensi Penerapan Pajak Karbon Di Indonesia. *Jurnal Reformasi Administrasi, 7*(1), 29–34. https://ojs.stiami.ac.id/index.php/reformasi/article/view/845

Sevik, N., & Yildirim, S. (2023). Sustainable Enterprises Post COVID-19 Pandemic: The Rise of Sustainable Fashion Enterprises. In *Handbook of Research on Current Advances and Challenges of Borderlands, Migration, and Geopolitics*. IGI Global Publishing.

Sukma Aisya, N. (2019). Dilema Posisi Indonesia dalam Persetujuan Paris tentang Perubahan Iklim. *Indonesian Perspective*, *4*(2), 118–132.

Yildirim, S. (2020). The consumer role for sustainable development: how consumers contribute sustainable development goals. In *Chkoniya, V., Madsen, A.O. and Bukhrashvili. In Anthropological Approaches to Understanding Consumption Patterns and Consumer Behavior*. IGI Global. doi:10.4018/978-1-7998-3115-0.ch018

Yildirim, S., Demirtas, I., & Yildirim. (2022). A Review of Alternative Economic Approaches to Achieve Sustainable Development: The Rising Digitalization and Degrowth Post COVID-19. In *Handbook of Research on Sustainable Development Goals, Climate Change, and Digitalization*. Hershey, PA: IGI Global.

Yildirim, S., & Yildirim, D. Ç. (2020). Achieving Sustainable Development Through a Green Economy Approach. In *Advanced Integrated Approaches to Environmental Economics and Policy: Emerging Research and Opportunities*. IGI Global. doi:10.4018/978-1-5225-9562-5.ch001

Yunis, J., & Aliakbari, E. (2020). Carbon Pricing in High-Income OECD Countries. *Fraser Institute*, 42. https://www.fraserinstitute.org/sites/default/files/carbon-pricing-in-high-income-oecd-countries.pdf

Chapter 10

Analysis of Energy Infrastructure for Sustainable Development:

Using Game Theory Within the Context of Rational Choices

Erkan Oflaz
Kocaeli University, Turkey

Şevket Alper Koç
Kocaeli University, Turkey

Ayhan Orhan
Kocaeli University, Turkey

ABSTRACT

Human beings have needed energy throughout history. Simple hand tools were used until the industrial revolution. In the agricultural and pre-agricultural society period, where humans and domesticated animals were used as energy sources, hydraulic and wind energy were used primitively. With the industrial revolution, steam energy, internal combustion engines, and electric motors began to be used in accordance with the increasing production speed. There are two important problems for new energy sources, just like human and animal power: efficiency and sustainability. Although the nature of the revolutions in human history is seen as administrative, class struggle is also a problem of energy efficiency and sustainability. An energy source that is not efficient and sustainable can be destructive in the process. In an agricultural society, slave labor or vassal peasants are a source of energy for their lords/seigneurs.

DOI: 10.4018/979-8-3693-1297-1.ch010

1. INTRODUCTION

Human beings have needed energy throughout history. Simple hand tools were used until the industrial revolution. In the agricultural and pre-agricultural society period, where humans and domesticated animals were used as energy sources, hydraulic and wind energy were used primitively. With the industrial revolution, steam energy, internal combustion engines and electric motors began to be used in accordance with the increasing production speed.

There are two important problems for new energy sources, just like human and animal power: efficiency and sustainability. Although the nature of the revolutions in human history is seen as administrative, class struggle is also a problem of energy efficiency and sustainability. An energy source that is not efficient and sustainable can be destructive in the process. In an agricultural society, slave labor or vassal peasants are a source of energy for their lords/seigneurs. If the number of slaves/peasants was not optimally proportional to the size of the land, housing and nutrition problems would arise, and these situations would harm production due to rebellions or diseases, depending on the administration.

The energy resources of our age, just like in the agricultural society, have efficiency-sustainability problems for social and economic reasons. The aim of our study is to test the effectiveness of selected energy sources in terms of their economic, social and ecological impacts. An answer will be sought to the question of what kind of infrastructure should be created for the energy need, which is one of the most important components of sustainable economic growth.

2. ENERGY-BASED CONFLICTS IN THE AGRICULTURAL SOCIETY

The individual socializes in order to preserve the value he has acquired during the socialization process and to exchange it for other products. Accumulating more is seen as the source of the pursuit of wealth. Simply owning more land is not a sufficient. Existing soil must also be cultivated. When Adam Smith said, *"It takes 500 poor people to make one rich man,"* he put forward this proposition not because he was not a humanist, but because he was a realist (Smith, Cited by Bauman, 2017 s:7). In Ottoman society, the tax collected from land was collected on a pair of oxen. This tax, called the double tax, was based on the judgment that the source of wealth was cultivated land (Pamuk, 2000, p:56).

Why did Adam Smith need five hundred poor people and why, in Ottoman society, the land that could be cultivated was more important than the size of the land. Essentially, both situations refer to the need for energy. Being rich does not involve a definitive judgment. Becoming rich should be thought of as a process. If wealth is not tied to a sustainable process of production and exchange, it can easily evolve into poverty. Energy is the basic requirement for production. The exchange process includes both tradable processes and the problem of sharing in production factors.

The production process in the agricultural society was basically based on an agreement between the owners of the land and the agricultural workers. In early patriarchal societies, this division of labor was based on the skills of the members of the community. Emerging civilizations resolved the workforce by legalizing the concept of slavery. Even though slavery became a social status, people rebelled against this status due to human nature. In order to oppose this status, both innate and acquired later, rebellions occurred in the Greek, Roman and Ancient Egyptian civilizations. There are also different approaches to the institution of slavery, which was regulated by following a methodology in line with Montesquieu's concept of "alienation" (Rousseau,2012-p:114). There is a practice that emerged with the promise of "buying freedom" in response to slave revolts in the ancient Greek city-states. The contracts made with Irish workers who wanted to go to the United States are a partial slavery model adapted to contemporary life. From a different perspective, European feudalism in the Middle Ages and caste practices in Indian and Russian geography are primitive solutions to agricultural energy demand.

It can be argued that the sustainability of energy in the agricultural society depends on the availability of sufficient labor force on the land. Adequate labor force which is directly related with agricultural output also provides profitability. Given the harvest obtained from unit land, the largest output is agricultural labor. The approach applied in France during the mercantilist period forms the basis of profitability in the production mechanism. The proposition that "French peasants consume less food will bring more exports" supports the assumption that the peasant population is not considered citizens. The cost of agricultural labor, which is the unit energy source, is at the root of the conflict. It is not surprising that Bouillonism was at the root of the French Revolution, one of the most famous rebellions of the agricultural society.

3. ENERGY-BASED CONFLICTS IN THE INDUSTRIAL SOCIETY

The uniformization of the need for labor is one of the most important features of the industrial revolution. Production lines and agricultural machines have emerged as an alternative to human labor. A new era has begun in which the non-substitutability of mastery and labor against capital has disappeared (Baudrillard,2021, s:60-61). Capital has moved to a new stage of production, first with steam machines and then with artificial intelligence. Although labor-capital relations have not completely disappeared in the new era, a more specialized workforce has become necessary. In the new type of energy projection, labor uses, manages and maintains other energy resources. Tasks on production lines have become uniform. Production lines, which reduce the expertise of the workforce to very simple processes, have brought the labor-capital relationship to a lower level. With the increasing population, the continuity of labor supply has become a relatively decreasing problem for capital.

The close ties between labor and capital have become substitutable in the new era, making the protection of labor an issue for the state. It has become necessary to regulate issues such as social rights, minimum wage tariffs and working hours with the regulatory power of the state. The social state and production mechanisms have led to the "Welfare Society" in our age. The new sociological structure has resulted in more consumption and more needs, and has also brought the need for energy to households. Heating and the widespread use of electrical appliances have made electricity production a basic need. Due to the decrease in the price elasticity of energy demand, there was a need for the state to regulate and to ensure supply security.

The state's regulation of both production factors and energy security in the new period is considered within the scope of the security needs of the society. From this perspective, energy security is a condition for establishing social peace. Another concern is the continuity of society's view on energy security and its selectiveness in terms of its impact on the environment. For the people who demand energy, social sensitivities are developing in terms of air pollution and/or environmental effects of energy. Like energy security, public health is also a security issue. The main aim of the state is to find resources that are accessible, sustainable and cause minimal damage to the environment. In our age, the privilege of governing democratic states directly depends on the level of public satisfaction. The chance of re-election of a government that cannot ensure energy security decreases. As recorded in Figure-1, natural gas demand in industry and housing is close to each other and constitutes 67% of the total demand. Public awareness

Figure 1. Usage areas of natural gas around the world
(https://enerji.gov.tr/bilgi-merkezi-enerji-dogalgaz)

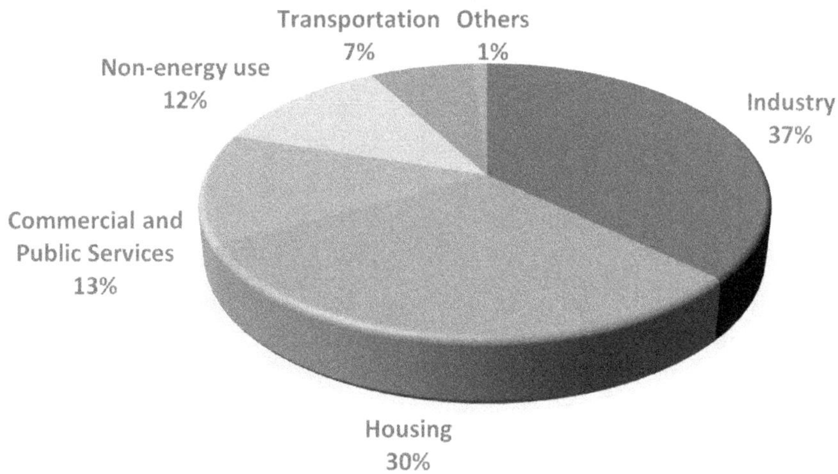

of the environment and ensuring the transmission and consumption of energy at an accessible level have become the most important propaganda for political parties.

The legitimacy of a democratic state is measured by the proportion of citizens voting in the system (Özbudun, 1964, p:26-31). Citizens' voting behavior depends on the policies proposed by the government and the opposition. Energy security propaganda is a phenomenon that attracts the public's attention. People may take a negative position due to environmental pollution and energy outages. For political parties, the proposition that "energy security and production factors within the scope of labor-capital relations are very important topics" is meaningful for the reasons explained above.

The goal of a welfare society is shaped around natural unemployment and sustainable economic policies. The concept of clean energy, with its production infrastructure that causes the least harm to the environment, is a matter of development. It is a natural tendency for developing countries to prioritize production and job opportunities compared to developed countries. The wealth and lifestyle of developed countries cause them to prioritize environmental sensitivities. Undoubtedly, the hierarchy of basic needs of humanity also creates different priorities. In line with this argument, it is understandable that developed countries establish and operate dirty industrial facilities in developing countries, or that developing countries establish dirtier industries due to both workforce structure and capital adequacy concerns. This makes the development level of the countries another reason for preference. The situation can be seen in the Kuznetz curve in Figure 2.

Energy security and sustainability is also an area of particular interest in the context of world peace.[1] The United Nations has a special field of study within the scope of energy security. There are main problems such as energy resources, environmental damage and meeting the increasing demand. Problems that may arise in energy supply and production and distribution processes that may pose a threat to public health are the natural areas of interest of every state. For the reasons explained above, the UN carries out studies under the title "Ensuring access to affordable, reliable, sustainable and modern energy".[2]

Figure 2. The relationship between carbon emission and GNP
(Stern, 2004, s: 1420)

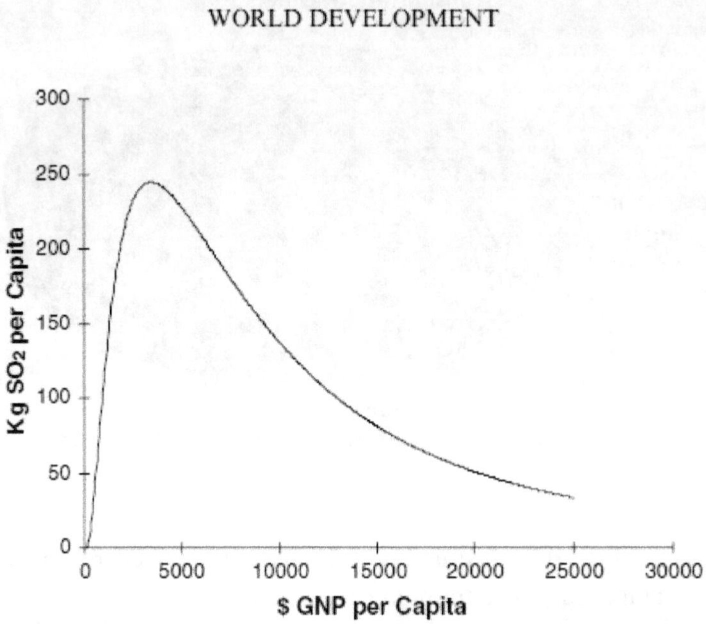

4. ENERGY INFRASTRUCTURE WITHIN THE SCOPE OF RATIONAL CHOICES

Countries have different trends within the scope of energy infrastructure. The decisions taken by decision makers are based on the country's economy, energy supply security and technology. Energy efficiency and sustainability are directly related to the production method. The dominant view in the literature is that renewable energy is directly related to development and has a positive effect (Demir,2023 p:274).

The classification of the resources to be used for energy production is given in the table below (Figure 3). In the study, the resources to be used are considered as Fossil Fuels and Renewable energy. The study aimed to examine the decision-making processes of the country and its citizens according to their income group and development level. In both groups of energy units, there are sources that are excluded from the list due to installation costs and technology requirements.

The effectiveness of energy resources in countries is based on various reasons in the study.

- (TR) type country refers to countries that have the capacity to establish and operate energy resources, have rich fossil fuel resources and technological infrastructure.
- (T) type country refers to countries that have a technological infrastructure in terms of establishing and operating energy resources, but are not sufficient in terms of fossil fuel resources.
- (R) type country refers to countries that are rich in fossil resources but lack technological infrastructure in terms of establishing and operating energy resources.
- (P) type country indicates countries that are inadequate in terms of both technological infrastructure and fossil resources in terms of establishing and operating energy resources.

Table 1. Classification of the resources used in energy production, listed in terms of the resources to be used

Classification of Resources Used in Energy Production	
Fossil fuels (carbon sources)	Coal
	Natural gas
Renewable energy	Solar energy
	Wind power
	Hydraulic Energy
	Geothermal energy
	Biomass Energy
	Hydrogen Energy

Within the scope of the study, two types of citizens were discussed;

- (D) Citizen with high environmental sensitivity, high welfare level and high energy consumption.
- (UD) Citizens with neutral environmental sensitivity, low welfare level and low energy consumption.

Citizens make different choices depending on the development levels of countries. Citizens' choices depend on their quality of life. Supply security is decisive for environmentally friendly energy demand. For decision makers, investment costs, energy production capacity, efficiency and sustainability are prioritized.

- (C) indicates carbon-based sources as energy production sources.
- (re) indicates renewable resources as the source of energy production.

Actors make their choices according to the variables given below;

- Installation Cost = **x**
- Operating Cost = **y**
- Sustainability = **z**
- Environmental Impact = **e**
- Efficiency= **f**

4.1. Country Model with Advanced Technology and Resource Adequacy (TR) (D)

The developed and resource-sufficient country model describes countries whose technological infrastructure is capable of establishing any energy production facility they want without any technological support and countries those have the raw materials required for the facility they establish on their own territory.

- Due to its technological infrastructure, its adaptation to renewable energy technologies is high.
- Energy efficiency is the prioritized investment criterion.

- The country's citizens attach importance to quality of life with high levels of welfare, education and environmental awareness.
- There is no capacity problem. It is assumed that the country's installed capacities are sufficient and that it has invested more than the population growth rate and the current GNP growth rate in energy.
- It is preferred to export reserve carbon-based raw materials instead of using them in energy production.

Table 2. Country with advanced technology and resource adequacy

		Payoffs of parties in energy infrastructure design	
		Country with Advanced Technology and Resource Adequacy (TR) (D)	
		Citizen	
		Vote	Not Vote
Government	carbon sources (c)	7,3	0,6
	Renewable energy (re)	10,8	0,4

Figure 3. In the country model with technology and resource sufficiency

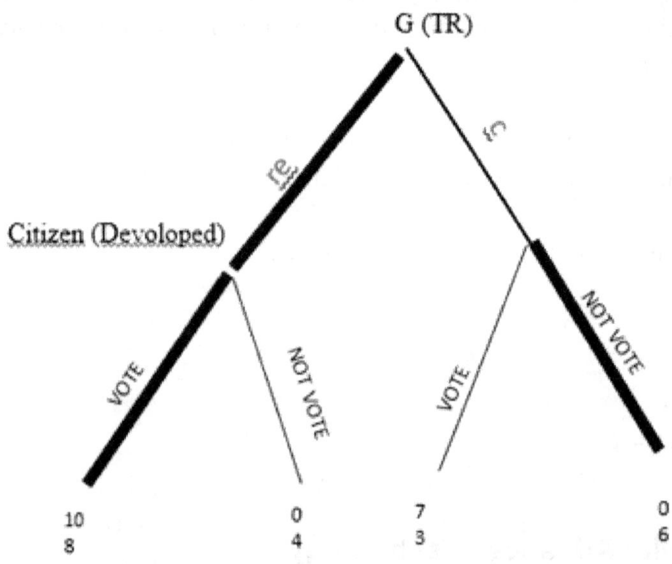

$$" x_{re}^{TR} + y_{re}^{TR} + z_{re}^{TR} + e_{re}^{TR} + f_{re}^{TR} < x_{c}^{TR} + y_{c}^{TR} + z_{c}^{TR} + e_{c}^{TR} + f_{c}^{TR} "$$

$$U_{citizen}^{D} = f(e,z) \quad \frac{\partial u}{\partial e} > 0 \quad \frac{\partial u}{\partial z} > 0$$

In the country model with technology and resource sufficiency, it is accepted that the country's installed energy infrastructure is sufficient and that there is an ecosystem in which new investments are made according to the foreseen increases in energy demand. It is assumed that renewable energy costs decrease with the use of technology (Sims, Rogner, and Gregory, 2003, pp: 1321-1322). The country can establish and operate both carbon and renewable energy platforms. While the operating cost for a renewable energy source is low, the initial investment cost is high. Exporting carbon resources instead of using them has a positive impact on the country's foreign trade. It has been taken as a given that the citizens of the model country are individuals with a high level of welfare and environmental sensitivity. Voters will not vote for carbon-based resource use due to environmental sensitivities.

The subgame perfect Nash equilibrium of this game is found with the state choosing "Re" in the first period and the citizens choosing "Vote" in the second period.

4.2. Country Model With Advanced Technology and Lack of Resource Sufficiency (T-D)

This model describes countries that can establish any energy production facility they want without any technological support, but do not have the raw materials required for the facility they establish on their own territory.

- Due to its technological infrastructure, its adaptation to renewable energy technologies is high.
- Energy efficiency is the prioritized investment criterion.
- Citizens have a high level of welfare, are educated and environmentally sensitive, and attaches importance to the quality of life.
- There is no capacity problem. It is assumed that the country's installed capacities are sufficient and that it has invested more than the population growth rate and the current GNP growth rate in energy.
- The country is dependent on foreign sources due to the lack of reserve carbon-based raw materials.
- Being dependent on foreign sources in terms of energy supply security raises sustainability concerns.

Table 3. Country with advanced technology and lack of resource adequacy

		Payoffs of parties in energy infrastructure design	
		Country with Advanced Technology and Lack of Resource Adequacy (T) (D)	
		Citizen	
		Vote	Not Vote
Government	carbon sources (c)	5,3	0,6
	Renewable energy (re)	10,8	0,4

In the country model with sufficient technology but without carbon fuel resources, it is accepted that the country's installed energy infrastructure is sufficient and there is an ecosystem in which new investments are made according to the foreseen increases in energy demand. It is assumed that renewable energy costs decrease with the use of technology. The country can establish and operate both carbon and

Figure 4. In the country model with sufficient technology but without carbon fuel resources

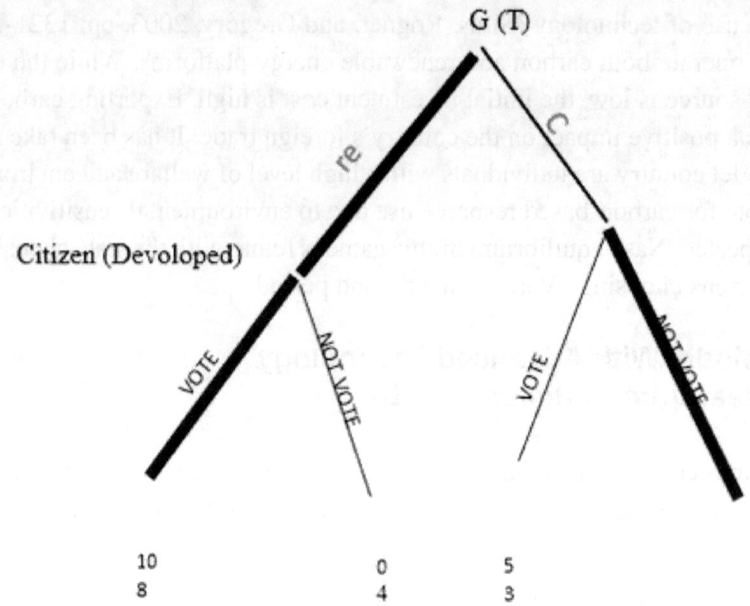

$$\text{“}\ x^T_{re}+y^T_{re}+z^T_{re}+e^T_{re}+f^T_{re}<x^T_c+y^T_c+z^T_c+e^T_c+f^T_c\ \text{”}$$

$$U^{TR}_{citizen}=f(e,z)\quad \frac{\partial u}{\partial e}>0\quad \frac{\partial u}{\partial z}>0$$

renewable energy platforms. While the operating cost for a renewable energy source is low, the initial investment cost is high. While using carbon resources has a negative impact on the country's foreign trade, it also means foreign dependency in terms of energy supply security. Model country citizens consist of individuals with a high level of welfare and environmental sensitivity. Voters will not vote for carbon-based resource use due to environmental sensitivities.

The subgame perfect Nash equilibrium of this game is found with the state choosing "Re" in the first period and the citizens choosing "Vote" in the second period.

4.3. Resource-Adequate Country Model With Insufficient Technology (R-UD)

The developing and resource-sufficient country model describes countries that have inadequate technological infrastructure and have the raw materials required for the facility they establish on their own lands.

- Due to its technological infrastructure, its adaptation to renewable energy technologies is weak.
- Energy capacity is the prioritized investment criterion.
- The welfare level of citizens is low. Environmental sensitivity does not find support from every segment of society.

- There is capacity problem. The country's installed capacity is not sufficient. It is assumed that energy investments are more than the population growth rate and the GNP growth rate.
- It is preferred to use reserve carbon-based raw materials in energy production.

Table 4. Country with ınsufficient technology and resource adequacy

		Payoffs of parties in energy infrastructure design	
		Country with Insufficient Technology and Resource Adequacy (R) (UD)	
		Citizen	
		Vote	Not Vote
Government	carbon sources (c)	10,8	0,6
	Renewable energy (re)	5,5	0,4

Figure 5. In a country that lacks technological competence but is rich in carbon fuel resources

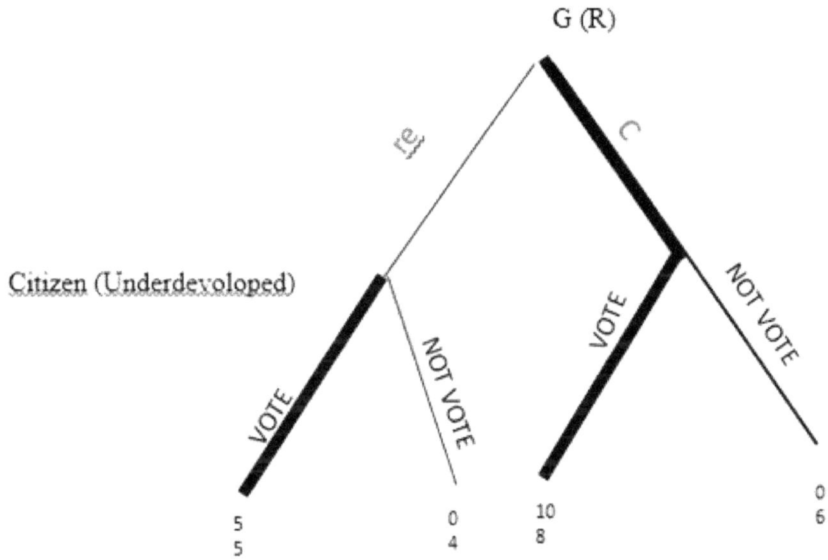

$$“\, x^T_{re}+ y^T_{re}+z^T_{re}+e^T_{re} + f^T_{re} > x^T_{c}+ y^T_{c}+z^T_{c}+e^T_{c} + f^T_{c}\,”$$

$$U^{TR}_{citizen}=\mathrm{f}(z) \qquad \frac{\partial u}{\partial z}>0$$

In a country that lacks technological competence but is rich in carbon fuel resources, it is accepted that there is an eco-system in which the country's installed energy infrastructure is not sufficient and new investments cannot be made according to the foreseen demand increases. Although renewable energy costs are decreasing with the use of technology, the country's energy infrastructure cannot meet the energy demand. The country is dependent on foreign sources to establish and operate both carbon and renewable energy platforms. While the operating cost for a renewable energy source is low, the initial investment cost is high. Using carbon resources has a negative impact on the country's foreign trade. The state attaches importance to the use of resources and prioritizes capacity increase. Citizens have low welfare levels and no environmental sensitivity. Individuals attach importance to meeting energy demands. They support all energy investments made.

The subgame perfect Nash equilibrium of this game is found with the state choosing "C" in the first period and the citizens choosing "Vote" in the second period.

4.4. Country Model With Insufficient Technology and Resources (P-UD)

The developing country model, which does not have sufficient resources, describes countries that have inadequate technological infrastructure and do not have the raw materials required for the facility they establish on their own lands.

- Due to its technological infrastructure, its adaptation to renewable energy technologies is weak.
- Energy capacity is the prioritized investment criterion.
- The welfare level of its citizens is low. Environmental sensitivity does not find support from every segment of society.
- There is capacity problem. The country's installed capacity is not sufficient. It is assumed that energy investments are more than the population growth rate and the GNP growth rate.
- It is dependent on foreign sources due to the lack of reserve carbon-based raw materials.
- Being dependent on foreign sources for energy supply security raises sustainability concerns.

Table 5. Country with insufficient technology and resource adequacy

		Payoffs of parties in energy infrastructure design	
		Country with Insufficient Technology and Resource (P) (UD)	
		Citizen	
		Vote	Not Vote
Government	carbon sources (c)	5,8	0,6
	Renewable energy (re)	10,5	0,4

In a country without technology and carbon fuel sufficiency, it is accepted that there is an ecosystem in which the country's installed energy infrastructure is not sufficient and new investments cannot be made according to the foreseen demand increases. Although renewable energy costs are decreasing with the use of technology, the country's energy infrastructure cannot meet the energy demand. The country is dependent on foreign sources to establish and operate both carbon and renewable energy platforms. While the operating cost for a renewable energy source is low, the initial investment cost is high. While using carbon resources has a negative impact on the country's foreign trade, it also means foreign dependency in terms of energy supply security. Citizens of model countries have low welfare levels and no environmental sensitivity. Individuals attach importance to meeting energy demands. They support all energy investments.

Figure 6. In a country without technology and carbon fuel sufficiency

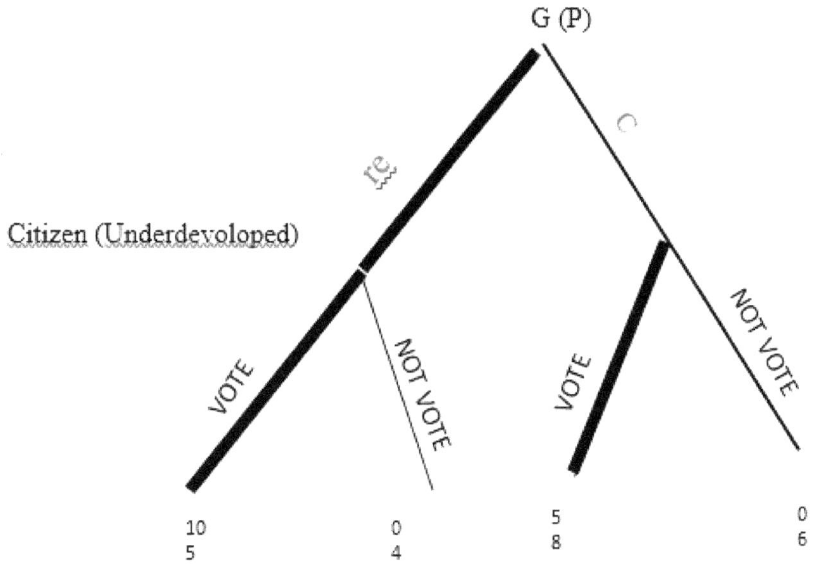

$$\text{“} x^T_{re} + y^T_{re} + z^T_{re} + e^T_{re} + f^T_{re} < x^T_c + y^T_c + z^T_c + e^T_c + f^T_c \text{”}$$

$$U^{TR}_{citizen} = \text{f (z)} \quad \frac{\partial u}{\partial z} > 0$$

The subgame perfect Nash equilibrium of this game is found with the state choosing “re” in the first period and the citizens choosing “Vote” in the second period.

5. CONCLUSION

Our study tested the interaction between the government and the citizen in the process of establishing the energy infrastructure with sub-game perfect Nash equilibrium. Establishing energy infrastructure is directly related to efficiency due to investment and operating costs, sustainability in terms of accessibility of natural resources, and prosperity in terms of environmental sensitivity. Although there are energy production sources excluded from the established model, tests have been carried out to rationalize the relationship between the government and the individual, which is the main argument.

While the government’s aim was considered to be re-elected, it was not evaluated only under the energy constraint. The optimum factor efficiency of resources available to the government is also included in the analysis as a decision-making process. It is assumed that citizens change their voting behavior in response to the government’s elections. In voting behavior, energy supply security and its impact on the environment are the reasons for preference for the individual.

Green and sustainable energy is the optimum situation supported by the citizen. While the impact of energy production on the environment depends on the welfare level of the society, sustainability does not.

The game has been examined in four main groups:

In the first group, technologically developed and resource-sufficient country model is chosen. The sub-game perfect Nash equilibrium of this game is that in the first period the state chooses "re" because it subjects its carbon resources to foreign trade and prefers to use renewable resources, and in the second period, citizens vote for this investment that they find green and sustainable.

For the second group, country model with technological competence but without carbon fuel resources is chosen. The perfect Nash equilibrium of this game is that in the first period the country, which is dependent on foreign sources in terms of carbon resources, chooses "re" in order to use its technological infrastructure instead of relying on external resources for its development, and in the second period, citizens "Vote" for this investment, which they find green and sustainable.

In third group, developing and resource-sufficient country model is chosen. The developing and resource-sufficient country model describes countries that have inadequate technological infrastructure and have the raw materials required for the facility they establish on their own lands. The sub-game perfect Nash equilibrium of this game is that in the first period the decision makers of the country choose "C" due to their desire to rapidly increase the energy capacity depending on the country's growth projection, and in the second period the citizens "Vote" this investment they find sustainable.

Lastly, the country model that does not have technology and carbon fuel sufficiency is chosen. The sub-game perfect Nash equilibrium of this game is that in the first period, the country, which is dependent on foreign sources in terms of carbon resources and technology, chooses "re" for the purpose of technology transfer instead of relying on external resources for its development, and in the second period, citizens "vote" this investment that they find sustainable.

REFERENCES

Baudrillard, J. (2021) *Tüketim Toplumu Ayrıntı.* Yayınları İstanbul

Bauman, Z. (2017). *Azınlığın Zenginliği Hepimizin Çıkarına mıdır?* Ayrıntı Yayınları İstanbul.

Cohen, D., & Hattatoğlu, D. (2000). *Dünyanın zenginliği, ulusların fakirliği*. İletişim Yayıncılık.

Demir, Y. (2023). Türkiye'de Yenilenebilir Enerji Tüketimi Ekonomik Büyümeye Katkı Sağlar mı? *Doğuş Üniversitesi Dergisi*, *24*(2), 271–281. doi:10.31671/doujournal.1209964

Özbudun, E. (1964). M. Duverger'in Siyasal Partileri ve Siyasal Partilerin İncelenmesinde Bazı Metodolojik Problemler. *Ankara Üniversitesi Hukuk Fakültesi Dergisi*, *21*(1), 23–51.

Pamuk, S. (2000). *A monetary history of the Ottoman Empire*. Cambridge University Press.

Rousseau, J. J. (2012). *Rousseau: The basic political writings: Discourse on the sciences and the arts, discourse on the origin of inequality, discourse on political economy, on the social contract, the state of war*. Hackett Publishing.

Sims, R. E., Rogner, H. H., & Gregory, K. (2003). Carbon emission and mitigation cost comparisons between fossil fuel, nuclear and renewable energy resources for electricity generation. *Energy Policy*, *31*(13), 1315–1326. doi:10.1016/S0301-4215(02)00192-1

Stern, D. I. (2004). The rise and fall of the environmental Kuznets curve. *World Development*, *32*(8), 1419–1439. doi:10.1016/j.worlddev.2004.03.004

ENDNOTES

1. https://www.worldenergy.org/assets/downloads/World_Energy_Trilemma_Index_2022.pdf?v=1669839605
2. https://un-energy.org/; last access date 02.10.2023

Chapter 11
Materials for Phase Change Heat Storage in Scheffler Reflectors:
A Sustainable and Perceptive Analysis of Renewable Energy

Dharmesh Dhabliya
https://orcid.org/0000-0002-6340-2993
Vishwakarma Institute of Information Technology, India

Ankur Gupta
https://orcid.org/0000-0002-4651-5830
Vaish College of Engineering, India

Nitin N. Sakhare
Vishwakarma Institute of Information Technology, India

Sharayu Ikhar
Yashika Journal Publications Pvt. Ltd., India

Ritika Dhabliya
Yashika Journal Publications Pvt. Ltd., India

Rahul Sharma
Auricle Global Society of Education and Research, India

Sabyasachi Pramanik
https://orcid.org/0000-0002-9431-8751
Haldia Institute of Technology, India

ABSTRACT

In order for humans to meet their fundamental needs, energy is required. The main sources of natural energy are carbon-based fuels such as biomass and fossil fuels. These fuels made of carbon are scarce and harmful to the environment. Innovative, clean, and environmentally friendly energy solutions are desperately needed. Particularly in light of the global issues posed by population expansion, the environment, and economic growth, solar energy may be a workable alternative for sustainable development. The Scheffler is a unique kind of solar concentrator that can quickly attain a high temperature. By adding a heat storage unit, Scheffler's capacity to retain heat may be greatly boosted. This study compares the thermal and physical properties, such as density, thermal conductivity, and melting point, of various thermal storage materials that are used to store heat energy for a longer amount of time, such as bricks, concrete, water, phase change material (PCM), latent heat storage material (LHS), aluminum, iron, molten salts, silicon, etc.

DOI: 10.4018/979-8-3693-1297-1.ch011

INTRODUCTION

The world's supply of fossil fuels is limited and will run out by 2088. A significant portion of the population in many countries still uses carbon fuels, such as wood, biomass, and other hydrocarbons (Patel, R. et al. 2022). A considerable amount of dangerous chemicals, including greenhouse gasses, are emitted during the burning of these carbon-based fuels. Since fossil fuels take millions of years to create, using them up rapidly might result in their depletion. Alternatives to these energy sources should be looked into in order to meet the basic energy demands of the population. Renewable energy (Kumar, A. et al. 2017) sources, especially solar energy, are clean and beneficial to the environment. Solar heaters, panels, concentrators, and their combinations are only a few of the devices and applications for solar energy. Solar concentrators are used for a variety of purposes, such as electricity generation, cooking, heating and cooling, and areas that need high temperatures. A Scheffler reflector (Reddy, D. S. et al. 2018) is a useful solar device that concentrates sunlight at a fixed focus (see image 1). It has to stay focused by tracking the daily and seasonal motions of the Sun. The tracking mechanism used by Scheffler to monitor the Sun's movement may be either automatic or human. Figure 1 shows the phases that a Scheffler goes through to operate. After striking the reflector, the sun's rays are concentrated on a fixed focus, or receiver (Hassan, F. et al. 2022), which transforms the incoming light into heat that may be used for a number of purposes. The receiver might be covered with a material that is good at retaining heat. Its primary usage is in cooking, while it may also be used in other high-heat operations (Ahmed, S. F. et al. 2022) including desalination, power generation, and cremation. Meals for a big group of people are prepared in community kitchens using it. Built by Brahma Kumari, the largest solar kitchen in the world can produce 38,500 meals a day. Because Scheffler runs on solar energy, it will not perform effectively on overcast or dreary days. This problem may be lessened by using heat-storage (Cárdenas, B. 2013) materials, which hold heat for extended periods of time and enable Scheffler to run for longer durations of time.

The way this research will be carried out is as follows: Part II compares the desired qualities of various heat storage (Chandel, S. S. et al. 2017) materials and covers the types of materials and their properties that are suitable for use in Scheffler reflectors. The challenges associated with producing heat using phase-change materials (Lingayat, A. B. et al. 2022) were discussed in Part III. The research's last portion addresses the topic's future and ongoing discussions.

Figure 1. Scheffler reflector used for desalination of water

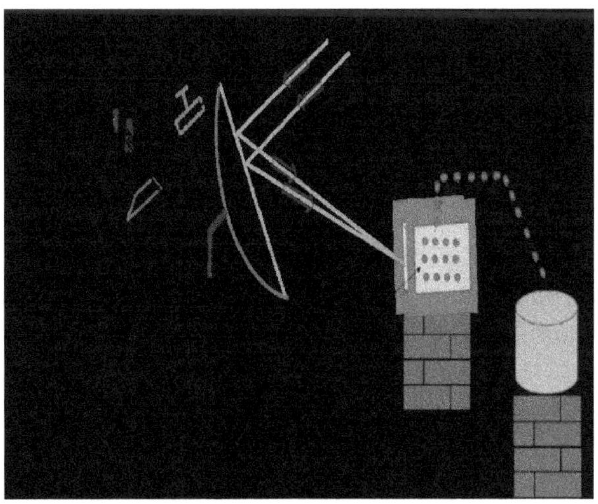

Energy may be stored as heat in two different ways: by changing its phase, or by storing it without changing it. Phase shift (Leong, K. Y. et al. 2019) heat storage seems more attractive than other useful heat storage techniques since it can store more heat for a given unit volume and maintains a steady temperature throughout the transfer process. When heat is delivered to a material, its temperature increases, and thermal energy is just stored there. This energy may be gathered from the approved medium when the temperature fell. They can work at a range of temperatures and accommodate a large number of applications (Veeraiah, V. et al. 2023). A substance that changes phases has the following properties:

- As phases change, there shouldn't be a significant difference in volume.
- A large latent heat capacity is required of the material.
- It must not be corrosive or react with the container it is stored in.
- Its thermos-physical characteristics shouldn't be lost too quickly during phase transitions.
- There should be no damage to the ecosystem.
- The material should be inexpensive.
- It must be easy to access.
- When functioning at a greater temperature, it shouldn't catch fire.

Table 1 displays the thermophysical properties and heat storage of the LHS and non-latent materials, respectively. Density, melting and boiling temperatures, thermal conductivity (Ding, W. et al. 2018), and heat capacity are some of these properties.

Non-LHS materials, such as silicon (Kg/m3), iron (7874 Kg/m3), aluminum, pebbles (1900 Kg/m3), and aluminum (2710 Kg/m3), have higher densities than LHS materials, as seen in Figure 3, but their heat capacities are much lower (0.45 J/gK, 0.89 J/gK, 0.88 J/gK, and 0.71 J/gK, respectively). As a result, density does not depend on heat capacity for any given material; rather, as was previously said, a material with a high density (Mondal, D. et al. 2023) would need less space than one with a low density. Table 2 illustrates that a suitable material (LHS) for a Scheffler Reflector may be one that has a compromised density and a strong heat capacity. Examples of such materials include sodium dihydrogen phosphate dodecahydrate (279.6 J/g-K and 1520 Kg/m3), erythritol (339.8 J/g-K and 1480 Kg/m3), and acetamide (263 J/g-K and 1159 Kg/m3).

Figure 4 shows that high heat capacities are often found in materials with low melting points (Pandey, B. K. et al. 2023). While iron and brick have high melting temperatures of 2000 K and 1811 K, respectively, they have low heat capacities of 0.45 J/g-K and 0.84 J/g-K. PCM materials, which have low melting points (355 K and 315 K, respectively) and high heat capacities (263 J/g-K and 200 J/g-K), with the exception of water, make them ideal candidates for use as storage materials in Scheffler reactors (Dhamodaran, S. S. et al. 2023).

Figure 5 illustrates how much less heat conductivity PCM material has than other typical materials as silicon (230 W/m-K), iron (79.5 W/m-K), aluminum (237 W/m-K), etc. As a result, it has been shown that materials with high heat storage characteristics but low heat storage (THS), such acetamide (0.5 W/m-K) and erythritol (0.326 W/m-K), will have poor thermal conductivity.

Table 1. Thermo-physical properties of various materials

MATERIALS *(PROPERTIES)*	VALUES
BRICKS	
Density	1700 kg/m^3
Melting Point	2000 K
Thermal Conductivity	1.31 W/m-K
Heat Capacity	0.84 J/g-K
CONCRETE	
Density	2400 kg/m^3
Melting Point	1800 K
Thermal Conductivity	2.25 W/m-K
Heat Capacity	0.88J/g-K
SAND	
Density	1442 kg/m^3
Melting Point	1973 K
Thermal Conductivity	2.05 W/m-K
Heat Capacity	0.830 J/g-K
PEBBLES	
Density	(1846 & 2399.8) kg/m^3
Melting Point	1753 K
Thermal Conductivity	2.5 W/m-K
Heat Capacity	0.88050 J/g-K
ALUMINUM	
Density	2710 Kg/m^3
Melting Point	933.47 K
Thermal Conductivity	237 W/m-K
Heat Capacity	0.89 J/g-K
IRON	
Density	7874 Kg/m^3
Melting Point335	1811 K
Thermal Conductivity	79.5 W/m-K
Heat Capacity	0.450 J/g-K
MOLTEN SALTS	
Density	1549 kg/m^3
Melting Point	773 K
Thermal Conductivity	0.652–0.927 W/m-K
Heat Capacity	1.53 J/g-K
SILICON	
Density	2330 Kg/m^3
Melting Point	1687 K
Thermal Conductivity	230 W/m-K
Heat Capacity	0.71 J/g-K

Table 2. Thermo-physical properties of PCM

PARAFFIN WAX	VALUES
Density	900 Kg/m3
Melting Point	643 K
Thermal Conductivity	7.1 W/m-k
Heat Capacity	(2.14–2.9) J/g-K
ACETAMIDE	
Density	1159 Kg/m3
Melting Point	355 K
Thermal Conductivity	0.5 W/m-K
Heat Capacity	263 J/g-K
STEARIC ACID	
Density	940 Kg/m3
Melting Point	337.5 K
Thermal Conductivity	1.60 W/m-K
Heat Capacity	196 J/g-K
MALIC ACID	
Density	860 Kg/m3
Melting Point	325 K
Thermal Conductivity	0.17 W/m-K
Heat Capacity	192 J/g-K
Calcium Chloride Hexahydrate	
Density	1710 Kg/m3
Melting Point	303 K
Thermal Conductivity	1.08 W/m-K
Heat Capacity	175 J/g-K
Magnesium Chloride Hexahydrate	
Density	1450 Kg/m3
Melting Point	390 K
Thermal Conductivity	0.570 W/m-K
Heat Capacity	168.6 J/g-K
PALMITIC ACID	
Density	942 Kg/m3
Melting Point	335 K
Thermal Conductivity	0.162 W/m-K
Heat Capacity	205 J/g-K
LAURIC ACID	
Density	862 Kg/m3
Melting Point	315 K
Thermal Conductivity	0.16 W/m-K

continued on following page

Table 2. Continued

Heat Capacity	**200 J/g-K**
ERYTHRITOL	
Density	**1480 Kg/m3**
Melting Point	**391 K**
Thermal Conductivity	**0.326 W/m-K**
Heat Capacity	**339.8 J/g-K**
Sodium Dihydrogen Phosphate Dodecahydrate	
Density	**1520 Kg/m3**
Melting Point	**313 K**
Thermal Conductivity	**0.476 W/m-K**
Heat Capacity	**279.6 J/g-K**
WATER	
Density	**998 kg/m3**
Melting Point	**373 K**
Thermal Conductivity	**0.598 W/m-K**
Heat Capacity	**4.182 J/g-K**

Figure 2. Graph between heat capacity and density

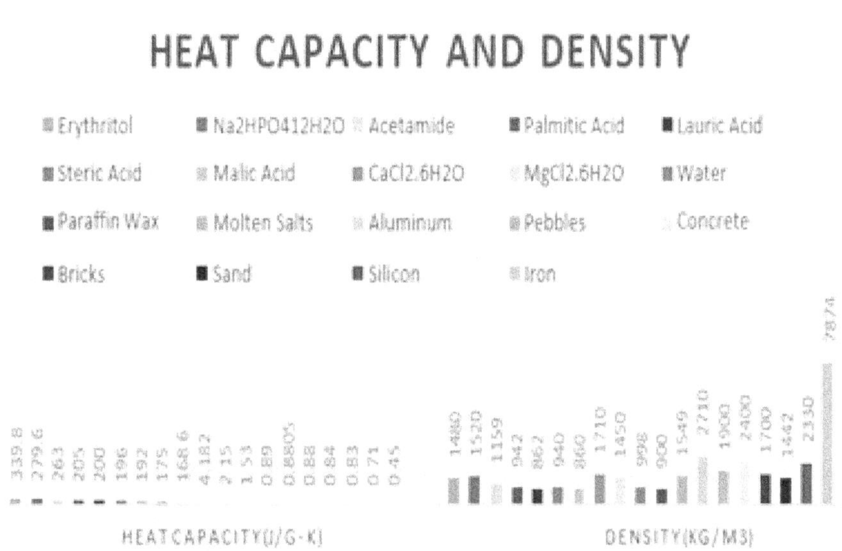

Figure 3. Graph between heat capacity and melting point

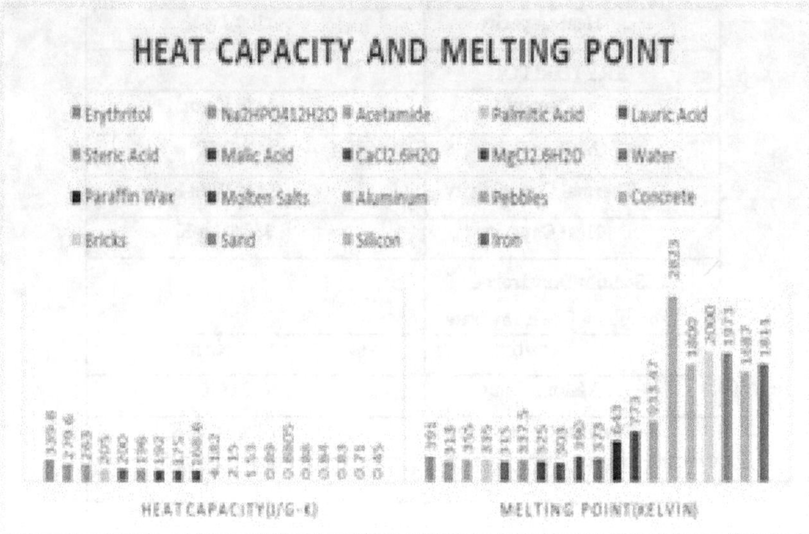

Figure 4. Graph between heat capacity and thermal conductivity

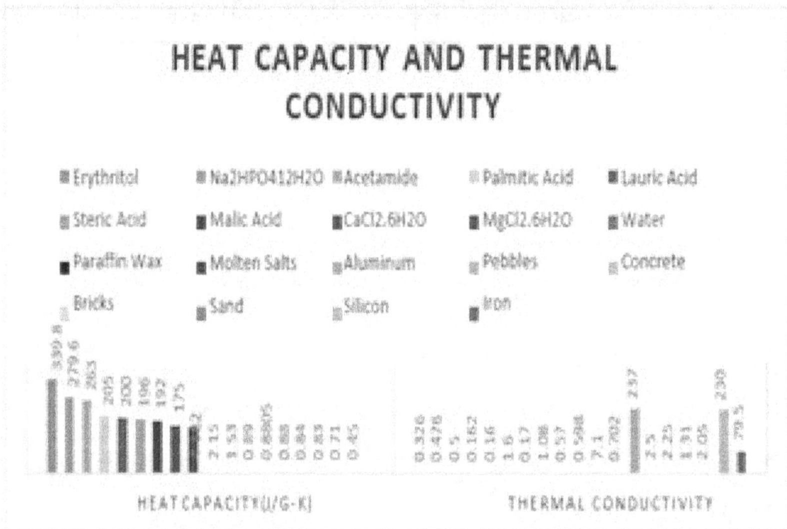

ACADEMIES

A. Safety

Given that safety is a key factor in choosing a heat storage material for a unit, it makes sense to choose one with greater LHS properties and enhanced safety. Paraffin and non-paraffin are examples of organic materials that are suitable LHS compounds even if they have a low ignition temperature. Only moderate temperatures may be used with them.

B. Expensive For High Density of Energy

Even if the equipment and the process are rather expensive, thermochemical storage is one option due to its high energy density of storage. It is preferred over thermal absorption because to its lower cost, particularly in applications that needs sun heat.

C. PCM Selection Standard

A phase-change material with both physical and thermal characteristics may be made. Fatty acid is used in high-temperature applications, whilst some molecules, such paraffin, are better suited for use in low-temperature applications.

D. Material Reactivity for Storage

Despite having excellent heat storage capacity and low associated costs (Chandan, R. R. et al. 2023), some substances, such as salt compounds and metal alloys (mainly used in heat-based applications in the solar energy area) are not suitable for use as heat-absorbing substances for Scheffler usage due to their corrosive nature and rapid temperature decrease.

CONCLUSION

The operation of the Scheffler reflector has been shown to be very beneficial to the production of thermal energy and its use as the primary source of renewable energy. For uses requiring a wide temperature range, the dish's size may be changed to deliver heat. The kind of material used to store heat has an impact on the management and control of heat in Scheffler. Based on thermos-physical characteristics such density, melting point, heat capacity, and thermal conductivity, a range of heat storage materials were compared and contrasted in order to manage heat over an extended period of time. A substance which emits or stores energy to create warmth or cooling when its phase changes are known as a phase-change material (PCM). PCMs are renowned for their extended heat retention times and high heat capacities. Latent heating has the potential to store the same amount of heat in a smaller area than specific heat storage since a substance's latent heat is much larger than its specific heat. The findings demonstrate that LHS materials have greater heat capacities than other heat storage materials, including erythritol, acetamide, and sodium dihydrogen phosphate dodecahydrate. The results also show that although density and specific heat do not always correspond, a high-density material would fit inside a thermal storage device more compactly. Therefore, compromised materials like erythritol (339.8 J/g-K and 1480 Kg/m3), sodium dihydrogen phosphate dodecahydrate (279.6 J/g-K and 1520 Kg/m3), and acetamide (263 J/g-K and 1159 Kg/m3) are the ideal materials for heat storage in a Scheffler reflector. According to research, materials with high heat capacities will also have low melting or boiling temperatures. For example, acetamide and lauric acid have high heat capacities of 263 J/g-K and 200 J/g-K, respectively, but low melting points of 355 K and 315 K. The materials with higher specific heat values exhibited lower thermal conductivities, according to the results. Because LHS materials offer a high heat-storage capacity, they are the best choice for heat storage units for Scheffler reflectors. LHS material has several applications in the Scheffler reflector business. The creative and industrial sectors should create focused awareness campaigns in order to expand the practical material's applications and social exposure. Thermochemical energy storage devices have shown good results, however building Scheffler instruments using this technology is now quite costly.

REFERENCES

Ahmed, S. F., Rafa, N., Mehnaz, T., Ahmed, B., Islam, N., Mofijur, M., Hoang, A. T., & Shafiullah, G. M. (2022, September). Integration of phase change materials in improving the performance of heating, cooling, and clean energy storage systems: An overview. *Journal of Cleaner Production*, *364*, 132639. doi:10.1016/j.jclepro.2022.132639

Chandan, R. R., Soni, S., Raj, A., Veeraiah, V., Dhabliya, D., Pramanik, S., & Gupta, A. (2023). Genetic Algorithm and Machine Learning. In Advanced Bioinspiration Methods for Healthcare Standards, Policies, and Reform. IGI Global. doi:10.4018/978-1-6684-5656-9

Chandel, S. S., & Agarwal, T. (2017). Review of current state of research on energy storage, toxicity, health hazards and commercialization of phase changing materials. Renewable and Sustainable Energy Reviews, 67. Elsevier Ltd17. doi:10.1016/j.rser.2016.09.070

Dhamodaran, S., Ahamad, S., Ramesh, J. V. N., Sathappan, S., Namdev, A., Kanse, R. R., & Pramanik, S. (2023). *Fire Detection System Utilizing an Aggregate Technique in UAV and Cloud Computing, Thrust Technologies' Effect on Image Processing*. IGI Global.

Ding, W., Bonk, A., & Bauer, T. (2018). Corrosion behavior of metallic alloys in molten chloride salts for thermal energy storage in concentrated solar power plants: A review," Frontiers of Chemical Science and Engineering 2018 12:3, vol. 12, no. 3, pp. 564–576, Oct. 2018, . doi:10.1007/s11705-018-1720-0

Hassan, F., Jamil, F., Hussain, A., Ali, H. M., Janjua, M. M., Khushnood, S., Farhan, M., Altaf, K., Said, Z., & Li, C. (2022, February). Recent advancements in latent heat phase change materials and their applications for thermal energy storage and buildings: A state of the art review. *Sustainable Energy Technologies and Assessments*, *49*, 101646. doi:10.1016/j.seta.2021.101646

Kumar, A., Prakash, O., & Kaviti, A. K. (2017, September). A comprehensive review of Scheffler solar collector. *Renewable & Sustainable Energy Reviews*, *77*, 890–898. doi:10.1016/j.rser.2017.03.044

Leong, K. Y., Abdul Rahman, M. R., & Gurunathan, B. A. (2019, February). Nano-enhanced phase change materials: A review of thermo-physical properties, applications and challenges. *Journal of Energy Storage*, *21*, 18–31. doi:10.1016/j.est.2018.11.008

Lingayat, A. B., & Suple, Y. R. (2022). *Review on Phase Change Material as Thermal Energy Storage Medium: Materials* (Vol. 3). Application.

Mondal, D., Ratnaparkhi, A., Deshpande, A., Deshpande, V., Kshirsagar, A. P., & Pramanik, S. (2023). Applications, Modern Trends and Challenges of MultiscaleModelling in Smart Cities. In *Data-Driven Mathematical Modeling in Smart Cities*. IGI Global. doi:10.4018/978-1-6684-6408-3.ch001

Pandey, B. K., Pandey, D., Nassa, V. K., George, A. S., Pramanik, S., & Dadheech, P. (2023). Applications for the Text Extraction Method of Complex Degraded Images. In *The Impact of Thrust Technologies on Image Processing*. Nova Publishers. doi:10.52305/ATJL4552

Patel, R. & Patel, V. (2022). Scheffler reflector for cooking application: a review. *International Journal of Ambient Energy*. Taylor and Francis Ltd. . doi:10.1080/01430750.2020.1758778

Reddy, D. S., Khan, M. K., Alam, M. Z., & Rashid, H. (2018, March). Design charts for Scheffler reflector. *Solar Energy*, *163*, 104–112. doi:10.1016/j.solener.2018.01.081

Veeraiah, V., Shiju, D. J., Ramesh, J. V. N., Ganesh Kumar, R., Pramanik, S., Gupta, A., & Pandey, D. (2023). *Healthcare Cloud Services in Image Processing, Thrust Technologies' Effect on Image Processing*. IGI Global.

KEY TERMS AND DEFINITIONS

Latent Heat Storage: Using the significant latent heat of phase shift during the melting of a solid into a liquid, latent heat storage involves storing heat in a phase-change substance. Heat is transformed into chemical bonds by thermochemical storage, which is advantageous for long-term storage applications and reversible.

Phase Change Materials: Phase change materials, or PCMs, are substances that, when they undergo a change in their physical state—that is, when they shift from a solid to a liquid and vice versa—absorb or release significant quantities of heat that is said to be "latent."

Scheffler: Since its introduction by Wolfgang Scheffler, fixed focus type Scheffler concentrators have found widespread usage in a variety of low- to medium-sized industrial process heat applications. The typical sizes of these Scheffler concentrators are 8 m2 and 16 m2.

Sustainable Development Goals: The seventeen interconnected Sustainable Development Goals, also known as the Global Goals, are intended to act as a "shared blueprint for peace and prosperity for people and the planet, now and into the future."

Sustainable Development: Development that is sustainable is one which satisfies current demands without jeopardising the capacity of future generations to satisfy their own needs.

Chapter 12
Engaging Stakeholders for a Sustainable Future:
Catalysts of Green Economy and Renewable Energy Transitions

Surjit Singha
https://orcid.org/0000-0002-5730-8677
Kristu Jayanti College (Autonomous), India

ABSTRACT

This chapter highlights the critical importance of stakeholder engagement as a catalyst for sustainable development in the green economy and renewable energy transitions. It transcends a mere procedural requirement by emphasizing its fundamental function as a catalyst for progress. Key takeaways include the significance of diverse stakeholder participation, objective alignment, and an all-encompassing approach to sustainability encompassing environmental, social, and economic dimensions. It highlights the importance of partnerships, effective policies, technological advancements, and ongoing monitoring. Future trends, such as localized approaches and data-driven decision-making, are investigated, along with emerging challenges, such as complex ecosystems of stakeholders and the digital divide. Despite obstacles, opportunities such as inclusive innovation and policy influence exist. The engagement of stakeholders arises as an indispensable factor in shaping a sustainable future.

INTRODUCTION

The introduction emphasizes the importance of stakeholder participation in accelerating the transition to a green economy and the widespread adoption of renewable energy sources. These transitions are not merely responses to environmental challenges but crucial measures towards ensuring a sustainable future for ourplanet and future generations. Stakeholder engagement lies at the core of these transformative shifts, involving the active involvement, consultation, and collaboration of various individuals, groups, organizations, and communities with vested interests in sustainability initiatives, green economy

DOI: 10.4018/979-8-3693-1297-1.ch012

practices, and renewable energy projects. There are numerous compelling reasons why its significance cannot be overstated. First, stakeholders contribute diverse perspectives, expertise, and experiences to decision-making, ensuring that decisions are informed by a comprehensive range of knowledge and attitudes, resulting in more balanced and practical solutions (Kabeyi & Olanrewaju, 2022).

Furthermore, successful transitions in the green economy and renewable energy fields require the support and acceptance of the general public. Engaging stakeholders fosters community trust and a sense of ownership, increasing the likelihood that initiatives will be embraced rather than met with opposition. In addition, stakeholder engagement fosters innovation by encouraging the exchange of ideas and integrating multiple approaches. Collaboration among stakeholders can result in innovative solutions that address our intricate sustainability challenges. Moreover, involving stakeholders can identify and address prospective risks and concerns early in the planning and implementation phases, maximizing project resilience and minimizing obstacles (Soderholm, 2020; Maqbool et al., 2020).

Transparency in decision-making is another essential advantage of stakeholder engagement, as it facilitates monitoring progress, allocating resources, and accountability for responsible actions. Engaging stakeholders ensures that the interests of all parties are considered, thereby contributing to the long-term viability of green economy practices and renewable energy solutions. In the following chapters, we will explore the multifaceted role of stakeholder engagement, examining strategies, best practices, and real-world examples that highlight the transformative potential of collaboration and engagement in building a more sustainable and prosperous future. By recognizing the importance of stakeholder engagement, we take a significant step toward attaining our sustainability objectives and ensuring a better future for all. This chapter emphasizes the centrality of stakeholder engagement, provides clear definitions, and establishes the context for readers to navigate subsequent chapters, where we investigate the intricate facets of this critical topic in greater depth (Wei et al., 2023).

This introductory section highlights the central role of stakeholder engagement in accelerating the transition to a green economy and the widespread adoption of renewable energy sources. The chapter highlights the fundamental significance of stakeholder engagement by describing its role in addressing complex sustainability challenges and fostering comprehensive, balanced solutions. It investigates the crucial relationship between stakeholder engagement and achieving sustainability goals. This section illustrates the contribution of an efficacious concentration to the success of green economy and renewable energy transitions. It defines key terms and concepts related to stakeholder engagement, green economy, renewable energy transitions, sustainability, and related topics clearly and concisely. It ensures that readers have a firm understanding of the subject matter. It clarifies the relationship between stakeholder engagement and broader sustainability objectives, emphasizing social, environmental, and economic integration. Recognizing that various stakeholder groups have distinct interests and levels of influence, this chapter introduces stakeholder categories, and this classification sets the groundwork for comprehending the wide variety of stakeholders involved in green economy and renewable energy initiatives. It serves predominantly as an introduction and provides a thematic foundation for subsequent relevant themes. It prepares the reader for a more in-depth examination of strategies, case studies, challenges, and solutions associated with stakeholder engagement in green economy and renewable energy transitions. The real-world relevance of stakeholder engagement is illustrated throughout the chapter through examples, case studies, and instances in which effective engagement has been instrumental in promoting sustainable initiatives and transitions (Kabeyi & Olanrewaju, 2020). The purpose of this introductory chapter is to emphasize the importance of stakeholder engagement in accelerating sustainability changes. It prepares the groundwork for readers to comprehend the significance, definitions, and context of stakeholder engagement and its importance in attaining a sustainable and equitable future. By recognizing the utmost relevance of stakeholder engagement, readers are prepared to explore the many facets of this crucial topic in greater depth. This introductory chapter's theory and context are firmly rooted in sustainability, sustainable development, and the central role of stakeholder engagement. Its main idea is that stakeholder engagement catalyzes the transition to a green economy and the widespread adoption of renewable energy sources. This theory recognizes the urgent need to resolve environmental issues and ensure a sustainable future for future generations.

The central concept of this chapter is sustainability, which encompasses the capacity to meet present requirements without compromising future generations' ability to meet their own. As a holistic approach, sustainable development strives to balance economic growth, social equity, and environmental protection. It is the foundation for transitioning to a green economy and adopting renewable energy sources. In these transitions, the theory of this chapter highlights stakeholder engagement as an indispensable process. The stakeholder engagement theory emphasizes the active participation, consultation, and collaboration of diverse individuals, groups, and communities with vested interests in sustainability initiatives, green economy practices, and renewable energy projects. It emphasizes the importance of diverse perspectives, expertise, and experiences in effectively making informed decisions and solving problems. The rationale for engaging stakeholders is firmly established, emphasizing its necessity. Several compelling arguments support the importance of stakeholder engagement, including its ability to bring diverse perspectives, build public support and trust, foster innovation, identify and mitigate risks, promote transparency, and ensure the consideration of all parties' present and future interests.

It provides a preview of a more in-depth examination of the multifaceted role of stakeholder engagement. It foreshadows the imminent discussion of strategies, best practices, and real-world examples that vividly illustrate the transformative potential of collaboration and engagement in building a more sustainable and prosperous future. The theory and context of this introductory chapter are firmly rooted in the principles of sustainability, sustainable development, and the vital importance of stakeholder engagement. It asserts unequivocally that stakeholder engagement is not only advantageous but a necessary propelling force in the transitions towards a green economy and renewable energy, paving the way for a thorough examination of this crucial topic in the following chapters.

THE SIGNIFICANCE OF STAKEHOLDER ENGAGEMENT

Pursuing sustainability objectives globally is necessary, and the central role of stakeholder engagement rests at the heart of this endeavour. Actively involving individuals, groups, organizations, and communities with a vested interest in sustainability initiatives constitutes stakeholder engagement. It is impossible to overstate its importance in attaining sustainability objectives. Stakeholder engagement fosters a comprehensive and balanced approach to addressing multifaceted sustainability challenges that frequently span economic, environmental, and social dimensions by bringing together diverse perspectives, knowledge, and experiences. It ensures that decisions are well-informed, considering both technical considerations and real-world consequences (Nonet et al., 2022; Wells et al., 2021). It fosters community trust and ownership, promoting social acceptance and minimizing resistance. Transparency in decision-making is a cornerstone, allowing stakeholders and the public to comprehend the process, thus enhancing accountability and tracking of progress.

Moreover, stakeholder engagement is an early warning system, identifying potential obstacles and challenges in advance and enhancing the project's resilience. It embodies the principles of inclusiveness and equity, ensuring that the interests of marginalized groups are incorporated into sustainability initiatives, thereby contributing to more equitable outcomes. Additionally, it fosters a long-term commitment to sustainability objectives, as individuals and groups who are actively engaged are more likely to remain committed to success over time. It provides a structured platform for conflict resolution and consensus building, thereby reducing the likelihood of conflicts that could impede progress toward sustainability. In essence, stakeholder engagement is an indispensable catalyst for attaining sustainability objectives, as it provides the support, insights, and resiliency required to confront the complex challenges facing our planet and society (Kujala et al., 2022; Wells et al., 2021; Herremans et al., 2015).

Concurrently, there is an undeniable connection between stakeholder engagement and successful transitions to a green economy and renewable energy. Participation of key stakeholders, such as government agencies, enterprises, and local communities and individuals, plays a fundamental role in generating support and buy-in for the transition process. Engaged stakeholders are likelier to partake actively, infusing the transition with the necessary change momentum. Collaboration is fundamental to successful transitions, and involving diverse stakeholders encourages integrating multiple approaches and innovative solutions to resolve the complex challenges posed by green economy and renewable energy transitions (Maqbool et al., 2020).

These transitions entail inherent technical, economic, and social complexities necessitating collaborative problem-solving. Engagement of stakeholders provides the necessary platform for identifying and addressing these challenges collectively, utilizing the collective intelligence of various stakeholders. In addition, it shapes the regulatory environment by involving stakeholders in policy development and regulatory processes, ensuring that frameworks are well-informed and aligned with sustainability objectives. These policies foster an environment conducive to adopting eco-friendly practices and renewable energy solutions. In addition, stakeholder engagement assists in addressing the concerns and requirements of communities and individuals affected by these transitions, promoting social acceptance and reducing resistance. It provides access to a wealth of resources and expertise contributed by various stakeholders, thereby enhancing the capacity to implement green practices and renewable energy initiatives effectively. Lastly, by maintaining a continuous feedback cycle, stakeholder engagement ensures that constant adjustments and enhancements are incorporated, making the transition adaptive and responsive to evolving challenges and opportunities. Stakeholder engagement is essential for realizing a more sustainable, environmentally responsible, and prosperous future, particularly in the context of green economy and renewable energy transitions.

IDENTIFYING STAKEHOLDERS

Effective stakeholder management requires categorizing stakeholders according to their interests and influence in the green economy and renewable energy transitions. These stakeholder groups comprise a vast array of entities, each with its own set of priorities and impact levels. The government and regulatory bodies exert considerable influence through policy development and regulation, ensuring environmental protection and energy security. Profitability, innovation, and sustainability drive businesses and industries with significant power due to their investment capacity. Non-Governmental Organizations (NGOs) and environmental advocacy organizations are crucial in shaping sustainability policies and increasing public awareness. As project hosts, local communities moderately influence public opinion and project acceptance. Investors and financial institutions wield significant influence through capital provision and investment decisions. Academic institutions contribute expertise and knowledge, resulting in a moderate impact on technological progression. Consumers and end-users moderately impact the market demand for sustainable products through purchasing decisions. As essential players in energy production and distribution, utilities and energy providers wield considerable influence (Wells et al., 2021; Gibson, 2012). Through negotiations, labour unions exert a moderate amount of influence on job creation and workforce development. Influential international organizations establish global sustainability standards and climate agreements. Technology providers and innovators exercise moderate to substantial impact on innovation and market expansion. With moderate influence, supply chain participants promote sustainability practices. Media and public opinion leaders have moderate to high effects on public perception and policy discourse. Local administrations and municipalities moderately impact the formulation of local policies and sustainable urban planning. This categorization helps stakeholders understand their roles and guides decision-makers in effectively engaging and prioritizing key stakeholders, promoting collaboration and consensus-building during the transition to a green economy and renewable energy (Friedrich, 2021; Da Silva et al., 2019).

Identifying and prioritizing critical stakeholders in the context of green economy and renewable energy transitions is a multifaceted process crucial for successful project implementation and stakeholder engagement. It begins with a comprehensive phase of identifying stakeholders, which includes developing a stakeholder map, conducting interviews and surveys, and reviewing existing data to identify potential stakeholders and their interests. Once identified, stakeholders thoroughly evaluate their claims, influence, prospective impact on transitions, and alignment with the project's objectives. This analysis is the foundation for categorizing stakeholders on an influence-interest matrix, which helps visualize which stakeholders are vital actors and informs the prioritization process (Zhang et al., 2021; Maqbool et al., 2020).

Prioritizing key stakeholders requires concentrating on those with high influence and a strong interest in the transitions, as they are likely to be key decision-makers, influencers, and supporters. It also entails engaging strategically with stakeholders who may have high influence but divergent interests and utilizing the input of stakeholders who have a high interest but lower leverage. It is essential to develop customized engagement strategies for each key stakeholder group, considering their individual requirements, concerns, and priorities. Continuous evaluation and regular updates to the stakeholder prioritization ensure that changing conditions and new stakeholders are considered. Involving key stakeholders in decision-making, problem-solving, and project planning increases the likelihood of reaching a consensus and gaining support. This ongoing and dynamic process of identifying and prioritizing stakeholders is essential for successfully navigating the complexities of green economy and renewable energy transitions, building solid relationships, and achieving sustainability objectives (Jager et al., 2023; Soderholm, 2020).

STAKEHOLDER ANALYSIS

Based on their distinct duties and interests, green economy and renewable energy transition stakeholders have diverse needs, expectations, and concerns. Government and regulatory authorities seek effective policy frameworks and clarity to support sustainability objectives, with expectations centred on compliance, environmentally responsible practices, and contributions to national energy security. Businesses and industries prioritize profitability and market expansion, anticipating regulatory consistency, incentives for investments in sustainability, and access to qualified labour while being concerned about regulatory burdens and market volatility. Non-governmental organizations (NGOs) and environmental advocacy groups prioritize ecological protection and sustainability advocacy, anticipating transparency and collaboration on environmental initiatives while remaining vigilant against greenwashing and insufficient commitment to Sustainability (Kabeyi & Olanrewaju, 2022; Soderholm, 2020).

Local communities expect economic benefits, employment opportunities, minimal environmental and social impacts, community engagement, fair compensation, and mitigation of project-related disruptions. Investors and financial institutions seek attractive investment returns and risk management, anticipating transparent reporting, sustainable practices, and long-term viability while being concerned about financial risks and project delays. Academic and research institutions prioritize research collaboration and technological advancement, anticipating knowledge exchange, access to research findings, and contributions to innovation while being concerned about limited research opportunities and insufficient data sharing (Bhuiyan et al., 2022; Soderholm, 2020).

Consumers and end users require affordable and sustainable energy products and services, expect access to renewable energy options and transparent pricing, and are concerned about rising energy costs and supply reliability. Utilities and energy providers concentrate on profitability and efficient energy production, anticipating regulatory support, market competition, and infrastructural investment while coping with regulatory restrictions and energy market volatility. Labour unions advocate for job creation, workforce development, and labour conditions, anticipating employment opportunities, equitable wages, and safe working conditions while being concerned about job losses and insufficient labour rights (Kabeyi & Olanrewaju, 2021).

International organizations prioritize global sustainability standards, climate agreements, and policy coordination, anticipating multilateral cooperation, adherence to global contracts, and leadership in sustainability while being concerned about failures to meet international obligations and environmental degradation. Technology providers and innovators emphasize technological innovation and market growth, expecting innovative solutions, collaboration on research, and market support, with concerns about sluggish technology adoption and market competition. Supply chain partners seek resource efficiency, compliance with sustainability standards, and supply chain resiliency, expecting sustainable sourcing, responsible supply chain practices, and collaboration on sustainability goals while being concerned about supply chain disruptions and noncompliance with sustainability standards (Su et al., 2021).

Media and public opinion leaders seek information dissemination, public awareness, and influence over public opinion, expecting accurate reporting, transparency, and the promotion of sustainability values while expressing concern regarding misinformation and insufficient coverage of sustainability issues. Local governments and municipalities focus on sustainable urban planning, local economic development, and environmental stewardship, expecting participation in decision-making, infrastructure support, and alignment with local sustainability goals while grappling with concerns regarding insufficient municipal resources, land use conflicts, and regulatory constraints. Recognizing and addressing these diverse stakeholder needs, expectations, and concerns is crucial for effective stakeholder engagement and the success of the green economy and renewable energy transitions (Hollmann et al., 2022; Kabeyi & Olanrewaju, 2022).

The systematic and dynamic mapping and analysis of stakeholders is essential to the success of green economy and renewable energy transitions. Initially, stakeholders must be identified exhaustively through research, documentation, or ideation sessions to account for all relevant parties. Classifying these stakeholders according to their roles, interests, and influence provides a structured framework for analysis. To understand their motivations and potential effects on transitions, background, affiliations, and previous interactions are defined (Kabeyi & Olanrewaju, 2021).

The Power-Interest Grid is a visual tool for prioritizing stakeholders based on their influence and level of interest. It facilitates the identification of essential stakeholders who should be the primary focus of engagement initiatives. A thorough analysis of stakeholders examines each group's needs, expectations, and concerns, considering their historical relationships with comparable industries and their perspectives. It is essential to assess the present level of participation and pinpoint any shortcomings to improve engagement methods. These tactics should be adapted to each stakeholder group's unique needs and concerns by utilizing various engagement platforms, including surveys, public consultations, and one-on-one sessions. Establishing methods for addressing possible disagreements is also necessary (Kabeyi & Olanrewaju, 202).

Continuous monitoring and feedback collection are essential components of stakeholder engagement, allowing for modifying strategies as conditions change. A well-structured communication plan ensures that information is communicated effectively through the proper channels and at the appropriate frequency. Lastly, maintaining meticulous recordings of stakeholder interactions and outcomes contributes to openness and accountability. Mapping and analysis of stakeholders serve as the basis for informed, strategic, and adaptable stakeholder engagement throughout the transitions toward a green economy and renewable energy. These processes are essential for garnering support, addressing concerns, and attaining sustainability goals.

STRATEGIES FOR EFFECTIVE ENGAGEMENT

Effective engagement of stakeholders is a multifaceted process crucial to the success of green economy and renewable energy transitions. Organizations and initiatives can establish trust and foster collaboration by implementing multiple strategies, such as early and continuous engagement, tailored communication, stakeholder consultation, and transparency. Mechanisms for conflict resolution, partnerships, and capacity-building programs strengthen engagement efforts. Prioritizing inclusivity and equity ensures that diverse voices are heard, while feedback loops and adaptable engagement strategies facilitate the ability to respond to changing requirements. Ethical considerations guide responsible engagement practices, facilitated by public awareness campaigns and long-term relationship development. Utilizing diverse engagement methods and regular reporting further strengthens transparency and accountability. These strategies empower stakeholders to contribute to the transition to sustainability by aligning their interests and resolving their concerns for a more equitable and environmentally responsible future.

Effective stakeholder engagement in green economy and renewable energy transitions requires a multifaceted strategy that includes effective communication techniques, collaboration frameworks, and negotiation abilities. Effective communication involves actively listening to the concerns of stakeholders, employing transparent and customized messaging, establishing feedback mechanisms, and, when necessary, employing contact for conflict resolution. Collaboration frameworks include the formation of partnerships with key stakeholders, the construction of stakeholder working groups, the promotion of co-creation and co-design, and the utilization of multi-stakeholder platforms to facilitate open dialogue. Negotiation skills are essential for conflict resolution, compromise, consensus-building, and ethical negotiations that respect fairness and transparency (Lennon et al., 2019). By incorporating these elements, organizations can navigate the complexities of stakeholder engagement, foster trust, and propel progress toward a sustainable and equitable future.

CASE STUDIES

Case Study 1: The Cape Wind Project

The Cape Wind Project, an ambitious proposal for an offshore wind farm off Cape Cod, Massachusetts, was marked by a succession of strategic efforts to engage stakeholders. Developers established early connections with local communities, government agencies, and environmental organizations at the project's onset. Regular consultations, workshops, and public forums were held, allowing stakeholders to voice their concerns and contribute to project decisions transparently—partnerships with local environmental groups and research collaborations assisted in the comprehensive assessment of potential environmental impacts. Possibly most notably, an adaptive approach was adopted, with project developers incorporating stakeholder feedback to refine the project's design, thereby minimizing its visual and environmental impact.

Nevertheless, this endeavour had obstacles. Opposition arose from local communities and concerned organizations, primarily due to worries about the potential visual impact on scenic views and effects on marine life. Complex permitting procedures and regulatory approvals proved to be a formidable obstacle.

Despite these obstacles, the Cape Wind Project accomplished significant results. It obtained crucial regulatory approvals, demonstrating the efficacy of stakeholder engagement in addressing concerns and navigating the permitting process. Moreover, stakeholder input significantly improved the project's design, reducing environmental impacts. Notably, persistent engagement fostered public support for offshore wind energy in the region, highlighting the significance of proactive and transparent stakeholder engagement in renewable energy initiatives.

Case Study 2: SolarCity's Community Solar Projects

SolarCity, now a subsidiary of Tesla, implemented an innovative community solar initiative across the United States, enabling residents to subscribe to solar power without installing rooftop panels. SolarCity employed several essential strategies to accomplish this. Extensive community outreach efforts, including town hall meetings, seminars, and informational campaigns, were implemented to ensure stakeholders were informed and involved. The company allowed stakeholders to subscribe to community solar initiatives, emphasizing solar energy's cost savings and environmental advantages. In addition, initiatives were launched to educate the public about the benefits of solar energy, resulting in a more informed populace.

However, the initiative was full of obstacles. The structuring of community solar programs could have been improved by differing state and local regulations, which required cautious navigation. In addition, continuous educational efforts were required to ensure that all stakeholders comprehended the subscription model and its benefits.

Significant outcomes were realized through SolarCity's community solar initiative. The model was widely adopted, making solar energy accessible to a larger population and reducing its overall cost. In addition, the success of stakeholder engagement efforts facilitated the expansion of community solar initiatives in several states through policy changes. Most importantly, these initiatives had a tangible environmental impact by reducing greenhouse gas emissions and increasing clean energy generation, showcasing the transformative potential of community solar in advancing renewable energy adoption.

Case Study 3: The Ivanpah Solar Electric Generating System

The Ivanpah Solar Electric Generating System in California is one of the world's most extensive solar thermal power facilities, producing renewable energy using concentrated solar power (CSP) technology. Various strategies were employed to navigate the complexities of such an undertaking. Extensive public consultations were held with local communities and environmental organizations to address concerns about the potential impacts on desert ecology and wildlife, particularly the population of desert tortoises. Environmental mitigation measures, including relocation efforts for desert tortoises, were implemented to mitigate ecological disruptions. Educational programs were implemented to improve the public's comprehension of CSP technology and its advantages.

Despite obstacles, the project produced substantial results, including environmental concerns and regulatory complexities associated with innovative CSP technology. It generates clean energy successfully, contributing to California's renewable energy objectives and supplying electricity to thousands of homes. Environmental monitoring and mitigation efforts ensured the safety of the desert tortoise population, demonstrating the viability of renewable energy development in tandem with wildlife conservation. Moreover, ongoing stakeholder engagement enhanced public perception and garnered support for renewable energy initiatives in the region. These case studies highlight the significance of effective stakeholder engagement in addressing obstacles, fostering support, and achieving positive results in green economy and renewable energy initiatives. Early and ongoing engagement, tailored communication, and adaptable approaches are indispensable for successfully implementing projects and advancing sustainability objectives.

OVERCOMING CHALLENGES IN STAKEHOLDER ENGAGEMENT

Engagement of stakeholders for sustainable development is unquestionably essential but fraught with obstacles. Often, stakeholders originate from diverse backgrounds and have varying interests and priorities, making it difficult to reconcile these disparities. The engagement process can be further complicated by limited resources and capacity, resistance to change, and the need to navigate complex regulatory environments. Considerations include establishing trust and credibility, bridging communication gaps, and harmonizing short-term and long-term objectives. Managing engagement fatigue, resolving conflicts, and ensuring accountability are crucial aspects of effective stakeholder engagement (Wells et al., 2021; Pedrini & Ferri, 2019).

However, there are methods to address these obstacles effectively. These include a comprehensive analysis of stakeholders' motivations, capacity-building programs, transparent communication, education and information dissemination, collaboration with regulatory authorities, and an emphasis on long-term benefits. Key strategies include encouraging open and respectful dialogue, providing translation services, demonstrating receptivity to stakeholder input, and periodically assessing and modifying engagement efforts (Franklin, 2020).

Organizations and initiatives can overcome these obstacles by implementing these solutions and best practices, cultivating positive relationships, and achieving sustainable development objectives. Such endeavours are necessary for establishing a more equitable and sustainable future for all parties involved.

BUILDING PARTNERSHIPS AND ALLIANCES

By creating collaborative networks and frameworks for addressing complex sustainability challenges, partnerships and alliances play a pivotal role in nurturing stakeholder engagement. In the context of green economy and renewable energy transitions, these alliances serve as bridges between various stakeholders, including government entities, businesses, non-governmental organizations (NGOs), and academic institutions. They allow diverse perspectives, knowledge, and resources to converge, promoting consensus and collective action toward shared sustainability objectives. Partnerships increase the influence and credibility of stakeholders, making it more straightforward to navigate regulatory complexities, mobilize resources, and engage in productive dialogue with broader audiences. In addition, they promote knowledge exchange, innovation, and the development of best practices, thereby contributing to the success of sustainable initiatives and enhancing the quality of decision-making. In pursuing a more sustainable and equitable future, partnerships and alliances are crucial for building trust, fostering collaboration, and attaining meaningful stakeholder engagement (Kabeyi & Olanrewaju, 2022).

Multiple successful partnerships have emerged in the context of green economy and renewable energy transitions, demonstrating the effectiveness of collaboration in fostering sustainability. The Renewable Energy Buyers Alliance (REBA) is a notable example of an organization that brings together significant corporations, such as Google, Facebook, and Walmart, to accelerate the procurement of renewable energy. REBA collaborates with NGOs and industry experts to develop tools, resources, and best practices that facilitate the renewable energy transition of organizations. The Renewable Energy Ministerial (CEM) is another example of a global forum that brings together governments, businesses, and other stakeholders to promote renewable energy. The CEM has led to initiatives like the Electric Vehicles Initiative, which seeks to advance the adoption of electric vehicles worldwide. In addition, the Global Wind Energy Council (GWEC) collaborates with governments, international organizations, and industry stakeholders to expand the global reach of wind energy. These partnerships illustrate how diverse stakeholder collaboration can drive the adoption of renewable energy, advance sustainability objectives, and accelerate the transition to a greener economy.

POLICY AND REGULATORY FRAMEWORKS

Government policies and regulations are crucial in encouraging stakeholder participation by providing a structured framework and incentives for sustainable development efforts. Frequently, these policies require or promote engagement practices that foster collaboration, transparency, and accountability. For example, requiring public consultations during project permit processes ensures that stakeholders' voices are heard and their concerns are addressed. Tax credits and subsidies motivate stakeholders, such as individuals and businesses, to actively partake in sustainability initiatives, such as renewable energy projects. Sustainability goals and targets established by the government provide a clear direction that encourages stakeholders to align their actions with broader environmental goals. Moreover, regulations that mandate transparency and reporting ensure that organizations and initiatives remain accountable to their stakeholders, fostering confidence and facilitating ongoing engagement. Therefore, government policies and regulations are crucial in promoting meaningful stakeholder engagement and advancing sustainable development objectives.

Legal structures play a crucial role in shaping and influencing sustainable development initiatives. Clear and comprehensive regulations and efficient enforcement mechanisms can facilitate and promote sustainability by providing direction, incentives, and accountability. They empower stakeholders, promote responsible conduct, and safeguard the environment. In contrast, weak, ambiguous, or contradictory legal frameworks, regulatory capture, and a narrow focus on short-term economic advantages can impede sustainability by creating uncertainty, permitting unsustainable practices, and restricting citizen participation. To cultivate a more sustainable world, it is crucial to design and implement legal frameworks that align with sustainable development objectives, prioritize the well-being of current and future generations, and encourage responsible and environmentally friendly practices.

TOOLS AND TECHNOLOGIES FOR STAKEHOLDER ENGAGEMENT

Technological advancements have transformed stakeholder engagement by providing organizations with tools and platforms to cultivate meaningful connections, collect data, and make informed decisions. Twitter, Facebook, and LinkedIn are examples of social media platforms that facilitate real-time interactions and dialogue with diverse stakeholder groups. Online surveys and feedback tools expedite data collection and analysis, allowing organizations to tailor their strategies based on stakeholder input. Software for Stakeholder Relationship Management (SRM) centralizes stakeholder data, improving engagement monitoring and management. Data analytics and visualization tools enable organizations to glean insights from stakeholder data, thereby contributing to the development of sustainable initiatives. Virtual meetings and webinars eliminate geographical barriers and allow remote stakeholder participation. Platforms for collaboration, geo-mapping, AI chatbots, and mobile applications augment engagement strategies. Blockchain technology increases transparency, whereas platforms for crowdsourcing and crowdfunding democratize participation. Voting and governance systems founded on the blockchain promote fairness in decision-making. Collectively, these tools permit organizations to navigate stakeholder engagement in the digital era, thereby facilitating sustainable development.

Social media, data analytics, and various digital tools have revolutionized stakeholder engagement, providing organizations with potent means to connect, communicate, and collaborate with their stakeholders effectively. Social media platforms like Twitter, Facebook, and LinkedIn have facilitated real-time communication, allowing organizations to share updates, engage in two-way dialogues with stakeholders, and reach a global audience. Data analytics tools have enabled organizations to gain insights into stakeholder sentiments and emergent trends, enabling personalized engagement and predictive strategies and improving performance evaluation. Online surveys and tools have expedited feedback collection, making it convenient and scalable, while virtual meetings and webinars have improved accessibility and interactivity in stakeholder engagement efforts. Chatbots powered by AI offer 24/7 support, facilitating data collection and scalability. Geomapping and GIS technologies enable the visualization and analysis of project impacts, while blockchain technology improves data sharing security and transparency. These digital tools have become indispensable as they facilitate effectiveness, scalability, and data-driven decision-making in stakeholder engagement for sustainability initiatives.

MONITORING AND EVALUATION

Organizations committed to sustainable development and meaningful stakeholder relationships must continuously monitor and evaluate their efforts to engage stakeholders. They function as compasses, guiding organizations through the intricate terrain of stakeholder interactions. Through assessments, organizations can determine the efficacy of their engagement strategies, adapt and fine-tune their approaches, demonstrate transparency and accountability, and make decisions based on facts and data. This continuous process also contributes to long-term success, ensuring that organizations remain on track to achieve their sustainability objectives despite the emergence of new obstacles. Monitoring and evaluation also cultivate a learning and knowledge-sharing culture, enabling organizations to gain valuable insights that benefit internal operations and the broader stakeholder community. By demonstrating the tangible impact of stakeholder input, organizations can enhance their credibility and trustworthiness, thereby driving their commitment to continuous stakeholder engagement enhancement.

For organizations committed to sustainability and responsible practices, evaluating the efficacy of stakeholder engagement activities is essential. The supplied metrics and indicators provide a comprehensive and adaptable framework for evaluating engagement efforts in diverse areas. By monitoring these metrics, organizations can assess their impact on stakeholders, monitor their progress toward sustainability objectives, and perpetually enhance their engagement strategies. In addition, these metrics enable organizations to demonstrate transparency, accountability, and responsiveness to stakeholders, thereby nurturing confidence and enhancing their reputation. Customizing the evaluation strategy to align with particular objectives and stakeholder dynamics ensures that engagement efforts remain pertinent and contribute to meaningful, long-term sustainability outcomes. In a swiftly changing environment, these metrics enable organizations to navigate challenges, seize opportunities, and form long-lasting stakeholder partnerships to drive positive change.

FUTURE TRENDS AND OUTLOOK

For effective planning and strategy development, it is essential to forecast future trends in stakeholder engagement for green economy and renewable energy transitions. Here are some anticipated products in this discipline. Future efforts to engage stakeholders will increasingly emphasize localized and community-centric strategies. This trend will emphasize the participation of local communities, indigenous groups, and grassroots organizations as essential stakeholders in renewable energy and sustainability initiatives. The prominence of community-owned renewable energy initiatives and regional plans for sustainable development will increase. Organizations will implement engagement models that combine in-person techniques with digital resources. This approach will ensure inclusivity by catering to stakeholders with varying digital access and literacy levels. Virtual engagement platforms will continue to develop immersive experiences, including virtual town halls and interactive webinars. Engagement with stakeholders will expand beyond an organization's immediate stakeholders to incorporate an ecosystem and value chain perspective. Organizations will collaborate with suppliers, consumers, and partners to address sustainability issues collectively. This trend will promote supply chain sustainability and transparency. Driven Organizations will increasingly seek innovation from stakeholders. The development of sustainable products, services, and solutions will result from the co-creation and co-innovation of stakeholders. Crowdsourcing and open innovation platforms will facilitate innovation processes driven by stakeholders. Artificial intelligence and machine learning will allow for personalized engagement with stakeholders. AI-powered chatbots and virtual assistants will provide customized information and assistance to stakeholders, boosting employment and responsiveness. Predictive analytics will anticipate the requirements and preferences of stakeholders. Concerns regarding data sovereignty and privacy will result in the creation of new regulations and standards. Organizations must navigate these complex issues while ensuring data-driven engagement is conducted ethically and securely.

Increasing emphasis will be placed on measuring and reporting the social impact of engagement efforts and environmental metrics. Job creation, community well-being, and social equity metrics will become more prevalent in sustainability reporting. Engagement of stakeholders will play an essential role in sustainable finance initiatives. To evaluate the viability of projects and investments, investors and financial institutions will solicit input and confirmation from stakeholders. Organizations will invest in stakeholder education and capacity building to facilitate meaningful engagement. It will include initiatives to improve stakeholders' comprehension of sustainability issues, allowing them to partake in decision-making processes more effectively. As data collection and analysis become increasingly sophisticated, organizations may need help managing and interpreting enormous quantities of stakeholder data. It will be crucial to ensure data relevance and actionable insights. Building and maintaining trust in engagement efforts, particularly in hostile environments, will remain challenging. Authenticity and transparency must be demonstrated for effective stakeholder engagement. Despite efforts to promote inclusivity, it will continue to be challenging to ensure that all stakeholders, including marginalized groups, have an equal voice in engagement processes. Collaborative Issue Resolution: The engagement of stakeholders will evolve into a collaborative problem-solving platform, enabling organizations to address complex sustainability challenges with diverse perspectives and expertise. Organizations that flourish at stakeholder engagement will be more competitive in the market. Positive stakeholder relationships can increase brand loyalty and facilitate market differentiation. Effective stakeholder engagement can create policies and regulations that expedite the transition to a green economy and renewable energy sources. By involving stakeholders in innovation processes, organizations can drive the development of sustainable products and solutions that satisfy the changing demands of the marketplace. Building Resilience: Involving stakeholders in climate and disaster preparedness initiatives can increase community resilience and reduce exposure to environmental risks by reducing vulnerability. Future trends in stakeholder engagement for the transitions to a green economy and renewable energy will prioritize inclusivity, innovation, and localized approaches. These organizations will be better positioned to accomplish their sustainability objectives and contribute to a more sustainable future if they adopt these trends and effectively navigate emerging challenges.

Emerging challenges and opportunities in stakeholder engagement for transitioning to a green economy and renewable energy create a dynamic landscape. These challenges and opportunities shape how organizations and stakeholders collaborate to achieve sustainability objectives. On the one hand, the increasing complexity of stakeholder ecosystems, the persisting digital divide, concerns over data privacy, and the need for authenticity present formidable obstacles. However, these obstacles are accompanied by intriguing opportunities, such as inclusive innovation, community-centric approaches, the use of artificial intelligence for personalization, data-driven decision-making, sustainability-linked financing, policy influence, and resilience building. Embracing these opportunities and addressing these challenges through ethical and data-driven engagement strategies can enable organizations to navigate this shifting landscape and meaningfully contribute to a more sustainable future.

DISCUSSION

This exhaustive examination of stakeholder engagement in the context of the green economy and renewable energy transitions has uncovered its profound significance as a catalyst for sustainable development. Engagement of stakeholders transcends a mere procedural requirement to become the very foundation of progress in sustainability. Local communities, governments, enterprises, and non-governmental organizations (NGOs) are just a few examples of the stakeholders involved. This inclusivity is not merely desirable but a fundamental requirement for attaining sustainability goals. Engaging these disparate stakeholders enables organizations to leverage their collective knowledge and contributions, ensuring that sustainability initiatives are comprehensive and representative. Effective stakeholder engagement is contingent on aligning the objectives of various stakeholders with those of the organization or industry. This alignment fosters a sense of shared purpose and dedication, which is essential for advancing sustainability. When stakeholders see their interests reflected in sustainability objectives, they become active contributors to progress. Engagement of stakeholders promotes a holistic approach to sustainability. It considers not only the environmental but also the social and economic aspects. This holistic perspective is necessary for developing sustainable practices that will benefit both present and future generations. It serves as a reminder that sustainability is a complex endeavour. Collaboration through partnerships and alliances emerges as a potent multiplier of stakeholder engagement efforts. These partnerships allow organizations to combine their resources, knowledge, and collective influence to advance sustainability initiatives. The concept of synergy and collective action is prominent. It is impossible to exaggerate the importance of government policies and regulations in fostering stakeholder engagement and shaping sustainability initiatives. Uncertain or lax laws can impede sustainable development, whereas effective legal frameworks can accelerate it. It highlights the interdependence of government actions and stakeholder participation in promoting sustainability. Technology's emergence is transforming stakeholder engagement. It provides many tools and platforms, including social media, data analytics, virtual meetings, and chatbots powered by artificial intelligence. These capabilities enable organizations to bolster their engagement strategies and expand their influence.

The significance of continuous surveillance and evaluation in determining the efficacy of efforts to engage stakeholders is emphasized. These practices provide indispensable insights for adaptation, enhancement, and accountability. They reaffirm that sustainability is a journey that requires vigilance because it is constantly changing. The chapter examines several emerging trends, challenges, and opportunities in stakeholder engagement with an eye toward the future. These trends, which include community-centric approaches, hybrid engagement models, and AI-powered personalization, reflect the character of stakeholder engagement as it evolves. They demonstrate a transition toward more inclusive, adaptable, and data-driven strategies. The difficulties, such as complex stakeholder ecosystems and the digital divide, emphasize the need for organizations to navigate complex dynamics and close participation and data privacy gaps. Opportunities like inclusive innovation and sustainability-linked financing allow organizations to foster innovation, collaborate with stakeholders on financial decisions, and influence policy changes.

Stakeholder engagement is a dynamic and transformative force that promotes sustainable development in the context of the green economy and renewable energy transitions. Organizations and initiatives can significantly contribute to a more sustainable and equitable world by actively involving stakeholders, nurturing collaboration, and addressing challenges while seizing opportunities. This chapter emphasizes that stakeholder engagement is not a one-time activity but rather an ongoing commitment that can influence the future of sustainability.

CONCLUSION

This chapter concludes by emphasizing the importance of stakeholder engagement as a fulcrum for fostering sustainable development within the green economy and the transition to renewable energy sources. It has been elucidated that stakeholder engagement is more than just a procedural requirement; it is a fundamental driver of progress. Key takeaways include recognizing the importance of diversified stakeholder engagement, aligning goals and objectives, and adopting an all-encompassing approach to sustainability that includes environmental, social, and economic dimensions. In addition, the importance of partnerships, effective policy frameworks, technological innovations, and ongoing monitoring and evaluation has been emphasized as essential factors for the success of engagement initiatives. In terms of the future, the chapter has cast light on emerging trends such as localized approaches, hybrid engagement models, and an increasing emphasis on social impact measurement. Concurrently, it has acknowledged the difficulties of complex stakeholder ecosystems, the digital divide, and data privacy. However, it remains optimistic regarding the opportunities for inclusive innovation, community-centred strategies, data-driven decision-making, and policy influence. This chapter has emphasized that stakeholder engagement is indispensable for positive change and enduring impact as we navigate the path towards a sustainable future.

REFERENCES

Bhuiyan, M. A., Zhang, Q., Khare, V., Mikhaylov, A., Pintér, G., & Huang, X. (2022). Renewable Energy Consumption and Economic Growth Nexus—A Systematic Literature Review. *Frontiers in Environmental Science*, *10*, 878394. doi:10.3389/fenvs.2022.878394

Da Silva, L. M., Bitencourt, C. C., Faccin, K., & Iakovleva, T. (2019). The role of Stakeholders in the context of Responsible Innovation: A Meta-Synthesis. *Sustainability (Basel)*, *11*(6), 1766. doi:10.3390u11061766

Franklin, A. L. (2020). Understanding stakeholder motivations. In Springer eBooks (pp. 65–96). doi:10.1007/978-3-030-47519-2_4

Friedrich, K. (2021). A systematic literature review concerning the different interpretations of the role of sustainability in project management. *Management Review Quarterly*, *73*(1), 31–60. doi:10.100711301-021-00230-z

Gibson, K. (2012). Stakeholders and Sustainability: An evolving theory. *Journal of Business Ethics*, *109*(1), 15–25. doi:10.100710551-012-1376-5

Herremans, I. M., Nazari, J. A., & Mahmoudian, F. (2015). Stakeholder relationships, engagement, and sustainability reporting. *Journal of Business Ethics*, *138*(3), 417–435. doi:10.100710551-015-2634-0

Hollmann, S., Regierer, B., Bechis, J., Tobin, L. T., & D'Elia, D. (2022). Ten simple rules on how to develop a stakeholder engagement plan. *PLoS Computational Biology*, *18*(10), e1010520. doi:10.1371/journal.pcbi.1010520 PMID:36227852

Jäger, J., Brutschin, E., Pianta, S., Omann, I., Kammerlander, M., Vishwanathan, S. S., Vrontisi, Z., MacDonald, J., & Van Ruijven, B. (2023). Stakeholder engagement and decarbonization pathways: Meeting the challenges of the COVID-19 pandemic. *Frontiers in sustainability*, *3*. doi:10.3389/frsus.2022.1063719

Kabeyi, M. J. B., & Olanrewaju, O. A. (2022). Sustainable energy transition for renewable and low carbon grid electricity generation and supply. *Frontiers in Energy Research*, *9*, 743114. doi:10.3389/fenrg.2021.743114

Kujala, J., Sachs, S., Leinonen, H., Heikkinen, A., & Laude, D. (2022). Stakeholder engagement: Past, present, and future. *Business & Society*, *61*(5), 1136–1196. doi:10.1177/00076503211066595

Lennon, B., Dunphy, N., & Sanvicente, E. (2019). Community acceptability and the energy transition: A citizens' perspective. *Energy, Sustainability and Society*, *9*(1), 35. doi:10.118613705-019-0218-z

Maqbool, R., Deng, X., & Rashid, Y. (2020). Stakeholders' satisfaction as a key determinant of critical success factors in renewable energy projects. *Energy, Sustainability and Society*, *10*(1), 28. doi:10.118613705-020-00259-0

Nonet, G. A., Gößling, T., Van Tulder, R., & Bryson, J. M. (2022). Multi-stakeholder engagement for the Sustainable Development Goals: Introduction to the special issue. *Journal of Business Ethics*, *180*(4), 945–957. doi:10.100710551-022-05192-0 PMID:36065323

Pedrini, M., & Ferri, L. M. (2019). Stakeholder management: A systematic literature review. *Corporate Governance (Bradford)*, *19*(1), 44–59. doi:10.1108/CG-08-2017-0172

Söderholm, P. (2020). The green economy transition: The challenges of technological change for sustainability. *Sustainable Earth*, *3*(1), 6. doi:10.118642055-020-00029-y

Su, M., Fang, M., Pang, Q., & Park, K. (2022). Exploring the role of sustainable logistics service providers in multinational supply chain cooperation: An integrated theory-based perspective. *Frontiers in Environmental Science*, *10*, 976211. doi:10.3389/fenvs.2022.976211

Wei, S., Jiandong, W., & Saleem, H. (2023). The impact of renewable energy transition, green growth, green trade and innovation on environmental quality: Evidence from top 10 green future countries. *Frontiers in Environmental Science*, *10*, 1076859. doi:10.3389/fenvs.2022.1076859

Wells, E. C., Lehigh, G. R., & Vidmar, A. M. (2021). Stakeholder engagement for sustainable communities. In Springer eBooks (pp. 1–13). doi:10.1007/978-3-030-38948-2_10-1

Zhang, W., Li, B., Xue, R., Wang, Y., & Cao, W. (2021). A systematic bibliometric review of clean energy transition: Implications for low-carbon development. *PLoS One*, *16*(12), e0261091. doi:10.1371/journal.pone.0261091 PMID:34860855

Chapter 13
Groundwater and Pesticides:
Effects on Health, the Environment, and the Relevance of Environmental Education in this Scenario

Luciana Cordeiro de Cordeiro de Souza-Fernandes
UNICAMP, Brazil

Roberta Oliveira Lima
UFF, Brazil

Giovanni de Farias Seabra
UFPB, Brazil

Rui Alexandre Castanho
https://orcid.org/0000-0003-1882-4801
WSB University, Poland

ABSTRACT

From the pandemic scenario to the current environmental problems, we present the issue of the indiscriminate and criminal use of pesticides in Brazil and their impacts on the soil. Its reflex on the groundwater, which supplies more than 50% of the Brazilian population, makes them inappropriate for human consumption; even so, they continue to be supplied to the population. Due to the various chemical compounds that make up pesticides, whether by ingesting water or food, irreversible damage to human health and the environment is being caused. Professionals have complained about the harmful effects of pesticide use in Brazil from different areas, and a legal reflection on such an important topic has been urgent.

DOI: 10.4018/979-8-3693-1297-1.ch013

INTRODUCTION

In the 21st century, water is being sought on Mars as an alternative to terrestrial life; Rivers of money are spent on prospecting the establishment of a new civilization on the red planet, and, in the same way, megalomaniacs sell tourist tickets for space travel. Meanwhile, planet Earth suffers from numerous environmental problems, such as scarcity and loss of water quality, the adverse effects of climate change, the new coronavirus pandemic, misery, poverty, and environmental contamination resulting from the toxicity of products. Chemicals used to 'produce food'—a true paradox of existence.

So much technology, financial resources, and scientific knowledge could be used to 'care' this House of ours, to clean up and decontaminate water and soil, combat deforestation, prevent fires, encourage biodynamic agriculture, mitigate climate change, among so many other challenges for a good life on Earth.

The loss of forests in territorially protected spaces translates not only into legal disrespect but into the loss of biodiversity, water, and the natural filter protecting urban and rural soil, states Rodrigues (2008: 8), as 'the preservation of green. It is essential for the quality of life of city populations".

Trees function as suction and spray pumps for surface and subsurface waters, releasing them as vapor into the atmosphere to form rain clouds, known as "flying rivers." In this work, we will look at these problems, presenting the indiscriminate use of pesticides and groundwater contamination and their effects on human and environmental health. Next, we highlight the importance of Environmental Education as an instrument of awareness and action to prevent the processes and deactivate perverse rural production systems that degrade the environment, putting planetary health, ecosystems, and human life at risk.

THE BRAZILIAN WATER SCENARIO

The pandemic that emerged on 12/31/2019 in the city of Wuhan in China of the new strain of coronavirus (2019-nCoV), better known as COVID-19, officially announced in early 2020 by the World Health Organization – WHO (UN NEWS, 2021), which seemed more like a health problem and local environmental imbalance, offered us a new look at the whole that surrounds us, as it exacerbated our structural deficiencies and allowed us more extraordinary environmental reflections.

By revealing inequality in access to water, it highlighted the existence of 'water poverty' (ANA, 2019) in Brazil, confirming that the 'address'/household should be seen as a risk factor for the pandemic, increasing the spread of the virus in underserved areas. sanitation (CIDADES SUSTENTÁVEIS, 2021). After all, the simple act of washing our hands can ward off contamination, and not everyone has access to this good of life, hence the need for an integrated and holistic vision of the city to achieve environmental balance in all its aspects, such as treating and distributing water through engineering works, for example.

In this sense, we can see in the survey (Figure 1) by Rebouças (2002), which presents a picture of water availability in Brazilian regions, proving that spatial distribution and availability are significantly unequal within the national territory. Moreover, based on this knowledge about sanitation, notably access to treated water in Brazilian regions, the data are presented in a much more conflicting way (Figure 2).

Given the information in the Table above (Figure 1), we can see that the Amazon region has the country's largest territory, the most considerable amount of water, and the second smallest population. In contrast, the southeast and northeast regions have the highest population density and the lowest water supply. However, having water quantity does not mean 'access to water' or quality water. This is proven by the study of piped water supply carried out by the National Sanitation Information System (SNIS) in

Figure 1. Table of water availability by Brazilian regions
(Adapted from Rebouças (2002) with population data updated by IBGE, 2010)

Regiões Brasileiras	Área Territorial (%)	População (%)	Disponibilidade Hídrica (%)
Região Amazônica (norte)	45,3	8,3	68,5
Região Centro Oeste	18,8	7,4	15,7
Região Sul	6,8	14,4	6,5
Região Sudeste	10,8	42,1	6,0
Região Nordeste	18,3	27,8	3,3

Figure 2. Supply of piped water in Brazil

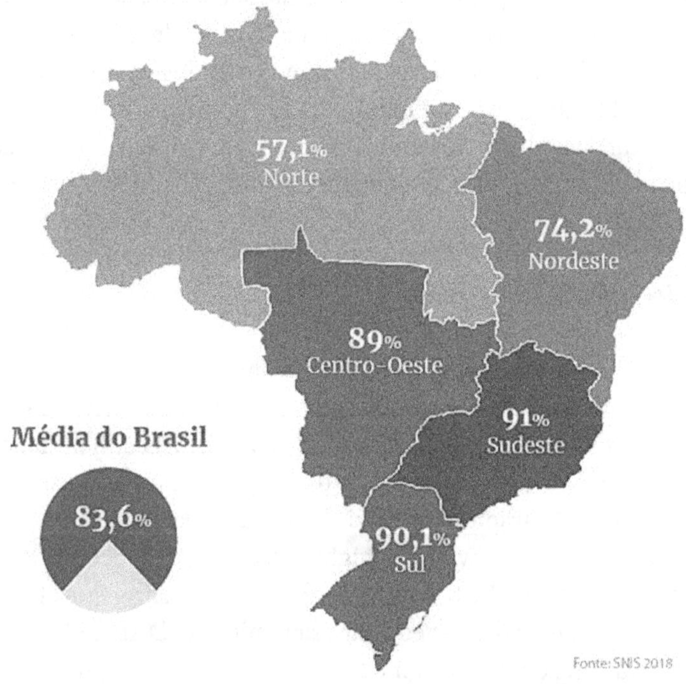

2018, demonstrating that the North region, the largest holder of water, has the lowest supply of treated water (Figure 2), another national paradox.

In the 'Table of water availability by Brazilian regions' (Figure 1), we emphasize that the availability percentages include the sum of surface and groundwater, with groundwater representing the most significant percentage in this calculation.

ABAS (2021) emphasizes the occurrence of groundwater in greater or lesser quantities in the subsoil throughout the country, and the combination of geological structures with geomorphological and climatic factors in Brazil resulted in the configuration of ten hydrogeological provinces, which are regions with aquifer systems with similar storage, circulation, and water quality conditions.

Furthermore, it is essential to clarify (SOUZA, 2009) that an aquifer is only those underground water deposits in which water can be exploited, that is, extracted, and that for managing the use and ordering of soil in cities, it is essential to identify and qualify the vulnerable areas of aquifers, since depending on the type of soil and contaminants used in the soil, such as in agriculture, groundwater may be contaminated through percolation, causing the loss of its potential for human supply.

From the moment the molecule of a particular pesticide is applied to the environment, regardless of the form of application, in most cases, it reaches the soil. In this environment, the molecule can follow different routes, reaching different ecosystems and interfering in the dynamics of countless living beings (STEFFEN; STEFFEN; ANTONIOLLI, 2011).

PESTICIDES: AN INDISCRIMINATE USE

On July 28, 2021, the date of the last data collection for this chapter's construction, we recorded 3376 pesticide products sold throughout Brazil. Since the beginning of his term, the Jair Bolsonaro government (2019-2022) published the approval of 1,310 new pesticide products TWITTER ROBOTOX, 2021).

It is essential to point out that Brazil has been leading the way in the use of pesticides for a long time. Since 2008, it has surpassed the United States of America (USA), assuming the position of the world's largest market for pesticides and the second-largest producer of transgenics (BOMBARDI, 2016).

The 2015 Dossier of the Brazilian Association of Public Health – ABRASCO (2021) informs that the Brazilian citizen consumes an average of 7.5 liters of poison per year through the consumption of water and food as a result of the use of pesticides. Moreover, in some regions, there are even higher consumption levels.

The indiscriminate use of pesticides is not the result of chance. However, it is symptomatic of the majority agricultural production model that features a vital role for large agribusiness corporations and the consequent dominance of capital over Brazilian politics. Thus, corroborating this statement, we must glimpse the fact that companies producing and selling commodities, seeds and various inputs, in addition to industries producing pesticides, slaughterhouses, and other investors in the sector, appropriate the country's institutional policy in such a way that, At the Brazilian legislative level, through the Agricultural Parliamentary Front, they have 243 deputies and 39 senators, representing 47.5% of support in the Federal Congress (FRIEDRICH, 2021).

In the Executive Branch, the release of large numbers of pesticides in recent years is not the result of chance but a reflection of the means created to make resources, policies, and programs viable that favor agro(toxic)productive macropolitics. These releases or relaxations, to use a popular term in the sector, are based on economic arguments, as many of the products authorized in Brazil are not allowed for use in other countries due to their proven harmful effects on health and the environment. Furthermore, the same government that intensively releases pesticides needs to invest in monitoring the local manufacture, use, and import of these products. It also does not meet the demand for investments in Technical Assistance and Rural Extension – ATER, for small farmers, which would guarantee specific guidance on use, further aggravating everyone's risks, given the contamination of water and food that reaches the farmers' table. consumers (FRIEDRICH, 2021).

Regarding the use of pesticides banned on other continents, we cite the recent work by Larissa Bombardi (2021), in which the author demonstrates (Figure 3) a graph of pesticide sales for Mercosur in the years 2018 and 2019, whose use is prohibited in the territories of the European Union – EU, thus clearly portraying how indiscriminate and criminal the use of pesticides is in the country.

Figure 3. Graph of sales of pesticides banned in the EU to Mercosur
(BOMBARDI, 2021, p. 28)

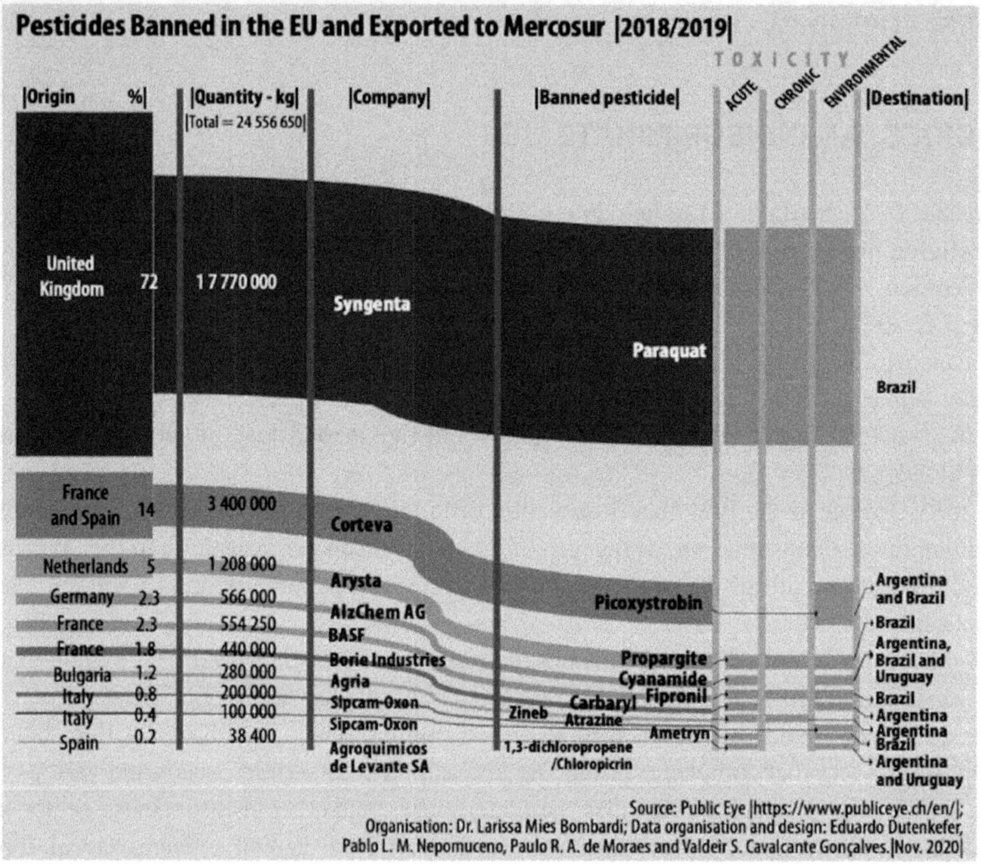

The UN Special Rapporteur, Baskut Tuncak (2021), on a mission to the country from December 2 to 13, 2019, warned of the rate of release of pesticides in Brazil, which has increased by more than 338% since 2000, ranking among the three most significant consumers of pesticides in the world, being the largest consumer for more than a decade. For the rapporteur, the enormous use of pesticides is resulting in severe impacts on human rights in Brazil, considering that food production and economic growth are not a legitimate excuse for these preventable violations and abuses, with countless victims experiencing everything from deaths to health problems, as well as cruel, inhumane and degrading treatments resulting from exposure to pesticides (UN, 2020). Environmental degradation, water contamination, and biodiversity loss, including bees, are serious effects.

AQUIFER CONTAMINATION IN BRAZIL

More fresh water is below the Earth's surface - in underground aquifers than in any other source, excluding ice sheets. Groundwater is essential for rivers worldwide, keeping them alive even when droughts reduce water volume. However, in recent decades, the rampant exploitation of several of these reservoirs and soil contamination, especially by pesticides, has led to an alarming reality: the loss of this water quality. Hence the importance of this work.

We verified the presence of aquifers throughout the Brazilian territory, and according to the Instituto Trata Brasil (2021), 52% of the 5,570 Brazilian municipalities are supplied totally (36%) or partially (16%) by groundwater.

Numerous scientific studies have highlighted groundwater contamination by pesticides in all regions of the country. To exemplify this scenario, we highlight examples in each geographic region, starting with the Northeast region of the country, with research carried out in 2019 in a sugar and alcohol area in the metropolitan region of João Pessoa, municipality of Santa Rita, in the state of Paraíba. As a result of the estimation of groundwater contamination, it was observed that of the 25 active ingredients evaluated by the methods (EPA and GUS), 52% showed a tendency towards potential contamination (ISMAEL; ROCHA, 2019). In the study by Canuto et al. (2010), in the area of the Municipality of Tianguá, located on the Ibiapaba Plateau, northwest of the state of Ceará, the presence of the pesticides atrazine and simazine was confirmed in water samples from underground springs and also in superficial.

In the Midwest, Soares' research, Faria and Rosa (2017) carried out in Campo Novo do Parecis, located in the middle north of Mato Grosso, in Chapada dos Parecis, identified through the survey carried out on the products used in the agricultural areas of the municipality, that there is the use of 114 agricultural products in the region. Of these, 17 do not register with the AGROFIT online system. The large number of pesticides reflects the increased production of large crops – soybeans and corn in the region. According to the authors: "the results obtained in this work showed that a large number of pesticides from highly toxicological classes and with a risk of environmental contamination are being applied in the region of Campo Novo do Parecis, Mato Grosso, since 45.6% of the products sold fall into classes I and II of the environmental classification, highly dangerous and very dangerous, respectively. It is also concluded that 26.1% of the listed active ingredients used in the region represent some risk of groundwater contamination.

In the South region, in the states of Rio Grande do Sul (RS) and Santa Catarina (SC), according to Silva et al. (2011), irrigated rice is one of the leading agricultural and economic activities, with a total area in both states of approximately 1.2 million hectares. The current irrigated rice production system demands a wide use of pesticides, with 29 herbicides, 12 insecticides, and eight fungicides recommended for the crop. Furthermore, a study carried out over three periods in 2007/2008 in six rice-producing regions in RS and one in SC. Within which three municipalities were selected, chosen based on the largest area cultivated with rice and their geographical position, the researchers found that "on average over the entire period and across all locations studied, the pesticides with the highest frequencies in groundwater were 'fipronil', 'imazethapyr', 'clomazone', 'imazapic' and 'quinclorac', detected in 87, 42, 23, 19 and 2% of the total samples monitored."

In the Southeast region, in an area under the Guarani Aquifer System - SAG, between Descalvado and Analândia, in the state of São Paulo, which has around 90% of the areas used for agriculture, represented by the planting of orange, sugar cane and brachiaria (pasture), considering the information obtained from the Cooperativa Agropecuária do Vale do Mogi-Guaçu (COOPERVAM) and the environmental characteristics of the leading products used in the region, scientific research (TAVANTI et al., 2009) identified the pesticides with the highest degree of toxicological impact and environmental impact for each crop, highlighting the presence of Furadan 350 (carbofuran), Regente Wg (Fipronil), Temik (aldicarb) and Actara (thiamethoxam). This study is very worrying because the municipality of Analândia, for example, has a highly vulnerable territory, which is considered a 100% SAG recharge area.

In the North region, in the Eastern Amazon, a study by Lima (2007) carried out in the micro-basin of the Cumaru stream, Igarapé-Açu, which makes up the Bragantina micro-region, located in the northeast of the state of Pará, they highlighted the presence of 'dimethoate' due to intensive use of pesticides in passion fruit and black pepper crops, given the high potential for leaching of these chemical compounds into the soil.

Despite the importance of agriculture for the country, both for supply and for the calculation of the Gross Domestic Product - GDP, for the trade balance and international trade, what is certain is that the indiscriminate use of pesticides - including products considered prohibited - contaminates the soil, surface and underground waters - and reflexively, affects fauna and flora, above all, human health, which we will now present.

EFFECTS OF PESTICIDES ON HUMAN AND ENVIRONMENTAL HEALTH

The COVID-19 pandemic is mentioned again because it highlights the relationship between the emergence of pandemics and the implementation of agribusiness, which is allocated on monoculture and agrochemical bases that have a negative impact on human and environmental health. In the book "Pandemic and Agribusiness: infectious diseases, capitalism and Science" by evolutionary biologist and phylogeographer Rob Wallace (2020), who has been researching, for more than two decades, the relationship between productive activities and the most fundamental origins of viruses with pandemic potential, argues that: 'Sars-Cov-2, the new coronavirus, causing the Covid-19 pandemic that has crossed the world, represents just one of the new strains of pathogens that have suddenly emerged as threats to human beings this century. Among them are the African swine fever virus, Campylobacter, Cryptosporidium, Cyclospora, Makona and Reston Ebolas, the bacteria Escherichia coli O157:H7, foot-and-mouth disease, hepatitis E, listeria, Nipah virus, Coxiella burnetii of Q fever, salmonella, vibrio, yersínia and some new variants of influenza A, such as H1N1 (2009), H1N2v, H3N2v, H5N1, H6N1, H7N1, H7N3, H7N7, H7N9 and H9N2. These outbreaks, however, are not just the result of bad luck. All are directly or indirectly linked to changes in production or land use associated with intensive agriculture. Capital-intensive monoculture – livestock and agriculture – drives deforestation and enterprises that increase the rate and taxonomic scope of pathogen spillover: from wild animals to livestock and, from there, to workers in the sector. [...] Through the global trade that characterizes the sector, newly developed strains can be exported worldwide.'

The Dossier against the Poison Package and in Defense of Life, launched in 2021 by ABRASCO and organized by Karen Friederich, similarly points out that the option for agribusiness is a determinant of risks that lead to illness and death in populations exposed to pesticides. The size and relevance, combined with its intervention in so many areas, means that the problem has a strategic dimension to be addressed by strengthening State organizations in the three spheres of government. Added to this is the need to inform and involve society, expand pesticide residue monitoring programs in food, and increase laboratory capacity to meet analysis demands – for example, water monitoring; in addition to training health services to diagnose, treat, and report cases of poisoning; review the registration of very toxic products already banned by other countries; extinguish the tax exemption for pesticides; value and invest in organic and agroecological food production experiences (FRIEDRICH, 2021), among other urgent measures to improve environmental protection and human health.

Talking about the damage caused by pesticides to the environment and human health is, therefore, also discussing the majority agribusiness model in our country. We even dare to say that the birth of "pre-polluted" children, fed with contaminated breast milk and attacked by cancer from an early age, as well as the illness of rural workers, suicides, pregnancies with fetal malformations, incidents of physical and mental disabilities and food allergies, in addition to all sorts of problems that affect human health in its most varied age stages (LIMA, 2019) are symptomatic of a predatory model of food production which, in turn, is symptomatic of the neoliberal capitalist modus operandi itself in its "sacrifice zones of global capital," a last expression coined by Rob Wallace (2020), generating potential "agrocide" and, at best, a kind of "molecular colonialism."

Friederich (2021) points out that: 'In the last decade, Brazil has stood out as a subservient country, restricted to secondary functions in the global economy, which place it among the largest consumers of pesticides, cultivators of transgenic plants and exporters of raw materials, moving towards the scrapping of industrial transformation bases. Pesticides, chemical fertilizers, and genetically modified (transgenic) seeds form pillars supporting the country's hegemonic agricultural production model. The scarce relationship between the productivity gains of those seeds and their demand for inputs is imposing a continuous need to expand crop areas to preserve the profitability of the farms. This dependence on the scale of production has been imposing changes in environmental legislation, facilitating the occupation of preservation areas. It is also associated with changes in land legislation, facilitating the occupation of territories of traditional populations, indigenous areas, and areas of agrarian reform settlements by exporting agribusiness. Large estates, environmental crimes, and the destruction of traditional ways of life and cultures characterize this production model. Despite representing a significant portion of the Brazilian GDP, this model generates social crises and irrecoverable environmental impacts, such as the loss of biodiversity and ecosystem changes resulting from toxic products. The concentration of land and income is associated with unfair labor relations, with records of super-exploitation and forms similar to slavery, and attacks and deaths of leaders of rural workers, indigenous peoples, and traditional communities are not rare".

The UN Report (2020), already mentioned in a previous topic in this chapter, also warns of the need for Brazil to act to combat the situation of chronic exposure of workers to dangerous substances, especially industrial chemicals, and pesticides, as workers in Brazil continue to be exposed to many dangerous substances and processes banned around the world.

Finally, dealing specifically with some pesticides, according to Jouzel (2019), it is essential to highlight that, in 2015, the International Cancer Research Center (CIRC), an agency linked to the World Health Organization (WHO), published a report that classified 'glyphosate,' 'diazinon' and 'malathion' as "probable carcinogens" for humans and 'tetrachlorvinphos and 'parathion' as "possible carcinogens." The contestation of the Report mentioned above for the 'glyphosate' case was immediate, both by the company responsible for its production at the time - Monsanto and by the national agencies responsible for evaluating such products. On the other hand, environmental NGOs, journalists, and political parties point out that what has already been reported at different times has only been confirmed: the extent to which these local agencies make their decisions are influenced by links they establish with interested companies, whether in the form of political pressure, financing, intimidation.

When we talk about the effects of pesticides on human health, we are faced with the issues highlighted above, which are located in the field of uncertainty in a purposefully designed way through the strategy of consistently "producing doubt" about the danger of pesticides and thus "capturing" the authorities responsible for controlling them. In addition, we emphasize that there are cases of direct poisoning by these products. It is vital to highlight that, concerning the topic, there is a significant number of under-reports of poisoning, approximately 1 in every 50 (LIMA; OLIVEIRA, 2020).

Internationally, the possibility of holding environmental and human health damages as an ecocidal practice is being discussed, that is, a type of crime against humanity (HAIA, 2016). In a critical and combative way and through the mobilization of civil society, we have the international NGO Greenpeace, which has been exposing and questioning the Brazilian agricultural model, as well as the use of GMOs, the expansion of agriculture over native forests, the massive use of pesticides and the resulting socio-environmental and climate impacts (GREENPEACE, 2017), in addition to the indiscriminate soil and groundwater contamination that supplies millions of people throughout Brazil.

ENVIRONMENTAL EDUCATION AS A TOOL FOR PROMOTING ENVIRONMENTAL INFORMATION

The Globalized World materializes through overproduction, compulsive consumption, and the disposal of an immeasurable amount of solid, liquid, and gaseous waste into the environment. Therefore, environmental degradation, the risk of ecological collapse, and the advancement of inequality and poverty are signs of the crisis in the globalized world (LEFF, 2009). Agribusiness is part of this context, whose ecologically overwhelming model destroys everything in front of it, causing an increase in energy expenditure and worsening air pollution, rivers, seas, and underground water reserves.

So, to begin with, it is good to clarify that in Brazil, Agribusiness operates outside the law, given that Federal Law No. 9,433 of 1/8/1997 (BRASIL, 1997), which established the National Water Resources Policy and creates the National System of Water Resources Management, which regulates the occupation and use of land, and limits the use of water resources, which are priorities for human consumption.

According to Federal Law No. 9,795/1999 (BRASIL, 1999), Environmental Education is defined as "the processes through which the individual and the community build social values, knowledge, skills, attitudes and competencies aimed at conserving the environment, a common asset for the people, essential to a healthy quality of life and its sustainability." Obviously, Environmental Education is closely linked to Nature, which in turn is synonymous with biodiversity; the concept refers to the variety among living organisms and their ecological complexities.

Socio-biodiversity, in turn, is the harmonious harmony between the multiplicity of animal and plant species with social diversity to preserve natural assets and cultural heritage. The concept of socio-biodiversity is extensive and inclusive of the traditional ancestral culture and worldview of original peoples. To justify this concept, we assume that the animal world and everything that exists on Earth and in the Universe are the work of divine creation and, therefore, within the scope of the inexplicable for human and artificial intelligence (SEABRA, 2011). In fact, this justifies the right to life of all living beings and guarantees the necessary means for the survival and perpetuation of the species.

The theory of Natural Evolution, proposed by Charles Darwin in the 19th century, points to a single origin of species: a unique "root" cell germinating millions of animal, plant, and protist species in the Earth's diverse morphoclimatic environments. Thus, all existing beings in the Universe, living and non-living, originate in the same physical-chemical elements that emerged billions of years ago along with the stars. Biodiversity, including bacteria and humans, carries the same basic genetic code composed of amino acids and phosphates. On Earth, elements as common as carbon, hydrogen, nitrogen, and oxygen are just a few examples; they organize themselves in unusual patterns, giving rise to life (Lynas, 2012). Having the chemical mentioned above elements as raw material, the emergence, and evolution of various life forms are also due to numerous environmental factors, such as climatic conditions, tectonic effects, geographic isolation, composition, temperature and pressure of atmospheric air, and natural selection. It is essential to add, as a determining factor in the elimination and emergence of new species in the current Anthropocene period, human interventions, with the use and application of new technologies and their devastating effects. Agro is planted in this context by extinguishing species and ecosystems and creating artificialized and polluted environments.

The global impacts of human interference are reflected in global warming, the expansion of deserts, the contamination of drinking water reservoirs, the sterilization of soil, air pollution, the spread of plagues and epidemics, nuclear radiation, hurricanes, and tsunamis. Attacks on biodiversity have alarming results, eliminating between 27,000 and 100,000 species per year (BARBAULT, 2011), many of which are unknown or identified. As a rule, when combined, human actions and natural cataclysms cause catastrophes of immeasurable dimensions, causing irreversible changes in biodiversity, irreparable material damage, and loss of thousands of human lives.

In the tangled web of life, each animal or plant species has a mutual vital association with other living beings and the surrounding environment. The set of things and energy is called the Geographical Stratum of the Earth (GRIGORIEV, 1968), a place where life is sown and evolves in a biodiverse scenario, whose stage is set in the spheres of earth, air, water, and fire. These are the four elements that allow and guarantee the existence of life in geographic space.

Arctic soil, called permafrost, has a high methane concentration, a gas 23 times more potent than carbon dioxide (CO2) for the greenhouse effect, which is stored in frozen humus and peat. As the soil warms, the amount of methane released through the decomposition of organic matter increases.

Like the Arctic region, the Brazilian Amazon, Cerrado, and Atlantic Forest biomes have many inert humus under the original vegetation mantle. As agribusiness removes vegetation on a large scale, thousands of tons of methane gas and other greenhouse gases are released into the atmosphere, increasing global warming. The population of deforested areas by cattle farming creates gigantic sources of methane gas, further contributing to the increase in atmospheric air temperature. We highlight that Brazil has 234 million heads of cattle (IBGE, 2022), the largest herd in the world.

The appropriation of Environmental Education by capital and corporations makes ecological projects, movements, and actions ineffective, given the destructive force of large economic groups allied with political forces. As an integral part of the process of saving the environment, the concept of natural capital emerges, which corresponds to the sum of all the benefits that balanced ecosystems provide to man, from the most tangible, such as drinking water, food, and wood, to the most abstract, as the spiritual and cultural value that natural environments represent for different communities. These ecosystem benefits result from a piece of highly complex machinery, whose parts comprise the various genes and species found on the Planet; that is, biodiversity (STRUMPF, 2023).

In a more financial and less ecological approach, natural capital is the monetization of nature, the transformation of everyone's goods into productive goods. The development model of modern society created the misconception that natural capital was endless. This vision implied the linear development of the economy, tracing a one-way street between natural resources and waste. Furthermore, it added externalities to the economic system interferences linked to the non-valuation of natural capital, which has resulted in the privatization of economic gains and the socialization of environmental losses.

In environmental-capitalist logic, ecological movements are financed by federal agencies and large national and multinational private corporations. These same bodies and companies encourage compulsive consumption and, consequently, pollution through mass media under the aegis of the Sustainable Planet slogan. This is the polluter/pays principle, which drives and sustains the green economy and environmental marketing. This system includes carbon credits and environmental compensation.

Reducing greenhouse gas emissions could mean profound changes for some developed countries, putting their economies at risk. According to the Kyoto Protocol, developed countries with goals to reduce carbon dioxide emissions can invest in projects that reduce pollution in any other country, counting emissions not realized in their quota.

For the approval of environmentally impactful projects, environmental compensation or compensation is provided; that is, a compensation value corresponding to the size or volume of the degradation. Environmental compensation, therefore, is a mechanism for holding entrepreneurs who cause significant environmental impact accountable for the damage they cause to the environment. As the economic activity they develop has a negative impact on the environment or everyday use of the people, a fundamental right of present and future generations, the entrepreneur must, in return, support mechanisms that promote environmental preservation.

The anthropization of the landscape by agribusiness, destructive and autophagic, accelerates the pace nowadays, putting planetary biodiversity and the survival of the human species at risk. Exponential global demographic growth is frighteningly reflected in the ecological footprint, defined as the total area of ecosystems necessary to sustain society's consumption of resources and assimilation of waste in a given inhabited area (WWF, 2023). The ecological footprint of a country or a population group corresponds to the size of the productive areas of land and sea necessary to generate products, goods, and services that support certain lifestyles. Therefore, the Earth's Ecological Footprint corresponds to the number of minerals, soils, nutrients, water, forests, pastures, sea, plankton, fisheries, and energy sufficient to maintain existing demand without compromising stocks. Currently, almost two planets equal to Earth are needed to meet the demands of the world population while maintaining current consumption patterns. Overload Day is a symbolic date indicating humanity's consumption, which the Earth can replenish during the year. In 2023, the overload day was August 2nd, recording the deadline for replacing consumed inputs. This means that, until December, the products and energy consumed would not be renewed. Conservation units, protected areas, and legal reserves are reserves of land, water, and biodiversity for Nature itself, favoring planetary homeostasis.

Environmental rationality requires the formation of new knowledge based on the interdisciplinary integration of knowledge necessary for understanding socio-environmental systems. Due to its holistic conception, environmental knowledge transcends environmental sciences, which results from the incorporation of ecological approaches to traditional disciplines, following a collision course against ethical values, practical knowledge, and traditional knowledge.

CONCLUSION

Brazil has an immense water potential distributed spatially unequally across its territory, with groundwater being a crucial supply source for its population. However, studies prove that this underground water source is being contaminated by the indiscriminate use of pesticides in all regions of the country, especially in vulnerable areas of aquifers. Pesticides are chemical compounds used in the most diverse crops, and when they percolate through the soil, they reach aquifers, compromising their quality by making their water unfit for consumption.

As mentioned throughout the article, "Agricultural Waters" is also about a food production model that is increasingly unsustainable and polluting with harmful effects on the health and environment of present and future generations. Brazil is a country that announces in prime time that "agro is tech, agro is everything, agro is Brazil's wealth" and that, therefore, the commercialization of new pesticide products increases every day, including those banned in other continents. It is necessary to pay close attention to the "currents" that lead us to food poisoning and violate the Human Right to Adequate Food – DHAA and quality water.

Faced with such evidence and environmental risks, ecological discourse and Environmental Education are, to say the least, superficial. It is only possible to transfer environmental-educational responsibility to the family or schools if there is governmental, business, and political support for an effective change in the current critical environmental situation. The exercise of citizenship, powerless in the face of governmental and private abuse, acquires colossal strength when manifested through collective organizational systems, such as schools, universities, and research centers, and popular communication channels, such as social networks.

Finally, given the above, it is possible to perceive, albeit in a strict summary, the danger that surrounds the environment and human health, precisely our water wealth, when opting for a mode of production allocated to monocultures and pesticides. The legal universe still treats the issue of pesticides, environmental contamination, and human health with a certain timidity, and further reflection on the topic is urgently needed.

REFERENCES

ABAS. 2021. Águas Subterrâneas O que são? Available at <https://www.abas.org/aguas-subterraneas-o-que-sao/>. 27 July, 2021.

Barbault, R. (2011). *Ecologia Geral: estrutura e funcionamento da biosfera*. Vozes.

Bombardi, L. M. (2016). *Pequeno ensaio cartográfico sobre o uso de agrotóxicos no Brasil*. Laboratório de Geografia Agrária da USP.

Bombardi, L. M. (2021). *Geography of Asymmetry: the vicious cycle of pesticides and colonialism in the commercial relationship between Mercosur and the European Union*. Commissioned by The Left group in the European Parliament. https://left.eu/events/eu-mercosur-the-vicious-circle-of-pesticides/

Calcagno, A. (2001). *Identificação de áreas para a execução de programas e ações piloto e definição de termos de referência. Atividade 09 do Projeto Aquífero Guarani*. ANA.

Canuto, T. G. (2010). Estimativa do risco potencial de contaminação por pesticidas de águas superficiais e subterrâneas do município de Tianguá-CE, com aplicação do método de Goss e índice de Gus. *Anais XVI Congresso Brasileiro de águas subterrâneas e XVII Encontro Nacional de Perfuradores de Poços*, São Luís, Maranhão.

Carneiro, F. F., Rigotto, R., Augusto, L., Friedrich, K., & Búrigo, A. (2015). *(Org.). Dossiê ABRASCO: um alerta sobre os impactos dos agrotóxicos na saúde. Rio de Janeiro: EPSJV*. Expressão Popular.

Friedrich, K. (2021). *(org.). Dossiê contra o Pacote do Veneno e em defesa da Vida!* Rede Unida.

Grigoriev, A. A. (1968). The theoretical fundaments of modern physical geography. In *The Interaction of Sciences in the Earth*. Moscou.

Ismael, L. L., & Rocha, E. M. R. (2019). Estimativa de contaminação de águas subterrâneas e superficiais por agrotóxicos em área sucroalcooleira, Santa Rita/PB, Brasil. *Ciencia & Saude Coletiva*, *24*(12), 4665–4675. doi:10.1590/1413-812320182412.27762017 PMID:31778516

Jouzel, J. N. (2019). *Pesticides. Comment ignorer ce que l'on sait*. Paris: Les Presses de Sciences Po, coll. Gouvernances.

Leff, E. (2009). *Saber Ambiental*. Editora Vozes.

Lima, L. M. (2007). Simulação da movimentação de agrotóxicos no solo com o uso de geotecnologias, como instrumento para avaliação do potencial de risco de contaminação de águas subterrâneas na Amazônia Oriental. *Anais XIII Simpósio Brasileiro de Sensoriamento Remoto, Florianópolis*, (abril), 21–26.

Lima, R. O. (2019). *Agro(tech) ou agro(tóxico)? Sustentabilidade, riscos, futuras gerações e justiça ambiental* (1st ed.). Editora Multifoco.

Londres, F. (2011). *Agrotóxicos no Brasil: um guia para ação em defesa da vida*. ASPTA.

Lynas, M. (2012). *A espécie divina: como o planeta pode sobreviver à era dos seres humanos*. Alta Books.

Rebouças, A. C. (2002). *Águas doces no Brasil*. Escrituras Editora.

Rodrigues, J. E. R. (2008). *Parque urbano: aplicação do Sistema Nacional de unidades de Conservação (SNUC) ao meio urbano. Tese de Doutorado*. Faculdade de Saúde Pública da USP.

Seabra, G. (2011). Educação Ambiental: caminhos para a conservação da sociobiodiversidade. In *SEABRA, Giovanni (Org.). Educação Ambiental no Mundo Globalizado: uma ecologia de riscos, desafios e resistência*. Editora Universitária da UFPB.

Silva, D. R. O., Avila, L. A., Agostinetto, D., Bundt, A. D. C., Primel, E. G., & Caldas, S. S. (2011). Ocorrência de agrotóxicos em águas subterrâneas de áreas adjacentes a lavouras de arroz irrigado. *Quimica Nova*, *34*(5), 748–752. doi:10.1590/S0100-40422011000500004

Soares, D. F., Faria, A. M., & Rosa, A. H. (2017, March/April). Análise de risco de contaminação de águas subterrâneas por resíduos de agrotóxicos no município de Campo Novo do Parecis (MT), Brasil. *Engenharia Sanitaria e Ambiental*, *22*(2), 277–284. doi:10.15901413-41522016139118

Souza, L. C. (2009). *Águas subterrâneas e a legislação brasileira*. Juruá.

Steffen, G.P.K., Steffen, R.B., & Antoniolli, Z.I. (2011). Contaminação do solo e da água pelo uso de agrotóxicos. *TECNO-LÓGICA, Santa Cruz do Sul*, *15*(1).

Wallace, R. (2020). *Pandemia e Agronegócio: Doenças infecciosas, capitalismo e ciência. Trad. Allan Rodrigo de Campos Silva*. Elefante.

Chapter 14
Greenpreneurship Pioneering Solutions for Climate Change: An Indian Perspective

Pooja Jain
https://orcid.org/0000-0003-1523-8460
Christ University, India

P. Aruna
Christ University, India

Geetanjali Purswani
Christ University, India

ABSTRACT

In an era marked by pressing global climate challenges, the role of green entrepreneurship, or "greenpreneurship," has gained paramount significance. The present chapter begins by elucidating the inherent connection between greenpreneurship and climate change, followed the contributions of the greenpreneurs appreciating their efforts to make a difference to the society. The chapter mentions certain skills and traits required by greenpreneurs to run their business. It states the challenges that the greenpreneurs face. The chapter then takes a dive into the realm of greenpreneurship from an Indian perspective. India, with its unique blend of environmental challenges and a burgeoning entrepreneurial ecosystem, presents an intriguing case study. The chapter illustrates how Indian greenpreneurs are contributing to a cleaner, greener future. It states the policies which the government has made to support greenpreneurs in the country. Finally, recommendations are given for existing greenpreneurs, budding entrepreneurs, the public, and the government to collectively drive green solutions.

DOI: 10.4018/979-8-3693-1297-1.ch014

INTRODUCTION

The world is facing the brunt of major climate change. It is a matter of concern for the entire globe. It impacts not only the environment, but also the economy, and the society. The United Nations framework convention on climate change (1992) defines Climate change as "change of climate which is attributed directly or indirectly to human activity that alters the composition of the global atmosphere and which is in addition to natural climate variability observed over comparable time periods." Climate change has led to many hazardous impacts on the world and it calls for immediate action to correct our ways so as to reduce the speed of this change.

According to NASA's Global Climate Change website (2023), there are two ways to respond to climate change, one is mitigation and the other is adaptation. The existing conditions of deterioration of climate are attributable to the prolonged human intervention in natural processes and abundant industrialisation which leads to continuous Greenhouse gases emission. Mitigation requires us to apply measures that can help reduce the emissions of greenhouse gases. On the other hand, certain environmental concerns cannot be dealt with in the short run and so the solution lies in adapting to these changes. Adaptation to climate change not only reduces the negative effects and risks posed by climate changes but also provides new opportunities to benefit the society as a whole.

Mitigation and adaptation requires rigorous human effort to make good our past deeds or at least, to reduce further damage to the environment. In this context, greenpreneurship has come up as a powerful approach. Greenpreneurs are individuals with strong green values who develop business ideas and adopt those green business practices that prioritize environmental sustainability (Schaper, 2002). Greenpreneurs are also called Ecopreneurs, as they aim to bring innovative ways to utilize the limited natural resources in an efficient and environmentally congenial way. As per the study conducted by Cohen and Winn (2007) sustainable entrepreneurs play an important role in improving local as well as global conditions. They also take care of social and environmental surroundings simultaneously giving a boost to the economy. According to Serio et al. (2020), upcoming business startups focused on environmentally sustainable production processes have been found to have relatively higher chances of surviving in the market.

GREENPRENEURS AND THEIR CONTRIBUTIONS

To overcome the environmental challenges and to shape more greener and sustainable future, greenpreneurs are likely to play a vital role. There are various sectors where already greenpreneurs have set the examples:

1. Renewable Energy Adoption: According to the International Renewable Energy Agency (IRENA) report (March, 2023), global renewable generation capacity increased to 3372 GW in 2022 as compared to 3077 GW in 2021. Significant steps have been taken by greenpreneurs to drive the adoption of renewable energy technologies.
2. Creating job opportunities:

Transition to net zero economy, which is the ultimate goal of greenpreneurs, will result in a wide range of new job skills. The new job roles may emerge across various disciplines such as engineering, retail, banking, manufacturing, education, health, etc. In India, for example, the Council on Energy, Environment, and Water (CEEW) report (2021) states that to achieve the target of 500 GW by the Indian government, the clean energy sector in India will grow at a rapid rate over the next decade. The latest technologies required for clean energy development may require a workforce of about one million.

3. Circular Economy Promotion

The circular economy is a diversion from the traditional linear economy model of "take-make-dispose" where raw materials are extracted, products are manufactured, used, and then discarded as waste. Contrary to this, the circular economy emphasizes on repairing, reusing and recycling the materials to ensure the Longevity. It emphasizes on sharing platforms and collaborative consumption models where multiple individuals can use the same product, such as car-sharing or bike-sharing services etc.

4. Transforming new knowledge into innovative business opportunities

Greenpreneurs adapt cutting-edge technologies into business opportunities for economic growth. They are more open to networking and sharing their ideas (Zahraie et al., 2016) thereby, access to resources, knowledge, and support for their ventures becomes viable. Being keen observers of consumer demand and market trends, greenpreneurs identify new markets and convert them into new and sustainable business opportunities. This results not only in positive environmental and social impacts but also acceleration in economic growth.

5. Environmental Education and Awareness

Some greenpreneurs are involved in drawing the attention of the Public towards increasing environmental concerns and giving guidance to them on adapting sustainable living options by supporting green businesses. They regularly organize awareness programmes, run educational campaigns and provide environmentally safe technological solutions. Continuous investment by these entities in the awareness regimes has led to growing interest in the people towards following greener practices and supporting sustainable products and services.

TRAITS AND SKILLS OF GREENPRENEURSHIP

Green entrepreneurs play an important role in providing innovative solutions to address environmental challenges while making a positive impact on society (Taylor, 2019). To be successful in this field, green entrepreneurs need to possess specific skills and traits. Here are some essential ones.

1. Innovative Thinking: Creativity and Innovative thinking is the primary trait of any entrepreneur, they should be always finding out new ways to develop sustainable products, services or operations that reduce negative environmental impacts and make people a little conscious concerning environmental issues (Demuth, 2014). Results of such innovative thinking are Solar energy Trade, Biofuel plants, Eco-friendly paper bags etc.
2. Passion for Sustainability: Green entrepreneurs must have a genuine passion for environmental and social issues. This passion serves as a driving force and makes them committed to creating

businesses that contribute to a more sustainable world. Farinelli et al. (2011) also stated that green entrepreneurs are intrinsically motivated and consciously aim at ensuring a more sustainable future. Sustainability also reduces environmental damage and combats climate change. It promotes the adoption of eco-friendly behaviours and ignites green innovation (Demuth, 2014). Aruna and Sunil (2020) state that competitive capabilities will result in sustainability.

3. Environmental knowledge: A strong understanding of environmental issues and their potential solutions is vital. This knowledge helps to identify opportunities and develop practical solutions that align with sustainability principles. Also, it creates value for customers and society while protecting the natural environment from pollution and waste generation (Benjamin Anabaraonye, 2019).
4. Business Acumen: Business Acumen is a combination of knowledge and skill based on experience. Successful green entrepreneurs must have sound business acumen to create and run a profitable and sustainable venture. This includes knowledge of business issues and skills in finance, marketing, operations and strategic planning (Cristina Martinez-Fernandez, 2010).
5. Resilience: It is the ability to adapt to difficult situations and bounce back quickly in times of stress. Building a green business may involve facing challenges and setbacks, both from a business perspective and when trying to push for sustainable practices. Resilience is crucial to overcoming obstacles and staying committed to their mission (Ik Muo and Adebayo Azeez, 2019).
6. Networking and Collaboration: Networking and collaborations are essential to green entrepreneurs because they facilitate the sharing of ideas and pooling of resources, also helping to drive innovation and creativity. Green entrepreneurs often work in a community of like-minded individuals, and building strong networks and collaborative relationships can lead to valuable partnerships and support (Bruton, 2010).
7. Long-term Vision: Green Entrepreneurs should take the time to develop a clear and well-defined vision for their business and use it to guide their decisions and actions over the long term. By doing so, they can increase their chances of success and create a lasting legacy in their field. The long-term vision should be able to communicate effectively to people.
8. Ethical and Transparent Practices: A business cultivates trustworthiness with its clients, customers and employees through honesty, transparency and reliability. Hence, Integrity and ethical behaviour are essential traits for green entrepreneurs. Being transparent about their sustainable practices builds trust with customers and stakeholders (Porter, 1995).

APPLICATION OF GREENPRENEURSHIP IN VARIOUS SECTORS

Creating green business models and strategies is essential for sustainable development across various sectors, including agriculture, ecotourism, renewable energy, automobiles, and solar systems. Below, an overview of green business models and strategies in different sectors is provided:

1. Agriculture:

- Organic Farming: Transitioning to organic farming practices reduces chemical use, conserves soil health, and improves crop yields (Mäder et al., 2002). Organic farming aims at bringing natural ways of doing agriculture, avoiding any use of chemicals in the entire process from cultivation, to dealing with the weeds.
- Precision Agriculture: Implementing precision agriculture technologies, like IoT sensors and data analytics, enhances resource efficiency and minimizes waste (Daberkow et al., 2010). It makes

use of technology to ensure the right quantity of necessary inputs is utilised at the right time in appropriate quantities to improve the yield of agriculture. This ensures minimal waste of scarce resources and their optimum utilization.

2. Ecotourism:

- Sustainable Accommodation: Eco-lodges and resorts can adopt sustainable practices such as energy-efficient design and local sourcing of materials (Butler, 2011). They aim at reducing the wasteful use of resources. Certain hotels install solar panels, and use non-toxic materials for their cleaning. All these products are sourced from the local community, thus, ensuring the local people are also benefited.
- Community Engagement: Engaging local communities in tourism development can foster economic growth while preserving the environment (Simpson, 2008). The natural habitat of the region remains intact in the long run and the residents of the area get a means of living for themselves.

3. Renewable Energy:

- Solar Power Purchase Agreements (PPAs): Businesses can enter into PPAs to buy solar power from third-party providers, reducing emissions and energy costs (Byrne, 2017). While their electricity needs are fulfilled through their own set arrangements, this also benefits the government as they are relieved of the burden to take care of the electricity requirements of these businesses.
- Wind Energy Cooperatives: Communities can establish wind energy cooperatives to generate clean energy and distribute profits locally (Bäckstrand et al., 2010). Community at large will be reaping the benefits of these investments, which are expensive to install initially but the benefits keep coming in the long run.

4. Automobiles:

- Electric Vehicles (EVs): Transitioning to EVs reduces carbon emissions and reliance on fossil fuels (Axsen & Kurani, 2013). Years of research has improved the technology in the area of EVs. EVs today are more efficient and reliable. Over the years such investments in technology can bring more support in sustainable living.
- Car-Sharing Programs: Encouraging car-sharing programs reduces the overall number of vehicles on the road (Shaheen et al., 2016). Reducing the number of vehicles on the road reduces pollution and also makes commutation more congenial for all.

5. Solar Systems:

- Net Metering: Installing solar panels with net metering allows businesses to sell excess energy to the grid, promoting energy self-sufficiency (Gross & Heptonstall, 2006). The energy stored can be utilized by the users later.
- Solar Leasing: Leasing solar systems enables businesses to access solar energy with minimal upfront costs (Feldman et al., 2013). These make, installing the expensive solar panels, a viable option for homeowners. A reduction in electricity bill will benefit them further. It becomes a unique funding opportunity for the businesses which are involved in this field.

CHALLENGES OF GREENPRENEURS

Greenpreneurs, or environmentally conscious entrepreneurs, face several challenges as they seek to create and grow sustainable businesses. These challenges encompass various aspects, including finance, market competition, and regulatory hurdles. Following are few of the many challenges faced by greenpreneurs in the functioning:

1. Access to Funding: Green businesses often require substantial upfront investments in sustainable technologies and practices. Although the importance of these businesses have been recognised worldwide, but the access to funding is still a significant challenge for greenpreneurs (Sarkar & Singh, 2010). They often struggle to secure funding for their eco-friendly initiatives due to a perceived higher risk and longer return on investment.
2. Regulatory Hurdles: As per International labour organisation report (2022), there is not much clarity among regulatory authorities about green businesses that act as a hurdle in enforcing environmental regulations and standards. Dealing with complex environmental regulations and policies can be time-consuming and costly.
3. Customer Awareness: Customers in developing economies lack awareness about environmentally friendly products .They are also not willing to bear the extra costs associated with these products (Yao et al. (2019). Building awareness and educating consumers about the benefits of green products and services can be a time-consuming and costly endeavor
4. Market Competition: Greenpreneurs often face competition from traditional, less environmentally friendly businesses, which can pose challenges in terms of market share and differentiation (Hockerts & Wüstenhagen, 2010). Competing with conventional businesses that may offer cheaper, non-sustainable alternatives can be daunting.
5. Supply Chain Sustainability: Ensuring sustainability throughout the supply chain, from sourcing materials to distribution, can be challenging and require coordination with various stakeholders (Seuring & Müller, 2008). This can be a logistical and financial challenge for the greenpreneurs.
6. Technological Advancements: Staying updated with the latest sustainable technologies and incorporating them into business operations can be demanding and costly (Dangelico & Pujari, 2010). To be able to compete with the existing incumbents, the greepreneurs have to invest in advancement in technology and its upgradation from time to time.
7. Changing Consumer Preferences: Rapid shifts in consumer preferences and attitudes toward sustainability can create uncertainties and challenges in product development. Pacing up with this change can be expensive for the greenpreneurs.
8. Scaling Up: Expanding a green business while maintaining its sustainable practices can be challenging due to resource limitations and increased complexity (Bansal, 2005). As the business expands, the complexity increases, finding environmentally sustainable solutions becomes very challenging then.
9. International Regulations: For green businesses operating globally, navigating different international environmental regulations can also be a challenge. Every country may have different norms for sustainable business practices. Dealing with varied practices at international level may be cumbersome for these businesses.

These challenges may vary depending on the specific nature and focus of the green business, but they are commonly encountered by greenpreneurs in their pursuit of environmentally sustainable and profitable ventures.

GREENPRENEURS- INDIAN CASE STUDIES

Greenpreneurs are individuals or businesses that focus on sustainable and environmentally friendly practices while also aiming for profitability. In India, there are several notable cases of greenpreneurship and sustainable initiatives. Here are a few examples:

1. Chakr Innovation: Chakr Innovation is a startup that has developed a device to capture and convert emissions from diesel generators into usable ink. The technology not only reduces air pollution but also repurposes waste into a valuable product. Another initiative taken by the organization was to take care of abundant waste which came as an outcome of Latest Pandemic. N95 masks were necessary to be worn to save Corona from spreading. There was abundant demand for these masks in the market and they were to be thrown away after the use. Chakr Innovation came with a device which can disinfect these N95 masks (*CHAKR Innovation – Revolution Through Pollution*, n.d.)
2. Saahas Zero Waste: Saahas Zero Waste is a social enterprise that focuses on sustainable waste management. They work with individuals, communities, and businesses to implement zero-waste practices by reducing, reusing, and recycling waste. They have various initiatives to promote responsible waste disposal. They have been able to divert the waste going to landfills and also generate employment opportunities for people from lower economic background (Saahas Zero Waste, 2023).
3. Boheco (Bombay Hemp Company): Boheco is a startup that promotes the use of hemp for various products such as textiles, food, and building materials. Hemp is a sustainable crop that requires fewer resources compared to traditional crops. Boheco is working to change the perception of hemp in India. They have applied scientific ways of utilising hemp to find solutions to day to day medical and other problems for people (Buy Hemp Products in India. n.d.).
4. Ecolibrium Energy: Ecolibrium Energy is a company that provides energy management solutions to industrial and commercial enterprises. Their platform helps businesses optimize their energy usage, reduce carbon emissions, and save on energy costs, thus contributing to a more sustainable future. They help to make the companies ESG compliant.
5. Banyan Nation: Banyan Nation is a recycling and waste management company that uses technology to streamline and optimize the recycling process. They work with municipalities, brands, and consumers to collect and recycle plastics effectively. The company uses the latest plastic cleaning technology that converts used plastic into high quality recycled granules. Thereby, it helps global companies to make use of recycled plastic in place of virgin plastic. They support the municipalities in their waste management practices using the latest technologies (Banyan nation, n.d.).
6. Ninjacart: Ninjacart is a technology-driven agritech B2B startup that connects farmers directly with retailers and businesses to reduce food wastage and improve the supply chain. By doing so, they aim to assist farmers to get better prices and maintain regular demand for their products. On the other hand, retailers also get the fresh vegetables at competitive prices directly from farmers. The integrated supply chain supported by latest technology, infrastructure and data led decisions facilitate company to offer its products at lower cost and at better speed (Ninjacart, n.d.).

7. Saral Design Solutions: Saral Design is a startup that focuses on sustainable menstrual hygiene solutions. They have developed machines which provide eco-friendly and affordable sanitary pads and similar hygiene and health related products to women in India, addressing both menstrual health and environmental concerns. During the time of Covid 19, they even developed machines to make affordable and good quality face masks to prevent the spread of Covid 19. They are the suppliers of these machines to other organizations ensuring bulk production (Saral design, n.d).
8. CleanMax Solar: CleanMax Solar is a solar energy company. They provide clean energy solutions to commercial and industrial clients, helping them reduce their carbon footprint and energy costs through solar power installations. Their recent innovation includes wind solar hybrid solutions for enterprises. Many companies have availed their services to make themselves self-sufficient for their electrical needs (CleanMax Solar, n.d.).
9. Elrhino: The name Elrhino clearly shows a culmination of Elephant and Rhinoceros. Elrhino wants to save the animals and natural habitat of Forests in Assam. It is involved in producing tree free paper. They produce paper by using rhinoceros and elephant dung and other locally sourced natural products to make paper, note books etc. They employ people from indigenous tribes in the region of Assam and provide an environmentally conscious alternative to traditional paper products (Elrhino dung paper, n.d.).
10. Ather Energy: Ather Energy is an electric scooter manufacturer that focuses on providing sustainable, electric mobility solutions. Their electric scooters are designed with energy efficiency and reduced carbon emissions in mind. Overtime, they have worked on the designs of their scooter making them look like a viable solution as compared to other speedy fuel based vehicles (Ather Energy, n.d.).
11. BetterPlace: BetterPlace is a technology platform that addresses the sustainability of gig economy workers. Companies which provide vehicle rental services or those which are involved in home delivery require abundant frontline workforce. BetterPlace provides a one-stop solution for managing the front line workers hired by these organizations from their hiring, payrolls, customer feedback, etc. This platform contributes to social and environmental sustainability (Better place, n.d.).
12. Uger: Uger is a startup that promotes sustainable and eco-friendly living by offering eco-conscious and reusable products, such as cloth diapers and cloth masks, reducing the environmental impact of single-use products (Usha Hariprasad (2021, March 8). The founder of the technology is a strong follower of Copyleft concept and has decided that she would not copyright her product development strategy, in fact, she wants more organizations to come forward and use her technology of making these reusable products and make the technique even better.
13. Sunbirdstraws: Sunbird straws is an initiative of Dr Saji Verghese which uses the coconut leaves to make drinking straws and eco-friendly pens. The material used in the products is all natural and the workers are rural women in the region. Their aim is to reduce the use of plastic and paper for these products. And also empower the women in that area (Sunbird straw, n.d).
14. Bhoomi Ka: Bhoomi Ka is a sustainable agriculture venture that provides eco-friendly and organic farming solutions to rural farmers. They focus on regenerative farming practices that are environmentally sustainable and financially viable. They have involved many small farmers from Jharkhand, Rajasthan, Madhya Pradesh, West Bengal, and Odisha in their regime to improve the conditions of organic farming in India (Bhoomi Ka, n.d.).
15. Yulu Bikes: is a bicycle-sharing service that provides convenient and eco-friendly transportation solutions in urban areas. The company offers a fleet of bicycles that can be rented through a mobile

app, allowing users to pick up and drop off bikes at designated stations throughout the city. Yulu Bikes aims to reduce traffic congestion and promote sustainable transportation options by making bikes readily available for short trips and commutes within the city (Upadhyay et al., 2020).

These greenpreneur cases in India reflect the growing interest and success in sustainable and eco-friendly entrepreneurship, addressing environmental and social challenges while also contributing to economic growth and development.

POLICY AND ADVOCACY FOR GREEN ENTREPRENEURSHIP IN INDIA

Policy and advocacy for green entrepreneurship in India are essential for ensuring eco-friendly economic growth, environmental conservation, and promotion of a green economy. Primarily, Green entrepreneurship refers to businesses and startups that prioritize environmental sustainability and social responsibility (OECD 2011). Here are some key aspects of policy and advocacy for green entrepreneurship in India:

1. National Green Tribunal (NGT): The NGT is a court which specializes in Environmental protection in India. It was established under the National Green Tribunal Act, 2010. It is located in total of five places of sittings namely: Bhopal, Pune, New Delhi, Kolkata, and Chennai, amongst which, New Delhi is the Principal place of sitting. Its main objective is effective and expeditious disposal of cases that are related to the protection and conservation of the environment, forests, and other natural resources, including those related to green entrepreneurship, by ensuring environmental compliance and enforcement (National Green Tribunal, n.d.).
2. Make in India: The Make in India initiative, launched by the Indian government as part of a wider set of nation-building initiatives by promoting manufacturing and entrepreneurship in various sectors, including green technologies and renewable energy. It ensures 'ease of doing business' as the single most important factor to promote entrepreneurship. It encourages investment in eco-friendly manufacturing prodcuts (Make in India, n.d.).
3. Startup India: The Startup India initiative supports the growth of startups across various sectors, including those focusing on green and sustainable technologies. It provides funding, tax benefits, R & D facilities and regulatory support for startups. The government has proposed to hold 2 startup fests annually both nationally and internationally to enable the various stakeholders of a startup to meet. This will provide huge networking opportunities (Stratup India, n.d.)
4. National Solar Mission (Jawaharlal Nehru National Solar Mission): The National Solar Mission is one of the important programs of the Indian government, focusing on encouraging the use of solar energy thus promoting green entrepreneurship in the sector of renewable energy. In order to create a sustained interest within the investor community, Ministry of New & Renewable Energy (MNRE), Govt. of India has decided to support viable business models with the objective to promote off-grid application of solar energy (both SPV & Solar Thermal). Under this scheme, Ministry shall provide Central Financial Assistance for setting up of Solar power (National Solar Mission, n.d.).
5. National Clean Energy Fund (NCEF): The sole purpose for establishing NCEF was to finance the research and promote innovative projects in clean energy. The Mission projects identified in the National Action Plan on Climate Change (NAPCC) that use more environmentally friendly technologies were also given assistance. It has been a crucial source of financial support for green entrepreneurs working

on renewable energy solutions. However it also collects Environment tax which is an excise duty on goods that cause environmental pollutants (National Clean Energy fund, n.d.).

6. Atal Innovation Mission (AIM): AIM, an initiative under NITI Aayog, promotes innovation and entrepreneurship in India. AIM's primary objective is to develop new programmes and policies for fostering innovation in different sectors of the economy, provide platforms and collaboration opportunities for different stakeholders, and create an umbrella structure to oversee the innovation & entrepreneurship ecosystem of the country. It also supports startups working on sustainable and green technologies through various programs and incubators (Atal Innovation Mission, n.d.).
7. Environmental Impact Assessment (EIA): EIA is termed as one of the best policy innovations in the 1900s. The main aim of EIA is to conserve the environment and bring out the best combination of economic and environmental costs and benefits. It is an essential policy tool for regulating industrial and infrastructure projects in India. It ensures that environmental concerns are addressed before project approvals and as a result the adverse impacts on the environment are avoided and promots sustainable practices (Environment Impact Assessment, n.d.).
8. National biodiversity Authority (NBA):NBA is responsible for conserving biodiversity in India. It focuses on advising the Central Government on matters relating to biodiversity conservation, sustainable use of its components, and equitable sharing of benefits arising from the utilization of biological resources. Anyone seeking intellectual property rights on research based on biological resources or knowledge and Entrepreneurs engaged in eco-friendly and biodiversity-related businesses may need to comply with NBA regulations and guidelines (Grover, 2023).
9. Faster Adoption and Manufacturing of Hybrid and Electric Vehicles in India (FAME India Scheme): FAME India is basically a subsidy scheme which was introduced by the government of India on April 1, 2019, for a period of three years, which was further extended for a period of two years up to March 31, 2024. Its main aim is to promote electric mobility and green entrepreneurship in the automotive sector by providing incentives for electric and hybrid vehicle manufacturers and users. The programme also finances the charging infrastructures (ET Online, 2023)
10. Renewable Purchase Obligation (RPO): RPO mandates the obligated entities of all the state and Union Territories that a specific percentage of total electricity consumption come from renewable sources. Obligated Entities (which includes Discoms, Open Access Consumers and Captive power producers) are obligated to purchase a minimum share of their electricity from renewable energy sources as per RPO targets. This encourages the growth of renewable energy businesses, including solar and wind power (Ministry of new and renewable energy, n.d.).
11. Waste Management Rules: India has implemented various waste management rules, such as E-Waste Management Rules, Solid wast management management rules and Plastic Waste Management Rules, which impact businesses involved in recycling and waste management in an environmentally friendly manner. The Government encourages the people and businesses to follow 3R's (Reduce, Re-use & Recycle) principles for waste management by adopting responsible waste management practices (Central Pollution control board, n.d.).
12. State-Level Policies: Many Indian states have their own policies and incentives to promote green entrepreneurship, renewable energy, and sustainable business practices. These policies can vary significantly from one state to another.

RECOMMENDATIONS

This section contains recommendations to various stakeholders. Beginning from budding Greenpreneurs, already established greenpreneurs, Public at large and finally government.

For Budding Greenpreneurs:

These people are at the beginning phase of their journey. They have an intention to do good to the society and nature together with making means for themselves. Their investments in this area will provide wealth to the nation simultaneously conserving resources for the future generations. Greenpreneurs should do the following to make their ventures even better:

1. Research and Education: Investing time in understanding environmental issues, green technologies, and market trends can be beneficial for the budding entrepreneurs. Formal education or specialized courses in sustainability can be invaluable for them. These trainings will add to the existing repository of their knowledge giving them more options to avail to support their cause.
2. Innovation: Innovation is possible when one seeks novel and unique solutions to environmental challenges. Greenpreneurs need to think outside the box and be open to unconventional ideas. Support from the team members with a variety of thoughts and acceptance to new ways of doing the old things will help.
3. Funding Support: Initially these green businesses may not be cost effective. Thus, it becomes difficult for greenpreneurs to arrange for funds. One way to overcome this challenge is to seek venture capital from impact investors who prioritize environmental and social impact alongside financial returns (Mrkajic et al., 2019).
4. Network Building: Networking always ensures more collaborative work. Budding greenpreneurs need to connect with existing greenpreneurs and environmental organizations to gain practical insights into the issues. They need to network extensively to gain insights, mentorship, and access to resources in their respective domain. Attending conferences, seminars, workshops in their area would help them get in touch with like minded people who already have experience in their industry. This would do away with the rule of thumb saving a lot of their time and energy by learning from the mistakes of others and not repeating the same for themselves.
5. Stay Informed: Greenpreneurs are working in very dynamic conditions. They are required to keep themselves up-to-date with the latest developments in sustainability and climate change. Their updated knowledge can be the key to developing new and innovative solutions.
6. Collaborate: In the initial phase of any organization's journey, it requires support from others. Partnering with like-minded organizations, NGOs, and government agencies can maximize the impact of upcoming greenpreneurs. Sometimes the support from other agencies like NGOs and Government, not only help them promote their products but also get expertise and monetary support for their ventures. Collective action is often more effective and this support can enhance the working of greenpreneurs. Collaboration with suppliers and adopting eco-friendly sourcing practices can help greenpreneurs improve the sustainability of their supply chain (Carter & Easton, 2011).
7. Advocate for Policies: Every business is impacted by the government policies; however, greenpreneurs are working in the area where governments look forward to getting the support of the people to understand ground level realities and seeking solutions. Greenpreneurs can support the government in this context. They can use their knowledge to advocate for policies that support climate action and sustainability, both locally and globally.

8. Educate and Engage: Sharing the knowledge opens many avenues for the future of your own organization and also motivates others to do well. Greenpreneurs should share their gained expertise with others to make a difference. They should make efforts to raise awareness and educate their customers and the public about climate change and sustainable practices. An informed customer also remains loyal to the organization that seems to be taking care of limited resources. Emphasizing the unique environmental benefits of the products or services and targeting eco-conscious consumers can help greenpreneurs carve out a niche in the market (Hockerts & Wüstenhagen, 2010).

FOR EXISTING GREENPRENEURS

Existing Greenpreneurs are already in the field and have established themselves. They may already have reached some milestones and may be enjoying the fruits of their efforts. However, they cannot settle with what they have but should put efforts to keep growing in their area. They are suggested to do the following for themselves:

1. Continuous Innovation: Existing greenpreneurs may be pioneers in their area, but the conditions are changing very frequently. They are also required to keep themselves abreast of the latest developments in sustainability and green technologies. They should regularly update and improve their products or services to remain competitive and impactful.
2. Scaling Up: Greenpreneurs are required to explore opportunities to scale their green business and expand its reach. They can collaborate, enter into partnerships, and even plan international expansion to maximize their climate impact.
3. Advocacy: Experienced greenpreneurs should engage in climate advocacy by supporting policies and initiatives that promote sustainability. They can advocate for green entrepreneurship at local, national, and international levels. Greenpreneurs can engage in policy advocacy and collaboration with environmental organizations to influence and shape policies in their favor.
4. Measure and Report: Ignorance can kill any business. In case of ventures which are working for sustainability, the conditions are all the more tough to manage. Existing greenpreneurs should regularly assess their environmental and social impact and share their results transparently. This fosters trust and accountability among people keeping them motivated to support such ventures.

RECOMMENDATIONS FOR THE PUBLIC

Public can create an environment congenial for the development of greenpreneurs. Support of the public to the business can increase the life of the business, and also keep the entrepreneurs motivated. On the other hand, public can also create pressure to reduce the business practices which are hazardous for nature. Following are few of the recommendations for the public:

1. Support Green Businesses: If the public supports any venture, it can survive in the long run. Public should choose to support businesses that prioritize sustainability. Consumer choices can drive change and motivate more entrepreneurs to apply sustainable business practices.

2. Reduce Carbon Footprint: Public is the final market and consumers for any product. If as consumers we decide to make changes in our daily life to reduce our carbon footprint, we can ensure that the businesses also start working in that direction. People can start using public transport, this would conserve energy, and reduce waste. They can purchase products which are environmentally more sustainable. It would provide a boost to sustainable businesses.
3. Advocate for Change: In a democratic set up like India, views of the public are of prime importance. Public can influence the decisions of policy makers. People can engage with their local and national representatives to push for policies that combat climate change. They can also join or support organizations dedicated to climate action.
4. Stay Informed: Awareness of the public can be a complete game changer. Public should stay informed about climate change and its effects. Knowledge empowers people to make informed decisions and advocate for change by supporting ventures which are taking care of nature in the long run.

RECOMMENDATIONS FOR GOVERNMENT

The ultimate power lies in the hands of policy makers. Their ideology would decide which business will flourish in their region. Government has to take many measures to support environmentally friendly practices. Government can involve in few of the following mentioned practices:

1. Set Clear Policies: Governments should establish clear policies and regulations that promote sustainability, renewable energy, and emissions reduction. This enhances nature friendly practices in their regions promoting more sustainable business practices.
2. Incentivize Green Innovation: Greenpreneurs are required to compete with existing players which are already well established in the market but their ways of functioning are harmful for nature. Support from the government can give boost to the efforts of greenpreneurs. Government can offer incentives for green businesses and startups, such as tax benefits, grants, and subsidies, to stimulate innovation in the green sector.
3. Invest in Infrastructure: Governments should invest in sustainable infrastructure, such as public transportation, renewable energy projects, and sustainable urban planning. Example can be Singapore where public transport is so strong that people do not purchase their own vehicles. Also, this would create a pressure on existing businesses to follow environment friendly techniques in their functioning.
4. Support Climate Education: Public awareness is a responsibility of the government. Government can implement climate education programs in schools and communities to raise awareness and encourage sustainable practices. Government can also promote research and development in green technologies and innovation.
5. Lead by Example: Governments can lead by example by adopting sustainable practices in their own operations and procurement processes. Government involves a lot of people and business to source its work. Governments can assign their tasks to the vendors who follow sustainable practices. Their can be wings of the governments fully dedicated to understanding the need of the hour and promoting greenpreneurship.
6. Policy Support: Government can develop and implement policies that promote green entrepreneurship. They can provide incentives, tax breaks, and funding opportunities to support sustainable startups.

7. Collaboration: Government can be a catalyst for promoting greenpreneurship and environmentally sustainable ways of living by the community. Government can foster collaboration between greenpreneurs, academia, and government agencies to work together on solutions for climate change and environmental sustainability. It can run programmes where the knowledge exchange can happen between all the stakeholders and solutions are also derived.

In India, with its significant environmental challenges and entrepreneurial spirit, greenpreneurship can be a powerful force for addressing climate change. It requires collective effort and commitment from existing greenpreneurs, budding entrepreneurs, the public, and the government to drive sustainable innovation and make a positive impact on the environment and society. The fight against climate change is a collective effort, with Greenpreneurs, the public, and governments each playing a crucial role. Collaboration and innovation will be a key in addressing this global challenge effectively.

CONCLUSION

By fostering a culture of innovation, sustainability, and responsible business practices, green entrepreneurship contributes significantly to combat climate change. These entrepreneurs are driving positive change, raising awareness, and inspiring others to adopt sustainable practices, thus contributing to a more sustainable and resilient future for our planet. They develop and implement innovative ideas, technologies, and practices that contribute to reducing greenhouse gas emissions, implementing sustainable agriculture and food systems, advocating for circular economy models, promoting renewable energy, and more. By integrating environmental considerations into their entrepreneurial endeavors, greenpreneurs play a vital role in shaping a greener and more sustainable future. Their contributions extend beyond economic growth; they actively work towards mitigating climate change, preserving ecosystems, promoting social equity, and inspiring others to adopt environmentally conscious practices. The significance of greenpreneurship lies in its potential to transform industries, engage local communities, influence policy, and drive systemic change towards a resilient and low-carbon society. It serves as a beacon of hope, showcasing that entrepreneurship can be a force for positive environmental change, and that sustainable business models can thrive while addressing the urgent global challenge of climate change.

REFERENCES

Aruna, P., & Sunil, D. B. (2020). Factors affecting the competitive capability of small and medium women entrepreneurs. *International Journal of Advanced Science and Technology*, *29*(5), 574–584.

Atal Innovation Mission, (n.d). *About AIM*. AIM. https://aim.gov.in/

Ather Energy. (n.d.) Wikipedia, Retrieved from https://en.wikipedia.org/wiki/Ather_Energy Ather Energy

Axsen, J., & Kurani, K. S. (2013). Social influence in the global diffusion of alternative fuel vehicles: A meta-analysis. *Journal of Transport Geography*, *31*, 94–103.

Bäckstrand, K., Khan, J., Kronsell, A., & Lövbrand, E. (2010). *Environmental politics and deliberative democracy: Examining the promise of new modes of governance*. Edward Elgar Publishing. doi:10.4337/9781849806411

Bansal, P. (2005). Evolving sustainably: A longitudinal study of corporate sustainable development. *Strategic Management Journal*, *26*(3), 197–218. doi:10.1002mj.441

Benjamin Anabaraonye, O. J. (2019, April). Green Entrepreneurial Opportunities in Climate Change Adaptation and Mitigation for Sustainable Development in Nigeria. *Journal of Environmental Pollution and Management*, *2*(1), 1–6.

Bruton, G. D., Ahlstrom, D., & Li, H.-L. (2010). Institutional theory and entrepreneurship: Where are we now and where do we need to move in the future? *Entrepreneurship Theory and Practice*, *34*(3), 421–440. doi:10.1111/j.1540-6520.2010.00390.x

Butler, R. (2011). Tourism area life cycle: Applications and modifications. In Tourism Area Life Cycle, Concepts and Applications (pp. 13-32). Channel View Publications.

Buy hemp products in India. (n.d.). BOHECO. https://boheco.com/

Byrne, J. (2017). The economics of solar power. In *Handbook of Clean Energy Systems* (pp. 1–24). Wiley.

Carter, C. R., & Liane Easton, P. (2011). Sustainable supply chain management: Evolution and future directions. *International Journal of Physical Distribution & Logistics Management*, *41*(1), 46–62. doi:10.1108/09600031111101420

CEEW. (2021, December 15). *India's journey towards 500 GW: Reaching the capacity and investment targets*. CEEW. https://www.ceew.in/events/indias-journey-towards-500-gw-reaching-capacity-and-investment-targets

Central Pollution control board. (n.d). *Waste Management*. CPCB. https://cpcb.nic.in/rules/

Cohen, B., & Winn, M. I. (2007). Market imperfections, opportunity and sustainable entrepreneurship. *Journal of Business Venturing*, *22*(1), 29–49. doi:10.1016/j.jbusvent.2004.12.001

Cristina Martinez-Fernandez, C. H. (2010). *Green jobs and skills:the local labour market implications of addressing climate change*. OECD. www.oecd.org/dataoecd/54/43/44683169.pdf?contentId=44683170

Daberkow, S. G., & McBride, W. D. (2010). Farm and operator characteristics affecting the awareness and adoption of precision agriculture technologies in the US. *Precision Agriculture*, *11*(4), 335–350.

Dangelico, R. M., & Pujari, D. (2010). Mainstreaming green product innovation: Why and how companies integrate environmental sustainability. *Journal of Business Ethics*, *95*(3), 471–486. doi:10.100710551-010-0434-0

Demuth, A. (2014). Green Entrepreneurship: A promising path towards a sustainable future in Tunisia and elsewhere. *Internationale Zusammenarbeit (GIZ) GmbH*, 4-51.

Development, S. A. (2017). Skills for Green Entrepreneurship Training Mannual. Swiszerland: Swiss Academy for Development.

Environmental Impact Assessment. (n.d.). *Biju's*. EIA. https://byjus.com/free-ias-prep/eia/

FAME scheme: What is it, and what's all the brouhaha? (2023, May 18). *ET Online*. https://economictimes.indiatimes.com/industry/renewables/fame-scheme-what-is-it-and-whats-all-the-brouhaha/articleshow/100325140.cms

Farinelli, F., Bottini, M., Akkoyunlu, S., & Aerni, P. (2011). Green entrepreneurship: The missing link towards a greener economy. *Atdf Journal*, *8*(3/4), 42–48.

Farinelli, F., Bottini, M., Akkoyunlu, S., & Aerni, P. (2011). Green entrepreneurship: The missing link towards a greener economy. *Atdf Journal*, *8*(3/4), 42–48.

Feldman, D., Barbose, G., Margolis, R., Wiser, R., & Darghouth, N. (2013). *Photovoltaic system pricing trends: Historical, recent, and near-term projections* (2013 edition). Lawrence Berkeley National Laboratory.

Field, C. B. (Ed.). (2012). Managing the risks of extreme events and disasters to advance climate change adaptation: special report of the intergovernmental panel on climate change. Cambridge University Press, 555-564. doi:10.1017/CBO9781139177245

Gross, R., & Heptonstall, P. (2006). *The costs and impacts of intermittency: An assessment of the evidence on the costs and impacts of intermittent generation on the British electricity network*. UK Energy Research Centre.

Grover, N. (2023, May 21). *Prepp by collegedunia*. prepp.in. https://prepp.in/news/e-492-the-national-biodiversity-authority-nba-environment-notes

Hockerts, K., & Wüstenhagen, R. (2010). Greening Goliaths versus emerging Davids—Theorizing about the role of incumbents and new entrants in sustainable entrepreneurship. *Journal of Business Venturing*, *25*(5), 481–492. doi:10.1016/j.jbusvent.2009.07.005

International Labour Organisation (ILO). (2022). *Promotion of Green Entrepreneurship for Youth.* ILO. https://www.ilo.org/wcmsp5/groups/public/---asia/---ro-bangkok/---ilo-colombo/documents/briefingnote/wcms_885924.pdf

IRENA. (2023). *Renewable capacity statistics 2023*. International Renewable Energy Agency.

Mäder, P., Fliessbach, A., Dubois, D., Gunst, L., Fried, P., & Niggli, U. (2002). Soil fertility and biodiversity in organic farming. *Science*, *296*(5573), 1694–1697. doi:10.1126cience.1071148 PMID:12040197

Mapping India's Energy Policy 2022: Aligning Support and Revenues with a Net-Zero Future. (2023b, March 7). CEEW. https://www.ceew.in/publications/energy-policy-research-india-2022

Ministry of new and renewable energy. (n.d.). *Home-Objectives*. RPO. https://rpo.gov.in/Home/Objective

Mrkajic, B., Murtinu, S., & Scalera, V. G. (2019). Is green the new gold? Venture capital and green entrepreneurship. *Small Business Economics*, *52*(4), 929–950. doi:10.100711187-017-9943-x

Muo, I., & Azeez, A. A. (2019). Green entrepreneurship: Literature review and agenda for future research. *International Journal of Entrepreneurial Knowledge*, *7*(2). Advance online publication. doi:10.37335/ijek.v7i2.90

NASA's Global Climate Change website. (2023, September 27). *Climate change adaptation and mitigation*. Climate Change: Vital Signs of the Planet. https://climate.nasa.gov/solutions/adaptation-mitigation/

National Clean Energy Fund. (n.d). *Biju's.* https://byjus.com/free-ias-prep/ncef-national-clean-energy-fund/

National Green Tribunal. (n.d.). *About us.* National Green Tribunal. https://www.greentribunal.gov.in/about-us

Neumann, T. (2022). Impact of green entrepreneurship on sustainable development: An ex-post empirical analysis. *Journal of Cleaner Production, 377*, 134317. doi:10.1016/j.jclepro.2022.134317

OECD. (2011). *Measuring Green Entrepreneurship. Entrepreneurship at a Glance,* 23-38. OECD. doi:10.1787/9789264097711-4-en

Porter, M. E., & Linde, C. (1995). Toward a new conception of the environment-comptitiveness relationship. *The Journal of Economic Perspectives*, *9*(4), 97–118. doi:10.1257/jep.9.4.97

Saahas Zero Waste. (2023, October 16). *Waste Management Company in India.* SAAHAS Zero Waste. https://saahaszerowaste.com/

Sarkar, A., & Singh, J. (2010). Financing energy efficiency in developing countries—Lessons learned and remaining challenges. *Energy Policy*, *38*(10), 5560–5571. doi:10.1016/j.enpol.2010.05.001

Schaper, M. (2002). *Introduction:* The Essence of Ecopreneurship. *Greener Management International, 38*, 26–30. https://www.jstor.org/stable/greemanainte.38.26

Serio, R. G., Dickson, M. M., Giuliani, D., & Espa, G. (2020). Green production as a factor of survival for innovative startups: Evidence from Italy. *Sustainability (Basel)*, *12*(22), 9464. doi:10.3390u12229464

Seuring, S., & Müller, M. (2008). From a literature review to a conceptual framework for sustainable supply chain management. *Journal of Cleaner Production*, *16*(15), 1699–1710. doi:10.1016/j.jclepro.2008.04.020

Shaheen, S., Cohen, A., & Zohdy, I. (2016). Mobility and the sharing economy: Potential to contribute to environmental and social sustainability. *Sustainability*, *8*(12), 1275.

Simpson, M. C. (2008). Community benefit tourism initiatives: Linking communities, tourism, and conservation in the southern Philippines. *Geoforum*, *39*(2), 946–960.

Taylor, E. (2019). Green Entrepreneurship: Literature review and agenda for future research. *International Journal of Entrepreneurial Knowledge*, 17 - 29.

Tyagi, A., Lata, C., Korsh, J., Nagarwal, A., Rai, D., Kwatra, S., & Saxena, P. (2021). *India's Expanding Clean Energy Workforce*.

Upadhyay, D., Purswani, G., & Jain, P. (2020). Yulu: Moving Towards a Sustainable Future. *South Asian Journal of Business and Management Cases*, *9*(3), 445–456. doi:10.1177/2277977920957954

Usha Hariprasad. (2021, March 8). *Uger: New beginnings in sustainable, safe, and dignified menstruation*. Vikalp Sangam. https://vikalpsangam.org/article/uger-new-beginnings-in-sustainable-safe-and-dignified-menstruation/

Yao, Q., Liu, J., Sheng, S., & Fang, H. (2019). Does eco-innovation lift firm value? The contingent role of institutions in emerging markets. *Journal of Business and Industrial Marketing*, *34*(8), 1763–1778. doi:10.1108/JBIM-06-2018-0201

Zahraie, B., Everett, A. M., Walton, S., & Kirkwood, J. (2016). Environmental entrepreneurs facilitating change toward sustainability: A case study of the wine industry in New Zealand. *Small Enterprise Research*, *23*(1), 39–57. doi:10.1080/13215906.2016.1188717

Chapter 15
A Case Study on a Beacon of Hope Transition:
India's Renewable Energy Integration and the Ujwal DISCOM Assurance Yojana (UDAY)

S. Baranidharan
https://orcid.org/0000-0002-7780-4045
Christ University, India

B. K. Mallika
Christ University, India

N. Thilaga
Kavery Arts and Science College, India

ABSTRACT

This case study examines the transformative impact of the Ujwal DISCOM Assurance Yojana (UDAY) on India's energy landscape, focusing on its role in facilitating renewable energy integration. India's energy sector faced daunting challenges, including financially distressed power distribution companies (DISCOMs) and high aggregate technical and commercial (AT&C) losses. UDAY's financial restructuring and operational efficiency improvements led to remarkable reductions in DISCOMs' debt burdens and AT&C losses, respectively. The policy aligned with India's renewable energy goals, driving DISCOMs to procure renewable energy sources. Consequently, India witnessed significant growth in its renewable energy capacity, environmental benefits through reduced emissions, and economic growth via job creation. This case study offers insights into the challenges faced, technological advancements incentivized, and the long-term sustainability of these reforms. Moreover, it presents broader lessons for energy sector reform and renewable energy integration, both within India and globally.

DOI: 10.4018/979-8-3693-1297-1.ch015

LEARNING OBJECTIVES

- Understand the challenges and constraints faced by India's energy sector, including financially distressed DISCOMs and high AT&C losses.
- Analyze the key objectives and components of Ujwal DISCOM Assurance Yojana (UDAY) and its role in addressing the financial and operational issues of DISCOMs.
- Evaluate the impact of UDAY on improving the financial health of DISCOMs through debt restructuring and reduced interest burdens.
- Examine the role of UDAY in reducing aggregate technical and commercial (AT&C) losses and its contribution to a more efficient distribution system.
- Investigate how UDAY aligned with India's renewable energy goals, including the incorporation of Renewable Purchase Obligations (RPOs) and preferential tariffs.
- Assess the environmental benefits of UDAY's promotion of renewable energy integration, including reductions in carbon emissions and fossil fuel dependence.

UDAY'S OBJECTIVES

UDAY's primary objectives were to improve the financial health of DISCOMs, reduce their aggregate technical and commercial (AT&C) losses, and promote operational efficiency. These objectives laid a solid foundation for the integration of renewable energy into the grid.

BACKGROUND

India, as one of the world's most populous and rapidly developing nations, has long grappled with significant challenges in its energy sector. The country's energy landscape was characterized by a heavy reliance on fossil fuels, financially distressed power distribution companies (DISCOMs), and inadequate infrastructure. These issues not only hindered the growth of the energy sector but also posed serious environmental and economic challenges. Amid these challenges, India recognized the need to transition to renewable energy sources to mitigate environmental concerns, enhance energy security, and foster sustainable economic growth. The Indian government introduced several policies and initiatives to promote renewable energy adoption, including the National Solar Mission and the National Wind Mission, both aimed at boosting solar and wind energy capacity.

- India's Energy Challenges: India's energy landscape was marred by financially ailing DISCOMs, mounting debt, and operational inefficiencies. High AT&C losses, inadequate infrastructure, and outdated metering systems contributed to the challenges.
- Renewable Energy Aspirations: India recognized the importance of renewable energy to mitigate environmental concerns, enhance energy security, and foster sustainable economic growth. Initiatives like the National Solar Mission and the National Wind Mission set ambitious targets for solar and wind power capacity.

The electricity sector in India is facing significant challenges, including high debt levels, inefficient distribution companies, and inadequate investment in infrastructure. The Ujwal Discom Assurance Yojana (UDAY) was launched in 2015 to address these challenges by providing financial support to distribution companies and encouraging them to reduce their losses. Several studies have examined the impact of UDAY on the Indian electricity sector. Bajaj and Sheoran (2022) found that UDAY has had a positive spillover impact on the economy by reducing electricity tariffs and increasing demand. Bhardwaj and Sharma (2022) found that UDAY has helped to improve the financial sustainability of distribution companies in Rajasthan. Singh and Vashishtha (2019) found that UDAY has empowered the power sector in Haryana by providing it with financial stability and reducing political interference.

However, other studies have raised concerns about the long-term sustainability of UDAY. Habeebur Rahman (2020) found that the electricity distribution sector in India is likely to face significant challenges in the future, including rising electricity demand and increasing environmental concerns. Kristoff (2019, 2020) argued that India needs to further reform its energy sector in order to address these challenges. Sharma et al. (2018) examined the impact of UDAY on tariff adjustments and distribution company performance in Uttar Pradesh. They found that UDAY led to a significant reduction in tariffs, but that this was not accompanied by a corresponding improvement in distribution company performance.

Overall, the evidence suggests that UDAY has had a mixed impact on the Indian electricity sector. While it has led to some positive outcomes, such as reduced tariffs and improved financial stability for distribution companies, there are concerns about its long-term sustainability.

However, the success of these renewable energy initiatives was closely tied to the health and efficiency of the power distribution sector. The struggling DISCOMs, weighed down by debt and inefficiency, were a major roadblock to integrating renewable energy into the grid. In this context, the Ujwal DISCOM Assurance Yojana (UDAY) was introduced in 2015 as a comprehensive reform program. It aimed to address the financial and operational issues faced by DISCOMs, thereby creating a conducive environment for the adoption of renewable energy. UDAY's inception marked a critical moment in India's energy history, offering hope for a more sustainable, reliable, and efficient energy future.

Problems Faced

Financial Distress of DISCOMs: Before the implementation of UDAY, India's power distribution companies (DISCOMs) were grappling with severe financial distress, characterized by high levels of debt and accumulated losses.

High Aggregate Technical and Commercial (AT&C) Losses: India's energy sector suffered from significant AT&C losses, which not only strained the financial health of DISCOMs but also hindered the efficient distribution of electricity.

Challenges in Renewable Energy Integration: Integrating renewable energy sources into the grid posed challenges related to grid stability, intermittency of renewable power generation, and the need for technological upgrades.

Timeline of Key Events

- 2015: Ujwal DISCOM Assurance Yojana (UDAY) was launched by the Indian government to address the financial distress of DISCOMs and improve the efficiency of the power distribution sector.
- 2016: UDAY gained momentum as states and DISCOMs signed agreements to participate in the program, signaling their commitment to reforming the sector.
- 2016-2019: UDAY's financial restructuring and operational efficiency measures were implemented, resulting in a reduction of DISCOMs' debt burdens and a gradual decrease in AT&C losses.
- 2016-2020: India's renewable energy capacity saw significant growth, driven in part by UDAY's alignment with Renewable Purchase Obligations (RPOs) and preferential tariffs.
- 2020: By this year, UDAY had successfully achieved significant milestones in debt takeover and financial restructuring of DISCOMs, along with substantial reductions in AT&C losses.
- Ongoing: Challenges persist, including the need for sustained reforms to ensure the long-term sustainability of DISCOMs' financial health and further enhance renewable energy integration.

This timeline outlines the key events and developments in the case study, highlighting the transformation of India's energy landscape through UDAY and the ongoing efforts to address challenges in the sector.

This case study explores the challenges faced by India's energy sector, the inception and key components of UDAY, its transformative impact on the power distribution sector, and its crucial role in accelerating India's renewable energy transition. It highlights the synergy between financial restructuring, operational improvements, and renewable energy integration, showcasing how a holistic approach can pave the way for a greener, more sustainable energy landscape. Key Components are:

1. Financial Restructuring: UDAY allowed state governments to take over 75% of the outstanding debt of DISCOMs, reducing their interest burden.
2. Operational Efficiency: The scheme emphasized measures such as reducing AT&C losses, improving metering, and implementing energy-efficient practices.
3. Tariff Rationalization: UDAY aimed to ensure tariff hikes to bridge the gap between the cost of power and revenue generated.

CASE QUESTIONS

1. What were the primary challenges faced by India's energy sector before the introduction of Ujwal DISCOM Assurance Yojana (UDAY), and how did these challenges hinder the transition to renewable energy sources?
2. Describe the key objectives and components of UDAY. How did UDAY aim to address the financial and operational issues of power distribution companies (DISCOMs)?
3. Explain how UDAY's financial restructuring component contributed to the improvement of DISCOMs' financial health. What impact did this have on the integration of renewable energy in India?
4. Discuss the role of UDAY in reducing aggregate technical and commercial (AT&C) losses in India's power distribution sector. How did this reduction create a more favorable environment for renewable energy integration?

5. How did UDAY align with India's renewable energy aspirations, and what regulatory measures were put in place to encourage DISCOMs to procure renewable energy?
6. Examine the technological advancements incentivized by UDAY in the power distribution sector. How did these advancements promote efficient renewable energy integration and reduce power losses?
7. Evaluate the environmental and economic impacts of UDAY's integration of renewable energy sources. How did this integration contribute to environmental sustainability and economic growth in India?

CRITICAL ANALYSIS

Positive Aspects

Financial Restructuring Success: UDAY's debt takeover was successful in improving the financial health of DISCOMs. By reducing their interest burden and providing financial support, it enabled DISCOMs to invest in renewable energy projects, contributing to India's renewable energy goals.

Reduction in AT&C Losses: UDAY's emphasis on reducing AT&C losses was effective in creating a more efficient distribution system. This reduction not only improved the financial sustainability of DISCOMs but also created an environment conducive to renewable energy integration.

Alignment with Renewable Energy Goals: The policy framework aligned with UDAY, including Renewable Purchase Obligations (RPOs) and preferential tariffs, encouraged DISCOMs to procure renewable energy. This alignment helped India make significant progress toward its renewable energy targets.

Environmental and Economic Benefits: The integration of renewable energy sources due to UDAY resulted in substantial environmental benefits, including reduced carbon emissions and fossil fuel consumption. Additionally, the policy created employment opportunities in the renewable energy sector, promoting economic growth.

Areas of Concern

Challenges in Implementation: UDAY faced initial resistance from DISCOMs and required significant political will and collaboration with state governments for successful implementation. The case study does not provide a detailed analysis of how these challenges were overcome.

Long-term Viability: While UDAY improved DISCOMs' financial health in the short term, there may be concerns about the long-term sustainability of these improvements. A critical analysis should address the potential for future financial challenges and the need for continued reforms.

Data and Metrics: The case study lacks specific data and metrics to quantify the impact of UDAY on renewable energy integration and DISCOM financial health. Real-time data on renewable energy capacity, AT&C losses, and financial performance would provide a more comprehensive analysis.

Social and Political Factors: The case study does not delve into the social and political factors that influenced UDAY's success. Understanding the role of public perception, political support, and public-private partnerships would enhance the analysis.

Technological Advancements: While the case mentions technological advancements, it does not provide specific examples or data on their impact. A more detailed analysis of how these technologies improved efficiency and reduced losses would be valuable.

Impact on Renewable Energy Transition

Improved Financial Health: UDAY's debt takeover relieved DISCOMs of their financial burdens, enabling them to invest in renewable energy projects, which were previously unfeasible.

Reduction in AT&C Losses: UDAY's focus on loss reduction created a conducive environment for renewable energy integration by improving the efficiency of the distribution system.

Regulatory Support: The policy framework aligned with UDAY, including Renewable Purchase Obligations (RPOs) and preferential tariffs, encouraged DISCOMs to procure renewable energy.

Technological Advancements: UDAY incentivized DISCOMs to adopt advanced technologies like smart meters and grid management systems, promoting efficient renewable energy integration and reducing power losses.

Environmental and Economic Impact

Environmental Impact: The integration of renewable energy sources due to UDAY significantly reduced carbon emissions and fossil fuel consumption, contributing to a cleaner environment and enhanced energy security.

Economic Benefits: UDAY created employment opportunities in the renewable energy sector, boosting economic growth and improving the financial viability of DISCOMs.

Challenges Overcome

UDAY faced initial challenges, including resistance from DISCOMs, the need for regulatory reforms, and the political will to implement the scheme. However, persistent efforts and collaboration with state governments helped overcome these hurdles.

Future Outlook

As India continues to set ambitious renewable energy targets, UDAY's legacy will continue to play a pivotal role in fostering sustainable economic growth and environmental stewardship. The case study illustrates how comprehensive reforms in the power distribution sector can serve as a powerful catalyst for renewable energy adoption. The UDAY case study highlights the positive impact of the policy on DISCOMs' financial health and its alignment with India's renewable energy goals.

However, a critical analysis should consider challenges in implementation, long-term viability, data and metrics, social and political factors, and technological advancements to provide a more comprehensive assessment of UDAY's effectiveness in transforming India's energy landscape. Real-time data and specific metrics would further strengthen the analysis.

FINDINGS FROM THE CASE STUDY

1. **Improved Financial Health of DISCOMs:** UDAY's debt takeover and financial restructuring significantly improved the financial health of DISCOMs by reducing their interest burdens and overall debt levels. This improvement enabled DISCOMs to invest in infrastructure upgrades, including renewable energy projects.
2. **Reduction in AT&C Losses:** UDAY's emphasis on reducing aggregate technical and commercial (AT&C) losses led to operational improvements in the distribution sector. These reductions not only enhanced the financial sustainability of DISCOMs but also created a more conducive environment for the integration of renewable energy sources.
3. **Alignment with Renewable Energy Goals:** UDAY's policy framework aligned with India's renewable energy objectives. The inclusion of Renewable Purchase Obligations (RPOs) and preferential tariffs encouraged DISCOMs to procure renewable energy, helping India progress significantly toward its renewable energy targets.
4. **Environmental Benefits:** The integration of renewable energy sources into the grid as a result of UDAY led to substantial environmental benefits. These benefits included reduced carbon emissions and decreased dependence on fossil fuels, contributing to a cleaner environment and climate change mitigation.
5. **Economic Growth:** UDAY's impact extended beyond the energy sector. The policy created employment opportunities in the renewable energy sector, boosting economic growth and improving the overall employment landscape.
6. **Challenges Overcome:** The case study highlights the challenges faced during the implementation of UDAY, such as initial resistance from DISCOMs and the need for regulatory reforms. It underscores the importance of persistent efforts and collaboration with state governments in overcoming these hurdles.
7. **Technological Advancements:** While not extensively detailed in the case study, technological advancements were incentivized by UDAY. These advancements included the adoption of smart meters and grid management systems, which promoted efficiency and reduced power losses.
8. **Long-Term Sustainability:** Although not explicitly addressed in the case study, the long-term sustainability of DISCOMs' financial health and the continued reduction in AT&C losses are critical factors that would influence the lasting impact of UDAY on India's energy landscape.

These findings collectively demonstrate how UDAY, through its financial restructuring, operational improvements, and alignment with renewable energy goals, has played a crucial role in transforming India's energy sector, making it more financially viable, efficient, and sustainable while contributing to the growth of renewable energy sources.

Suggestions for Pre-Reading Materials and Additional Sources of Information That Can Provide Context and Enhance Understanding of the Case Study

1. **Official Government Documents:** Access official documents, reports, and publications related to UDAY and India's renewable energy policies. These documents can provide detailed information and statistics:
   - Ujwal DISCOM Assurance Yojana (UDAY) official website.
   - Ministry of Power, Government of India reports and publications.
   - Ministry of New and Renewable Energy (MNRE) reports and policies.

2. **International Energy Agency (IEA) Reports:** IEA often publishes reports on India's energy sector and renewable energy transitions. These reports offer valuable insights into the broader context and international perspectives:
   - IEA's "India Energy Outlook."
3. **Academic Research:** Look for academic papers, articles, and studies that analyze UDAY's impact on India's energy landscape and renewable energy integration. Academic sources can provide in-depth analysis and data:
   - Search academic databases like Google Scholar or databases specific to energy and environmental studies.
4. **Case Studies and Articles:** Explore case studies and articles from reputable sources that examine similar energy transition initiatives in other countries. Comparing India's experiences with global best practices can provide valuable lessons:
   - Harvard Business Review articles on energy transitions.
   - Case studies from academic institutions or consulting firms.
5. **Renewable Energy and Energy Transition Books:** Read books on renewable energy and energy transition to gain a comprehensive understanding of the global context and the importance of such transitions:
   - "Renewable Energy: Power for a Sustainable Future" by Godfrey Boyle.
   - "Energy Transitions: History, Requirements, Prospects" by Vaclav Smil.
6. **Energy Policy Journals:** Browse through energy policy journals, such as Energy Policy and Renewable Energy, for articles and research related to India's energy transition and policies:
   - Energy Policy journal.
   - Renewable Energy journal.
7. **Government Reports on Renewable Energy:** Explore reports and publications by government agencies related to renewable energy in India:
   - Reports by the Central Electricity Regulatory Commission (CERC).
   - Reports by the National Institution for Transforming India (NITI Aayog).
8. **TED Talks and Podcasts:** Look for TED Talks and podcasts featuring experts discussing renewable energy, energy transitions, and sustainable development. These can provide accessible insights:
   - TED Talks on renewable energy.
   - Renewable energy-related podcasts.

CONCLUSION

In conclusion, the Ujwal DISCOM Assurance Yojana (UDAY) has played a pivotal role in transforming India's energy landscape, achieving significant milestones in renewable energy integration and power distribution sector reforms. The following facts summarize the key takeaways from this case study:

1. **Financial Resurgence of DISCOMs:** UDAY's debt takeover and financial restructuring reduced the interest burden on DISCOMs, allowing them to channel resources into infrastructure upgrades, including renewable energy projects. By 2020, UDAY had successfully led to the takeover of over 94% of the debt burden of DISCOMs, amounting to approximately ₹2.69 trillion (Source: Ministry of Power, Government of India).

2. **Reduction in AT&C Losses:** UDAY's focus on reducing AT&C losses led to operational efficiencies, cutting losses from approximately 21.34% in 2015 to around 17.52% in 2020 (Source: Power Finance Corporation, Government of India). This improvement not only bolstered the financial sustainability of DISCOMs but also facilitated the integration of renewable energy into the grid.
3. **Renewable Energy Capacity Growth:** As a result of UDAY's support, India's renewable energy capacity witnessed remarkable growth. By 2020, India had achieved over 89 GW of installed renewable energy capacity, including solar, wind, and biomass (Source: Ministry of New and Renewable Energy, Government of India).
4. **Environmental Impact:** The integration of renewable energy sources, facilitated by UDAY, led to significant environmental benefits. India's carbon emissions were reduced, and the country's dependence on fossil fuels declined, aligning with global climate change mitigation efforts.
5. **Alignment with Renewable Energy Goals:** UDAY's policy framework aligned with India's renewable energy objectives. It incorporated Renewable Purchase Obligations (RPOs) and preferential tariffs, driving DISCOMs to procure renewable energy and contributing to India's progress toward its renewable energy targets.
6. **Technological Advancements:** UDAY incentivized the adoption of advanced technologies like smart meters and grid management systems. These technologies improved operational efficiency and reduced power losses.
7. **Economic Growth and Employment Opportunities:** The integration of renewable energy sources generated employment opportunities, promoting economic growth. The renewable energy sector became a significant contributor to job creation.

While UDAY has achieved notable successes in India's energy sector, it is crucial to acknowledge that challenges remain, including the long-term sustainability of DISCOMs' financial health and the need for continued reforms. The case study illustrates that comprehensive reforms in the power distribution sector, coupled with a commitment to renewable energy integration, can serve as a powerful catalyst for achieving a greener, more sustainable energy future.

TEACHING OBJECTIVES

1. **Understanding the Energy Sector Challenges:**

To introduce students to the challenges faced by India's energy sector, including financial distress among power distribution companies (DISCOMs), high aggregate technical and commercial (AT&C) losses, and the need for sustainable energy solutions.

2. **Analyzing UDAY's Objectives and Components:**

To examine the key objectives of UDAY and its components, including financial restructuring, operational efficiency improvements, and tariff rationalization, to gain a comprehensive understanding of the policy framework.

3. **Assessing Financial Restructuring:**

To evaluate how UDAY's financial restructuring component reduced the debt burden on DISCOMs and analyze the impact of this financial relief on the power distribution sector.

4. **Exploring Reduction in AT&C Losses:**

To understand how UDAY's focus on reducing AT&C losses led to operational improvements, decreased losses, and enhanced the efficiency of the distribution system.

5. **Investigating Renewable Energy Integration:**

To explore the role of UDAY in promoting renewable energy integration and understand how it aligned with India's renewable energy goals, including Renewable Purchase Obligations (RPOs) and preferential tariffs.

6. **Analyzing Environmental and Economic Impacts:**

To assess the environmental benefits of UDAY's renewable energy integration, such as reduced carbon emissions, and examine the economic impact, including job creation and economic growth.

7. **Discussing Implementation Challenges:**

To facilitate a discussion on the challenges encountered during the implementation of UDAY, including resistance from DISCOMs and the need for regulatory reforms, and how these challenges were overcome.

8. **Evaluating Technological Advancements:**

To analyze the technological advancements incentivized by UDAY, such as smart meters and grid management systems, and their role in improving operational efficiency.

9. **Reflecting on Long-Term Sustainability:**

To encourage critical thinking about the long-term sustainability of the improvements achieved through UDAY and the need for continued reforms in the power distribution sector.

10. **Drawing Broader Lessons:**

To facilitate a discussion on the broader lessons and implications of UDAY as a case study in energy sector reform and renewable energy integration, both within India and for other countries facing similar challenges.

TEACHING NOTES

Teaching Approach

This case study is designed to facilitate a comprehensive understanding of India's energy transition and the role of the Ujwal DISCOM Assurance Yojana (UDAY) in promoting renewable energy integration. It touches upon the challenges faced by India's energy sector, the objectives and components of UDAY, its impact on financial restructuring and AT&C loss reduction, and its alignment with renewable energy goals. The teaching approach should be interactive and engaging, encouraging critical thinking and discussion among students.

Teaching Strategy

1. **Introduction to the Case:**
    - Begin by introducing the case study and its relevance to India's energy landscape and global energy transitions.
    - Highlight the importance of understanding the challenges faced by India's energy sector and the role of policy interventions like UDAY.
2. **Pre-Reading Assignment:**
    - Assign pre-reading materials, including relevant reports, articles, and government documents, to provide students with background knowledge.
    - Encourage students to prepare questions or discussion points based on their pre-reading.
3. **Classroom Discussion:**
    - Engage students in a guided discussion by asking open-ended questions related to the case study.
    - Encourage students to share their insights and observations from the pre-reading materials.
    - Facilitate a discussion on the challenges faced by India's energy sector, including financial distress and high AT&C losses.
4. **Exploration of UDAY's Components:**
    - Dive into the key components of UDAY, including financial restructuring, operational efficiency improvements, and tariff rationalization.
    - Use case-related data and statistics (where available) to illustrate the impact of UDAY on DISCOMs' financial health and operational efficiency.
5. **Analysis of Renewable Energy Integration:**
    - Explore how UDAY aligned with India's renewable energy goals and promoted the integration of renewable energy sources.
    - Discuss the environmental and economic benefits of UDAY's renewable energy initiatives.
6. **Challenges and Solutions:**
    - Examine the challenges faced during the implementation of UDAY, such as resistance from DISCOMs and the need for regulatory reforms.
    - Encourage students to brainstorm potential solutions to these challenges.

7. **Technological Advancements:**
    - Analyze the technological advancements incentivized by UDAY, such as smart meters and grid management systems, and their impact on the distribution sector.
8. **Long-Term Sustainability:**
    - Foster a discussion on the long-term sustainability of the improvements achieved through UDAY and the importance of ongoing reforms in the power distribution sector.
9. **Broader Lessons and Implications:**
    - Encourage students to reflect on the broader lessons and implications of UDAY as a case study in energy sector reform and renewable energy integration.
    - Discuss how the experiences of India can offer insights to other countries facing similar energy challenges.
10. **Case Study Conclusion:**
    - Summarize the key findings and takeaways from the case study.
    - Emphasize the transformative role of UDAY in India's energy landscape.

Assessment

- Evaluate students' understanding of the case through assignments, quizzes, or class discussions.
- Assign research projects or presentations related to renewable energy policies in other countries, allowing students to draw comparisons with India's experiences.

Additional Resources

- Provide students with a list of additional resources, including academic papers, government reports, and articles, for further exploration of the topics discussed in the case study.

By following this teaching approach and strategy, educators can facilitate an engaging and informative learning experience for students, enabling them to grasp the complexities of energy transitions and the impact of policy interventions in real-world contexts.

TEACHING PLAN

Duration: 90 minutes
Audience: Undergraduate (UG) and Postgraduate (PG) students in relevant disciplines (e.g., Energy Studies, Environmental Science, Economics, Public Policy).
Objective: To provide UG and PG students with a comprehensive understanding of UDAY and its role in India's renewable energy transition through a mix of lectures, discussions, and group activities.

Materials Needed:

- Projector and screen for presentations.
- Handouts of key case study points.

- Whiteboard and markers.
- Laptop with internet access (for accessing online resources, if needed).

Teaching Plan: Introduction (10 minutes):

- Begin with a brief introduction to the topic and its relevance.
- Highlight the objectives of the session and the case study's importance in the context of India's energy transition.

Lecture on India's Energy Challenges (15 minutes):

- Present an overview of the challenges faced by India's energy sector, including financial distress among DISCOMs, high AT&C losses, and environmental concerns.
- Use statistics and facts to illustrate the severity of these challenges.

Interactive Discussion (15 minutes):

- Engage students in a discussion about the importance of addressing these challenges and the role of policy interventions.
- Encourage students to share their perspectives and experiences related to energy issues.

Lecture on UDAY (20 minutes):

- Provide an in-depth explanation of UDAY, its objectives, and key components.
- Use visuals, such as charts or graphs, to illustrate the impact of UDAY on DISCOMs' finances and operational efficiency.

Group Activity (15 minutes):

- Divide the class into small groups.
- Assign each group a specific component of UDAY (e.g., financial restructuring, AT&C loss reduction, renewable energy integration).
- Instruct groups to discuss and present the key points and outcomes related to their assigned component.

Discussion on Renewable Energy Integration (10 minutes):

- Facilitate a discussion on how UDAY aligned with India's renewable energy goals.
- Encourage students to reflect on the environmental and economic benefits of renewable energy integration.

Case Study Analysis (10 minutes):

- Distribute handouts summarizing the key findings and takeaways from the case study.
- Invite students to ask questions or seek clarification on specific points.

Critical Thinking Exercise (5 minutes):

- Present a hypothetical energy policy scenario related to the case study and ask students to brainstorm potential solutions.
- Encourage creative thinking and problem-solving.

Conclusion and Q&A (5 minutes):

- Summarize the key points covered during the session.
- Open the floor for questions and answers to address any remaining doubts or inquiries.

Assignment (5 minutes):

- Announce an assignment related to the case study. For UG students, this could be a short essay or discussion post. For PG students, it could involve a more in-depth research project or presentation.

Wrap-up (5 minutes):

- Thank students for their participation and engagement.
- Provide information on additional resources for further exploration of the topic.

TARGET AUDIENCE

1. **Students Community**
    - **Undergraduate (UG) Students:** UG students pursuing degrees in disciplines related to energy, environmental science, economics, and public policy. They are looking to understand real-world applications of their coursework and explore career opportunities in the energy sector.
    - **Postgraduate (PG) Students:** PG students with a deeper academic and research interest in energy studies, sustainable development, and policy analysis. They seek in-depth knowledge and critical analysis of energy policies and their impact.
2. **Teaching and Academia**
    - **Educators and Lecturers:** Faculty members and instructors in universities and colleges who want to use this case study as part of their curriculum. They aim to educate and engage students in discussions about renewable energy policies and energy sector reforms.
    - **Academic Researchers:** Researchers interested in energy transitions, renewable energy policies, and their implications. They may use this case study as a reference for their research.
3. **Policymakers**
    - **Government Officials:** Policymakers at both the central and state levels in India who are involved in energy policy formulation. They seek insights into the effectiveness of policies like UDAY and its impact on energy transition.
    - **Policy Analysts:** Professionals and researchers in think tanks and policy analysis organizations who want to assess the outcomes and lessons learned from UDAY for designing effective energy policies.

4. **Indian Government**
   - **Energy Ministry and Regulatory Authorities:** Officials responsible for energy policy implementation, monitoring, and regulation in India. They are interested in understanding the success and challenges of UDAY to inform future policy decisions.
   - **Finance Ministry:** Officials responsible for budgetary and financial considerations related to energy sector reforms. They need to assess the fiscal impact of policies like UDAY.
5. **Societal Impact**
   - **General Public:** Citizens of India who want to understand the implications of energy sector reforms on their daily lives, including access to reliable electricity, environmental sustainability, and economic growth.
   - **Environmental Organizations:** NGOs and environmental advocacy groups interested in assessing the environmental benefits of renewable energy integration facilitated by UDAY.
   - **Energy Industry Stakeholders:** Businesses and investors in the energy sector who want to assess the impact of UDAY on market dynamics and opportunities in renewable energy.

DISCUSSION QUESTIONS

1. **Policy Objectives and Implementation:**
   - What were the primary objectives of Ujwal DISCOM Assurance Yojana (UDAY), and how were these objectives expected to address India's energy sector challenges?
   - What were the key components of UDAY, and how were they implemented to achieve the policy's objectives?
2. **Financial Restructuring and DISCOMs:**
   - How did UDAY's financial restructuring component relieve the financial burden on DISCOMs, and what impact did this have on their operations and investment decisions?
   - Can you identify specific examples of how DISCOMs utilized the financial relief provided by UDAY to invest in renewable energy projects?
3. **Reduction in AT&C Losses:**
   - Explain the significance of reducing aggregate technical and commercial (AT&C) losses in the context of India's energy sector. How did UDAY contribute to this reduction?
   - What strategies and initiatives were adopted by DISCOMs to achieve the goal of reducing AT&C losses, and were they effective?
4. **Alignment with Renewable Energy Goals:**
   - How did UDAY align with India's renewable energy goals, including Renewable Purchase Obligations (RPOs) and preferential tariffs for renewable energy procurement by DISCOMs?
   - What role did UDAY play in encouraging DISCOMs to procure renewable energy, and what were the outcomes of this alignment?
5. **Technological Advancements:**
   - Discuss the technological advancements incentivized by UDAY, such as smart meters and grid management systems. How did these technologies improve the efficiency of the distribution system and support renewable energy integration?

6. **Environmental and Economic Impact:**
    - Evaluate the environmental impact of UDAY's promotion of renewable energy integration. How did it contribute to reducing carbon emissions and dependence on fossil fuels?
    - Explore the economic benefits of renewable energy integration facilitated by UDAY, including job creation and economic growth.
7. **Challenges Faced and Solutions:**
    - What were the main challenges encountered during the implementation of UDAY, and how were they overcome?
    - Can you identify any ongoing challenges or issues that need to be addressed to sustain the benefits of UDAY?
8. **Long-Term Sustainability:**
    - Reflect on the long-term sustainability of the improvements achieved through UDAY, especially in terms of DISCOMs' financial health and AT&C loss reduction. What factors could influence their sustainability?
9. **Broader Lessons and International Comparisons:**
    - Discuss the broader lessons that can be drawn from the UDAY case study for energy sector reform and renewable energy integration in other countries.
    - Are there international examples of similar policies or initiatives that can be compared to UDAY?
10. **Future Outlook:**
    - What is the potential role of UDAY in India's future energy landscape, considering the country's ambitious renewable energy targets?
    - How can the experiences and outcomes of UDAY inform future energy policies and reforms in India and globally?

REFERENCES

Bajaj, S., & Sheoran, A. (2022). Spillover impact of debt takeover of electricity distribution utilities: Evidence from India's Ujwal discom assurance Yojana (Uday). SSRN *Electronic Journal*. doi:10.2139/ssrn.4090569

Bhardwaj, N., & Sharma, D. (2022, January 18). *Achieving financial sustainability through digitalization of the Indian power sector: Analysis of post UDAY performance of Rajasthan distribution companies.* Presented at the *2nd International Conference on Sustainability and Equity (ICSE-2021)*, Bhubaneswar, India. 10.2991/ahsseh.k.220105.015

Habeebur Rahman, T. (2020). *Prediction of electricity consumption and emission for india till 2050 using various forecasting techniques.* AC. https://shodhganga.inflibnet.ac.in/handle/10603/333987

Kristoff, M. M. (2019). *IEEFA India: Post-election, India must formalise energy reforms already long deliberated.* Policy Commons. https://policycommons.net/artifacts/2247234/ieefa-india/3005931/

Kristoff, M. M. (2020). *India's Power Distribution Sector Needs Further Reform - unshackling from the woes inflicting the sector.* Policy Commons. https://policycommons.net/artifacts/2249185/indias-power-distribution-sector-needs-further-reform/3007882/

Ministry of Power, Government of India. (2023). Ujwal DISCOM Assurance Yojana (UDAY). Ministry of Power. https://powermin.nic.in/en/content/ujwal-discom-assurance-yojana-uday and htttps://www.uday.gov.in/about.php

Sharma, S., Moerenhout, T., & Garg, V. (2018). *Electricity Sector Reform in Uttar Pradesh: Analysis of tariff adjustments and the Ujwal Discom Assurance Yojana Plan (UDAY)*. Policy Commons. https://policycommons.net/artifacts/614370/electricity-sector-reform-in-uttar-pradesh/1594618/

Singh, K., & Vashishtha, S. (2019). Empowering the power sector through UDAY: A study of Haryana. *ZENITH International Journal of Multidisciplinary Research, 9*(5), 1–7. https://mpra.ub.uni-muenchen.de/id/eprint/99266

Chapter 16
Green Jobs in Green Transformation Story

Buket Alkan
Fenerbahçe University, Turkey

ABSTRACT

Governments around the world are enacting green recovery and transition programs in collaboration with international agencies. Their coordinated efforts attempt to balance economic growth with environmental preservation, emphasizing that for a sustainable and green future the green transformation is an urgent requirement. The employment component of the green transformation has significant social and economic repercussions. Depending on how prepared countries are for the transition process, skill adaptation and the creation of new job opportunities can provide socioeconomic benefits. "Green jobs" are discussed in the chapter as an important part of the transition strategy to a green economy. The chapter outlines what a "green job" is and is not, presents the connection between employment and skills, and emphasizes the relevance of green jobs in the transition process.

1. INTRODUCTION

Human populations have been utilizing more natural resources than the earth can renewably produce on a global scale since at least the mid 1970s (McLellan et al., 2014). So called "ecological overshoot" occurs when human demand surpasses the regenerative capacity of a natural ecosystem. The ecological overshoot day for 2023 was set at August 2. The world does not have time to grow up irresponsibly and then clean up after itself. It must develop cleanly.

So, green growth isn't a challenge for tomorrow. It is an imperative for today. In fact, positive examples from early starters in the environmental transformation, especially in developed countries, demonstrate that a trade-off between growth and environmental agendas is not a must. It is possible for the economies while they are economically growing and the energy consumption has remained more or less constant and CO2 emissions have been reduced. Governments around the world are striving to establish policies to foster a green recovery and a green transition with the help of the institutions such as Organization

DOI: 10.4018/979-8-3693-1297-1.ch016

for Economic Cooperation and Development (OECD), World Bank (WB), Development Banks, World Trade Organization (WTO), International Labour Organization (ILO) etc.

There is a wealth of information available on green transition and sustainable development. The common feature of the studies is what they omit that the importance of providing employment to everybody in order to assure improving quality of life as a vital precondition for sustainable development (Mehmet, 1995). This was a statement of 1995. However, it is not possible to say that many things have changed. The job section of this literature is fairly tiny.

ILO's "Policy Brief on Methodologies for assessing green jobs" starts with this key question "What about jobs?". The question of whether to prioritize sustainable economic development initiatives, policymakers around the world frequently ponder this essential question. Let's pursue this question in this chapter of the book.

Chasing this question, the chapter discusses green jobs, as an important aspect of the transition mechanism to a green economy. The employment component of the green transformation has both social and economic implications. Depending on how prepared countries are for the transition process, skill adaptation and the creation of new professions can provide socioeconomic benefits.

In recent years, the concept of green jobs has received more attention from policymakers and researchers alike. Green skilled workers are required in the transition to a green economy.

The shock of covid-19 has profoundly impacted various processes in people's lives. Aside from having a significant influence on health, the pandemic process had an economic and social consequence. Employment is one of the most impacted aspects of the economy. The figures clearly demonstrate this. It has unquestionably paved the way for a fundamental revolution. Similarly, it is easy to see how the climate crisis has caused and will continue to cause such fundamental changes. However, because the climate change is not a sudden shock like Covid-19, its consequences are gradual, cumulative, and irreversible. We will be late unless we shape ourselves against this insidious structural change.

This chapter of the book focuses on the employment effect of green transition so the environmental regulation and of innovation. The adaptation of work activities to environmental criteria is so crucial than it seems. Main objectives of the chapter are to define what is and not the "green job", to explain why this issue is crucial for inclusive and sustainable growth, to present the connection between jobs and skills and importance of them in the transition process.

2. FROM THE EMPLOYMENT PERSPECTIVE: GREEN TRANSITION THAT LEAVES NO ONE BEHIND

It is critical for sustainable development to minimize our reliance on fossil-fuel-derived energy, which is the fundamental cause of climate change. The term "energy transition" refers to the global energy sector's shift away from fossil-based systems of energy production and consumption (oil, natural gas, and coal) and toward renewable energy sources (wind and solar, as well as lithium-ion batteries). This means signaling a chain change all at once. Production and consumption patterns, as well as working lives, are changing. Switching to the green economy, we are becoming acquainted with the term "*green jobs*". Green transition may only offer new job opportunities if the workforce is equipped with the relevant skills (*green skills*). As a result of the transition to a green economy, some new employment opportunities may be created while others will be eliminated, and some existing employees may be retrained to adapt to changing conditions (OECD/Cedefop, 2014). Adjusting training programs of the workers to ongoing and upcoming green changes is a transversal task.

The shift to a green economy is necessary for the fight against ecological crisis. However, our main priority should be a just and inclusive transition to a green economy. It would surely be acceptable to strive for carbon-zero output (production of services and goods) to make the transition to a green economy. But switching to a green economy does not guarantee growth that is both employment-rich and socially equitable. A structure should be put in place to ensure that everyone has access to green career possibilities.

In a macroeconomic perspective the effect of environmental policies on employment is a complex issue, and no clear-cut conclusion (Consolia et al., 2016). Some scholars believe it is either inefficient (Michaels and Murphy, 2009; Hughes, 2011) or harmful to jobs (Alvarez, 2009; Morriss et al., 2009). The professor Gabriel Calzada Álvarez states in a speech of him by referring their study of the effects on employment of public aid renewable energy resources, in 2009 that "for every 1 green job financed by Spanish taxpayers, 2.2 jobs were lost as an opportunity cost." However, on the other side there are hopeful perspectives based on the notion that policy has the capacity to stimulate the expansion of markets for labor-intensive environmental goods and services (Engel and Kammen, 2009; Selwyn and Leverett, 2006; UNEP, 2008).

The green transition will affect all populations in one way or other. It is also possible that the green transformation will lead to distribution problems. However, it should not be forgotten that distribution problems are always the result of political decisions. Some current jobs are likely to be lost as new, environmentally friendly ones are formed, but careful policy design will be required to prevent employees who leave their lost jobs. Therefore, the transition process needs to be designed very carefully.

Macroeconomic and growth policies, industrial and sectoral policies, business policies, talent development, occupational health and safety, social protection, and active labor market policies are the primary policy areas necessary to achieve green transformation (ILO, 2015). This should be accomplished by investing both publicly and privately in environmentally sustainable initiatives. The goal is to create green jobs across the supply chain in dynamic, high-value-added sectors, while also encouraging skill development and productivity in labor-intensive businesses. It is critical to promote sustainable development in all areas and to guarantee coordination among employment authorities and diverse sectors.

3. GREEN JOBS DEFINITIONS

"Definition" is the most crucial point! How should the term "green jobs" be defined? We can't measure where we are on the path if we can't define it well. It is critical for economies to adapt to greener jobs. Furthermore, green jobs need green skills. Hence, the adaptation of the workers' skills is suggested for a successful transition.

The body of research on green jobs that is now available can be divided into mainly two definitional approach: output, and process approaches (CEPS, 2023).

In the literature, the output technique is the most common. A green job, according to this method, is one that provides a product that is valuable to the environment or prevents harm to the environment while protecting natural resources. The output approach evaluates the amount of goods and services generated by aggregating them on a sectoral level, the Environmental Goods and Services Sector (EGSS).

The EGSS, according to Eurostat[1], is comprised of a diverse group of companies that produce goods and services that measure, control, restore, prevent, treat, minimize, and research environmental damages to air, water, and soil as well as issues with waste, noise, biodiversity, and landscapes. They also raise awareness of resource depletion. These goods and services must meet the end purpose criterion, which states that they must have resource management or environmental preservation as their main goals (Eurostat, 2009). However, such a sectoral strategy runs the risk of overlooking potentially 'green' jobs in other sectors that do not generally fall under the EGSS, such as education, healthcare, and retail (CEPS, 2023).

Other definitional approach is process approach. The process approach views jobs as green when work-related activities help make the organization's production processes more resource-efficient or ecologically sustainable (CEPS, 2023).

The ILO, in particular, has seen an increase in demand for statistical data on green jobs that would supplement existing labor market information at the international and country levels. The ILO has already made efforts to count the number of green jobs in various nations. This exercise revealed that the concept is exceedingly complex and that 1- a standard conceptual framework is required (*policy definition*); and 2- practical measurement aspects should not be neglected (*statistical definition*). As a result, we should define both the framework and the measurement.

3.1. Policy Definitions

Policy definition supports the countries to make their own policies and strategic plans. In general, there are two different policy definitions of "green jobs". One is according to ILO-UNEP (International Labour Organization- United Nations Environment Programme) and the other one according to ILO Green Jobs Programme (GJP). In 2008, the ILO and UNEP published a report entitled Green Jobs: Towards Decent Work in a Sustainable, Low-carbon World. Hence the first UN policy concept definition of green jobs came as follows (ILO, 2023):

"Green jobs are positions in agriculture, manufacturing, construction, installation, and maintenance, as well as scientific and technical, administrative, and service-related activities, that contribute substantially to preserving or restoring environmental quality. Specifically, but not exclusively, this includes jobs that help to protect and restore ecosystems and biodiversity; reduce energy, materials, and water consumption through high-efficiency and avoidance strategies; de-carbonize the economy; and minimize or altogether avoid generation of all forms of waste and pollution. But green jobs, also need to be good jobs that meet longstanding demands and goals of the labor movement, i.e., adequate wages, safe working conditions, and worker rights, including the right to organize labor unions (ILO and UNEP 2008, pp. 35–36)."

ILO– Green Jobs Programme (GJP) definition is as follows:

"Green jobs are decent jobs that contribute to preserve or restore the environment, be they in traditional sectors such as manufacturing and construction, or in new, emerging green sectors such as renewable energy and energy efficiency. Furthermore, green jobs help to improve energy and raw materials efficiency, to limit greenhouse gas emissions, to minimize waste and pollution, to protect and restore ecosystems and to support adaptation to the effects of climate change."

The policy definitions of "green jobs" are very important to understand the framework but they are not enough. Since, there should be some conflicts on the inclusion a job as green or not. For example, should driving a bus be considered a green job because it is more environmentally friendly than driving a car? Should a bus driver's job be called green only if the bus runs on biofuel (ILO, 2013a)? So, it needs also a statistical definition.

3.2. Statistical Definition

Because of the difficulty in estimating existing and potential job numbers, the influence of green transformation on employment is a somewhat avoided subject. Statistical definition is important for create comparable data both among countries and within a country among years. ILO presents some methodologies for assessing the green jobs in its Policy Brief report in 2013. There are mainly three types of methodologies for assessing the green jobs. Will it, for example, solely strive to quantify direct job creation (Employees of a geothermal energy plant) or will it also seek to quantify indirect and induced job creation (businesses that supply the computers and stationery for the plant)?

Inventory, Survey and Employment method that the questionnaire for the survey is distributed to relevant enterprises, government offices, or analysts, whereas an inventory typically draws on a national or regional database to offer employment statistics. Using this method is easy and it allows simple extrapolations for employment projection in the short-term. Furthermore, inventories and surveys, if conducted consistently over a long period of time, can also give a good indicator of the extent of new employment created by sustainable sectors.

Input-output analysis (I-O) and Social Accounting Matrices (SAMs) are empirical procedures that rely on the building of a matrix or table listing all subsectors in an economy and explaining how outputs from one sector are used as inputs in others. These models, which use data from national accounts, are the most extensively used tool for evaluating green jobs. While IO tables give a disaggregation of the production system and can highlight interactions within it, SAMs go a step further by describing the interdependence of income and transfer flows between different institutional units.

Computable General Equilibrium (CGE) models method that many of these models are based on IO analysis or SAMs, but they include extra assumptions to provide a more thorough, dynamic, and long-term examination of employment implications. These models enable policymakers to calculate the long-term effects of policies. Such CGE models include the OECD's Environmental Linkages Model and the Millennium Institute's Threshold21 (T21)model, which is used by UNEP's Green Economy effort.

3.3. Taxonomies for Green Jobs

The ILO developed three pillars as a derivative of the original definition by UNEP to evaluate whether jobs can be classified as green. The employment in the production of green products and services, employment in environmentally friendly processes, and decent jobs (see Figure 1). To be classified as green in this taxonomy, a job must benefit the environment while meeting the criteria for decent work. As a result, green jobs exist at the crossroads of employment in environmental outputs or employment in environmental processes and decent labor. An employment in waste management, for example, would be termed 'green' if social protection measures were available and health and safety at work were ensured (van der Ree, 2019).

Figure 1. ILO taxonomy for green jobs
(Adapted from: ILO, 2013b)

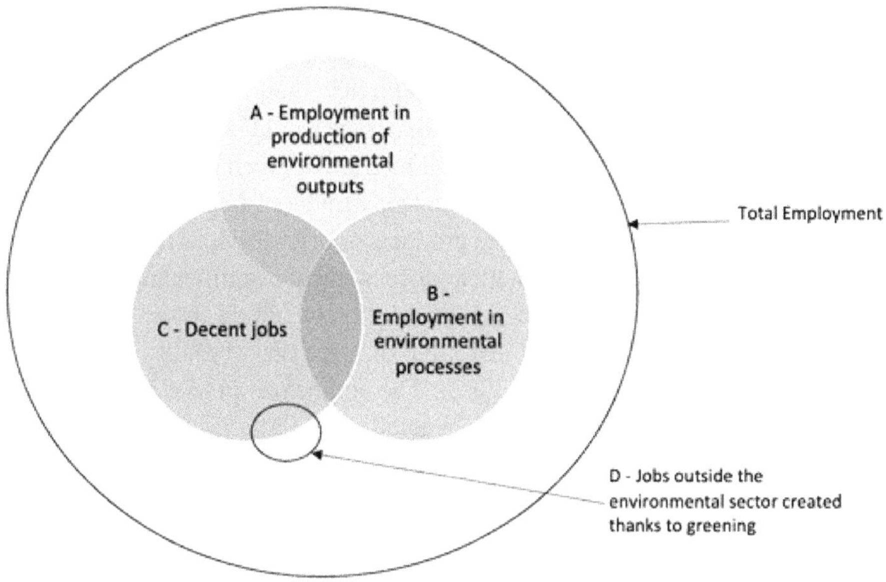

Employment in production of environmental outputs = A
Employment in environmental (friendly) processes = B
Decent jobs = C
Jobs outside the environmental sector created thanks to greening = D
Employment in the environmental sector = $A \cup B$
Employment created thanks to greening = $A \cup B \cup D$
Green jobs (employment in the environmental sector that is decent) = $(A \cup B) \cap C$
Is everything getting better now? I'm curious if it's now easier to settle on all of these definitions, measures, and constraints.

4. IS IT A GREEN OR BROWN JOB?

The brown job is the term generally used to emphasize jobs in the dominant economic structure before the development of the concept of green jobs. So, there is no specific definition for brown jobs, they only refer non-green jobs.

Measuring the greenness of a job is not an easy task. The beer is a product that consumes a lot of water in its production process. If a beer company intends to "cut the amount of water used to brew each hectoliter of beer by 25%." In addition, If the corporation intends to limit its use of fossil fuels and strive toward well-defined sustainability goals. When the plans come true, do you thing the workers of the company are now having a green job?

Furthermore, it is also difficult to decide a job is green or brown through the outputs. For example, a farmer producing corn for human consumption is not considered to be a green job by most classifications, but it becomes a green job if the corn is used to make ethanol[2] (Furchtgott-Roth, 2012).

Suppose that a job is defined as green. Another difficult task is calculating the "greenness" of the job. It is a continuous measurement of a job's greenness. It is not 0 (brown) or 1 (green), but some value in the interval. For example, an Electric Vehicle (EV) job can be categorized as green. However, besides EV cars for example Toyota or Mercedes also have other type production. In other words, even though these works are green on one side, they remain brown on the other.

Although assigning a ranking or classification to this issue would be difficult, every country/government has begun and should continue to include a road map about green jobs in its policy documents. For example, U.S.'s the Bureau of Labor Statistics at the Department of Labor (BLS), defines "green jobs" as they are either jobs in companies that produce products or offer services that benefit the environment or conserve natural resources, or jobs in which employees' responsibilities include reducing the use of natural resources or making their establishment's production processes more environmentally friendly. According to their definition BLS has compiled a list of more than 300 distinct industry clusters that can be classified as green (Furchtgott-Roth, 2012). The companies in that industry must achieve one of five objectives in order to be deemed "green," including (1) Energy from Renewable Sources, (2) Energy Efficiency, (3) Pollution Reduction and Removal, (4) Natural Resource Conservation, and (5) Environmental Compliance, Education, and Training and Public Awareness. Furthermore, there are a large number of "green jobs" and persons employed there can be considered "green workers". The BLS lists examples of jobs that persons in the relevant industries might hold in order to qualify as "green workers".

On the other hand, monitoring the transition from brown to green jobs is another aspect of the transformation. In general, while the number of employees shifting from brown jobs to green jobs remains small, the rate of transition from dirty to green jobs is rising rapidly (Curtis et al., 2023). The observed increase in this rate correlates to an increase in the number of available green jobs. If this trend continues, we can expect a significant number of people who are currently working in filthy jobs to switch to green jobs. However, officials must carefully plan the transition period. It is possible to establish how much of the skills/knowledge available in brown color works can be used in the transition to green color works. By examining the Economic Complexity literature (Hidalgo & Hausmann, 2009), the skills/knowledge set proximity of brown occupations to green ones may be proven on a sectoral level, and a strategy plan can be constructed in this context.

4.1. While Greening the Economy What About the Skills?

While jobs are turning green, skills must adapt to this change; yet, there will be no skills gap in this situation.

The empirical studies show that green jobs have a higher intensity of high-level cognitive skills than brown jobs. Furthermore, occupations that are changing qualitatively, that is, in terms of skill content, have more formal education, more work experience, and more on-the-job training than non-green employment (Consolia et al., 2016).

Green skills include (i) technical knowledge and abilities that enable professionals to effectively use green technology and processes; and (ii) transversal skills, as well as knowledge, beliefs, and attitudes that assist people in making pro-environmental decisions in their work and lifestyles. These overall green abilities are already being implemented into training programs around the world (EFT, 2020).

However, the skill gap is becoming a big issue as the demand for employees who can install and service heat pumps, solar panels, electric vehicle batteries, or chargers grows (TSKB, 2023). Let us not forget that the green transformation would necessitate more employment in particular industries that will play a key role in the transformation. It will be too late to build abilities for this once we face this reality. Developing skills is a policy and time issue. As a result of the necessity to be front-loaded, it should be included in policy documents as soon as possible.

In the report of World Economic Forum (WEF) a phrase was defined "unmet need" which is a gap between the green jobs in most economies today and the number of green jobs that could help countries achieve inclusion and emissions-reduction aspirations in 2030 (WEF, 2023). The report calculated this gap for 10 countries[3] and each of the ten countries need an increase in the number of green jobs. Totals of 10 countries result is seen in Figure 2.

Figure 2. Unmet needs according to sectors
(Adapted from: World Economic Forum)

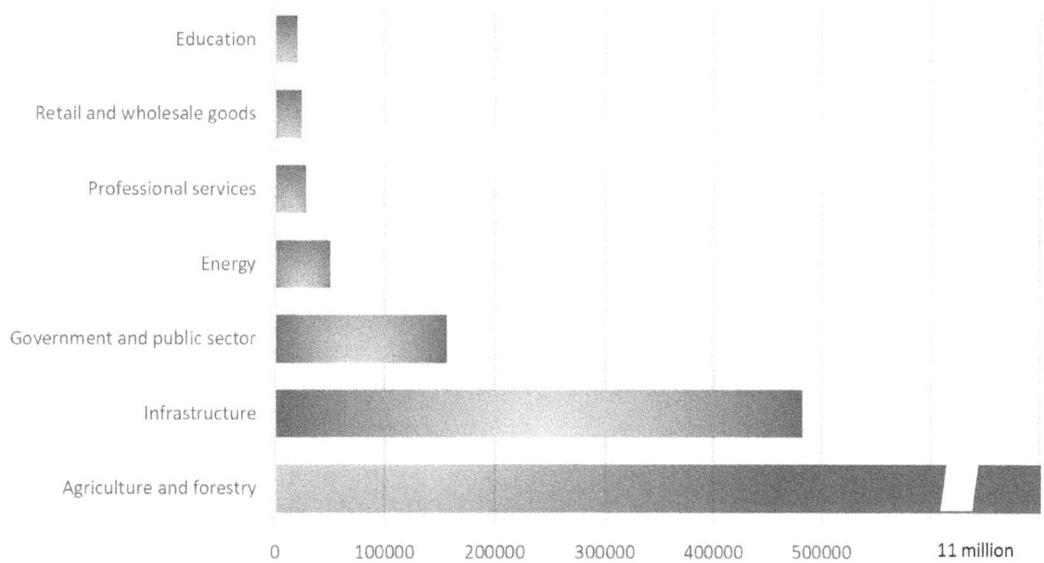

Green structural change is most likely to have a negative impact on high-carbon emitting sectors. Mining, fossil-fuel-based energy generation, industry, forestry, and agriculture are examples. Workers transitioning from declining to expanding industries may need to retrain (ILO, 2011).

Of course, the mining sector will be one of the most affected by the energy transition, which is the foundation of the green transformation. Green technologies, clean coal, and carbon capture and storage are all examples of changes that necessitate major skill upgrades. However, it is undeniable that the agriculture sector is one of the areas that must be made more ecologically friendly. In 2018, agriculture and related land use emissions accounted for 17 percent of global greenhouse gas (GHG) emissions from all sectors (FAO, 2020). Reducing emissions will necessitate the adoption of sustainable agriculture practices, which will necessitate the acquisition of new skills.

5. CONCLUSION

Even what is discussed in this section demonstrates the need of focusing on "green jobs" in terms of securing and sustaining the transition to a green economy and its justice.

Different estimations and scenarios yield differing perspectives on the medium- to long-term employment consequences of green restructuring, however most believe that the net effect will be beneficial.

Significant regulatory reforms and emissions targets are likely to result in industry reorganization and downsizing in emissions-intensive sectors.

It is important for local policymakers to understand which jobs or sectors most likely to become green and as soon as possible should become green. Which brown industries (skills) are how much far away from being green. It should be assessed which business lines are vanishing and what potential business lines exist. In this aspect, skill sets must be modified. It should not be overlooked that access to green jobs is critical for a just transition to a green economy, and that this is also a policy design issue.

REFERENCES

Alvarez, G. C. (2009). *Testimony Before the House Select Committee on Energy Independence and Global Warming*.

CEPS. (2023). *Jobs for Green Transition: Definitions*. Classifications and Emerging Trends.

Consolia, D., Marinb, G., Marzucchie, A., & Vona, F. (2016). Do green jobs differ from non-green jobs in terms of skills and human capital? *Research Policy*, *45*(5), 1046–1060. doi:10.1016/j.respol.2016.02.007

Curtis, E., O'Kane, L., & Park, R. (2023). *Workers and The Green-Energy Transition: Evidence from 300 Million Job Transition*. NATIONAL BUREAU OF ECONOMIC RESEARCH. doi:10.3386/w31539

Engel, D., & Kammen, D. M. (2009) Green Jobs and the Clean Energy Economy. In *Proceedings of the 2009 UN Climate Change Conference (COP15)*, Copenhagen, Denmark, 7–18 December 2009; pp. 160–171.

European Training Foundation (2020) ETF Policy Briefing: Skilling for the Green Transition.

Eurostat. (2009). *The environmental goods and services sector*. Luxembourg: Office for Official Publications of the European Communities.

FAO. (2020). Emissions due to agriculture. Global, regional and country trends 2000–2018. FAOSTAT Analytical Brief Series No 18. Rome.

Furchtgott-Roth, D. (2012). *Green Jobs in the U.S. Economy*. Manhattan Institute for Policy Research.

Hidalgo, C., & Hausmann, R. (2009). The Building Blocks of Economic Complexity. *Proceedings of the National Academy of Sciences of the United States of America*, *106*(26), 10570–10575. doi:10.1073/pnas.0900943106 PMID:19549871

Hughes, G. 2011. The myth of green jobs, Report No.3. London: The Global Warming Foundation

ILO, & UNEP. (2008). *Green Jobs: Towards Decent Work in a Sustainable, Low-carbon World.* ILO.

ILO. (2011). *Skills for Employment-Policy Brief.* Greening the Global Economy-The Skills Challenge.

ILO. (2013a). Methodologies for assessing green jobs. *Policy Brief.*

ILO. (2013b). *19th International Conference of Labour Statisticians.* Geneva: ILO.

ILO. (2015). *Guidelines for a just transition towards environmentally sustainable economies and societies for all.*

ILO. (2023). *Green jobs, green economy, just transition and related concepts: A review of definitions developed through intergovernmental processes and international organizations.* ILO.

Kees van der Ree. (2019). *Promoting Green Jobs: Decent Work in the Transition to Low-Carbon.* Green Economies, International Development Policy.

McLellan, R., Iyengar, L., Jeffries, B., & Oerlemans, N. (2014). Living [Species and Spaces, People and Places. Gland: WWF International.]. *The Planetary Report*, 2014.

Mehmet, O. (1995). Employment creation and green development strategy. *Ecological Economics, 15*(1), 11–19. doi:10.1016/0921-8009(95)00035-8

Michaels, R., & Murphy, R. P. (2009). *Green jobs: fact or fiction?* Institute for Energy Research.

Morriss A. P., Bogart W. T. & Meiners R. E., (2009) 7 Myths About Green Jobs.

OECD/Cedefop. (2014). *Greener Skills and Jobs, OECD Green Growth Studies.* OECD Publishing.

Selwyn, J., & Leverett, (2006). Emerging Markets in the Environmental Industries Sector, The UK Centre for Economic and Environmental Development.

TSKB. (2023). Climate Review, Issue No.12, July-September, 2023. İstanbul.

World Economic Forum. (2023). *Jobs of Tomorrow: Social and Green Jobs for Building Inclusive and Sustainable Economies.* WEF.

ENDNOTES

1 See the handbook on EGSS https://ec.europa.eu/eurostat/web/products-manuals-and-guidelines/-/ks-ra-09-012

2 Ethanol is a renewable energy source. Corn-based ethanol contributes to *reduces* greenhouse gas emissions.

3 Australia, Brazil, China, Germany, India, Japan, South Africa, Spain, the United Kingdom and the United States.

APPENDIX

ILO: International Labour Organization
GJP: Green Jobs Programme
OECD: Organization for Economic Co-operation and Development
UNEP: United Nations Environment Programme
WB: World Bank
EGSS: Environmental Goods and Services Sector
BLS: Bureau of Labor Statistics
SAMs: Social Accounting Matrices
I-O: Input – Output
CGE: Computable General Equilibrium
EV: Electric Vehicle
WEF: World Economic Forum
GHG: Greenhouse gas
WTO: World Trade Organization
ETF: European Training Foundation
FAO: Food and Agriculture Organization of the United Nations

Compilation of References

AA. (2022). *Avrupa Birliği 2022'de savaş, enerji krizi ve enflasyonun etkileriyle mücadele etti (European Union grapples with effects of war, energy crisis and inflation in 2022)*. Terhaber. https://www.trthaber.com/haber/dunya/avrupa-birligi-2022de-savas-enerji-krizi-ve-enflasyonun-etkileriyle-mucadele-etti-732611.html

AA. (2023). *COVID-19, salgın ilan edilişinin 3. yılında da "küresel acil durum" olarak nitelendiriliyor (COVID-19 is described as a "global emergency" in the 3rd year since it was declared an epidemic)*. Terhaber. https://www.trthaber.com/haber/dunya/covid-19-salgin-ilan-edilisinin-3-yilinda-da-kuresel-acil-durum-olarak-nitelendiriliyor-752265.html

ABAS. 2021. Águas Subterrâneas O que são? Available at <https://www.abas.org/aguas-subterraneas-o-que-sao/>. 27 July, 2021.

Acheampong, A. O., Adams, S., & Boateng, E. (2019). Do globalization and renewable energy contribute to carbon emissions mitigation in Sub-Saharan Africa? *The Science of the Total Environment*, *677*, 436–446. doi:10.1016/j.scitotenv.2019.04.353 PMID:31059886

Acheampong, A. O., & Dzator, J. (2020). Managing environmental quality: does institutional quality matter? In C. M. Hussain (Ed.), *Handbook of environmental materials management* (pp. 1–24). Springer. doi:10.1007/978-3-319-58538-3_215-1

Adams, S., Boateng, E., & Acheampong, A. O. (2020). Transport energy consumption and environmental quality: Does urbanisation matter? *The Science of the Total Environment*, *744*, 140617. doi:10.1016/j.scitotenv.2020.140617 PMID:32712414

Agbiboa, D. E., Mignouna, H. D., & Diallo, M. (2019). The "waste" perspective on social enterprise in Africa: The Wecyclers example. In T. Koh & G. M. Idowu (Eds.), *Social Responsibility and Sustainability in Africa* (pp. 221–243). Springer.

Ahmed, S. F., Rafa, N., Mehnaz, T., Ahmed, B., Islam, N., Mofijur, M., Hoang, A. T., & Shafiullah, G. M. (2022, September). Integration of phase change materials in improving the performance of heating, cooling, and clean energy storage systems: An overview. *Journal of Cleaner Production*, *364*, 132639. doi:10.1016/j.jclepro.2022.132639

Ajmi, A. N., Hammoudeh, S., Nguyen, D. K., & Sato, J. R. (2015). On the relationships between CO2 emissions, energy consumption and income: The importance of time variation. *Energy Economics*, *49*, 629–638. doi:10.1016/j.eneco.2015.02.007

Akadiri, S. S., Alola, A. A., Akadiri, A. C., & Alola, U. V. (2019). Renewable energy consumption in EU-28 countries: Policy toward pollution mitigation and economic sustainability. *Energy Policy*, *132*, 803–810. doi:10.1016/j.enpol.2019.06.040

Akhmat, G., Zaman, K., Shukui, T., Sajjad, F., Khan, M. A., & Khan, M. Z. (2014). The challenges of reducing greenhouse gas emissions and air pollution through energy sources: Evidence from a panel of developed countries. *Environmental Science and Pollution Research International*, *21*(12), 7425–7435. doi:10.100711356-014-2693-2 PMID:24584642

Ali, H. S., Zeqiraj, V., Lin, W. L., Law, S. H., Yusop, Z., Bare, U A A., & Chin, L. (2019). Does quality institutions promote environmental quality? *Environmental Science and Pollution Research International*, *26*(11), 10446–10456. doi:10.100711356-019-04670-9 PMID:30891699

Alkhathlan, K., & Javid, M. (2013). Energy consumption, carbon emissions and economic growth in Saudi Arabia: An aggregate and disaggregate analysis. *Energy Policy*, *62*, 1525–1532. doi:10.1016/j.enpol.2013.07.068

Al-Shetwi, A. Q. (2022). Sustainable development of renewable energy integrated power sector: Trends, environmental impacts, and recent challenges. *The Science of the Total Environment*, *822*, 153645. doi:10.1016/j.scitotenv.2022.153645 PMID:35124039

Altun, T., & Tarhan, M. (2022). *2023'te dünyayı Rusya-Ukrayna krizinin etkileri ve enerji krizi riski bekliyor (The effects of the Russia-Ukraine crisis and the risk of energy crisis await the world in 2023)*. AA. https://www.aa.com.tr/tr/ekonomi/2023te-dunyayi-rusya-ukrayna-krizinin-etkileri-ve-enerji-krizi-riski-bekliyor/2776757

Alvarez, G. C. (2009). *Testimony Before the House Select Committee on Energy Independence and Global Warming*.

Andrei, J. V., Mieila, M., & Panait, M. (2017). The impact and determinants of the energy paradigm on economic growth in European Union. *PLoS One*, *12*(3), e0173282. doi:10.1371/journal.pone.0173282 PMID:28301505

An, M., Xie, P., He, W., Wang, B., Huang, J., & Khanal, R. (2022). Spatiotemporal change of ecologic environmental quality and human interaction factors in three gorges ecologic economic corridor, based on RSEI. *Ecological Indicators*, *141*, 109090. doi:10.1016/j.ecolind.2022.109090

Anselin, L. (1988). *Spatial econometrics: Methods and models*. Kluwer Academic. doi:10.1007/978-94-015-7799-1

Anselin, L. (1995). Local indicators of spatial association-LISA. *Geographical Analysis*, *2*(2), 93–115. doi:10.1111/j.1538-4632.1995.tb00338.x

Apergis, N., Aye, G. C., Barros, C. P., Gupta, R., & Wanke, P. (2015). Energy efficiency of selected OECD countries: A slacks based model with undesirable outputs. *Energy Economics*, *51*, 45–53. doi:10.1016/j.eneco.2015.05.022

Arief, A. Y. (2004). *Poverty and Environmental Degradation: Searching for Theoretical Linkages*. (Working Paper in Economics and Development Studies). Equitable Policy. http://www.equitablepolicy.org/

Arimura, T. H., & Matsumoto, S. (2020). *Carbon Pricing in Japan*. Springer. https://link.springer.com/book/10.1007/978-981-15-6964-7

Aruna, P., & Sunil, D. B. (2020). Factors affecting the competitive capability of small and medium women entrepreneurs. *International Journal of Advanced Science and Technology*, *29*(5), 574–584.

Asafu-Adjaye, J. (2000). Environmental Economics for Non-Economists. World Scientific Publishing Co. Pte. Ltd. Singapore.

Asafu-Adjaye, J. (2000). The Relationship Between Energy Consumption, Energy Prices and Economic Growth: Time Series Evidence From Asian Developing Countries. *Energy Economics*, *22*(6), 615–625. doi:10.1016/S0140-9883(00)00050-5

Atal Innovation Mission, (n.d). *About AIM*. AIM. https://aim.gov.in/

Ather Energy. (n.d.) Wikipedia, Retrieved from https://en.wikipedia.org/wiki/Ather_Energy Ather Energy

Axsen, J., & Kurani, K. S. (2013). Social influence in the global diffusion of alternative fuel vehicles: A meta-analysis. *Journal of Transport Geography*, *31*, 94–103.

Aydın, K., Yıldırım, S., & Çizer, E. Ö. (2023). Big dilemma in face mask consumption: Environmental sensitivity versus the fear of COVID-19 [IJGW]. *International Journal of Global Warming*, *29*(3), 207–226. doi:10.1504/IJGW.2023.129490

Ayres, R. (1997). Comments on Georgescu-Roegen. *Ecological Economics*, *22*(3), 285–287. doi:10.1016/S0921-8009(97)00082-7

Ayres, R. (2000). Commentary on the Utility of the Ecological Footprint Concept. *Ecological Economics*, *32*, 347–349.

Ayres, R. U., Van Den Berg, J. C. J. M., Lindenberger, D., & Warr, B. (2013). The Underestimated Contribution of Energy to Economic Growth. *Structural Change and Economic Dynamics*, *27*, 79–88. doi:10.1016/j.strueco.2013.07.004

Ayunisari, M. K. (2022). *Home*. Video. [Youtube.] https://d1wqtxts1xzle7.cloudfront.net/61020782/UN-DESA__20UNCTAD_20Transition_20GE20191025-7038-1yz04en-with-cover-page-v2.pdf?Expires=1669460288&Signature=LP6jRRpaX2ELVcf-jKZ0qOs6ZmjQo9s0B211~6nV5jnsuScrXsTbS1QhQ~QewQ8sw7KiobHCm0aNLv5O-2EZcQq~xRiOZXFVJvty. Accessed 26 November 2022.

Azam, M., Khan, A. Q., Zafeiriou, E., & Arabatzis, G. (2016). Socio-economic determinants of energy consumption: An empirical survey for Greece. *Renewable & Sustainable Energy Reviews*, *57*, 1556–1567. doi:10.1016/j.rser.2015.12.082

Bäckstrand, K., Khan, J., Kronsell, A., & Lövbrand, E. (2010). *Environmental politics and deliberative democracy: Examining the promise of new modes of governance*. Edward Elgar Publishing. doi:10.4337/9781849806411

Bajaj, S., & Sheoran, A. (2022). Spillover impact of debt takeover of electricity distribution utilities: Evidence from India's Ujwal discom assurance Yojana (Uday). SSRN *Electronic Journal*. doi:10.2139/ssrn.4090569

Baldwin, R. (1995). Does sustainability require growth? In I. Goldin & L. Alan Winters (Eds.), *Economics Of Sustainable Growth* (pp. 51–77). Cambridge University Press.

Bansal, P. (2005). Evolving sustainably: A longitudinal study of corporate sustainable development. *Strategic Management Journal*, *26*(3), 197–218. doi:10.1002mj.441

Bappenas. (2014). *Model Ekonomi Hijau Provinsi Kalimantan Tengah (KT-GEM) Model Ekonomi Hijau Provinsi Kalimantan Tengah (KT-GEM)*. Bappenas.

Bappenas. (2021). A GREEN ECONOMY FOR A NET-ZERO FUTURE: How Indonesia can build back better after COVID-19 with the Low Carbon Development Initiative (LCDI). In *Ministry of National Development Planning, 12*(4).

Baranzelli, C., Lavalle, C., Sgobbi, A., Aurambout, J. P., Trombetti, M., & Jacobs-Crisioni, C. (2016) *Regional patterns of energy production and consumption factors in Europe*. [EUR 27697] Exploratory Project EREBILAND2016. . doi:10.2788/357099

Barbault, R. (2011). *Ecologia Geral: estrutura e funcionamento da biosfera*. Vozes.

Barkley, P. W., & David, W. S. (1972). *Economic Growth and Environmental Decay: The Solution Becomes The Problem*. Harcourt Brace Jovanovich.

Bartelmus, P. (2008). *Quantitative Eco-nomics: How Sustainable Are Our Economies?* Springer. doi:10.1007/978-1-4020-6966-6

Batista, T., Torre, S., Fermoso, J., Morais, N., Avila, R., Pinto Gomes, C., Castanho, R.A. and Cabezas, J. (2022). Nature-Based Solutions for Climate Change Adaptation in Scholar and Social Buildings: Concepts and Pilot Solutions for Portugal and Spain. *INTECH Book: Urban Green Spaces*. Intech Open. doi:10.5772/intechopen.105701

Baudrillard, J. (2021) *Tüketim Toplumu Ayrıntı.* Yayınları İstanbul

Bauman, Z. (2017). *Azınlığın Zenginliği Hepimizin Çıkarına mıdır?* Ayrıntı Yayınları İstanbul.

Bayhaqi, A. (2019). Ketidakpastian Dalam Pemodelan Perubahan Iklim. *Oseana, 44*(1), 38–53. doi:10.14203/oseana.2019.Vol.44No.1.30

Becchetti, L., Castriota, S., & Pelligra, V. (2020). Social cooperatives, a niche or a viable model for future food provision? Evidence from Italy. *Sustainability, 12*(19), 8066.

Beckerman, W. (1992a). *Economic Development and the Environment — Conflict or Complementarity?* (Working Paper No. 961). World Bank.

Beckerman, W. (1992b). Economic Growth and the Environment: Whose Growth? Whose Environment? *World Development, 20*(4), 481–496. doi:10.1016/0305-750X(92)90038-W

Belaid, F. (2017). Untangling the complexity of the direct and indirect determinants of the residential energy consumption in France: Quantitative analysis using a structural equation modelling approach. *Energy Policy, 110*, 246–256. doi:10.1016/j.enpol.2017.08.027

Benjamin Anabaraonye, O. J. (2019, April). Green Entrepreneurial Opportunities in Climate Change Adaptation and Mitigation for Sustainable Development in Nigeria. *Journal of Environmental Pollution and Management, 2*(1), 1–6.

Bhardwaj, N., & Sharma, D. (2022, January 18). *Achieving financial sustainability through digitalization of the Indian power sector: Analysis of post UDAY performance of Rajasthan distribution companies*. Presented at the *2nd International Conference on Sustainability and Equity (ICSE-2021)*, Bhubaneswar, India. 10.2991/ahsseh.k.220105.015

Bhattacharya, M., Churchill, S. A., & Paramati, S. R. (2017). The dynamic impact of renewable energy and institutions on economic output and CO_2 emissions across regions. *Renewable Energy, 111*, 157–167. doi:10.1016/j.renene.2017.03.102

Bhuiyan, M. A., Zhang, Q., Khare, V., Mikhaylov, A., Pintér, G., & Huang, X. (2022). Renewable Energy Consumption and Economic Growth Nexus—A Systematic Literature Review. *Frontiers in Environmental Science, 10*, 878394. doi:10.3389/fenvs.2022.878394

Bina, O. (2013). *Home*. Video. [Youtube.] https://journals.sagepub.com/doi/epdf/10.1068/c1310j..

Bin-Nashwan, S.A., Hassan, M.K. & Muneeza, A. (2022), Russia–Ukraine conflict: 2030 Agenda for SDGs hangs in the balance. *International Journal of Ethics and Systems*. doi:10.1108/IJOES-06-2022-0136

Blazquez, L., Boogen, N., & Filippini, N. (2013). Residential electricity demand in Spain: New empirical evidence using aggregate data. *Energy Economics, 36*, 648–657. doi:10.1016/j.eneco.2012.11.010

Bombardi, L. M. (2021). *Geography of Asymmetry: the vicious cycle of pesticides and colonialism in the commercial relationship between Mercosur and the European Union*. Commissioned by The Left group in the European Parliament. https://left.eu/events/eu-mercosur-the-vicious-circle-of-pesticides/

Bombardi, L. M. (2016). *Pequeno ensaio cartográfico sobre o uso de agrotóxicos no Brasil*. Laboratório de Geografia Agrária da USP.

Borozan, D. (2018). Regional-level household energy consumption determinants: The European perspective. *Renewable & Sustainable Energy Reviews, 90*, 347–355. doi:10.1016/j.rser.2018.03.038

Boyce, J. K. (2018). Carbon Pricing: Effectiveness and Equity. *Ecological Economics, 150*(November 2017), 52–61. doi:10.1016/j.ecolecon.2018.03.030

Bozlağan, R. (2005). Sürdürülebilir Gelişme Düşüncesinin Tarihsel Arka Planı. *Sosyal Siyaset Konferansları Dergisi*, (50), 1012–1028.

Brandl, J., & Zielinska, I. (2020). Reviewing the smart city Vienna framework strategy's potential as an eco-social policy in the context of quality of work and socio-ecological transformation. *Sustainability (Basel)*, *12*(3), 1–17. doi:10.3390u12030859

Braun, V., & Clarke, V. (2006). Using thematic analysis in psychology. *Qualitative Research in Psychology*, *3*(2), 77–101. doi:10.1191/1478088706qp063oa

Breiman, L. (1996). Bagging predictors. *Machine Learning*, *24*(2), 123–140. doi:10.1007/BF00058655

Breiman, L. (2001). Random forests. *Machine Learning*, *45*(1), 5–32. doi:10.1023/A:1010933404324

Broad, R. (1994). The Poor and Environment: Friends or Foes? *World Development*, *22*(6), 811–822. doi:10.1016/0305-750X(94)90055-8

Bruton, G. D., Ahlstrom, D., & Li, H.-L. (2010). Institutional theory and entrepreneurship: Where are we now and where do we need to move in the future? *Entrepreneurship Theory and Practice*, *34*(3), 421–440. doi:10.1111/j.1540-6520.2010.00390.x

Bryceson, D. F., & Jonsson, J. B. (2019). Can Social Enterprises Create Sustainable Livelihoods in Sub-Saharan Africa? Evidence from Zambia. *Sustainability*, *11*(19), 5305.

Bull, M. (2007). Fair Trade labeling: The globalization of social entrepreneurship. In *Social entrepreneurship* (pp. 121–135). Palgrave Macmillan.

Burton, E. (2000). The compact city: Just or just compact? A preliminary analysis. *Urban Studies (Edinburgh, Scotland)*, *37*(11), 1969–2006. doi:10.1080/00420980050162184

Busch, T., Bassen, A., Lewandowski, S., & Sump, F. (2020). Corporate Carbon and Financial Performance Revisited. *Organization & Environment*. doi:10.1177/1086026620935638

Butler, R. (2011). Tourism area life cycle: Applications and modifications. In Tourism Area Life Cycle, Concepts and Applications (pp. 13-32). Channel View Publications.

Buy hemp products in India. (n.d.). BOHECO. https://boheco.com/

Byrne, J. (2017). The economics of solar power. In *Handbook of Clean Energy Systems* (pp. 1–24). Wiley.

Calcagno, A. (2001). *Identificação de áreas para a execução de programas e ações piloto e definição de termos de referência. Atividade 09 do Projeto Aquífero Guarani*. ANA.

Canh, N. P., Schinckıs, C., Thanh, S. D., & Chong, F. H. L. (2021). The determinants of the energy consumption: A shadow economy-based perspective. *Energy*, *225*, 120210. doi:10.1016/j.energy.2021.120210

Canuto, T. G. (2010). Estimativa do risco potencial de contaminação por pesticidas de águas superficiais e subterrâneas do município de Tianguá-CE, com aplicação do método de Goss e índice de Gus. *Anais XVI Congresso Brasileiro de águas subterrâneas e XVII Encontro Nacional de Perfuradores de Poços*, São Luís, Maranhão.

Carattini, S., Carvalho, M., & Fankhauser, S. (2018). Overcoming public resistance to carbon taxes. *Wiley Interdisciplinary Reviews: Climate Change*, *9*(5), 1–26. doi:10.1002/wcc.531 PMID:31031823

Carneiro, F. F., Rigotto, R., Augusto, L., Friedrich, K., & Búrigo, A. (2015). *(Org.). Dossiê ABRASCO: um alerta sobre os impactos dos agrotóxicos na saúde. Rio de Janeiro: EPSJV*. Expressão Popular.

Carson, R. (1962). *Silent spring*. Houghton Mifflin.

Carter, C. R., & Liane Easton, P. (2011). Sustainable supply chain management: Evolution and future directions. *International Journal of Physical Distribution & Logistics Management*, *41*(1), 46–62. doi:10.1108/09600031111101420

Cassar, A., Healy, A., & Von Kessler, C. (2017). Trust, risk, and time preferences after a natural disaster: Experimental evidence from Thailand. *World Development*, *94*, 90–105. doi:10.1016/j.worlddev.2016.12.042

Castanho, R. A. (2017).*Sustainable Urban Planning in Transboundary Areas: Analysis of Critical Factors for Territorial Success* [Doctoral Thesis, Universityof Extremadura (UEx)].

Castanho, R. A. (2021). *Handbook of Research on Sustainable Development Goals, Climate Change, and Digitalization*. IGI Global. doi:10.4018/978-1-7998-8482-8

CEEW. (2021, December 15). *India's journey towards 500 GW: Reaching the capacity and investment targets*. CEEW. https://www.ceew.in/events/indias-journey-towards-500-gw-reaching-capacity-and-investment-targets

Central Pollution control board. (n.d). *Waste Management.* CPCB. https://cpcb.nic.in/rules/

CEPS. (2023). *Jobs for Green Transition: Definitions*. Classifications and Emerging Trends.

Chandan, R. R., Soni, S., Raj, A., Veeraiah, V., Dhabliya, D., Pramanik, S., & Gupta, A. (2023). Genetic Algorithm and Machine Learning. In Advanced Bioinspiration Methods for Healthcare Standards, Policies, and Reform. IGI Global. doi:10.4018/978-1-6684-5656-9

Chandel, S. S., & Agarwal, T. (2017). Review of current state of research on energy storage, toxicity, health hazards and commercialization of phase changing materials. Renewable and Sustainable Energy Reviews, 67. Elsevier Ltd17. doi:10.1016/j.rser.2016.09.070

Chen, C., Pınar, M., & Stengos, T. (2021). Determinants of renewable energy consumption: Importance of democratic institutions. *Renewable Energy*, *179*, 75–83. doi:10.1016/j.renene.2021.07.030

Chiu, Y. J., & Wuepper, D. (2021). Harnessing clean energy for all: Social enterprises in off-grid renewable energy. *Energy Policy*, *149*, 112111.

Chopra, M., Singh, S. K., Gupta, A., Aggarwal, K., Gupta, B. B., & Colace, F. (2022). Analysis & prognosis of sustainable development goals using big data-based approach during COVID-19 pandemic. *Sustainable Technology and Entrepreneurship*, *1*(2), 100012. doi:10.1016/j.stae.2022.100012

Christoff, P. (1996). Ecological Modernisation, Ecological Modernities. *Environmental Politics*, *5*(3), 476–500. doi:10.1080/09644019608414283

Cohen, B. (2019). *Social and sustainable enterprise: Changing the nature of business*. Routledge.

Cohen, B., & Winn, M. I. (2007). Market imperfections, opportunity and sustainable entrepreneurship. *Journal of Business Venturing*, *22*(1), 29–49. doi:10.1016/j.jbusvent.2004.12.001

Cohen, D., & Hattatoğlu, D. (2000). *Dünyanın zenginliği, ulusların fakirliği*. İletişim Yayıncılık.

Colander, D. C. (1993). *Microeconomics*. Irwin Publishes.

Coldwellsolar, (n.d.). *Causes, Effects, and Solutions to the Global Energy Crisis*. Coldwellsolar. https://coldwellsolar.com/commercial-solar-blog/causes-effects-and-solutions-to-the-global-energy-crisis/

Cole, M. A. (1999). Limits to Growth, Sustainable Development and Environmental Kuznets Curves: An Examination of the Environmental Impact of Economic Development. *Sustainable Development (Bradford)*, *7*(2), 87–97. doi:10.1002/(SICI)1099-1719(199905)7:2<87::AID-SD102>3.0.CO;2-5

Collins, P. (2021). Sustainable development: Definition, objectives and examples. *Climate Selectra*. https://climate.selectra.com/en/environment/sustainable-development.

Common, M., & Stagl, S. (2005). *Ecological Economics: An Introduction*. Cambridge University Press. doi:10.1017/CBO9780511805547

Consolia, D., Marinb, G., Marzucchie, A., & Vona, F. (2016). Do green jobs differ from non-green jobs in terms of skills and human capital? *Research Policy*, *45*(5), 1046–1060. doi:10.1016/j.respol.2016.02.007

Copeland, B. R., & Taylor, M. S. (2004). Trade, growth, and the environment. *Journal of Economic Literature*, *42*(1), 7–71. doi:10.1257/.42.1.7

Costanza, R., Cumberland, J., Daly, H., Goodland, R., & Noorgard, R. (1997). *An Introduction to Ecological Economics. St. Lucie Press*. Florida e ISEE International Society for Ecological Economics. doi:10.1201/9781003040842

Crespo, A., Velázquez, J., Herráez, F., Gülçin, D., Ugur O'zcan, A., Hernando, A., & Castanho, R. A. (2023). Territorial planning of rustic land constructions and their adaptation to climate change in the province of Málaga, Spain. *Land Use Policy*, *129*, 106644. doi:10.1016/j.landusepol.2023.106644

Creswell, J. W., & Miller, D. L. (2000). Determining validity in qualitative inquiry. *Theory into Practice*, *39*(3), 124–130. doi:10.120715430421tip3903_2

Cristina Martinez-Fernandez, C. H. (2010). *Green jobs and skills:the local labour market implications of addressing climate change*. OECD. www.oecd.org/dataoecd/54/43/44683169.pdf?contentId=44683170

Curtis, E., O'Kane, L., & Park, R. (2023). *Workers and The Green-Energy Transition: Evidence from 300 Million Job Transition*. NATIONAL BUREAU OF ECONOMIC RESEARCH. doi:10.3386/w31539

Czech, B. (2009). *Ecological Economics*. Center for the Advancement of Steady State Economy. http://steadystate.org/wp-content/uploads/Czech_ Ecological_Economics.pdf

Da Silva, L. M., Bitencourt, C. C., Faccin, K., & Iakovleva, T. (2019). The role of Stakeholders in the context of Responsible Innovation: A Meta-Synthesis. *Sustainability (Basel)*, *11*(6), 1766. doi:10.3390u11061766

Daberkow, S. G., & McBride, W. D. (2010). Farm and operator characteristics affecting the awareness and adoption of precision agriculture technologies in the US. *Precision Agriculture*, *11*(4), 335–350.

Daly, H. (1990). Towards Some Operational Principles of Sustainable Development. *Ecological Economics*, *2*(1), 1–6. doi:10.1016/0921-8009(90)90010-R

Daly, H. (2007). *Ecological Economics and Sustainable Development: Selected Essays of Herman Daly*. Edward Elgar. doi:10.4337/9781847206947

Daly, H. E., & Farley, J. (2004). *Ecological Economics: Principles and Applications*. Island Press.

Dangelico, R. M., & Pujari, D. (2010). Mainstreaming green product innovation: Why and how companies integrate environmental sustainability. *Journal of Business Ethics*, *95*(3), 471–486. doi:10.100710551-010-0434-0

De Araujo, G. T., Ribeiro, L. C., & Fernandes, A. M. (2020). Innovation processes in social enterprises for sustainable development: A multiple case study in Brazil. *Sustainability*, *12*(17), 7086.

Demir, Y. (2023). Türkiye'de Yenilenebilir Enerji Tüketimi Ekonomik Büyümeye Katkı Sağlar mı? *Doğuş Üniversitesi Dergisi*, *24*(2), 271–281. doi:10.31671/doujournal.1209964

Demuth, A. (2014). Green Entrepreneurship: A promising path towards a sustainable future in Tunisia and elsewhere. *Internationale Zusammenarbeit (GIZ) GmbH*, 4-51.

Departmental news. (2022). *Report: COVID-19 slows progress towards universal energy Access*. WHO. https://www.who.int/news/item/01-06-2022-report--covid-19-slows-progress-towards-universal-energy-access

Development, S. A. (2017). Skills for Green Entrepreneurship Training Mannual. Swiszerland: Swiss Academy for Development.

Dhamodaran, S., Ahamad, S., Ramesh, J. V. N., Sathappan, S., Namdev, A., Kanse, R. R., & Pramanik, S. (2023). *Fire Detection System Utilizing an Aggregate Technique in UAV and Cloud Computing, Thrust Technologies' Effect on Image Processing*. IGI Global.

Dietz, S., & Neumayer, E. (2007). Weak and Strong Sustainability in the SEEA: Concepts and Measurements. *Ecological Economics*, *61*(4), 617–626. doi:10.1016/j.ecolecon.2006.09.007

Dietz, T. E. A. R., & York, R. (2007). Driving the Human Ecological Footprint. *Frontiers in Ecology and the Environment*, *5*(1), 13–18. doi:10.1890/1540-9295(2007)5[13:DTHEF]2.0.CO;2

Dijkstra, L., & Poelman, H. (2010). A *revised urban-ruraltypology. In: Feldmann B, Önnerfors A (Eds) Eurostatregional yearbook 2010* (pp. 239–253). Publications Office of the European Union, Luxembourg. https://www.researchgate.net/publication/254266928_Downscaling_

Dijkstra, L., Garcilazo, E., & McCann, P. (2013). The economic performance of European cities and city regions: Myths and realities. *European Planning Studies*, *21*(3), 334–354. doi:10.1080/09654313.2012.716245

Dijkstra, L., Garcilazo, E., & McCann, P. (2015). The effects of the global financial crises on European regions and cities. *Journal of Economic Geography*, *15*(5), 935–949. doi:10.1093/jeg/lbv032

Ding, W., Bonk, A., & Bauer, T. (2018). Corrosion behavior of metallic alloys in molten chloride salts for thermal energy storage in concentrated solar power plants: A review," Frontiers of Chemical Science and Engineering 2018 12:3, vol. 12, no. 3, pp. 564–576, Oct. 2018, . doi:10.1007/s11705-018-1720-0

Dogaru, L. (2021). Green Economy and Green Growth—Opportunities for Sustainable Development. *MDPI*. https://www.mdpi.com/2504-3900/63/1/70.

Doytch, N., & Klein, Y. L. (2018). The impact of natural disasters on energy consumption: An analysis of renewable and non-renewable energy demand in the residential and industrial sectors. *Environmental Progress & Sustainable Energy*, *37*(1), 37–45. doi:10.1002/ep.12640

Duflo, E. (2012). Women's empowerment and economic development. *Journal of Economic Literature*, *50*(4), 1051–1079. doi:10.1257/jel.50.4.1051

Duraiappah, A. (1996). *Poverty and Environmental Degradation: a Literature Review and Analysis*. (CREED Working Paper Series No: 8). CREED. http://www.ce.cmu. edu

Durán Sosa, R., Araya Ramírez, I., & Castanho, R. A. (2021). *Environmental Sanitation in Heredia: A Relevant Challenge in Costa Rica. Chapter #8 in the IGI GLOBAL Handbook of Research: Handbook of Research on Sustainable Development Goals*. Climate Change, and Digitalization., doi:10.4018/978-1-7998-8482-8.ch008

EC. (1999). *The Load Sharing Agreement is Found in the Annex of the Commission Communication to the Council and the European Parliament Preparing for the Application of the Kyoto Protocol COM230 Final of 19.05.1999.* Council and the European Parliament. https://ec.europa.eu/clima/sites/clima/files/ets/ docs/com_1999_230_en.pdf.

EC. (2022) *Energy efficiency targets.* EC. https://energy.ec.europa.eu/topics/energy-efficiency/energy-efficiency-targets-directive-and-rules/energy-efficiency-targets_en

Edwards, M. G. (2021). The growth paradox, sustainable development, and business strategy. *Business Strategy and the Environment*, *30*(7), 3079–3094. doi:10.1002/bse.2790

EEA. (2017). *Renewable energy in Europe-2017 update: Recent growth and knock-on effects. European Environment Agency Report no. 23/2017.* Publications Office of the European Union, Luxembourg.

EEA. (2022). *Total greenhouse gas achievement trends and projections in Europe.* EEA. https://www.eea.europa.eu/ims/total-greenhouse-gas-emission-trends.

Enders, W. (2009). *Applied econometric Time Series* (3rd ed.). Wiley.

Engel, D., & Kammen, D. M. (2009) Green Jobs and the Clean Energy Economy. In *Proceedings of the 2009 UN Climate Change Conference (COP15)*, Copenhagen, Denmark, 7–18 December 2009; pp. 160–171.

Engin, B. (2007). *Avrupa Birliği Özelinde Çevre Politikalarının Etkinliği.* İstanbul Üniversitesi Sosyal Bilimler Enstitüsü İktisat Ana Bilim Dalı. Yayımlanmamış Doktora Tezi.

Environmental Impact Assessment. (n.d.). *Biju's.* EIA. https://byjus.com/free-ias-prep/eia/

Ertürk, H. (1998). Çevre Bilimlerine Giriş (3. Baskı). Bursa:Vipaş Yayınları

Esseghir, A., & Khouni, L. H. (2014). Economic growth, energy consumption and sustainable development: The case of the Union for the Mediterranean countries. *Energy*, *71*, 218–225. doi:10.1016/j.energy.2014.04.050

Euronews, (2023). *Avrupa, Rusya'ya karşı enerji savaşını kazandı mı? [Has Europe won the energy war against Russia?].* Euronews. https://tr.euronews.com/2023/01/11/avrupada-rusyanin-ukrayna-isgaliyle-baslayan-enerji-krizi-sona-erdi-mi

European Commission (2022b) *Background.* Brussels. https://ec.europa.eu/eurostat/web/nuts/.

European Commission. (2023). *EU energy security and the war inUkraine: From sprint to marathon, BRIEFING.* European Commission. https://www.europarl.europa.eu/RegData/etudes/BRIE/2023/739362/EPRS_BRI(2023)739362_EN.p df

European Training Foundation (2020) ETF Policy Briefing: Skilling for the Green Transition.

Eurostat. (2009). *The environmental goods and services sector.* Luxembourg: Office for Official Publications of the European Communities.

Eurostat. (2022a). *Urban and rural living in the EU.* Brussels. https://ec.europa.eu/eurostat/web/products-eurostat-news/-/edn-20200207-1.

Eurostat. (2023). *Renewable energy statistics.* Brussels. https://ec.europa.eu/eurostat/statistics-explained/index.php?title=Renewable_energy_statistics

FAME scheme: What is it, and what's all the brouhaha? (2023, May 18). *ET Online.* https://economictimes.indiatimes.com/industry/renewables/fame-scheme-what-is-it-and-whats-all-the-brouhaha/articleshow/100325140.cms

Fan, Y., Liu, L. C., Wu, G., Tang, T. H., & Wei, Y. M. (2007). Changes in carbon intensity in China: Empirical findings from 1980-2003. *Ecological Economics*, *62*(3-4), 683–691. doi:10.1016/j.ecolecon.2006.08.016

Fan, Y., & Xia, Y. (2012). Exploring energy consumption and demand in China. *Energy*, *40*(1), 23–30. doi:10.1016/j.energy.2011.09.049

FAO. (2020). Emissions due to agriculture. Global, regional and country trends 2000–2018. FAOSTAT Analytical Brief Series No 18. Rome.

Farinelli, F., Bottini, M., Akkoyunlu, S., & Aerni, P. (2011). Green entrepreneurship: The missing link towards a greener economy. *Atdf Journal*, *8*(3/4), 42–48.

Feldman, D., Barbose, G., Margolis, R., Wiser, R., & Darghouth, N. (2013). *Photovoltaic system pricing trends: Historical, recent, and near-term projections* (2013 edition). Lawrence Berkeley National Laboratory.

Ferdian, D. (2021). *Mencermati Peluang dan Tantangan Pajak Karbon di Indonesia.* Www.Mongabay.Co.Id. https://www.mongabay.co.id/2021/07/24/mencermati-peluang-dan-tantangan-pajak-karbon-di-indonesia/

Fertner, C. (2012). Downscaling European urban-rural typologies. *Geografisk Tidskrift*, *112*(1), 77–83. doi:10.1080/00167223.2012.707805

Field, C. B. (Ed.). (2012). Managing the risks of extreme events and disasters to advance climate change adaptation: special report of the intergovernmental panel on climate change. Cambridge University Press, 555-564. doi:10.1017/CBO9781139177245

Filipovic, S., Verbic, M., & Radovanovic, M. (2015). Determinants of energy intensity in the European Union: A panel data analysis. *Energy*, *92*(3), 547–555. doi:10.1016/j.energy.2015.07.011

Finco, M. V. A. (2009). Poverty and Environment Linkages: A Vicious Circle Hypothesis Analysis in the Brazilian Amazon Region. *International Science Conference on the Human Dimensions of Global environmental Change*. Bonn.

Fisher-Vanden, K., Jefferson, G., Liu, H., & Tao, Q. (2004). What is driving China's decline in energy intensity? *Resource and Energy Economics*, *26*(1), 77–97. doi:10.1016/j.reseneeco.2003.07.002

Foody, G. M., & Arora, M. K. (1997). An evaluation of some factors affecting the accuracy of classification by an Artificial Neural Network. *International Journal of Remote Sensing*, *18*(4), 799–810. doi:10.1080/014311697218764

Franklin, A. L. (2020). Understanding stakeholder motivations. In Springer eBooks (pp. 65–96). doi:10.1007/978-3-030-47519-2_4

Friedman, B. (2005). *The Moral Consequences of Economic Growth*. Alfred A. Knopf.

Friedrich, K. (2021). *(org.). Dossiê contra o Pacote do Veneno e em defesa da Vida!* Rede Unida.

Friedrich, K. (2021). A systematic literature review concerning the different interpretations of the role of sustainability in project management. *Management Review Quarterly*, *73*(1), 31–60. doi:10.100711301-021-00230-z

Fuerst, F., Kavarnou, D., Singh, R., & Adan, H. (2020). Determinants of energy consumption and exposure to energy price risk: A UK study. *Immobilienökonomie*, *6*(1), 65–80. doi:10.136541056-019-00027-y

Furchtgott-Roth, D. (2012). *Green Jobs in the U.S. Economy*. Manhattan Institute for Policy Research.

GEC. (2020). The 5 Principles of Green Economy. *Green Economy Coalition*. https://www.greeneconomycoalition.org/news-and-resources/the-5-principles-of-green-economy.

Gibson, K. (2012). Stakeholders and Sustainability: An evolving theory. *Journal of Business Ethics*, *109*(1), 15–25. doi:10.100710551-012-1376-5

Gowdy, J. M. (2004). Toward a New Welfare foundation for Sustainability. *Ecological Economics*, *55*, 211–222.

Grigoriev, A. A. (1968). The theoretical fundaments of modern physical geography. In *The Interaction of Sciences in the Earth*. Moscou.

Grossman, G. M., & Helpman, E. (1994). Endogenous Innovation in the Theory of Growth. *The Journal of Economic Perspectives*, *8*(1), 23–44. doi:10.1257/jep.8.1.23

Grossman, M., & Krueger, A. B. (1995). Economic Growth and the Environment. *The Quarterly Journal of Economics*, *110*(2), 353–377. doi:10.2307/2118443

Gross, R., & Heptonstall, P. (2006). *The costs and impacts of intermittency: An assessment of the evidence on the costs and impacts of intermittent generation on the British electricity network*. UK Energy Research Centre.

Grover, N. (2023, May 21). *Prepp by collegedunia*. prepp.in. https://prepp.in/news/e-492-the-national-biodiversity-authority-nba-environment-notes

Güney, E. (2004). *Çevre Sorunları*. Ankara: Nobel yayıncılık.

Guo, M. (2020). Green Technology and Sustainable Development: Assessment and Green Growth Frameworks. *MDPI*. https://www.mdpi.com/2071-1050/12/16/6571.

Guo, H., Tan, J., Liao, S., & Liang, Z. (2021). Exploring the spatial aggregation and determinants of energy intensity in Guangdong province of China. *Journal of Cleaner Production*, *282*, 124367. doi:10.1016/j.jclepro.2020.124367

Gyamfi, S., Krumdieck, S., & Urmee, T. (2013). Residential peak electricity demand response–highlights of some behavioural issues. *Renewable & Sustainable Energy Reviews*, *25*, 71–77. doi:10.1016/j.rser.2013.04.006

Habeebur Rahman, T. (2020). *Prediction of electricity consumption and emission for india till 2050 using various forecasting techniques*. AC. https://shodhganga.inflibnet.ac.in/handle/10603/333987

Haber, T. R. T. (2023). *Rusya-Ukrayna Savaşı küresel ekonomiyi nasıl etkiledi? (How did the Russia-Ukraine War affect the global economy?)*. Terhaber. https://www.trthaber.com/haber/dunya/rusya-ukrayna-savasi-kuresel-ekonomiyi-nasil-etkiledi-752972.html

Hamilton, K. (1995). Sustainable Development, the Hartwick Rule and Optimal Growth. *Environmental and Resource Economics*, *5*(4), 393–411. doi:10.1007/BF00691576

Hamilton, N. (2016). The impact of open hiring on employers. *Journal of Occupational Rehabilitation*, *26*(2), 217–232.

Harris, M. (2000). *Basic Principles of Sustainable Development*. (Working Paper). Global Development and Environment Institute. https://notendur.hi.is/bdavids/UAU101/Readings/Harris_2000_Sustainable_development.pdf.

Hartwick, J. M. (1977). Intergenerational Equity and the Investing of Rents from Exhaustible Resources. *The American Economic Review*, *67*(5), 972–974.

Hartwick, J. M. (1978a). Substitution Among Exhaustible Resources and Intergenerational Equity. *The Review of Economic Studies*, *45*(2), 347–354. doi:10.2307/2297349

Hartwick, J. M. (1978b). Investing Returns From Depleting Renewable Resource Stocks and Intergenerational Equity. *Economics Letters*, *1*(1), 85–88. doi:10.1016/0165-1765(78)90102-7

Hassan, F., Jamil, F., Hussain, A., Ali, H. M., Janjua, M. M., Khushnood, S., Farhan, M., Altaf, K., Said, Z., & Li, C. (2022, February). Recent advancements in latent heat phase change materials and their applications for thermal energy storage and buildings: A state of the art review. *Sustainable Energy Technologies and Assessments*, *49*, 101646. doi:10.1016/j.seta.2021.101646

Hepburn, C. & Bowen, A. (2012). *Prosperity With Growth: Economic Growth, Climate Change and Environmental Limits*, (Working Paper No: 109). Centre For Climate Change Economics and Policy. http://www.lse.ac.uk/ GranthamInstitute/ wp-content/uploads/2014/02/WP93-prosperity-with-growth-climate-change.pdf

He, R., Baležentis, T., Štreimikienė, D., & Shen, Z. (2022). Sustainable green growth in developing economies: An empirical analysis on the belt and road countries. *Journal of Global Information Management*, *30*(6), 1–15. doi:10.4018/ JGIM.20221101.oa1

Hermann, B. G., & Oels, A. (2020). From waste to value—A systematic review on social business models for the circular economy. *Sustainability*, *12*(14), 5545.

Hermanto Sirait, Y. (2019). Komitmen Terkait Deforestasi Dan Perubahan Iklim: Perspektif Dari Doktrin Parens Patriae. *Jurnal Jatiswara*, *34*(1), 1. doi:10.29303/jatiswara.v34i1.196

Herremans, I. M., Nazari, J. A., & Mahmoudian, F. (2015). Stakeholder relationships, engagement, and sustainability reporting. *Journal of Business Ethics*, *138*(3), 417–435. doi:10.100710551-015-2634-0

Herrington, G. (2021). Update to limits to growth: Comparing the World3 model with empirical data. *Journal of Industrial Ecology*, *25*(3), 614–626. doi:10.1111/jiec.13084

Hidalgo, C., & Hausmann, R. (2009). The Building Blocks of Economic Complexity. *Proceedings of the National Academy of Sciences of the United States of America*, *106*(26), 10570–10575. doi:10.1073/pnas.0900943106 PMID:19549871

Hidayattuloh, M. H., Bambang, A. N., & Amirudin, A. (2020). The Green Economy Concept as Development Strategy of Cempaka Tourism Village toward Sustainable Tourism Development. *The Indonesian Journal of Planning and Development*, *5*(1), 30–37. doi:10.14710/ijpd.5.1.30-37

Hoang, A. T., Sandro Nižetić, Olcer, A. I., Ong, H. C., Chen, W.-H., Chong, C. T., Thomas, S., Bandh, S. A., & Nguyen, X. P. (2021, July). Impacts of COVID-19 pandemic on the global energy system and the shift progress to renewable energy: Opportunities, challenges, and policy implications. *Energy Policy*, *154*, 112322. doi:10.1016/j.enpol.2021.112322 PMID:34566236

Hockerts, K., & Wüstenhagen, R. (2010). Greening Goliaths versus emerging Davids—Theorizing about the role of incumbents and new entrants in sustainable entrepreneurship. *Journal of Business Venturing*, *25*(5), 481–492. doi:10.1016/j. jbusvent.2009.07.005

Hollmann, S., Regierer, B., Bechis, J., Tobin, L. T., & D'Elia, D. (2022). Ten simple rules on how to develop a stakeholder engagement plan. *PLoS Computational Biology*, *18*(10), e1010520. doi:10.1371/journal.pcbi.1010520 PMID:36227852

Huang, W.-H. (2015). The determinants of household electricity consumption in Taiwan: Evidence from quantile regression. *Energy*, *87*, 120–133. doi:10.1016/j.energy.2015.04.101

Hueting, R. (1991). Correcting National Income For Environmental Losses: A Practical Solution For A Theoretical Dilemma. In R. Costanza (Ed.), *Ecological Economics: The Science and Management of Sustainability*. Colombia University Pres.

Hughes, G. 2011. The myth of green jobs, Report No.3. London: The Global Warming Foundation

Hussen, A. M. (2004). *Principles of Environmental Economics* (2nd ed.). Routledge. doi:10.4324/9780203507421

Hu, W., & Fan, Y. (2020). City size and energy conservation: Do large cities in China consume more energy? *Energy Economics*, *92*, 104943. doi:10.1016/j.eneco.2020.104943

Hyman, D. N. (1999). *Public Finance: A Contemporary Application of Theory To Policy* (6th ed.). The Dryden Press.

İbrahim, M. H., & Law, S. H. (2016). Institutional quality and CO2 emission-trade relations: Evidence from sub-saharan Africa. *The South African Journal of Economics*, *84*(2), 323–340. doi:10.1111aje.12095

IEA. (2020). *Power systems in transition: Challenges and opportunities ahead for electricity security*. IEA. https://iea.blob.core.windows.net/assets/cd69028a-da78-4b47-b1bf-7520cdb20d70/Power_systems_in_transition.pdf

IEA. (n.d.). *Russia's War on Ukraine Analysing the impacts of Russia's invasion of Ukraine on global energy markets and international energy security*. IEA. https://www.iea.org/topics/russias-war-on-ukraine

ILO, & UNEP. (2008). *Green Jobs: Towards Decent Work in a Sustainable, Low-carbon World.* ILO.

ILO. (2011). *Skills for Employment-Policy Brief.* Greening the Global Economy-The Skills Challenge.

ILO. (2013a). Methodologies for assessing green jobs. *Policy Brief.*

ILO. (2013b). *19th International Conference of Labour Statisticians*. Geneva: ILO.

ILO. (2015). *Guidelines for a just transition towards environmentally sustainable economies and societies for all.*

ILO. (2023). *Green jobs, green economy, just transition and related concepts: A review of definitions developed through intergovernmental processes and international organizations*. ILO.

International Labour Organisation (ILO). (2022). *Promotion of Green Entrepreneurship for Youth.* ILO. https://www.ilo.org/wcmsp5/groups/public/---asia/---ro-bangkok/---ilo-colombo/documents/briefingnote/wcms_885924.pdf

International Organization for Standardization. (2006). *Environmental management - Life cycle assessment - Principles and framework*. ISO.

IRENA. (2023). *Renewable capacity statistics 2023*. International Renewable Energy Agency.

Ismael, L. L., & Rocha, E. M. R. (2019). Estimativa de contaminação de águas subterrâneas e superficiais por agrotóxicos em área sucroalcooleira, Santa Rita/PB, Brasil. *Ciencia & Saude Coletiva*, *24*(12), 4665–4675. doi:10.1590/1413-812320182412.27762017 PMID:31778516

Jackson, T. (2005). *Motivating sustainable consumption: A review of evidence of consumer behaviour and behavioural change. Sustainable Development Research Network*. DEFRA.

Jäger, J., Brutschin, E., Pianta, S., Omann, I., Kammerlander, M., Vishwanathan, S. S., Vrontisi, Z., MacDonald, J., & Van Ruijven, B. (2023). Stakeholder engagement and decarbonization pathways: Meeting the challenges of the COVID-19 pandemic. *Frontiers in sustainability, 3*. doi:10.3389/frsus.2022.1063719

Jamil, M. N. (2022). Critical analysis of energy consumption and its impact on countries economic growth: An empirical analysis base on countries income level. *J Environ Sci Econ*, *1*(2), 1–12. doi:10.56556/jescae.v1i2.11

Janicke, M., Binder, M., & Mönch, H. (1997). Dirty Industries: Patterns of Change in Industrial Countries. *Environmental and Resource Economics*, *9*(4), 467–491. doi:10.1007/BF02441762

Jenkins, T., & Simms, A. (2020). CHALLENGE PAPERS. *Stakeholder Forum.* https://stakeholderforum.org/wp-content/uploads/2020/06/PAPER-1_Green-Economy_Final_vj.pdf.

Jouzel, J. N. (2019). *Pesticides. Comment ignorer ce que l'on sait.* Paris: Les Presses de Sciences Po, coll. Gouvernances.

Kabeyi, M. J. B., & Olanrewaju, O. A. (2022). Sustainable energy transition for renewable and low carbon grid electricity generation and supply. *Frontiers in Energy Research*, *9*, 743114. doi:10.3389/fenrg.2021.743114

Kaiser, M., Bernauer, M., Sunstein, C. R., & Reisch, L. A. (2020). The power of green defaults: The impact of regional variation of opt-out tariffs on green energy demand in Germany. *Ecological Economics*, *174*, 106685. doi:10.1016/j.ecolecon.2020.106685

Kander, A., Malanima, P., & Warde, P. (2014). *Power to the people: energy in Europe over the last five centuries*. Princeton University Press.

Kasztelan, A. (2017). Green growth, green economy and sustainable development: Terminological and relational discourse. *Prague Economic Papers*, *26*(4), 487–499. doi:10.18267/j.pep.626

Kaushik, V. (2021). What is Green Economy? *Analytics Steps*. https://www.analyticssteps.com/blogs/what-green-economy.

Kees van der Ree. (2019). *Promoting Green Jobs: Decent Work in the Transition to Low-Carbon*. Green Economies, International Development Policy.

Khalili, S. J., & Yusoff, R. B. (2019). Role of social enterprises in waste management: An empirical investigation. *Resources, Conservation and Recycling*, *141*, 66–74.

Khan, H., Khan, I., & Binh, T. T. (2020). The heterogeneity of renewable energy consumption, carbon emission and financial development in the globe: A panel quantile regression approach. *Energy Reports*, *6*, 859–867. doi:10.1016/j.egyr.2020.04.002

Khastar, M., Aslani, A., & Nejati, M. (2020). How does carbon tax affect social welfare and emission reduction in Finland? *Energy Reports*, *6*, 736–744. doi:10.1016/j.egyr.2020.03.001

Khor, M. (2011). Risks and uses of the green economy concept in the context of sustainable development, poverty and equity. *EconStor*. https://www.econstor.eu/bitstream/10419/232158/1/south-centre-rp-040.pdf.

Khosla, R., Urmila, T., Gupta, T., Goyal, V., & Verma, A. (2018). Sarvajal: Water for all in Rural India. *Case Research Journal*, *38*(2), 140–162.

Kılıçay, İ. (2023). *Rusya-Ukrayna savaşı enerji piyasalarına nasıl yansıdı?(How did the Russia-Ukraine war affect the energy markets?)*. Bloomberght. https://www.bloomberght.com/rusya-ukrayna-savasi-enerji-piyasalarina-nasil-yansidi-2325960

Kirikkaleli, D., Castanho, R. A., Deniz Özbay, R., Yılmaz Genç, S., & Ahmed, Z. (2023). *Does Resource Efficiency Matter for Environmental Quality in Canada?* (Vol. 11). Front. Environ. Sci. Sec. Environmental Economics and Management. doi:10.3389/fenvs.2023.1276632

Klisberg, B. (2004). *Más ética más desarrollo*. Temas Grupo Editorial.

Kosec, K., & Mo, C. H. (2017). Aspirations and the role of social protection: Evidence from a natural disaster in rural Pakistan. *World Development*, *97*, 49–66. doi:10.1016/j.worlddev.2017.03.039

Kristoff, M. M. (2019). *IEEFA India: Post-election, India must formalise energy reforms already long deliberated*. Policy Commons. https://policycommons.net/artifacts/2247234/ieefa-india/3005931/

Kristoff, M. M. (2020). *India's Power Distribution Sector Needs Further Reform - unshackling from the woes inflicting the sector*. Policy Commons. https://policycommons.net/artifacts/2249185/indias-power-distribution-sector-needs-further-reform/3007882/

Kriström, B., & Riera, P. (1996). Is The Income Elasticity of Environmental Improvements Less Than One? *Environmental and Resource Economics*, *7*(1), 45–55. doi:10.1007/BF00420426

Krugman, P. (2010). Climate Change - Building a Green Economy. *NYTimes.com.* https://cobblab.eas.gatech.edu/energy/Readings/envEcon_krugman.pdf.

Kth. (2020). Global objectives for sustainable development. *KTH.* https://www.kth.se/en/om/miljo-hallbar-utveckling/utbildning-miljo-hallbar-utveckling/verktygslada/sustainable-development/fn-s-globala-mal-for-hallbar-utveckling-1.612059.

Kujala, J., Sachs, S., Leinonen, H., Heikkinen, A., & Laude, D. (2022). Stakeholder engagement: Past, present, and future. *Business & Society*, *61*(5), 1136–1196. doi:10.1177/00076503211066595

Kula, E. (1998). *History of Environmental Economic Thought.* Routledge.

Kumala, R., Ulpa, R., Rahayu, A., & Martinah. (2021). Pajak Karbon: Perbaiki Ekonomi dan Solusi Lindungi Bumi. *Prosiding Seminar Stiami, 8*(1), 66–73. https://ojs.stiami.ac.id/index.php/PS/article/view/1370

Kumar, A., Prakash, O., & Kaviti, A. K. (2017, September). A comprehensive review of Scheffler solar collector. *Renewable & Sustainable Energy Reviews*, *77*, 890–898. doi:10.1016/j.rser.2017.03.044

Labandeira, X., Labeaga, J.M., & Rodríguez, M. (2006). A residential energy demand system for Spain. *Energy, 27,* 87e112.

Larsen, J., Bojö, J., Larsson, J., & Lindgren, M. (2019). Business models for sustainable urban mobility: A literature review. *Sustainability*, •••, 11.

Lau, L. S., Choong, C. K., & Eng, Y. K. (2014). Carbon dioxide emission, institutional quality, and economic growth: Empirical evidence in Malaysia. *Renewable Energy*, *68*, 276–281. doi:10.1016/j.renene.2014.02.013

Lee, C.-C., Wang, C.-W., Ho, S.-J., & Wu, T.-P. (2021). The impact of natural disaster on energy consumption: International evidence. *Energy Economics*, *97*, 105021. doi:10.1016/j.eneco.2020.105021

Leff, E. (2009). *Saber Ambiental.* Editora Vozes.

Lennon, B., Dunphy, N., & Sanvicente, E. (2019). Community acceptability and the energy transition: A citizens' perspective. *Energy, Sustainability and Society*, *9*(1), 35. doi:10.118613705-019-0218-z

Leong, K. Y., Abdul Rahman, M. R., & Gurunathan, B. A. (2019, February). Nano-enhanced phase change materials: A review of thermo-physical properties, applications and challenges. *Journal of Energy Storage*, *21*, 18–31. doi:10.1016/j.est.2018.11.008

Leopold, A. (1996). *Equilibrio Ecológico: Almanaque de un condado arenoso*. Ediciones Gernika.

Lescano, J., Valdéz, L., Vegas, E., Reyes, C., & Belaúnde, M. (2013). *Manual del Desarrollo Sostenible*. Guevara Garay S.A. y Geo Lab SRL.

Lima, L. M. (2007). Simulação da movimentação de agrotóxicos no solo com o uso de geotecnologias, como instrumento para avaliação do potencial de risco de contaminação de águas subterrâneas na Amazônia Oriental. *Anais XIII Simpósio Brasileiro de Sensoriamento Remoto, Florianópolis*, (abril), 21–26.

Lima, R. O. (2019). *Agro(tech) ou agro(tóxico)? Sustentabilidade, riscos, futuras gerações e justiça ambiental* (1st ed.). Editora Multifoco.

Lin, B., & Li, X. (2011). The effect of carbon tax on per capita CO2 emissions. *Energy Policy*, *39*(9), 5137–5146. doi:10.1016/j.enpol.2011.05.050

Lingayat, A. B., & Suple, Y. R. (2022). *Review on Phase Change Material as Thermal Energy Storage Medium: Materials* (Vol. 3). Application.

Liu, K., & Lin, B. (2019). Research on influencing factors of environmental pollution in China: A spatial econometric analysis. *Journal of Cleaner Production*, *206*, 356–364. doi:10.1016/j.jclepro.2018.09.194

Liu, Y., Lu, S., & Chen, Y. (2013). Spatio-temporal change of urban-rural equalized development patterns in China and its driving factors. *Journal of Rural Studies*, *32*, 320–330. doi:10.1016/j.jrurstud.2013.08.004

Lomborg, B. (2001). *The Skeptical Environmentalist: Measuring the Real State of the World.* Cambridge University Press. doi:10.1017/CBO9781139626378

Londres, F. (2011). *Agrotóxicos no Brasil: um guia para ação em defesa da vida.* ASPTA.

Long, R., Shao, T., & Chen, H. (2016). Spatial econometric analysis of China's province-level industrial carbon productivity and its influencing factors. *Applied Energy*, *166*, 210–219. doi:10.1016/j.apenergy.2015.09.100

Lopez, R. (1992). The Environment As A Factor of Production: The Economic Growth and Trade Policy Linkages. In P. Low (ed.): *International Trade and Environmet*, World Bank.

López, J. A., Mireles, A. I., & Jaramillo, A. C. (2020). E-waste management in Mexico: Current situation, policies, and prospects. *Sustainability*, *12*(3), 1024.

Lopez, R. (1994). The Environment as a Factor of Production: The Effects of Economic Growth and Trade Liberalization. *Journal of Environmental Economics and Management*, *27*(2), 163–184. doi:10.1006/jeem.1994.1032

Lopez, R., & Toman, M. A. (2006). *Economic Development and Environmental Sustainability*. Oxford University Press. doi:10.1093/0199298009.001.0001

Lynas, M. (2012). *A espécie divina: como o planeta pode sobreviver à era dos seres humanos*. Alta Books.

Mäder, P., Fliessbach, A., Dubois, D., Gunst, L., Fried, P., & Niggli, U. (2002). Soil fertility and biodiversity in organic farming. *Science*, *296*(5573), 1694–1697. doi:10.1126cience.1071148 PMID:12040197

Maginn, P. J. (2016). Affordable housing, social enterprise, and the elusive logic of scale. *Housing Studies*, *31*(1), 1–18.

Malthus, T. (1798). An Essay on the Principle of Population, London, UK.

Mapping India's Energy Policy 2022: Aligning Support and Revenues with a Net-Zero Future. (2023b, March 7). CEEW. https://www.ceew.in/publications/energy-policy-research-india-2022

Maqbool, R., Deng, X., & Rashid, Y. (2020). Stakeholders' satisfaction as a key determinant of critical success factors in renewable energy projects. *Energy, Sustainability and Society*, *10*(1), 28. doi:10.118613705-020-00259-0

Marron, D. B., & Morris, A. C. (2016). How to Use Carbon Tax Revenues. SSRN *Electronic Journal*. doi:10.2139/ssrn.2737990

Mashhoodi, B., Stead, D., & van Timmeren, A. (2020). Local and national determinants of household energy consumption in the Netherlands. *GeoJournal*, *85*(2), 393–406. doi:10.100710708-018-09967-9

McLellan, R., Iyengar, L., Jeffries, B., & Oerlemans, N. (2014). Living [Species and Spaces, People and Places. Gland: WWF International.]. *The Planetary Report*, 2014.

Meadows, D. H., Meadows, D. L., Randers, J., & Behren, W. W., III. (1972). *The Limits to Growth, A reportfor the club of Rome's Project on the predicament of mankind.* Donella Meadows. https://www.donellameadows.org/wp-content/userfiles/Limits-to-Growth-digital-scan-version.pdf

Meadows, D. H., Meadows, D. L., Randers, J., & Behrens, W. (1972). *The limits to growth.* Universe.

Meadows, K., & Bruijn, E. J. D. (2020). Measuring the impact of social enterprises on sustainable development goals: A study of 60 social enterprises in 9 European countries. *Sustainability*, *12*(9), 3613.

Mehmet, O. (1995). Employment creation and green development strategy. *Ecological Economics*, *15*(1), 11–19. doi:10.1016/0921-8009(95)00035-8

Merriam, S. B. (2009). *Qualitative research: A guide to design and implementation*. Jossey-Bass.

Michaels, R., & Murphy, R. P. (2009). *Green jobs: fact or fiction?* Institute for Energy Research.

Miles, M. B., Huberman, A. M., & Saldana, J. (2014). *Qualitative data analysis: A methods sourcebook*. Sage Publications.

Mill, J. S. (1848). *Principles of Political Economy with some of their Applications to Social Philosophy*. Oxford University Press.

Ministry of new and renewable energy. (n.d.). *Home-Objectives*. RPO. https://rpo.gov.in/Home/Objective

Ministry of Power, Government of India. (2023). Ujwal DISCOM Assurance Yojana (UDAY). Ministry of Power. https://powermin.nic.in/en/content/ujwal-discom-assurance-yojana-uday and htttps://www.uday.gov.in/about.php

Mirkhani, S., Abdolshah, M., & Rashidi, K. (2020). The role of social entrepreneurship in solving environmental problems: A case study of a recycling social enterprise in Iran. *Sustainability*, *12*(6), 2404.

Mondal, D., Ratnaparkhi, A., Deshpande, A., Deshpande, V., Kshirsagar, A. P., & Pramanik, S. (2023). Applications, Modern Trends and Challenges of MultiscaleModelling in Smart Cities. In *Data-Driven Mathematical Modeling in Smart Cities*. IGI Global. doi:10.4018/978-1-6684-6408-3.ch001

Morriss A. P., Bogart W. T. & Meiners R. E., (2009) 7 Myths About Green Jobs.

Mrkajic, B., Murtinu, S., & Scalera, V. G. (2019). Is green the new gold? Venture capital and green entrepreneurship. *Small Business Economics*, *52*(4), 929–950. doi:10.100711187-017-9943-x

Munasinghe, M. (2007). *Making Development More Sustainable*. http://www.eoearth.org/article/Sustainable_development_triangle

Munasinghe, M. (2002). The Sustainomics Trans-disciplinary Meta-framework for making Development more Sustainable: Applications to energy issues. *International Journal of Sustainable Development*, *4*(2), 6–54. doi:10.1504/IJSD.2002.002563

Muo, I., & Azeez, A. A. (2019). Green entrepreneurship: Literature review and agenda for future research. *International Journal of Entrepreneurial Knowledge*, *7*(2). Advance online publication. doi:10.37335/ijek.v7i2.90

Murali, D., Morisetty, S., & Sengupta, S. (2020). *Hasiru Dala: Transforming the lives of waste pickers through social entrepreneurship*. Ivey Publishing.

NASA Global Climate Change web site. (n.d.). *The Causes of Climate Change, Vital Signs of the Planet*. NASA. https://climate.nasa.gov/causes/

NASA's Global Climate Change website. (2023, September 27). *Climate change adaptation and mitigation*. Climate Change: Vital Signs of the Planet. https://climate.nasa.gov/solutions/adaptation-mitigation/

National Clean Energy Fund. (n.d). *Biju's*. https://byjus.com/free-ias-prep/ncef-national-clean-energy-fund/

National Green Tribunal. (n.d.). *About us*. National Green Tribunal. https://www.greentribunal.gov.in/about-us

Navamuel, E. L., Morollon, F. R., & Cuartas, B. M. (2018). Energy consumption and urban sprawl: Evidence for the Spanish case. *Journal of Cleaner Production*, *172*, 3479–3486. doi:10.1016/j.jclepro.2017.08.110

Neumann, T. (2022). Impact of green entrepreneurship on sustainable development: An ex-post empirical analysis. *Journal of Cleaner Production*, *377*, 134317. doi:10.1016/j.jclepro.2022.134317

Nguyen, C. P., Schinckus, C., Su, T. D., & Chong, F. H. L. (2022). The energy consumption: The global contributions from financial development and institutions. *Environmental Science and Pollution Research International*, *29*(13), 18721–18740. doi:10.100711356-021-17134-w PMID:34697709

Nonet, G. A., Gößling, T., Van Tulder, R., & Bryson, J. M. (2022). Multi-stakeholder engagement for the Sustainable Development Goals: Introduction to the special issue. *Journal of Business Ethics*, *180*(4), 945–957. doi:10.100710551-022-05192-0 PMID:36065323

Nordhaus, W. (2007b). To Tax or Not to Tax: Alternative Approaches to Slowing Global Warming. *Review of Environmental Economics and Policy*, *1*(1), 26–45. doi:10.1093/reep/rem008

Nordhaus, W., Stavins, R. N., & Weitzman, M. L. (1992). Lethal Model 2: The Limits to Growth Revisited. *Brookings Papers on Economic Activity*, *23*(2), 1–60. doi:10.2307/2534581 PMID:12287537

Nurdiawansyah, Lindrianasari, & Komalasari, A. (2018). Carbon Emission Issues in Indonesia. *Review of Integrative Business and Economics Research*, *7*(3), 20–33. http://repository.lppm.unila.ac.id/7178/1/RIBER 2018%28a%29.pdf

OEC. (2019). Taxing Energy Use 2019: Country Note - Colombia. X, 1–8. https://www.oecd.org/tax/tax-policy/taxing-energy-use-colombia.pdf

OECD (2023c), *Electricity generation (indicator)*. (Accessed on 09 November 2023) doi:10.1787/c6e6caa2-en

OECD. (2011). *Measuring Green Entrepreneurship. Entrepreneurship at a Glance*, 23-38. OECD. doi:10.1787/9789264097711-4-en

OECD. (2020). *Renewable energy feed-in tariffs*. OECD. https://stats.oecd.org/Index.aspx?DataSetCode=RE_FIT

OECD. (2023). *Economic Outlook for Southeast Asia, China and India 2023 Reviving Tourism Post-Pandemic*.

OECD. (2023a), *Primary energy supply (indicator)*. OECD. doi:10.1787/1b33c15a-en

OECD. (2023b). *Crude oil production (indicator)*. OECD. doi:10.1787/4747b431-en

OECD. (2023d). *Renewable Energy*. OECD. doi:10.1787/aac7c3f1-en

OECD. (2023e). *Nuclear power plants (indicator)*. OECD. doi:10.1787/3cc1191d-en

OECD/Cedefop. (2014). *Greener Skills and Jobs, OECD Green Growth Studies*. OECD Publishing.

Ojha, H., & Schofield, N. (2022). *Climate change and water security in the Indo-Pacific region: risks, responses, and a framework for action.*

Otsuka, A. (2019). Natural disasters and electricity consumption behaviour: A case study of the 2011 Great East Japan Earthquake. *Asia-Pasific J Region Sci*, *3*(3), 887–910. doi:10.100741685-019-00129-4

Özbudun, E. (1964). M. Duverger'in Siyasal Partileri ve Siyasal Partilerin İncelenmesinde Bazı Metodolojik Problemler. *Ankara Üniversitesi Hukuk Fakültesi Dergisi*, *21*(1), 23–51.

Pais-Magalhaes, V., Moutinho, V., & Robaina, M. (2020). Determinants of the household electricity consumption efficiency of an ageing population: Evidence for the EU-28. *Energy Reports*, *6*(8), 415–422. doi:10.1016/j.egyr.2020.11.193

Pamuk, S. (2000). *A monetary history of the Ottoman Empire*. Cambridge University Press.

Pandey, B. K., Pandey, D., Nassa, V. K., George, A. S., Pramanik, S., & Dadheech, P. (2023). Applications for the Text Extraction Method of Complex Degraded Images. In *The Impact of Thrust Technologies on Image Processing*. Nova Publishers. doi:10.52305/ATJL4552

Papaspyropoulos, K. G., Karamanolis, D., Sokos, C. K., & Birtsas, P. K. (2016). Enhancing Sustainability in Forestry Using Material Flow Cost Accounting. *Open Journal of Forestry*, *06*(05), 324–336. doi:10.4236/ojf.2016.65026

Papiez, M., Smiech, S., & Frodyma, K. (2018). Determinants of renewable energy development in the EU countries. A 20-year perspective. *Renewable & Sustainable Energy Reviews*, *91*, 918–934. doi:10.1016/j.rser.2018.04.075

Patel, R. & Patel, V. (2022). Scheffler reflector for cooking application: a review. *International Journal of Ambient Energy*. Taylor and Francis Ltd. . doi:10.1080/01430750.2020.1758778

Patton, M. Q. (2002). *Qualitative research and evaluation methods* (3rd ed.). Sage Publications.

Paul, I. D., Bhole, G. P., & Chaudhari, J. R. (2014). A Review on Green Manufacturing: It's Important, Methodology and its Application. *Procedia Materials Science, 6*(Icmpc), 1644–1649. doi:10.1016/j.mspro.2014.07.149

Pearce, D. W. And R. K. Turner. (1990). Economics of Natural Resources And The Environment, Hertfordshire: Harvester Wheatseaf Publishes.

Pearce, D., & Barbier, E. (2000). *Blueprint for a Sustainable Economy*. Earthscan Publications. doi:10.4324/9781849774239

Pedrini, M., & Ferri, L. M. (2019). Stakeholder management: A systematic literature review. *Corporate Governance (Bradford)*, *19*(1), 44–59. doi:10.1108/CG-08-2017-0172

Pepper, D. (1998). Sustainable Development and Ecological Modernization: A Radical Homocentric Perspective. *Sustainable Development (Bradford)*, *6*(1), 1–7. doi:10.1002/(SICI)1099-1719(199803)6:1<1::AID-SD83>3.0.CO;2-8

Pereira, P., Zhao, W., Symochko, L., Inacio, M., Bogunovic, I., & Barcelo, D. (2022). The Russian-Ukrainian armed conflict will push back the sustainable development goals. *Geography and Sustainability*, *3*(3), 277–287. doi:10.1016/j.geosus.2022.09.003

Popescu, G. H., Mieila, M., Nica, E., & Andrei, J. V. (2018). The emergence of the effects and determinants of the energy paradigm changes on European Union economy. *Renewable & Sustainable Energy Reviews*, *81*(1), 768–774. doi:10.1016/j.rser.2017.08.055

Porter, M. E., & Linde, C. (1995). Toward a new conception of the environment-comptitiveness relationship. *The Journal of Economic Perspectives*, *9*(4), 97–118. doi:10.1257/jep.9.4.97

Poumanyvong, P., & Kaneko, S. (2010). Does urbanisation lead to less energy use and lower CO_2 emissions? A cross-country analysis. *Ecological Economics*, *70*(2), 434–444. doi:10.1016/j.ecolecon.2010.09.029

Qadir, S. A., Al-Motairi, H., Tahir, F., & Al-Fagih, L. (2021). Incentives and strategies for financing the renewable energy transition: A review. *Energy Reports*, *7*, 3590–3606. doi:10.1016/j.egyr.2021.06.041

Rabe, B. G., & Borick, C. P. (2012). Carbon Taxation and Policy Labeling: Experience from American States and Canadian Provinces. *The Review of Policy Research*, *29*(3), 358–382. doi:10.1111/j.1541-1338.2012.00564.x

Rakshit, B. (2021). Impact of natural disasters on energy consumption: Evidence from Indian states. *Energy Res Let*, *2*(3). doi:10.46557/001c.27017

Ratnawati, D. (2016). Carbon Tax Sebagai Alternatif Kebijakan Untuk Mengatasi Eksternalitas Negatif Emisi Karbon di Indonesia. *Indonesian Treasury Review Jurnal Perbendaharaan Keuangan Negara Dan Kebijakan Publik, 1*(2), 53–67. doi:10.33105/itrev.v1i2.51

Rebouças, A. C. (2002). *Águas doces no Brasil.* Escrituras Editora.

Reddy, D. S., Khan, M. K., Alam, M. Z., & Rashid, H. (2018, March). Design charts for Scheffler reflector. *Solar Energy, 163*, 104–112. doi:10.1016/j.solener.2018.01.081

Rees, W. E. (1990). The Ecology of Eustainable Development. *The Ecologist, 20*(1), 18–23.

Rees, W. E. (1992). Ecological Footprints and Appropriated Carrying Capacity: What Urban Economics Leaves Out. *Environment and Urbanization, 4*(2), 121–130. doi:10.1177/095624789200400212

Reiss, P. C., & White, M. W. (2002). *Household electricity demand, revisited.* Stanford University Publication.

Reyes, R. C. (2011). The Green Solow Model with Natural Resources Constraint: A Theoretical Note. *DLSU Business and Economics Review, 21*(1), 111–116.

Rodrigues, J. E. R. (2008). *Parque urbano: aplicação do Sistema Nacional de unidades de Conservação (SNUC) ao meio urbano. Tese de Doutorado.* Faculdade de Saúde Pública da USP.

Roggenkamp, M., & Diestelmeier, L. (2020). Energy market reforms in the EU: A new focus on energy consumers, energy poverty, and energy (in)justice? In I. del Guayo, L. Godden, D. D. Zillman, M. F. Montoya, & J. J. Gonzalez (Eds.), *Energy justice and energy law* (pp. 160–177). Oxford University Press. doi:10.1093/oso/9780198860754.003.0010

Romero-Jordan, D., del Río, P., & Penasco, C. (2014). Analysing the determinants of household electricity demand in Spain. An econometric study. *Int J Electr Power Energy Syst, 63*, 950e961.

Rounaghi, M. M. (2019). Economic analysis of using green accounting and environmental accounting to identify environmental costs and sustainability indicators. *International Journal of Ethics and Systems, 35*(4), 504–512. doi:10.1108/IJOES-03-2019-0056

Rousseau, J. J. (2012). *Rousseau: The basic political writings: Discourse on the sciences and the arts, discourse on the origin of inequality, discourse on political economy, on the social contract, the state of war.* Hackett Publishing.

Saahas Zero Waste. (2023, October 16). *Waste Management Company in India.* SAAHAS Zero Waste. https://saahaszerowaste.com/

Sachs, J. (2015). *La era del Desarrollo Sostenible.* Ediciones Deusto.

Sadorsky, P. (2014). The effect of urbanisation on CO2 emissions in emerging economies. *Energy Economics, 41*, 147–153. doi:10.1016/j.eneco.2013.11.007

Salari, M., & Javid, R. J. (2016). Residential energy demand in the United States: Analysis using static and dynamic approaches. *Energy Policy, 98*, 637–649. doi:10.1016/j.enpol.2016.09.041

Sanchez-Molina, R., & Iniesta-Bonillo, M. A. (2020). Sustainable waste management practices and social entrepreneurship: A systematic literature review. *Journal of Cleaner Production, 246*, 119029.

Saputra, A. I. (2021). Pajak Karbon Sebagai Sumber Penerimaan Negara Dan Sistem Pemungutannya. [AKURASI]. *Jurnal Anggaran Dan Keuangan Negara Indonesia, 3*(1), 56–71. doi:10.33827/akurasi2021.vol3.iss1.art96

Sarkar, A., & Singh, J. (2010). Financing energy efficiency in developing countries—Lessons learned and remaining challenges. *Energy Policy, 38*(10), 5560–5571. doi:10.1016/j.enpol.2010.05.001

Sarkodie, S. A., & Adams, S. (2018b). Renewable energy, nuclear energy, and environmental pollution: Accounting for political institutional quality in South Africa. *The Science of the Total Environment, 643*, 1590–1601. doi:10.1016/j.scitotenv.2018.06.320 PMID:30189575

Sarkodie, S. A., & Adom, P. K. (2018a). Determinants of energy consumption in Kenya: A NIPALS approach. *Energy, 159*, 696–705. doi:10.1016/j.energy.2018.06.195

Schaper, M. (2002). *Introduction:* The Essence of Ecopreneurship. *Greener Management International, 38*, 26–30. https://www.jstor.org/stable/greemanainte.38.26

Schroff, F., Criminisi, A., & Zisserman, A. (2008). *Object class segmentation using Random Forests*. BMVC. doi:10.5244/C.22.54

Seabra, G. (2011). Educação Ambiental: caminhos para a conservação da sociobiodiversidade. In *SEABRA, Giovanni (Org.). Educação Ambiental no Mundo Globalizado: uma ecologia de riscos, desafios e resistência*. Editora Universitária da UFPB.

Selvi, R. N., & Rachmatulloh, I. (2020). Urgensi Penerapan Pajak Karbon Di Indonesia. *Jurnal Reformasi Administrasi, 7*(1), 29–34. https://ojs.stiami.ac.id/index.php/reformasi/article/view/845

Selwyn, J., & Leverett, (2006). Emerging Markets in the Environmental Industries Sector, The UK Centre for Economic and Environmental Development.

Serio, R. G., Dickson, M. M., Giuliani, D., & Espa, G. (2020). Green production as a factor of survival for innovative startups: Evidence from Italy. *Sustainability (Basel), 12*(22), 9464. doi:10.3390u12229464

Seuring, S., & Müller, M. (2008). From a literature review to a conceptual framework for sustainable supply chain management. *Journal of Cleaner Production, 16*(15), 1699–1710. doi:10.1016/j.jclepro.2008.04.020

Sevik, N., & Yildirim, S. (2023). Sustainable Enterprises Post COVID-19 Pandemic: The Rise of Sustainable Fashion Enterprises. In *Handbook of Research on Current Advances and Challenges of Borderlands, Migration, and Geopolitics*. IGI Global Publishing.

Shahbaz, M., Shahzad, S. J. H., Mahalik, M. K., & Sadorsky, P. (2018). How strong is the casual relationship between globalization and energy consumption in developed economies? A country-specific time-series and panel analysis. *Applied Economics, 50*(13), 1479–1494. doi:10.1080/00036846.2017.1366640

Shaheen, S., Cohen, A., & Zohdy, I. (2016). Mobility and the sharing economy: Potential to contribute to environmental and social sustainability. *Sustainability, 8*(12), 1275.

Sharma, S., Moerenhout, T., & Garg, V. (2018). *Electricity Sector Reform in Uttar Pradesh: Analysis of tariff adjustments and the Ujwal Discom Assurance Yojana Plan (UDAY)*. Policy Commons. https://policycommons.net/artifacts/614370/electricity-sector-reform-in-uttar-pradesh/1594618/

Siksnelyte-Butkiene, I. (2021). Impact of the COVID-19 Pandemic to the Sustainability of the Energy Sector. *Sustainability (Basel), 13*(23), 12973. doi:10.3390u132312973

Silva, D. R. O., Avila, L. A., Agostinetto, D., Bundt, A. D. C., Primel, E. G., & Caldas, S. S. (2011). Ocorrência de agrotóxicos em águas subterrâneas de áreas adjacentes a lavouras de arroz irrigado. *Quimica Nova, 34*(5), 748–752. doi:10.1590/S0100-40422011000500004

Simonis, U. E. (1997). Reorientación ecológica de la sociedad industrial. In *La protección del medio ambiente, conceptos y políticas. CIEDLA*. Editores Josef Thesing y Wilhelm Hofmeister.

Simon, J. (1980). Resources, Population, Environment: An Oversupply of False Bad News. *Science*, *208*(4451), 1431–1437. doi:10.1126cience.7384784 PMID:7384784

Simon, J. (1981). *The Ultimate Resource*. Robertson.

Simpson, M. C. (2008). Community benefit tourism initiatives: Linking communities, tourism, and conservation in the southern Philippines. *Geoforum*, *39*(2), 946–960.

Sims, R. E., Rogner, H. H., & Gregory, K. (2003). Carbon emission and mitigation cost comparisons between fossil fuel, nuclear and renewable energy resources for electricity generation. *Energy Policy*, *31*(13), 1315–1326. doi:10.1016/S0301-4215(02)00192-1

Sineviciene, L., Sotnyk, I., & Kubatko, O. (2017). Determinants of energy efficiency and energy consumption of Eastern Europe post-communist economies. *Energy & Environment*, *28*(8), 870–884. doi:10.1177/0958305X17734386

Singh, K., & Vashishtha, S. (2019). Empowering the power sector through UDAY: A study of Haryana. *ZENITH International Journal of Multidisciplinary Research*, *9*(5), 1–7. https://mpra.ub.uni-muenchen.de/id/eprint/99266

Soares, D. F., Faria, A. M., & Rosa, A. H. (2017, March/April). Análise de risco de contaminação de águas subterrâneas por resíduos de agrotóxicos no município de Campo Novo do Parecis (MT), Brasil. *Engenharia Sanitaria e Ambiental*, *22*(2), 277–284. doi:10.15901413-41522016139118

Söderholm, P. (2020). The green economy transition: The challenges of technological change for sustainability. *Sustainable Earth*, *3*(1), 6. doi:10.118642055-020-00029-y

Solow, R. (1956). A Contribution to the Theory of Economic Growth. *The Quarterly Journal of Economics*, *70*(1), 65–94. doi:10.2307/1884513

Solow, R. M. (1974). Intergenerational equity and exhaustible resources. *The Review of Economic Studies*, *14*, 29–45. doi:10.2307/2296370

Solow, R. M. (1986). On the Intergenerational Allocation of Natural Resources. *The Scandinavian Journal of Economics*, *88*(1), 141–149. doi:10.2307/3440280

Sönmez, S. (1987). *Kamu Ekonomisi Teorisi: Kamu Harcamalarında Etkinlik Arayışı*. Teori Yayınları.

Sorrell, S. (2015). Reducing energy demand: A review of issues, challenges and approaches. *Renewable & Sustainable Energy Reviews*, *47*, 74–82. doi:10.1016/j.rser.2015.03.002

Souza, L. C. (2009). *Águas subterrâneas e a legislação brasileira*. Juruá.

Srivastava, A., Sharma, R. K., & Suresh, A. (2020). Impact of Covid-19 on Sustainable Development Goals. *International Journal of Advanced Science and Technology*, *29*(No. 9s), 4968–4972.

Stake, R. E. (1995). *The art of case study research*. Sage Publications.

Steffen, G.P.K., Steffen, R.B., & Antoniolli, Z.I. (2011). Contaminação do solo e da água pelo uso de agrotóxicos. *TECNO-LÓGICA, Santa Cruz do Sul, 15*(1).

Steiner, A. (2014). Resilience and Adaption. *The Economist*. https://impact.economist.com/sustainability/resilience-and-adaptation/bringing-the-green-economy-to-the-blue-world?gclid=CjwKCAiAhKycBhAQEiwAgf19ejdQ0-_l8rACjFf-57BARdoZRBJG8b0Yf3vqR1K4I2kmMSJOCmjYftxoCREYQAvD_BwE&gclsrc=aw.ds

Stern, D. (1997). Van Den Berg: Ecological Economics. *Economic Journal (London)*, *107*(445), 1905–1907.

Stern, D. I. (2004). The rise and fall of the environmental Kuznets curve. *World Development*, *32*(8), 1419–1439. doi:10.1016/j.worlddev.2004.03.004

Stoddart, H. (2022). *earthsummit2012*. Stakeholder Forum. https://stakeholderforum.org/wp-content/uploads/2020/06/Earth-Summit-2012-Principles-for-the-Green-Economy-1.pdf.

Sturm, D., & Ulph, A. (2002). "Environment, Trade, Political Economy And Imperfect Information – A Survey". Discussion Papers in Economics and Econometrics, http://www.soton.ac.uk/ (23.02.2015).

Sukma Aisya, N. (2019). Dilema Posisi Indonesia dalam Persetujuan Paris tentang Perubahan Iklim. *Indonesian Perspective*, *4*(2), 118–132.

Su, M., Fang, M., Pang, Q., & Park, K. (2022). Exploring the role of sustainable logistics service providers in multinational supply chain cooperation: An integrated theory-based perspective. *Frontiers in Environmental Science*, *10*, 976211. doi:10.3389/fenvs.2022.976211

Taylor, E. (2019). Green Entrepreneurship: Literature review and agenda for future research. *International Journal of Entrepreneurial Knowledge*, 17 - 29.

Temurshoev, U. (2006). "Pollution Haven Hypothesis or Factor Endownment Hypothesis: Theory and Empirical Examination for US and China". Charles University Center for Economic Research and Graduate Education, Working paper series. http://iweb.cerge-ei.cz/pdf/wp/Wp292.pdf (23.02.2015).

The Lancet Public Health. (2020, September). The Lancet Public Health. (2020). Will the COVID-19 pandemic threaten the SDGs? *The Lancet. Public Health*, *5*(9), e460. doi:10.1016/S2468-2667(20)30189-4 PMID:32888438

Tilt, B. (2019). China's air pollution crisis: Science and policy perspectives. *Environmental Science & Policy*, *92*, 275–280. doi:10.1016/j.envsci.2018.11.020

Tinbergen, J., & Hueting, R. (1992). GNP and Market Prices. In R. Goodland, H. Daly, & S. El Serafy (Eds.), *Population, Technology and Lifestyle: the Transition to Sustainability* (pp. 52–62). Island Press.

Todaro, M. P., & Smith, S. C. (2009). *Economic Development* (10th ed.). Addison-Wesley.

TSKB. (2023). Climate Review, Issue No.12, July-September, 2023. İstanbul.

Tu, Y.-X., Kubatko, O., Piven, V., Sotnyk, I., & Kurbatova, T. (2022). Determinants of renewable energy development: Evidence from the EU countries. *Energies*, *15*(19), 7093. doi:10.3390/en15197093

Tyagi, A., Lata, C., Korsh, J., Nagarwal, A., Rai, D., Kwatra, S., & Saxena, P. (2021). *India's Expanding Clean Energy Workforce*.

Tzeiranaki, S. T., Bertoldi, P., Diluiso, F., Castellazzi, L., Economidou, M., Labanca, N., Serrenho, T. R., & Zangheri, P. (2019). Analysis of the EU residential energy consumption: Trends and determinants. *Energies*, *12*(6), 1065. doi:10.3390/en12061065

UN. (2022). Green economy: Sustainable Development Knowledge Platform. *Sustainable Development Goals*, https://sustainabledevelopment.un.org/index.php?menu=1446.

UNEP. (2022). Green economy. *UNEP.* https://www.unep.org/regions/asia-and-pacific/regional-initiatives/supporting-resource-efficiency/green-economy

UN-HABITAT. (2020). *The Strategic Plan 2020-2023*. UN. https://unhabitat.org/sites/default/files/ documents/2019-09/strategic_plan_2020-2023.pdf.

United Nations Economic and Social Council. (2021). *Enhancing energy security in the context of the coronavirus disease pandemic for a greener, more resilient and inclusive energy future in the region,* ESCAP/77/17. UN. https://www.unescap.org/sites/default/d8files/event-documents/ESCAP_77_17_E.pdf

United Nations Educational, Scientific and Cultural Organization. (2014). *Roadmap for implementing the Global Action Programme on Education for Sustainable Development.* UNESCO.

United Nations Sustainable Development Group. (2022). *Global Impact of war in Ukraine on food, energy and finance systems - BRIEF NO.2.* UN. https://unsdg.un.org/resources/global-impact-war-ukraine-food-energy-and-finance-systems-brief-no2

United Nations, Department of Economic and Social Affairs, Population Division. (2018). *World urbanization prospects: The 2018 revision.* UN, New York. https://ec.europa.eu/eurostat/web/products-eurostat-news/-/ddn-20220617-1.

United Nations. (2015). *Transforming Our World: The 2030 Agenda For Sustainable Development,* A/RES/70/1. UN. https://sustainabledevelopment.un.org/content/documents/21252030%20Agenda%20for%20Sustainable%20Development%20web.pdf

United Nations. (2015). *Transforming our world: The 2030 Agenda for Sustainable Development.* United Nations.

United Nations. (2022). *Global impact of war in Ukraine: Energy crisis UN GLOBAL CRISIS RESPONSE GROUP ON FOOD, ENERGY AND FINANCE AUGUST 2022.* UN. https://unsdg.un.org/sites/default/files/2022-08/GCRG_3rd-Brief_Aug3_2022_.pdf

UNPD. (2022). *The impact of the war in Ukraine on sustainable development in Africa, Rapid Assessment by the Regional Bureau for Africa.* UNDP. file:///C:/Users/hp/Downloads/UNDP%20RBA%20-%20IMpact%20of%20the%20war%20%20in%20Ukraine%20on%20Africa%20-%2024%20May%202022%20(1).pdf

UNRIC. (2022). *Green economy: a path towards development and poverty eradication.* UNRIC. https://unric.org/en/green-economy-a-path-towards-sustainable-development-and-poverty-eradication/.

Upadhyay, D., Purswani, G., & Jain, P. (2020). Yulu: Moving Towards a Sustainable Future. *South Asian Journal of Business and Management Cases, 9*(3), 445–456. doi:10.1177/2277977920957954

Usha Hariprasad. (2021, March 8). *Uger: New beginnings in sustainable, safe, and dignified menstruation.* Vikalp Sangam. https://vikalpsangam.org/article/uger-new-beginnings-in-sustainable-safe-and-dignified-menstruation/

Usman, M., Ma, Z., Zafar, M. W., Waheed, A., & Li, M. (2021). Analyzing the determinants of clean energy consumption in a sustainability strategy: Evidence from EU-28 countries. *Environmental Science and Pollution Research International, 28*(39), 54551–54564. doi:10.100711356-021-14473-6 PMID:34018103

Van Den Bergh, J. C. J. M. (1996). *Ecological Economics and Sustainable Development: Theory, Methods and Applications.* Edward Elgar.

Van Den Bergh, J. C. J. M. (2001). Ecological Economics: Themes, Approaches, and Differences with Environmental Economics. *Regional Environmental Change, 2*(1), 13–23. doi:10.1007101130000020

Van den Bergh, J. C. J. M., & Grazi, F. (2010). On the Policy Relevance Of Ecological Footprints. *Environmental Science & Technology, 44*(13), 4843–4844. doi:10.1021/es1003582 PMID:20441197

Van den Bergh, J. C. J. M., & Grazi, F. (2014). Ecological Footprint Policy: Land Use as an Environmental Indicator. *Journal of Industrial Ecology, 18*(1), 10–19. doi:10.1111/jiec.12045

Van den Bergh, J. C. J. M., & Verbruggen, H. (1999). Spatial Sustainability, Trade And Indicators: An Evaluation of the Ecological Footprint. *Ecological Economics*, *29*(1), 61–72. doi:10.1016/S0921-8009(99)00032-4

Veeraiah, V., Shiju, D. J., Ramesh, J. V. N., Ganesh Kumar, R., Pramanik, S., Gupta, A., & Pandey, D. (2023). *Healthcare Cloud Services in Image Processing, Thrust Technologies' Effect on Image Processing*. IGI Global.

Vegas, E. (2003). *Hacia un Perú sustentable. Colección Perú Sustentable*. Repositorio institucional de la Universidad Peruana de Ciencias e Informática. repositorio.upci.edu.pe

Vegas, E. (2018). *Biodiversidad de la macro región norte del Perú: Estado y estrategia para su conservación y usos sustentable*. Repositorio institucional de la Universidad Nacional de Piura, Perú. https://repositorio.unp.edu.pe/handle/UNP/1580

Vegas, E., & Vegas, W. (2022). *Los Objetivos de Desarrollo Sostenible en tiempo pos-Covid-19 y en la mirada de los derechos humanos. Revista 131: enero-junio 2022. POLÍTICA INTERNACIONAL*. Academia Diplomática del Perú.

Victor, P. A., & Jacson, T. (2012). *Home*. CloudFront. https://d1wqtxts1xzle7.cloudfront.net/57512350/j.ecolecon.2012.02.02820181005-18531-a8youb-with-cover-page-v2.pdf?Expires=1669460251&Signature=W~mm1Wn175O2ZBMs8yy6KcEQwRpOxMnsJ93yaI~5GGM3lA0uQdoJKrHJlghkjCuXziSAlgUuMePH8PvnlFYVQniNdY6mJsRFMK5KrqGr9QEGUU67S.

Wallace, R. (2020). *Pandemia e Agronegócio: Doenças infecciosas, capitalismo e ciência. Trad. Allan Rodrigo de Campos Silva*. Elefante.

Wei, S., Jiandong, W., & Saleem, H. (2023). The impact of renewable energy transition, green growth, green trade and innovation on environmental quality: Evidence from top 10 green future countries. *Frontiers in Environmental Science*, *10*, 1076859. doi:10.3389/fenvs.2022.1076859

Wells, E. C., Lehigh, G. R., & Vidmar, A. M. (2021). Stakeholder engagement for sustainable communities. In Springer eBooks (pp. 1–13). doi:10.1007/978-3-030-38948-2_10-1

Wiesmann, D., Lima Azevedo, I., Ferrao, P., & Fernandez, J. E. (2011). Residential electricity consumption in Portugal: Findings from top-down and bottom-up models. *Energy Policy*, *39*(5), 2772–2779. doi:10.1016/j.enpol.2011.02.047

William, N. (2007a). *The Challenge of Global Warming: Economic Models and Environmental Policy. Yale*. Yale University.

World Bank. (2022). *Population total-European Union*. World Bank. https://data.worldbank.org/indicator/.

World Economic Forum. (2023). *Jobs of Tomorrow: Social and Green Jobs for Building Inclusive and Sustainable Economies*. WEF.

Yao, Q., Liu, J., Sheng, S., & Fang, H. (2019). Does eco-innovation lift firm value? The contingent role of institutions in emerging markets. *Journal of Business and Industrial Marketing*, *34*(8), 1763–1778. doi:10.1108/JBIM-06-2018-0201

Yildirim, S., Demirtas, I., & Yildirim. (2022). A Review of Alternative Economic Approaches to Achieve Sustainable Development: The Rising Digitalization and Degrowth Post COVID-19. In *Handbook of Research on Sustainable Development Goals, Climate Change, and Digitalization*. Hershey, PA: IGI Global.

Yildirim, S. (2020). The consumer role for sustainable development: how consumers contribute sustainable development goals. In V. Chkoniya, A. O. Madsen, & P. Bukhrashvili (Eds.), *Anthropological Approaches to Understanding Consumption Patterns and Consumer Behavior* (pp. 325–341). IGI Global. doi:10.4018/978-1-7998-3115-0.ch018

Yıldırım, S. (2021). Do green women influencers spur sustainable consumption patterns? Descriptive evidences from social media influencers. *Ecofeminism and Climate Change*, *2*(4), 198–210. doi:10.1108/EFCC-02-2021-0003

Yildirim, S. (2023). Greenwashing: A rapid escape from sustainability or a slow transition? *LBS Journal of Management & Research, 21*(1), 53–63. doi:10.1108/LBSJMR-11-2022-0077

Yıldırım, S., & Candan, B. (2015). Segmentation of Green Product Buyers Based on Their Personal Values and Consumption Values, *Environmental Values* [October.]. *White Horse Press, 24*(5), 641–661.

Yildirim, S., Demirtas, I., & Yildirim, D. C. (2022). A Review of Alternative Economic Approaches to Achieve Sustainable Development: The Rising Digitalization and Degrowth Post COVID-19. In R. Castanho (Ed.), *Handbook of Research on Sustainable Development Goals, Climate Change, and Digitalization* (pp. 288–307). IGI Global. doi:10.4018/978-1-7998-8482-8.ch018

Yildirim, S., Kaplan, M., & Yildirim, D. C. (2023). Climate Change and the Ocean Economy: A Review on OECD's Ocean Economy. In A. Pego (Ed.), *Handbook of Research on Bioeconomy and Economic Ecosystems* (pp. 212–232). IGI Global. doi:10.4018/978-1-6684-8879-9.ch012

Yıldırım, S., & Yıldırım, D. Ç. (2020). Achieving Sustainable Development Through a Green Economy Approach. In S. Patti & G. Trizzino (Eds.), *Advanced Integrated Approaches to Environmental Economics and Policy: Emerging Research and Opportunities* (pp. 1–22). IGI Global. doi:10.4018/978-1-5225-9562-5.ch001

Yıldırım, S., Yıldırım, D. Ç., & Gedikli, A. (2016). Sustainable Consumption Trends in the World in the Context of Green Economy and Sustainability. In M. Erdoğdu, T. Arun, & I. Ahmad (Eds.), *Handbook of Research on Green Economic Development Initiatives and Strategies* (pp. 65–84). IGI Global. doi:10.4018/978-1-5225-0440-5.ch004

Yin, R. K. (2014). *Case study research: Design and methods* (5th ed.). Sage Publications.

Yu, B., Fang, D., Yu, H., & Zhao, C. (2021). Temporal-spatial determinants of renewable energy penetration in electricity production: Evidence from EU countries. *Renewable Energy, 180*, 438–451. doi:10.1016/j.renene.2021.08.079

Yunis, J., & Aliakbari, E. (2020). Carbon Pricing in High-Income OECD Countries. *Fraser Institute*, 42. https://www.fraserinstitute.org/sites/default/files/carbon-pricing-in-high-income-oecd-countries.pdf

Zafari, A., Zurita-Milla, R., & Izquierdo-Verdiguier, E. (2019). Evaluating the performance of a Random Forest kernel for land cover classification. *Remote Sensing (Basel), 11*(5), 575. doi:10.3390/rs11050575

Zahraie, B., Everett, A. M., Walton, S., & Kirkwood, J. (2016). Environmental entrepreneurs facilitating change toward sustainability: A case study of the wine industry in New Zealand. *Small Enterprise Research, 23*(1), 39–57. doi:10.1080/13215906.2016.1188717

Zhang, F. (2013). The energy transition of the transition economies: An empirical analysis. *Energy Economics, 40*, 679–686. doi:10.1016/j.eneco.2013.09.001

Zhang, W., Li, B., Xue, R., Wang, Y., & Cao, W. (2021). A systematic bibliometric review of clean energy transition: Implications for low-carbon development. *PLoS One, 16*(12), e0261091. doi:10.1371/journal.pone.0261091 PMID:34860855

About the Contributors

Rui Alexandre Castanho holds an International Ph.D. on Sustainable Planning in Borderlands. Nowadays, he's a Professor at the WSB University, Poland, and the Coordinator of International Relations on the Research Institute on Territorial Cooperation and Inter-Organizational Cooperation. Also, he is a pos-doc researcher on the GREAT Project, University of Azores, Ponta Delgada, Portugal. Furthermore, he collaborates with the Environmental Resources Analysis Research Group (ARAM) - University of Extremadura (UEx); VALORIZA - Research Center for the Enhancement of Endogenous Resources, Polytechnic Institute of Portalegre (IPP), Portugal; CITUR - Madeira - Centre for Tourism Research, Development and Innovation, Madeira, Portugal; and AQUAGEO Research Group - University of Campinas (UNICAMP), Brazil. Moreover, he has Graduated in Green Spaces Engineering and Agricultural Engineering and holds a Master's Degree in Planning, Audit, and Control in Urban Green Spaces.

Şahin Akkaya, having his BA,MA and Phd degrees in the field of Public Finance,has been working at Istanbul University,Faculty of Economics since 1985. He teaches environmental economics, the theory of public finance,tax theory and policy,globalization and fiscal system,taxation and welfare,and international public finance in undergraduate and graduate programs of public finance. Dr.Şahin Akkaya,who studies especially in the fields of international public finance, global public goods, tax policy,environmental economics, climate change and carbon tax, has many scientific publications on these subjects.He has published three academic books in the fields of environmental taxes and tax policies in the globalization age.

Mallika B K working as assistant professor at Christ University. She has 15 years of teaching and research experience. She has published research articles in international and national journals

Seyfettin Erdogan works at Istanbul Medeniyet University in Turkey. He is an expert in economics and studies on economy, energy, health and sustainability. He has many books and book chapters in IGI Global Publishing.

Miguel Angel Esquivias Padilla is a Senior lecture and researcher at the Department of Economics, Faculty of Economics and Business, Universitas Airlangga, Surabaya, Indonesia.

Ankur Gupta has received the B.Tech and M.Tech in Computer Science and Engineering from Ganga Institute of Technology and Management, Kablana affiliated with Maharshi Dayanand University, Rohtak in 2015 and 2017. He is an Assistant Professor in the Department of Computer Science and

Engineering at Vaish College of Engineering, Rohtak, and has been working there since January 2019. He has many publications in various reputed national/ international conferences, journals, and online book chapter contributions (Indexed by SCIE, Scopus, ESCI, ACM, DBLP, etc). He is doing research in the field of cloud computing, data security & machine learning. His research work in M.Tech was based on biometric security in cloud computing.

Pooja Jain is Associate Professor in Department of Commerce in School of Commerce, Finance and Accountancy at CHRIST (Deemed to be University). She has more than 15 years of experience in the field of teaching. Her area of specialization is Marketing and Research Methodology.

I. Made Laut Mertha Jaya is a Senior Lecture accounting at Universitas Mahakarya Asia, Indonesia, with a research interest about fraud and financial technology crime.

Thilaga N. has three years teaching experiences and five years of Research experience.

Aruna P. is working as Associate Professor in School of Commerce, Finance and Accountancy at Christ University, Bangalore.She is specialised in Accounting, Finance and Entrepreneurship.

Sabyasachi Pramanik is a professional IEEE member. He obtained a PhD in Computer Science and Engineering from Sri Satya Sai University of Technology and Medical Sciences, Bhopal, India. Presently, he is an Associate Professor, Department of Computer Science and Engineering, Haldia Institute of Technology, India. He has many publications in various reputed international conferences, journals, and book chapters (Indexed by SCIE, Scopus, ESCI, etc). He is doing research in the fields of Artificial Intelligence, Data Privacy, Cybersecurity, Network Security, and Machine Learning. He also serves on the editorial boards of several international journals. He is a reviewer of journal articles from IEEE, Springer, Elsevier, Inderscience, IET and IGI Global. He has reviewed many conference papers, has been a keynote speaker, session chair, and technical program committee member at many international conferences. He has authored a book on Wireless Sensor Network. He has edited 8 books from IGI Global, CRC Press, Springer and Wiley Publications.

Geetanjali Purswani is Assistant Professor in Department of Commerce in School of Commerce, Finance and Accountancy at CHRIST (Deemed to be University). She has more than 13 years of experience in the field of teaching. Her areas of specialization are Finance and Accountancy.

Baranidharan S. specialized in Finance Economics and Econometrics. Having 5 years research experience, 2 years of Industrial experience and 6 years of teaching experience. Published 6 patent, 45 research articles in international and national journal which are indexed in Scopus, WoS, Proquest, ABDC, etc.,

Nitin N. Sakhare is currently working as an Assistant Professor in the department of Computer Engineering, Vishwakarma Institute of Information Technology having 10 years of teaching experience.

Surjit Singha is a dedicated researcher interested in UN Sustainable Development Goals, Organizational Climate, Workforce Diversity, Organizational Culture, HRM, Marketing, Finance, IB, Global Business, Business, AI, Women Studies, and Cultural Studies. Currently serving as a faculty member in the Department of Commerce at Kristu Jayanti College (Autonomous), Dr. Surjit holds prestigious positions as Editor, reviewer, and author for renowned Global Publications and Journals, including Editorial review board member at Information Resources Management Journal; Reviewer and author at IGI Global. With over 13 years of extensive experience in Administration, Teaching, and Research, both in Industry and Higher Education Institutions (HEIs), Dr. Surjit is committed to imparting knowledge and guiding students in their research pursuits. As a research mentor, Dr. Surjit is vital in nurturing young minds and fostering academic growth. Leading a team of approximately 35 faculty members, Dr. Surjit also heads website management, promotion, and social media publicity efforts. Dedicated to continuous learning, Dr. Surjit boasts certifications as a Life Skill Trainer by RGNYID, a Microsoft Innovative Educator by Microsoft, and a Yoga Volunteer certified by The Yoga Certification Board, Ministry of AYUSH, Gov. of India. A trailblazer in academia, Dr. Surjit has guided and mentored 21 student projects in the academic year 2022-23, resulting in all 21 students publishing papers under Dr. Surjit's astute guidance. As NSS Faculty Mentor, Dr. Surjit has successfully mentored 65 students in the academic year 2022-23, ensuring all students achieve credits and qualifications. Dr. Surjit Singha has made substantial contributions to research with an impressive track record of over 65 publications as articles, including chapters in books, edited books, and various textbooks. Dr. Surjit continues to excel in academia after being granted 2 US Copyrights and receiving two fully funded minor research projects (Completed and Published) from Kristu Jayanti College (Autonomous). With a firm commitment to excellence in education and research, Dr. Surjit Singha elevates the institution's status and fosters an environment of knowledge dissemination and growth.

Eda Ustaoglu has a PhD in Planning and Public Policy from the School of Architecture, Planning and Environmental Policy, University College Dublin, and until 2015 she worked at the European Commission-Joint Research Centre-Ispra as a scientific officer. In the following periods, she worked as a post-doc researcher at the Department of Geomatics Engineering at Gebze Technical University and College of Social Sciences and Humanities at Koc University in Turkey. She is currently working as an Assistant Professor at the Department of Economics at Abdullah Gul University, Turkey. Over the past years, she has been involved in various projects, university studies and research activities in line with her graduate and post-graduate studies, which are directly related to the field of urban and environmental studies. Her research interests include urban economics, transport policy and planning, transport infrastructure appraisal, spatial economics and land use research.

Seda Yıldırım currently works at Tekirdag Namık Kemal University in Turkey. She studies on sustainable development, 2030 sustainable development goals, sustainable consumption patterns, Islamic finance and banking, consumption patterns, environmental quality and food security. She is married and has two children She won Emerald literati award- Outstanding Paper Award 2022.

Durmuş Çağrı Yıldırım works at Tekirdağ Namık Kemal University in Türkiye. He is an expert in economics. He studies on sustainable development, climate change, energy policies, education and health policies in general. He has many book chapter and book in IGI Global publishing. He has several publications in journal indexed by Web of Science and SCOPUS.

Index

F

G

H

I

L

O

P

R

S

T

U

W

www.ingramcontent.com/pod-product-compliance
Lightning Source LLC
LaVergne TN
LVHW080640011026
849160LV00014B/1271